Romantic CROCHET

Lyric Books Limited

66B, The Broadway, Mill Hill, London NW7 3TF, England

ISBN 0 7111 0031 4

Printed in Belgium by
Proost International Book Production

Series Technical Editor: Jenny McIvor
Production Editor: Pauline Moss

Introduction

You will already know how enjoyable the creative challenge of crochet can be if you like making clothes and accessories with a crochet hook. Now 'Romantic Crochet' offers you the chance to create for yourself the best of Continental-style furnishings in the same way. This clearly written and beautifully illustrated book will introduce you to a collection of patterns for decorative items to suit both traditional and contemporary interiors.

Assisted by the clear row-by-row patterns, tables of abbreviations and terms, and inspired by the colour photographs, you can choose from the simplicity of white filet curtains for the kitchen to the more ambitious table cloth borders and table centres featured. Why not give your bedroom or bathroom an individual look with flowered or geometric edgings for your towels, or perhaps use them to border your bedside table? Each project is rated for its degree of intricacy so that you can be certain which is right as you develop your level of skill. Both the charts and enlargements of each piece will ensure that your work stays accurate.

Whether you want to furnish your home in a personal way, create an heirloom to hand down to your children, or simply pass a few relaxing hours, you will find this book, the first in a series, a valuable source of ideas and enjoyment.

General Information

Abbreviations

Beg = beginning; **blk**(s) = block(s); **ch** = chain; **dec** = decrease; **dc** = double crochet; **dtr** = double treble; **htr** = half treble; **inc** = increase; **quadtr** = quadruple treble; **quintr** = quintuple treble; **rep** = repeat; **sl st** = slip stitch; **sp(s)** = space(s); **st(s)** = stitch(es); **tr** = treble; **ttr** = triple treble; **tog** = together.

■ = **1 block (blk)** = work 4tr for first blk, then 3tr for each additional blk.

□ = **1 space (sp)** = work 1tr, 2ch, 1tr for first sp, then 2ch, 1tr for each additional sp.

To inc 1 blk at beg of row = make 5ch, work 1tr into 4th ch from hook, 1tr into next ch, 1tr into next tr. - work 3 more ch (3 more tr) for each additional blk to be increased.

To inc 1 blk at end of row = work to last tr, yo, insert crochet hook into last tr and draw loop through, yo and through 1 loop on hook (1 base ch made), [yo and through 2 loops on hook] twice, *yo, insert hook into last base ch made and draw loop through, yo and through 1 loop on hook (another base ch made), [yo and through 2 loops on hook] twice, rep from * twice more - work from * 3 times more for each additional blk to be increased.

To dec 1 blk at beg of row = Sl st into each of first 4tr - sl st into 3 more tr for each additional blk to be decreased.

To dec 1 blk at end of row = work to last 3tr, turn - work 3tr less for each additional blk to be decreased.

Levels of Difficulty

The patterns in this book have been given levels of difficulty.

✪ = Beginners
✪✪ = Intermediate
✪✪✪ = Experienced
✪✪✪✪ = Expert

Notes

Repeat instructions following an asterisk, (*), as many more times as specified in addition to the original.

Repeat instructions in square brackets, [ ], as many times as specified.

To make counting easier when making a large number of chain, tie a length of contrasting yarn into every 20th or 50th ch made.

In order to simplify the instructions, some patterns state to start a row or a round with a tr (or dtr, or ttr), in these cases always start with 3ch (or 4, or 5ch), these ch replace the first tr (or dtr, or ttr) to bring the hook to the correct level to work the next st, the following stitch is then worked into 2nd stitch of previous row (thus missing the first, i.e. the last of previous row).

Washing and Pressing Instructions

Crochet items should not be washed when work is still in progress. The assembled article should be washed on completion.

Make a warm lather of pure soap flakes and wash in the usual way, either by hand or washing machine. If required, the article may be spin-dried until it is damp, or left until it is half dry. Place a piece of paper, either plain white or squared on top of a clean, flat surface. Draw the shape of the finished article onto the paper, using a ruler and set square for squares and rectangles and a pair of compasses for circles. Using rustless pins, pin the crochet onto the pencilled shape, taking care not to strain the crochet. Pin out the general shape first, then finish by pinning each picot, arch or space into position.

Special points to note carefully when pinning out are: -

1) When pinning arches, make sure the pin is in the centre of each loop to form balanced lines.

2) When pinning scallops, make all the scallops the same size and regularly curved.

3) Pull out all picots.

4) Where there are flowers, pull out each petal in position.

5) When pinning filet crochet, make sure that the spaces and blocks are square and that all edges are even and straight.

If the crochet requires to be slightly stiffened, use a solution of starch - 1 dessertspoonful to ½ litre hot water, and dab lightly over the article. Raise the crochet up off the paper to prevent it sticking as it dries. When dry, remove the pins and press the article lightly with a hot iron.

Materials

Throughout this publication we have recommended products by Coats Patons Crafts. This, however, is only a suggestion and any equivalent yarn, needle or sewing thread of the correct gauge may be substituted if preferred.

Yarn Equivalent

U.K.	Australia
Opera 5	Pellicano
Opera 20	Coats Mercer Crochet Cotton tkt 20
Opera 30	Coats Mercer Crochet Cotton tkt 30
Musica 5	Pellicano
Musica 8	South Maid
Sylko Sewing Thread	Duet sewing thread

BATAILLE

1

1

Table Centre

✪✪✪

Materials

Coats Patons Opera Crochet Cotton Shade 500 - 50 grams

0.75mm Milward Steel Crochet Hook

Special Abbreviations

1 picot = make 3ch, sl st into first of these ch.

Dtr2tog over next 3dc = working until 1 loop of each dtr remains on hook, work 1dtr into next dc, miss 1dc, 1dtr into next dc, yo and through all 3 loops on hook.

Dtr5tog over next 9dc = working until 1 loop of each dtr remains on hook, work 1dtr into next dc, [miss 1dc, 1dtr into next dc] 4 times, yo and through all 6 loops on hook.

Main Centre Piece

1st row: Make 171ch, work 1dc into 12th ch from hook, [7ch, miss 3ch, 1dc into next ch] 39 times, 5ch, miss 3ch, 1tr into last ch, turn.

2nd row: 5ch, work 1dc into first arch, [7ch, 1dc into next arch] 40 times, 4ch, 1tr into 3rd ch of previous row, turn.

3rd row: 10ch, miss first arch, [1dc into next arch, 7ch] 40 times, 1tr into next arch, turn.

Rep the last 2 rows 61 times more, then 2nd row again (126 rows worked).

127th row: 8ch, miss first arch, [1dc into next arch, 5ch] 39 times, 1tr into next arch, **do not** turn.

Edging

Next row: Working down side edge, work 2dc into each arch to corner arch, 7dc into corner arch, 5dc into each arch formed in first row to next corner arch, 7dc into corner arch, 2dc into each arch up other side edge to corner arch, 7dc into corner

arch, then 5dc into each arch formed in last row to last corner arch, 5dc into corner arch, sl st into first dc. Fasten off.

Flowers

Work 75 flowers regularly spaced on filet in 15 rows of 5. Each flower consists of 4 petals worked from 1dc on filet (centre of flower) and each petal secured to a dc immediately connected to this centre dc.

Rejoin yarn with a sl st to a dc on filet, *5ch, dtr3tog into same dc, 1dc into next dc immediately connected to centre dc, 5ch, 1dc into centre dc; rep from * 3 times more, rotating work as each petal is worked into next connecting dc. Fasten off.

Outer Border

Side Flowers (Make 38)

Make 8ch, sl st into first ch to form a ring.

1st round: 3ch, work 15tr into ring, sl st into 3rd of 3ch at beg of round.

2nd round: 3ch, 1 picot, [1tr into next tr, 1 picot] 15 times, sl st into 3rd of 3ch.

3rd round: 13ch, work 1tr into 4th ch from hook, 1tr into each of next 4ch, 1ttr into next tr on 2nd round, [8ch, 1tr into 4th ch from hook, 1tr into each of next 4ch, 1ttr into next tr on 2nd round] 6 times. 7 petals made. Fasten off.

Corner Flowers (Make 4)

Work 1st and 2nd rounds as given for Side Flowers.

3rd round: 13ch, work 1tr into 4th ch from hook, 1tr into each of next 4ch, 1ttr into next tr on 2nd round, [8ch, 1tr into 4th ch from hook, 1tr into each of next 4ch, 1ttr into next tr on 2nd round] 11 times. 12 petals made. Fasten off.

Leaves (Make 42)

1st round: Make 12ch, work 1dc into 3rd ch from hook, 1htr into next ch, 1tr into next ch, 1dtr into each of next 4ch, 1tr into next ch, 1htr into next ch, 1dc into last ch.

2nd round: 5ch, then continuing on other side of starting ch, work [1tr, 2ch] twice into first ch, 2ch, [miss 1ch, 1tr into next ch, 2ch] 4 times, [1tr, 2ch, 1tr] into 2ch arch at tip of leaf, then continue on other side as follows: 2ch, 1tr into next dc, [2ch, miss 1st, 1tr into next st] 4 times, 2ch, sl st into 3rd of 5ch at beg of round.

3rd and joining round: Into first 2ch arch work [1dc, 1ch, 1dc, 1ch, join with a border flower as follows: drop loop from hook, insert hook into 2nd free picot at left of last ttr of flower, pick up dropped loop and draw through picot, 1dc], [1dc, 1ch, 1dc] into each of next 6 arches, into next arch work [1dc, 1ch, 1dc, join as before to 2nd free picot at right of next border flower, 1dc], [1dc, 1ch, 1dc] into each of next 6 arches, sl st into first dc. Fasten off.

Make 7 leaves in this way joining them to 8 side flowers for each short side, and 10 leaves joining them to 11 side flowers for each long side. Make 2 leaves for each corner joining the first to side flower as before and into 2nd free picot of corner flower, and the second one to next picot of same corner flower and to another side flower, **at the same time** joining the 2 corner leaves together as illustrated.

Complete the remaining 3 corners in the same way.

Edging

With right side facing, rejoin yarn with a sl st to ch space of centre arch on outer edge of a leaf, *1dc into base of first tr of next petal on left-hand flower, 7tr into 3ch arch at top of petal, 1dc into top of first tr; rep from * on remaining petals of flower, sl st into ch space of centre arch on outer edge of next leaf, continue in this way to end of round, sl st into same ch space as sl st at beg of round. Fasten off.

Filling Flowers (Make 42)

Make 6ch, sl st into first ch to form a ring.

First round: 10ch (count as 1htr, 8ch), 1dc into ch space of 2nd arch on leaf before link with flower, *working on the last 8 ch, work 1dc into each of the first 2ch, 1htr into each of next 5ch, 1dc into next ch, then work 1htr into ring* (first petal make), 8ch, 1dc into 2nd free picot of flower after link with leaf and work from * to * as for first petal (second petal made), 8ch, miss next picot on flower, 1dc into next picot, then work from * to * as given for first petal (third petal made), 8ch, 1dc into ch space of 2nd arch on next leaf after link with flower and work from * to * as given for first petal (fourth petal made), then continuing working into ring, work 1 picot, [1htr, 1 picot] 6 times, sl st into 2nd ch at beg of round. Fasten off.

Work remaining filling flowers in the same way each side, joining them to flowers and leaves as before.

In each corner, work the filling flower in the same way but joining the first petal to same st on corner leaf where last filling flower was joined, miss 1 space on same leaf, join second petal into next space, then join third and fourth petal symetrically to next corner leaf.

Inner Border

1st round: With right side facing, rejoin yarn with a sl st to centre picot of corner filling flower, 1dc into picot, 11ch, *1dc into centre picot of next filling flower, 19ch, 1dc into ch space of centre arch on next leaf, 19ch; rep from * to last filling flower before corner filling flower, 1dc into centre picot of next filling flower, 11ch, 1dc into centre picot of centre filling flower, 11ch; rep from * 3 times more, omitting 11ch and 1dc at end of last rep, sl st into first dc.

2nd round: Work 1dc into each ch to end, sl st into first dc.

3rd round: 4ch, miss next dc, dtr2tog over next 3 dc, [1ch, miss 1dc, 1dtr into next dc] 11 times, miss 1dc, *dtr2tog over next 3dc, [1ch, miss 1dc, 1dtr into next dc] 17 times; rep from * to corner arch, dtr2tog over next 3dc, [1ch, miss 1dc, 1dtr into next dc] 11 times, 1ch, miss 1dc, dtr5tog over the 9 corner dc, [1ch, miss 1dc, 1dtr into next dc] 11 times, continue in this way to end of round and ending last corner dtr2tog over next 3dc, sl st into dtr2tog at beg of round.

4th round: Work 1dc into first ch space, [1dc, 1ch, 1dc] into each of next 10 spaces, 1dc into each of next 2 spaces, [1dc, 1ch, 1dc] into each of next 16 spaces, 1dc into each of next 2 spaces, [1dc, 1ch, 1dc] into each of next 16 spaces, continue in this way working 1dc only into each of the ch spaces either side of dtr2tog and dtr5tog, sl st into first dc. Fasten off.

5th round: Rejoin yarn into 2nd ch space after corner and work 6ch (count as 1tr, 3ch), miss 1 space, 1dc into next space, 7ch, miss 2 spaces, 1dtr into next space, *7ch, miss 6 spaces, 1dtr into next space, 7ch, miss 2 spaces, [1dc into next space, 3ch] 3 times, 1dc into next space, 7ch, miss 2 spaces, 1dtr into next space; rep from * to last space before corner, 7ch, miss 6 spaces, 1dtr into next space, 7ch, miss 2 spaces, 1dc into next space, 3ch, miss 1 space, 1 tr into next space until 2 loops remain on hook, miss 2 spaces, 1tr into next space until 3 loops remain on hook, yo and through all 3 loops on hook, 3ch, miss next space, 1dc into next space, 7ch, miss 2 spaces, 1tr into next space; continue in this way to end of round, omitting the tr2tog into last corner but ending with 1tr, sl st into 3rd of 6ch at beg of round.

6th round: 3ch (count as 1tr), 1tr into next dc, counting each ch as 1 st, continue as follows: *1ch, miss 1 st, 1htr into next st, rep from * to dc before corner, 1ch, work 1tr into dc until 2 loops remain on hook, 1tr into top of tr2tog until 3 loops remain on hook, 1tr into next dc until 4 loops remain on hook, yo and through all 4 loops on hook, continue in this way to end of round but ending with 1tr into dc, sl st into 3rd of 3ch at beg of round.

7th and joining round: 4ch (count as 1dtr), miss 2 ch spaces, 1dtr into next space, 1dc into corner dc on main piece, *5ch, miss 3 spaces on border, 1dc into next space, 5ch, miss 5dc on main piece, 1dc into next dc, 5ch, miss 3 spaces on border, 1dc into next space, continue in this way along side of main piece to next corner dc, 5ch, 1dc into corner dc, miss 3 spaces on border, 1dtr into next space until 2 loops remain on hook, 1dtr into top of tr3tog until 3 loops remain on hook, miss 3 spaces, 1dtr into next space until 4 loops remain on hook, yo and through all 4 loops on hook, 1dc into same corner st on main piece; rep from * 3 times more but working 1dtr only in last corner, 1dc into corner dc of main piece. Fasten off.

2
Colori
Centro Botanico
Harebell
Rosemary Verey
Centro Botanico
Wild Cornflower
Foxglove
Wild Flowers from Suttons Seeds
Wild Pansy
Wild Flowers from Suttons Seeds
Suttons Seeds

2

Irish Crochet Border

✪✪✪

Materials

Coats Patons Opera No. 20 Crochet Cotton Shade 500 - 50 grams

1.00mm Milward Steel Crochet Hook

Small amount of cotton wool

Special Abbreviations

Dc2tog = [insert hook into next st, yo and draw a loop through] twice, yo and through all 3 loops on hook.

Ttr2tog = work 2ttr into sts as indicated until 1 loop of each remains on hook, yo and through all 3 loops on hook.

Dtr3tog = working until 1 loop of each dtr remains on hook, work 1dtr into same dc as last dtr, miss 2dc, 1dtr into next dc, miss 2dc, 1dtr into next dc, yo and through all 4 loops on hook.

1 picot = 3ch, sl st into first of these ch.

Triple picot = 4ch, sl st into first of these ch, [3ch, sl st into same ch as last sl st] twice.

Flower

Make 10ch, sl st into first ch to form a ring.

1st round: Work 30dc into ring, sl st into first dc.

2nd round: 5ch (count as 1dtr, 1ch), [1dtr into next dc, 1ch] 29 times, sl st into 4th of 5ch at beg of round, turn.

First Petal

1st row (wrong side): 3ch (count as 1tr), counting each ch sp and each dtr as 1 st, continue as follows: 1tr into each of next 4 sts, 2tr into next st, 1tr into each of next 5 sts, turn

2nd row: Sl st into first tr, 1dc into next tr, 1htr into next tr, 1tr into next tr, 2tr into each of next 4tr, 1tr into next tr, 1htr into next tr, 1dc into next tr, sl st into next tr. Fasten off.

2nd Petal

1st row: With wrong side facing, miss next 4dtr on ring at right of previous petal, rejoin yarn to next dtr with a sl st, 1dc into same st as sl st, 3ch, 1tr into each of next 4 sts, 2tr into next st, 1tr into each of next 4 sts, then work 1tr into same dtr as first tr of previous petal.

2nd row: As 2nd row of first petal.

Work 4 more petals in the same way, starting last petal in same st as last tr of first petal.

Next row: Rejoin yarn on 2nd round between 2 petals and work *3sl sts into stem of tr at side of next petal, then working **into back loop only** of each st, work 1dc into each of next 16 sts, sl st into each of next 3ch at beg of same petal; rep from * around each of the remaining 5 petals. Fasten off.

Pistil

Make 2ch, work 4dc into first of these ch, sl st into first dc.

2nd round: 1ch, 2dc into each dc to end, sl st into first dc. 8dc.

3rd round: 1ch, 2dc into each dc to end, sl st into first dc. 16dc.

4th round: 1ch, work 1dc into each dc to end, sl st into first dc.

5th round: 1ch, [dc2tog] 8 times, sl st into first st. 8dc remain.

Insert a small tuft of cotton wool into the ring.

6th round: 1ch, [dc2tog] 4 times, sl st into first dc. Fasten off.

Sew pistil neatly into centre of flower. Arrange petals neatly so that they overlap slightly as illustrated.

Work 3 more flowers in the same way.

Leaf

1st row: Make 13ch, work 1dc into 2nd ch from hook, 1htr into next ch, 1tr into each of next 3ch, 1dtr into each of next 3ch, 1tr into each of next 2ch, 1htr into next ch, 1dc into last ch, sl st into back of 5th st on 3rd row of a flower petal.

Next round: Working on other side of ch, work 1dc into each of 11ch, 3dc into next ch, then work 1dc into each st of first row. Fasten off.

Make a second leaf in the same way **but** joining it to free tip of first leaf.

Work 2 more leaves in the same way, joining the first to 13th st of 3rd petal at right of petal previously joined, then work a pair of leaves at either side of each of the remaining 3 flowers.

Upper Edging

1st round: With right side facing, rejoin yarn with a sl st halfway along top edge of first leaf, work 15ch, *1dc between the 2 leaves, 10ch, ttr2tog working halfway along top edge of next leaf and into back of 4th st on 3rd row of next free petal, 6ch, miss 3sts on same petal, then continuing to work into back of 3rd row of petals, work 1tr into next st, 7ch, 1tr into 4th st on next petal, 6ch, miss 3sts, work ttr2tog working into next st of petal and into st halfway along top edge of next leaf, 10ch, 1tr between the 2 leaves, 10ch, ttr2tog working into st halfway along top edge of each of next 2 leaves, 10ch; rep from * 3 times more, thus joining the 4 groups of flowers and leaves, **but** omitting ttr2tog at end of last rep, work 1ttr halfway along top edge of last leaf, turn.

2nd row: 1ch, work 1dc into each ch and each st to end, turn.

3rd row: 4ch (count as 1dtr), miss first dc, 1dtr into each of next 2dc, *3ch, miss 3dc, 1dtr into each of next 3dc; rep from * to end, turn.

4th row: 1ch, 1dc into first dtr, 2ch, into next dtr work [1dtr, triple picot, 1dtr], *2ch, 1dc into next arch, 2ch, miss 1dtr, into next dtr work [1dtr, triple picot, 1dtr]; rep from * to end, 2ch, 1dc into last dtr. Fasten off.

Lower Edging

1st row: With wrong side facing, rejoin yarn to tip of first leaf with a sl st, 1dc into st, 9ch, *ttr2tog working halfway along edge of same leaf and halfway along edge of next leaf, 9ch, 1ttr into petal just below joining st with leaf, 12ch, 1dc into centre of next petal, 12ch, 1ttr into next petal

just below joining st with leaf, 9ch, ttr2tog working halfway along each of next 2 leaves, 9ch, 1dc inserting hook into tip of both leaves together; rep from * to end, working last dc into tip of last leaf, turn.

2nd row: 1ch, work 1dc into each ch and each st to end, turn.

3rd row: 6ch (count as 1dtr, 2ch), miss first 2dc, 1dtr into next dc, *2ch, miss 1dc, 1dtr into next dc; rep from * to end, turn.

4th row: 1ch, work 3dc into each 2ch space to end, turn.

5th row: 5ch (count as 1dtr, 1ch), miss first dc, 1dtr into next dc until 2 loops remain on hook, miss 2dc, 1dtr into next dc until 3 loops remain on hook, yo and through all 3 loops on hook, 1dtr into same dc as last dtr of dtr2tog, *dtr3tog, 2ch, 1dtr into same dc as last dtr of dtr3tog, 2ch; rep from * to last 4dc, 1dtr into same dc as last dtr until 2 loops remain on hook, 1dtr into last dc until 3 loops remain on hook, yo and through all 3 loops on hook, 1ch, 1dtr into last dc, turn.

6th row: 4ch (count as 1tr, 1ch), miss first st, *into next 2ch space work [1tr, 1ch] twice, 1tr into next st, 1ch; rep from * to end, omitting 1ch at end of last rep, turn.

7th row: 1ch, work 2dc into each ch space to end, turn.

8th row: 5ch (count as 1ttr), miss first dc, 1ttr into each of next 4dc, *1ch, 1 picot, 1ch, miss 2dc, 1ttr into each of next 5dc; rep from * to end.

9th row: 8ch (count as 1dtr, 4ch), miss first ttr, 1dtr into each of next 3ttr, *4ch, miss 2ttr, 1dtr into each of next 3ttr; rep from * to last ttr, 4ch, 1dtr into 5th of 5ch at beg of previous row.

10th row: 1ch, 1dc into first dtr, *3ch, miss 1dtr, into next dtr work [1tr, triple picot, 1tr], 3ch, 1dc into next arch; rep from * to end, placing last dc into 4th of 8ch at beg of previous row. Fasten off.

— ♦ —

TIP

Crochet work will acquire a lustre if ironed with a cotton cloth sprinkled with alcohol.

3

Table Centre in Filet

✪✪

Materials

Coats Patons Opera No. 5 Crochet Cotton Shade 500 - 100 grams

1.75mm Milward Steel Crochet Hook

Special Abbreviations

▣ = **block (blk)** = work 4dtr for first blk, then 3dtr for each additional blk.

- To inc 1 blk at beg of row: make 6ch, work 1dtr into 5th ch from hook, 1dtr into next ch, 1dtr into next dtr (work 3 more ch - 3 more dtr - for each additional block increased).

- To inc 1 blk at end of work: work to last dtr, [yo] twice, insert hook into last dtr and draw loop through, yo and through 1 loop on hook (1 base ch made), [yo and through 2 loops on hook] 3 times, *[yo] twice, insert hook into last base ch made and draw loop through, yo and through 1 loop on hook (another base ch made) then complete dtr as before; rep from * twice more to increase 1 block (rep from * 3 times more for each additional block increased).

□ = **space (sp)** = work 1dtr, 2ch, 1dtr for first sp, then 2ch, 1dtr for each additional sp.

To Make

Work the 3 separate scallops as follows:

★ **1st row**: Make 16ch, work 1dtr into 5th ch from hook, 1dtr into each of remaining 11ch, turn. 4 blks.

2nd row: Inc 3 blks, work 1dtr into each of next 12dtr (3 blks worked over 3 blks), inc 3 blks. 10 blks.

3rd row: Inc 3 blks, work 3 blks over 3 blks, [2ch, miss 2dtr, 1dtr into next dtr] 4 times (4 sps worked over 4 blks), 3 blks over 3 blks, inc 3 blks. 16 squares. Fasten off ★.

Rep from ★ to ★ twice more **but** do not fasten off at end of last scallop.

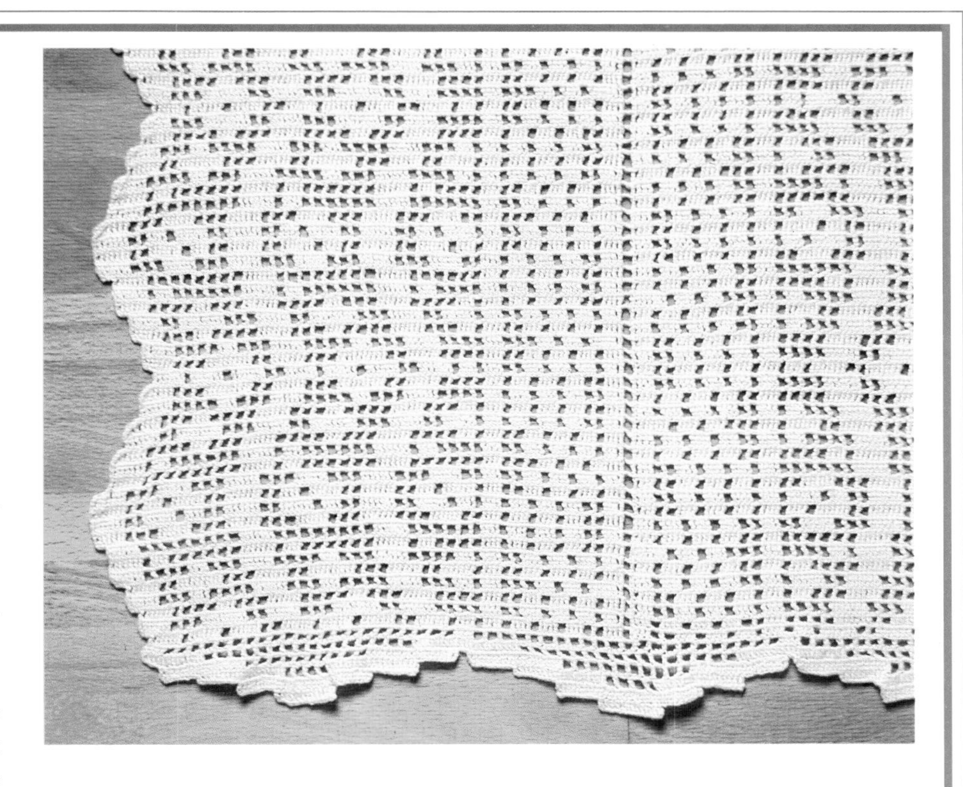

4th and joining row: *Inc 3 blks, work 3 blks, 3 sps over 3 blks, [2ch, 1dtr into next dtr] 4 times (4 sps worked over 4 sps), 3 sps over 3 blks, 3 blks, inc 3 blks, 2ch, rep from * twice more working across next 2 scallops, omitting 2ch at end of last rep, turn.

5th row: Inc 1 blk, *3 blks, 3 sps over 3 blks, 10 sps over 10 sps, 3 blks over 3 blks, 1dtr into each of next 2ch, rep from * twice more omitting 2dtr at end of last rep, inc 1 blk. (70 squares).

Continue following chart to 45th row inclusive, increasing and decreasing blks as shown, rep from 27th to 45th row 4 times more, then work in reverse order from 6th to 1st rows inclusive. Fasten off.

Key ■ = **Block** □ = **Space**

Gelée Extra
de
Pomme
Chutney
SONS LTD
SUCCO D'UVA
KIWI
SEYCHELLES

3/4

4

Kitchen Shelf Border

✪✪

Materials

Coats Patons Opera No. 20 Crochet Cotton Shade 500 - 100 grams

1.00mm Milward Steel Crochet Hook

1 reel Sylko Sewing Thread

1 sewing needle

20 cm x 105 cm white linen

Note

Border is worked lengthwise.

To Make

Make 72ch.

1st row: Work 1tr into 4th ch from hook, 1tr into each of next 2ch, 2ch, miss 2ch, 1tr into each of next 4ch, [2ch, miss 2ch, 1tr into next ch] 12 times, 1tr into each of next 6ch, [2ch, miss 2ch, 1tr into next ch] 4 times, 1tr into each of last 6ch, turn. 23 squares.

2nd row: Inc 3 blks, 2ch, miss 2tr, 1tr into each of next 4tr (1 sp worked over 1 blk and 1 blk over 1 blk), 2ch, 1tr into next tr (1 sp worked over 1 sp), 2tr into next sp, 1tr into next tr (1 blk worked over 1 sp), [2ch, 1tr into next tr] twice (2 sps worked over 2 sps), 1tr into each of next 6tr (2 blks worked over 2 blks), 2tr into next sp, 1tr into next tr (1 blk worked over 1 sp), [2ch, 1tr into next tr] 11 times (11 sps worked over 11 sps), 1tr into each of next 3tr (1 blk worked over 1 blk), 2ch, 1tr into each of next 3tr (1 sp worked over 1 sp and 1 blk over 1 blk), turn. 26 squares.

3rd row: 3ch, miss first tr, 1tr into each of next 3tr (1 blk at beg of row), 1 sp over sp, 1 blk over blk, 11 sps over 11 sps, 2 blks over 2 blks, 1 sp over blk, 1 sp over sp, 1 blk over sp, [1 blk over blk, 1 sp over sp] twice, 1 sp over blk, 2 blks over 2 blks, inc 2 blks, turn. 28 squares.

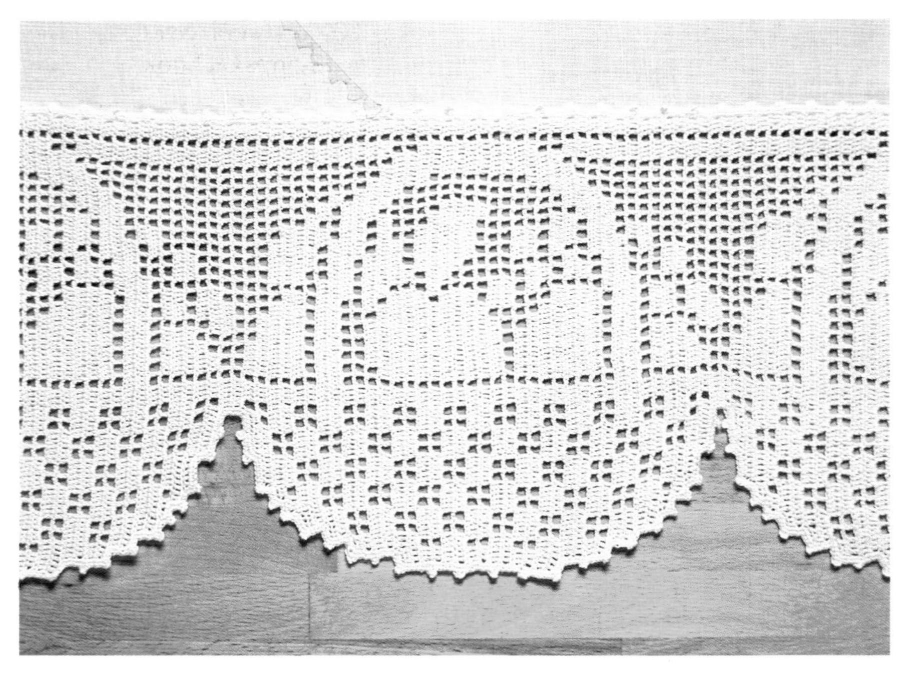

Continue following chart to 40th row inclusive, increasing and decreasing blks as shown.

Rep these 40 rows until border is of required length, **do not** fasten off at end of last row, but work evenly all round border as follows: *5dc, 3ch, sl st into first of these ch to form a picot; rep from * to end **but** working 12dc without picot between each 40 row repeat, sl st into first dc. Fasten off.

Making Up

Make a narrow hem all round fabric and sew border as illustrated.

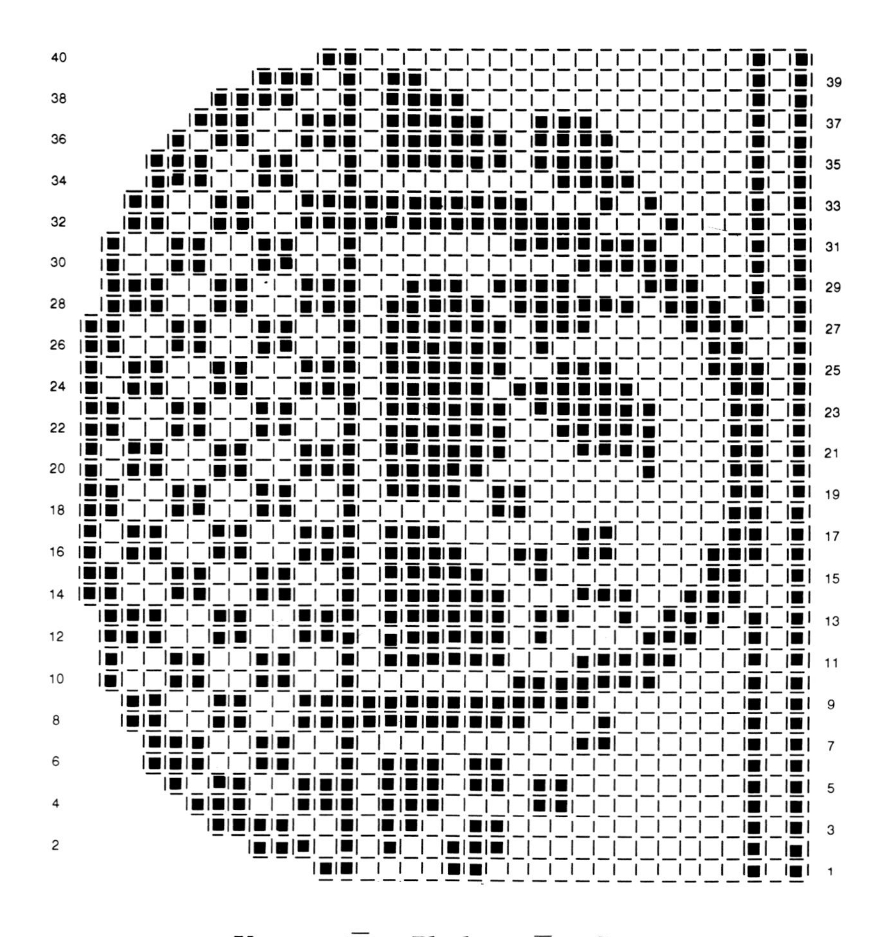

5

Square Mat

✪✪✪

Materials

Coats Patons Opera No. 30 Crochet Cotton Shade 500 - 150 grams

0.75mm Milward Steel Crochet Hook

1 reel Sylko Sewing Thread

1 sewing needle

67cm x 67cm piece of white linen

Size

The border is approximately 9cm [3½ ins] deep.

Special Abbreviations

Tr3tog or tr4tog = work 1tr into each of next 3 (or 4) sts until 1 loop of each tr remains on hook, yo and through all 4 (or 5) loops on hook.

Dc3tog = [insert hook into next st, yo and draw a loop through] 3 times, yo and through all 4 loops on hook.

Picot = make 3ch, sl st into first of these ch.

Side Motifs

Make 24ch.

★ **1st row** Work 1tr into 9th ch from hook, 1tr into each of next 15ch, turn.

2nd row: 3ch (count as 1tr), miss first tr, work 1tr into each of next 14tr, [3tr, 5ch, 1dtr] into arch, turn.

3rd row: 9ch, 3tr into first arch, 1tr into each of next 18tr, turn.

4th row: 3ch, miss first tr, 1tr into each of next 20tr, [3tr, 5ch, 1dtr] into arch, turn.

5th row: 5ch, 3tr into arch, 1tr into each of next 24tr, turn.

6th row: 3ch, miss first tr, 1tr into each of next 23tr, 3ch, 1dtr into arch, turn.

7th row: 7ch, miss 3tr, 1tr into each of next 21tr, turn.

8th row: 3ch, miss first tr, 1tr into each of next 17tr, 3ch, 1dtr into arch, turn.

9th row: 7ch, miss 3tr, 1tr into each of next 15tr.

Make 54ch ★ ★ .

Rep from ★ to ★ ★ 5 times more, **do not** fasten off.

Corner Motif

1st and 2nd rows: As 1st and 2nd rows of Side Motifs.

3rd row: 9ch, 3tr into arch, 1tr into each of next 6tr, 1htr into each of next 4tr, 1dc into each of next 8tr, turn.

5

6
Caffè
Zucchero

4th row: 1ch, 1dc into each of first 10 sts, 1htr into each of next 3 sts, 1tr into each of last 8tr, [3tr 5ch, 1dtr] into arch, turn.

5th row: 7ch, 3tr into arch, 1tr into each of next 10tr, 1htr into each of next 3 sts, 1dc into each of last 11 sts, turn.

6th row: 1ch, 1dc into each of first 12 sts, 1htr into each of next 2 sts, 1tr into each of last 13tr, 3ch, 1dtr into arch, turn.

7th row: 5ch, 1tr into each of next 13tr, 1htr into each of next 3 sts, 1dc into each of last 11dc, turn.

8th and 9th rows: Rep the last 2 rows once more.

10th row: 1ch, 1dc into each of first 11dc, 1htr into each of nedt 3 sts, 1tr into each of next 10tr, 3ch, 1dtr into arch, turn.

11th row: 7ch, miss 3tr, 1tr into each of next 10tr, 1htr into each of next 3 sts, 1dc into each of last 8dc, turn.

12th and 13th rows: As 8th and 9th rows of Side Motifs.

Make 54ch ★ .

Rep from ★ to ★ 3 times more, but make only 30ch at end of last repeat instead of 54 and sl st into first of starting ch. **Do not** fasten off.

Outer Edging

1st round: *Working on other side of starting ch of motif, miss first ch, then continue round motif as follows: work 1dc into each of next 14ch, 5dc into each of next 9 arches, 1dc into each of next 14tr, 1dc into each of next 30ch connecting two motifs; rep from * to end, working 5dc into each of the 13 arches of corner motif, sl st into first dc.

2nd round: Sl st into each of first 2dc, *1tr into each dc to centre dc of centre arch of motif, 3tr into next dc, 1tr into each dc on other side of motif to last 2dc, tr4tog, 1tr into each of next 26ch, tr4tog, rep from * to end, working tr4tog at end of last rep into last 2dc and first 2sl sts, sl st into first tr.

3rd round: 1ch, work 1dc into each st to end, sl st into first dc. Fasten off.

Flower

Make 6ch, sl st into first ch to form a ring.

1st round: Work 12dc into ring, sl st into first dc.

2nd round: 1ch, work [1dc into each of next 2dc, 3ch] 6 times, sl st into first dc.

3rd round: 1ch, [1dc into next dc, 5ch, miss 1dc] 6 times, sl st into first dc.

4th round: 1ch, work 7dc into each of first 3 arches, into next arch work [3dc, sl st into 9th dc on one motif before inner corner, 3dc], into next arch work [3dc, sl st into inner corner st, 3dc], into last arch work [3dc, miss 8dc on motif, sl st into next dc, 3ch], sl st into first dc. Fasten off.

Work a 2nd Flower symetrically in the same way **but** joining it also to the first flower as illustrated.

Work 2 flowers between each of the motifs in the same way.

Braid

With wrong side facing, rejoin yarn with a sl st to centre dc of 2nd free petal of 2nd flower before a corner motif, *5ch, sl st into centre dc of first free petal of next flower, 9ch, sl st into centre dc of next petal, 5ch, miss 2tr on side of next motif, sl st into next tr, turn and work 5dc over the first 5ch, 1 picot, then 5dc over the next 9ch, turn, **15ch, miss 4tr on motif, sl st into next tr, turn and work [4dc, 1 picot, 4dc] over the 15ch, turn**, rep from ** to ** 3 times more, turn, 15ch, miss 4tr on motif, sl st into next tr, turn and work [5dc, 1 picot, 5dc] over the 15ch (centre bar with picot), turn, work from ** to ** 4 times, 15ch, miss 4tr on motif, sl st into next tr, turn and work [5dc, 1 picot, sl st into centre dc of first free petal of next flower, 5dc] over the 15ch, turn, 6ch, sl st into centre dc of next petal, rep from * to end, **but** working 7 dc bars with picot at either side of centre dc bar on corner motifs, sl st into first sl st, turn.

2nd round: Work 5dc into arch between 2 flowers, 6dc into next arch, *1dc into side of dc on next bar with picot, 8dc into next arch, rep from * to last dc bar of motif, 1dc into side of dc on next bar with picot, 6dc into next arch, 5dc into arch between 2 flowers; rep from * to end, sl st into first dc.

3rd round: At inner corner between 2 flowers, work 3ch (count as 1tr), miss first dc, tr3tog over next 3dc, 1tr into next dc, *work 1tr into each dc all round next motif, then at next inner corner between 2 flowers work 1tr into first dc, tr3tog over next 3dc and 1tr into next dc, rep from * to end, sl st into 3rd of 3ch at beg of round.

4th round: *Work 1dc into each of first 10tr, turn, 5ch, sl st into corresponding st on previous motif, turn and work [5dc, 1 picot, 5dc] over the 5ch, 1tr into each of next 9tr, turn, 15ch, sl st into corresponding st on previous motif, turn and work [7dc, 1 picot, 7dc] over the 15ch, **1dc into each of next 9tr, 1 picot; rep from ** 6 times more, 1dc into each of next 24tr, rep from * to end, **but** working 11 picot around each corner motif. Fasten off.

Inner Edging

1st round: With right side facing rejoin yarn to first st after a corner motif and work 1dc into each st and 2dc into side of each tr on motifs, sl st into first dc.

2nd round: 3ch (count as 1tr), miss first dc, work 1tr into each dc and tr3tog into each of the 4 corners, sl st into 3rd of 3ch at beg of round.

3rd round: 1ch, *work 1dc into each of next 10tr, 1 picot; rep from * to end but working dc3tog into each corner. Fasten off.

Making Up

Work a narrow hem all round fabric, pin crochet border evenly all round fabric and slip stitch in place.

TIP

Before starting any crochet work make sure that your hands are scrupulously clean, and it is as well to check while you are working, particularly if your hands are inclined to perspire a little.

6

Table Centre with Flowers

✪✪✪

Materials

Coats Patons Opera No. 20 Crochet Cotton Shade 500 - 50grams

1.00mm Milward Steel Crochet Hook

Size

Finished Table Centre measures approximately 47cm [18 3/4 ins] square.

Special Abbreviations

Tr3tog = working until 1 loop of each tr remains on hook, work 1tr into next st, miss 1 st, 1tr into next st, miss 1 st, 1tr into next st, yo and through all 4 loops on hook.

Dtr3tog = work 1dtr into each of next 3tr until 1 loop of each dtr remains on hook, yo and through all 4 loops on hook.

Main Piece

Flowers (Make 6)

Make 8ch, sl st into first ch to form a ring.

1st round: 3ch (count as 1tr), work 15tr into ring, sl st into 3rd of 3ch at beg of round.

2nd round: 4ch (count as 1tr, 1ch), miss first tr, [1tr into next tr, 1ch] 15 times, sl st into 3rd of 4ch at beg of round.

3rd round: 1ch, work [1dc, 3ch (picot), 1dc] into each ch space to end. Fasten off.

Leaves (Make 6 pairs)

1st row: Make 15ch and work 1dc into 3rd ch from hook, 1htr into next ch, 1tr into each of next 2ch, 1dtr into each of next 5ch, 1tr into each of next 2ch, 1htr into next ch, 1dc into last ch, **do not** turn, but continue in rounds as follows:

1st round: 4ch (count as 1tr, 1ch), work [1tr, 1ch] twice into same st as last dc, [1tr into next ch, 1ch, miss ch] 6 times, into last ch work [1tr, 1ch] 3 times, [miss 1 st, 1tr into next st, 1ch] 6 times, sl st into 3rd of 4ch at beg of round.

3rd round: 1ch, work [1dc, 3ch (picot), 1dc] into first ch sp, into next tr work [1dc, 1ch, sl st into a picot on a flower, 1ch, 1dc], [1dc, 3ch, 1dc] into each of next 9 spaces, [1dc, 3ch, 1dc] into next tr, [1dc, 3ch, 1dc] into each of last 8 spaces, sl st into first dc. Fasten off.

Make a 2nd leaf in the same way **but** joining it to opposite picot of same flower and do not fasten off at end.

Next round: Sl st to picot at point of leaf, work 1dc into picot, *[7ch, miss 1 picot, 1dc into next picot] 4 times, 3ch, 1dc into next picot, 1dc into next free picot of flower, 3ch, 1dc into next picot, [7ch, miss 1 picot, 1dc into next picot] twice, 3ch, 1dc into next picot, 1dc into next picot of 2nd leaf, 3ch, 1dc into next picot, [7ch, miss 1 picot, 1dc into next picot] 4 times, rep from * once more. Fasten off.

Background Net

1st row: Make 197ch and work 1dc into 9th ch from hook, *5ch, miss 3ch, 1dc into next ch; rep from * to last 4ch, 3ch, 1tr into last ch, turn. 48 arches.

2nd row: 1ch, 1dc into tr, *5ch, 1dc into next 5ch arch; rep from * to last arch, 3ch, 1tr into 4th ch, turn.

3rd row: 1ch, 1dc into tr, *5ch, 1dc into next 5ch arch; rep from * to end, 3ch, 1tr into dc, turn.

Rep the last row 10 times more.

14th row: 1ch, 1dc into tr, [5ch, 1dc into next 5ch arch] 5 times, *2ch, sl st into tip of a leaf, 2ch, 1dc into next arch on background net, 2ch, sl st into next arch on leaf, 2ch, 1dc into next arch on background net, [5ch, 1dc into next arch] 13 times, rep from * once more, then join in 1 more leaf as before, work to end, turn.

Work 34 rows of background net separately at each side and between each motif, joining in each motif diagonally by working 1 more arch on one side of motif and 1 arch less on other side. Work 15 rows of background net across the whole width, then join 3 more motifs as before, then work 13 rows across the whole width. Fasten off.

Border

Work 8 flowers and 7 leaves alternately for each side, joining them as for main piece, thus having 2 flowers at each corner joined together at 3 picots so that 5 picots remain free on the inside and 7 on the outside as illustrated. Fasten off.

2nd round: With right side facing rejoin yarn with a sl st into 4th picot of flower on the right of one corner, 1dc into picot, *1dc into corresponding picot of next corner flower, 15ch, miss 2 picots, 1quintr into next picot, **7ch, 1dc into centre picot of leaf, 7ch, [miss 1 free picot on next flower, 1quintr into next picot, 13ch] twice, miss 1 picot, 1quintr into next picot, rep from ** 5 times more, 7ch, 1dc into centre picot of next leaf, 7ch, 1quintr into first free picot of next flower, 15ch, miss 2 picots, 1dc into next picot; rep from * 3 times more omitting 1dc at end of last rep, sl st into first dc.

3rd round: 1ch, work 1dc into each st and each ch to end, sl st into first dc.

4th round: 4ch (count as 1tr, 1ch), *miss next dc, 1tr into next dc, 1ch; rep from * to end, **at the same time** working tr3tog into each angle as illustrated, sl st into 3rd of 4ch at beg of round.

5th round: 1ch, *2dc into next ch space, [1dc, 3ch (picot), 1dc] into next ch space; rep from * to end omitting a picot at either side of tr3tog of previous round, sl st into first dc. Fasten off.

6th round: Rejoin yarn to first of 5 picots on first arch after a corner, 1dc into picot, *[5ch, 1dc into next picot] 4 times, 13ch, 1dc into 2nd picot on next arch, rep from * **at the same time** working into each corner as follows: 1dtr into centre of first small arch until there are 2 loops on hook, 1ttr into corner st until there are 3 loops on hook, 1dtr into centre of next small arch until there are 4 loops on hook, yo and through all 4 loops on hook, end round with a sl st into first dc.

7th round: 4ch (count as 1tr, 1ch), miss 1 st, *1tr into next st, 1ch, miss 1 st, rep from * to end **at the same time** working tr3tog into each corner, end round with a sl st into 3rd of 4ch. Fasten off.

8th round: With right side facing rejoin yarn with a sl st into a corner st, 4ch, sl st into corner st of background net, work 1dtr into next tr on border, sl st into same corner st of background net as before *4ch, miss 1tr on border, 1dc into next tr, 4ch, 1dc into next st on background net, rep from * to end **at the same time** working dtr3tog over the 3 corner sts, sl st into corner of background net. Fasten off.

— ♦ —

7

Tablecloth Border

✪✪✪

Materials

Coats Patons Opera No. 20 Crochet Cotton Shade 500 - 200 grams

1.00mm Milward Steel Crochet Hook

1 reel Sylko Sewing Thread

1 sewing needle

85cm x 85cm piece of white linen

Size

Finished Border is approximately 10cm [4 ins] deep.

TIP

When the base chain has over 100 stitches it becomes hard to keep count. If you insert a marker of coloured thread every 20 stitches, you can count the groups without going back to the beginning every time.

Special Abbreviation

Tr3tog = work 1tr into each of next 3 sts until 1 loop of each tr remains on hook, yo and through all 4 loops on hook.

To Make

Make 1900ch, sl st into first ch to form a ring.

1st round: *[Work 1tr into each of first 21ch, [tr3tog] twice, 1tr into each of next 4ch] 14 times, [1tr into each of next 6ch, 5tr into next ch] 3 times for corner, 1tr into each of next 10ch, [tr3tog] twice, 1tr into each of next 4ch; rep from * 3 times more, sl st into first tr.

2nd round: Sl st into first 6tr, *[1dc into each of next 5tr, 15ch, miss 6tr, **1dc into next tr, 2ch, miss 2tr, tr2tog by working 1tr into next st until 2 loops remain on hook, miss 2 sts, (the 2 tr3tog of previous round), 1tr into next tr until 3 loops remain on hook, yo and through all 3 loops on hook, 2ch, miss 2tr, 1dc into next tr**, 15ch, miss 6tr] 14 times, [1dc into each of next 5tr, 15ch, miss 6tr] 3 times, rep from ** to ** once, 15ch, miss 6tr; rep from * 3 times more, sl st into first dc.

3rd round: Sl st into first 2dc, ★ *1dc into next dc, 1tr into each of next 15ch, 1tr into each of first 6ch of next arch of 15ch, turn, 3ch, miss next 2tr, sl st into next tr, 21ch, miss 2tr on next arch, sl st into next tr, 3ch, miss 1tr, sl st into next tr, turn, 1tr into each of 21ch, sl st into last tr before turning, then continuing on same arch work 1tr into each of remaining 9ch, miss 2dc*, rep from * to * 13 times more, **1dc into 3rd of 5dc, 1tr into each of first 12ch of next arch, turn, 3ch, miss 2tr, sl st into next tr, 13ch, turn, 1tr into 4th ch from hook,

1tr into each of next 9ch, sl st into last tr before turning, 1tr into each of remaining 6ch of arch, rep from ** once more, miss 2dc, rep from * to * once, then rep from ★ 3 times more. Fasten off.

4th round: With right side facing, miss first 9tr of an arch, rejoin yarn to next tr and work 1dc into tr, 1dc into each of next 2tr, 49ch, *miss 9tr on next arch, 1dc into each of next 3tr, 49ch; rep from * to end, working the 3dc into end of bars at each corner, sl st into first dc.

5th round: *Tr3tog over the 3tr, [2ch, miss 2ch, 1tr into next ch] 8 times, 2ch, 1tr into next ch, 2ch, miss 2ch, [1tr into next ch, 2ch] twice, [miss 2ch, 1tr into next ch, 2ch] 7 times; rep from * to end, sl st into first st.

6th round: Sl st into each of first 2ch, *[1tr into next tr, 2tr into next 2ch space] 16 times, 1tr into next tr, miss 2 spaces; rep from * to end, missing 1 space only at end of last rep, sl st into first tr.

7th round: Sl st into each of next 4tr, *[1tr into next tr, 2ch, miss 2tr] 6 times, 1tr into next tr, 2ch, miss 1tr, [1tr, 2ch, 1tr] into next tr, 2ch, miss 1tr, 1tr into next tr, [2ch, miss 2tr, 1tr into next tr] 6 times, miss 4tr on next arch; rep from * to end, sl st into first tr.

8th round: Sl st to 2nd space, *[1dc, 3htr, 1dc] into each of next 13 spaces, 1ch, miss 1 space on next arch; rep from * to end, sl st into first dc. Fasten off.

Outer Border

1st round: With right side facing rejoin yarn between 3rd and 4th shell on right side of a scallop, *work 1tr between these 2 shells, 11ch, 1dtr between 6th and 7th shell, 7ch, 1dtr between 7th and 8th shell, 11ch, 1tr between 10th and 11th shell, 7ch; rep from * to end, sl st into first tr.

2nd round: 1ch, *1dc into next tr, 3ch, work [1tr, 3ch] 3 times into 11ch arch, 3ch, 1tr into next dtr, 3ch, [1tr, 3ch] twice into 7ch arch, 1tr into next dtr, 3ch, [1tr, 3ch] 3 times into next 11ch arch, 3ch, 1dc into next tr, 2ch, [1tr, 2ch] twice into next 7ch arch, 2ch; rep from * to end, sl st into first dc.

3rd round: 1ch, *2dc into next space, [1dc, 1htr, 1tr, 1htr, 1dc] into each of next 9 spaces, 2dc into each of next 2 spaces, [1dc, 1htr, 1tr, 1htr, 1dc] into next space, 2dc into next space; rep from * to end, sl st into first dc. Fasten off.

Filling

1st row: With right side facing and working inside an oval, rejoin yarn with a sl st to base of 3rd tr to the right of centre space at tip of oval, 1dc into base of tr, 3ch, work 3tr into centre space, 3ch, 1dc into base of corresponding tr on other side of the oval, 2ch, 1dc into base of next tr, turn.

2nd row: 3ch, 3tr into first tr, 2ch, miss 1tr, 3tr into next tr, 3ch, 1dc into base of next tr, 2ch, 1dc into base of next tr, turn.

3rd row: 3ch, 1tr into each of next 3 tr, 3ch, 1dc into 2ch arch, 3ch, 1tr into each of next 3tr, 3ch, 1dc into base of next tr, 2ch, 1dc into base of next tr, turn.

4th row: 3ch, 1tr into each of next 3tr, 3ch, 1dc into next arch, 5ch, 1dc into next arch, 3ch, 1tr into each of next 3tr, 3ch, 1dc into base of next tr, 2ch, 1dc into base of next tr, turn.

5th row: 3ch, 1tr into each of next 3tr, 5ch, 1dc into next arch, 5ch, 1tr into each of next 3tr, 3ch, 1dc into base of next tr, 2ch, 1dc into base of next tr, turn.

Rep the last 2 rows once more, then rep these 2 rows once more, **but** joining into tr of tr arches as follows: 1dc into next tr, miss 2tr, 1dc into next tr, turn.

Work 3 more rows in the same way, **but** working 2ch instead of 3 on the outside edges of the 3tr.

13th row: 1tr into each of 3tr **at the same time** joining them with a sl st to first 3 free tr on arch, 2ch, miss next 2tr on arch, 1dc into next tr, 3ch, 1dc into 5ch arch, 3ch, miss 3tr on next arch, 1dc into next tr, 2ch, 1tr into each of 3tr **at the same time** joining them with a sl st to last 3tr on arch. Fasten off.

Making Up

Using small invisible stitches, sew first round of border onto edge of fabric as illustrated. Make a narrow hem on wrong side.

PAVESE
1989
LIVIO PAVESE
DOLCETTO
D'ALBA
VENDEMMIA
PAVESE
1989
LIVIO PAVESE
DOLCETTO
D'ALBA

8

Motif for Mat

✪✪✪

Materials

Coats Patons Opera No. 30 Crochet Cotton Shade 500 - 60 grams

0.75mm Milward Steel Crochet Hook

1 reel Sylko Sewing Thread

1 sewing needle

30cm x 30cm piece of white linen

Special Abbreviations

1 picot = make 3ch, sl st into first of these ch.

Triple picot = [make 3ch, sl st into first of these ch] 3 times.

Ovals (Make 2 the same)

Leaves

1st row: *Make 10ch and sl st into 2nd ch from hook, 1dc into next ch, 1htr into each of next 2ch, 1dc into next ch, sl st into next ch (1 small leaf made)*, [12ch, work 1dc into 2nd ch from hook, 1htr into next ch, 1tr into each of next 3ch, 1htr into next ch, 1dc into next ch, sl st into next ch] 4 times, rep from * to * once, [6ch, sl st into 2nd ch from hook, 1dc into next ch, 1htr into each of next 2ch, 1dc into next ch] twice, sl st into dc of first of last 3 small leaves.

2nd row: Work along other side of vertical ch as follows: [1dc into each of first 4ch between 2 leaves, 8ch, 1dc into 2nd ch from hook, 1htr into next ch, 1tr into each of next 3ch, 1htr into next ch, 1dc into next ch, sl st into sl st] 4 times, 1dc into each of next 4ch, 6ch, sl st into 2nd ch from hook, 1dc into next ch, 1htr into each of next 2ch, 1dc into next ch, sl st into next sl st, 1dc into each of last 4ch.

Border

1st round: 1ch, 1dc into dc, *10ch, 1dc into tip of first leaf, 4ch, [1dc into tip of next leaf, 6ch] 3 times, 1dc into tip of next leaf, 4ch, 1dc into next leaf, 10ch, 1dc into tip of next leaf; rep from * once more, sl st into first dc.

2nd round: Work 1dc into each ch and each dc to end, sl st into first dc.

3rd round: 1dc into each dc to end, sl st into first dc.

4th round: 5ch (count as 1tr, 2ch), miss next dc, [1tr into next dc, 2ch, miss 1dc] twice, [1tr into next dc, 2ch, miss 2dc] 13 times, [1tr into next dc, 2ch, miss 1dc] 6 times, [1tr into next dc, 2ch, miss 2dc] 13 times, [1tr into next dc, 2ch, miss 1dc] 3 times, sl st into 3rd of 5ch at beg of round.

5th round: Work 1dc into each tr and 2dc into each 2ch space to end, sl st into first dc.

6th round: Work 1dc into each dc to end, sl st into first dc. Fasten off.

Centre Square

1st row: Make 7ch and work 1tr into 4th ch from hook, 1tr into each of next 3ch, turn.

2nd row: 3ch, miss first tr, 1tr into each of next 3tr, 1tr into next ch.

Continue in rounds as follows:

1st round: 4ch (count as 1tr, 1ch), into last tr of 2nd row work [1tr, 1ch] twice, miss 1tr, *1tr into next tr, 1ch, miss 1tr, into next corner work [1tr, 1ch] 3 times; rep from * 3 times more working the single tr into top of tr on first row where necessary, 1tr into 3rd of 3ch at beg of first row, 1ch, sl st into 3rd of 4ch at beg of round.

2nd round: 1dc into same st as last sl st, [1dc into next ch space, 1dc into next tr] 5 times, sl st into centre dc on one side of an oval, [1dc into next ch space, 1dc into next tr] 8 times, sl st into centre dc on side of second oval, [1dc into next ch space, 1dc into next tr] twice, 1dc into last ch space, sl st into first dc. Fasten off.

Fan

1st row: With right side facing and taking care not to twist work, miss 2dc on oval, rejoin yarn to next dc with a sl st, 5ch, 1tr into side tr on square, 5ch, 1dc into corner dc on square, 5ch, 1tr into side tr on square, 5ch, sl st into 3rd dc on side of 2nd oval, turn.

2nd row: Sl st into each of next 3dc on oval, 6ch, miss first arch, 1dc into next arch, 5ch, 1dc into next arch, 6ch, miss 2dc on oval, sl st into next dc, turn.

3rd row: Sl st into each of next 3dc on oval, 6ch, miss first arch, work 1dtr into next arch, [1ch, 1dtr] 6 times into same arch as last dtr, 6ch, miss 2dc on oval, sl st into next dc, turn.

4th row: Sl st into each of next 3dc on oval, 4ch, 2dtr into first ch space, [2ch, 2dtr into next ch space] 5 times, 4ch, miss 2dc on oval, sl st into next dc, turn.

5th row: Sl st into each of next 3dc on oval, 2ch, [2dtr into next dtr, 1dtr into next dtr, 2ch] 6 times, miss 2dc on oval, sl st into next dc, turn.

6th row: Sl st into each of next 3dc on oval, 2ch, [2dtr into next dtr, 1dtr into each of next 2dtr, 2ch] 6 times, miss 2dc on oval, sl st into next dc, turn.

7th row: Sl st into each of next 3dc on oval, 2ch, [1dtr into each of next 3dtr, 2dtr into next dtr, 2ch] 6 times, miss 2dc on oval, sl st into next dc, turn.

8th row: Sl st into each of next 3dc on oval, 2ch, [1dtr into each of next 4dtr, 2dtr into next dtr, 2ch] 6 times, miss 2dc on oval, sl st into next dc, turn.

9th row: Sl st into each of next 3dc on oval, 2ch, [1dtr into each of next 5dtr, 2dtr into next dtr, 2ch] 6 times, miss 2dc on oval, sl st into next dc. Fasten off.

Work a 2nd Fan in the same way on other side of square and ovals, **but do not** fasten off at end.

Border

Work evenly all round the 2 ovals and 2 fans as follows: *5dc, 1 triple picot, 5dc, 1 picot; rep from * to end, sl st into first dc. Fasten off.

Making Up

Using small invisible stitches, sew motif to one corner of fabric. Carefully cut away fabric under crochet motif and make a narrow hem. Work a narrow hemstitch all round remaining sides of hankerchief.

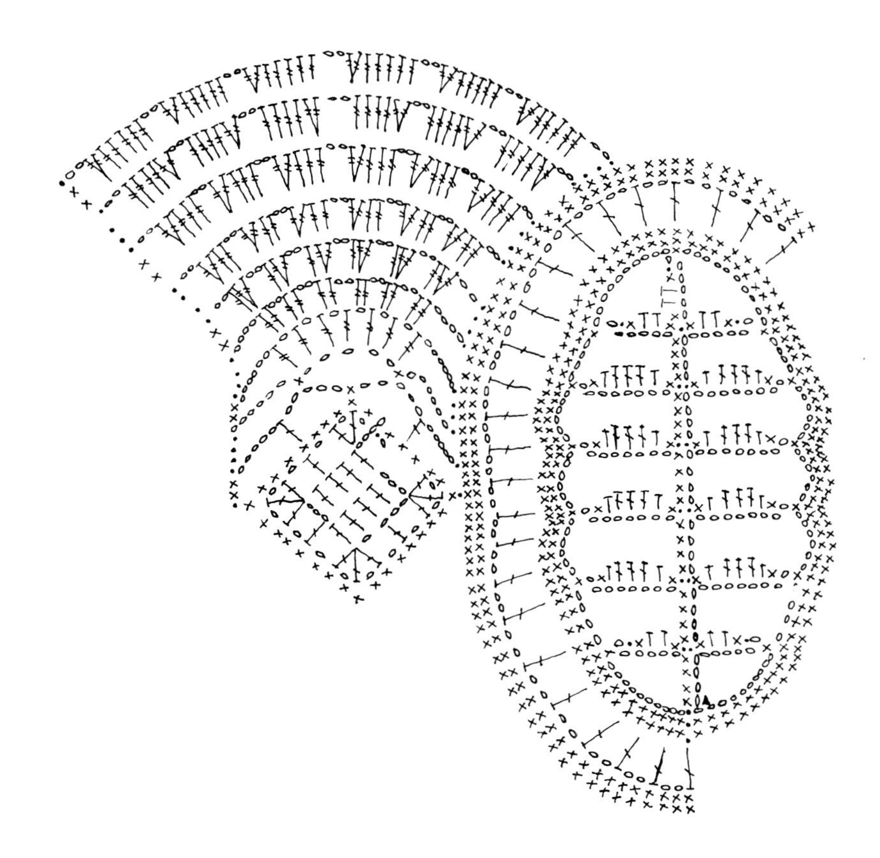

9

Tablecloth in Irish Crochet

✪✪

Materials

Coats Patons Opera No. 5 Crochet Cotton Shade 500 - 250 grams

1.75mm Milward Steel Crochet Hook

1 reel Sylko Sewing Thread

1 sewing needle

90cm x 120cm piece white linen

Size

Finished tablecloth measures approximately 75cm x 93 cm [30 x 37¼ ins].

Leaves (Make 39)

1st row: Make 13ch and work 1dc into 2nd ch from hook, 1dc into each of next 10ch, 3dc into last ch, then on other side of starting ch, work 1dc into each of next 11ch, turn.

2nd row: 1ch, **working into back loop only** of each dc, work 1dc into each of first 12dc, 3dc into next dc, 1dc into each of next 11dc, turn.

Rep the last row 20 times more. Fasten off.

Flowers (Make 39)

Make 12ch, sl st into first ch to form a ring.

1st round: Work 24dc into ring, sl st into first dc.

2nd round: 6ch (count as 1tr, 3ch), [miss 2dc, 1tr into next dc, 3ch] 7 times, sl st into 3rd of 6ch at beg of round.

3rd round: Work [1dc, 1htr, 3tr, 1htr, 1dc] into each 3ch arch to end, sl st into first dc. 8 petals.

4th round: [Work 1dc **into back loop only** of first dc of next petal, 6ch] 8 times, sl st into first dc.

5th round: Work [1dc, 1htr, 5tr, 1htr, 1dc] into each 6ch arch to end, sl st into first dc. Fasten off.

10

Curtain in Filet with Houses

✪✪

Materials

Coats Patons Opera No. 20 Crochet Cotton Shade 500 - 100 grams

1.00mm Milward Steel Crochet Hook

To Make

Work individual scallops as follows:

Right Scallop

1st row: Make 9ch, work 1tr into 4th ch from hook, 1tr into each of remaining 5ch, turn. 2 blks.

2nd row: Inc 1 blk, 1tr into each of next 6tr, inc 1 blk. 4 blks.

3rd row: 3ch, miss first tr, 1tr into each of next 12tr, inc 1 blk. 5lks. Fasten off.

★ Next Scallop

1st row: Make 9ch, work 1tr into 4th ch from hook, 1tr into each of remaining 5ch, turn. 2 blks.

2nd row: Inc 1 blk, 1tr into each of next 6tr, inc 1 blk. 4 blks.

3rd row: Inc 1 blk, 1tr into each of next 12tr, inc 1 blk. 6 blks. Fasten off ★.

Rep from ★ to ★ 8 times more.

Left Scallop

1st row: Make 9ch, work 1tr into 4th ch from hook, 1tr into each of remaining 5ch, turn. 2 blks.

2nd row: Inc 1 blk, work 1tr into each of next 6tr, inc 1 blk. 4 blks.

3rd row: Inc 1 blk, 1tr into each of next 12tr, turn. 5 blks.

4th and joining row: Work 5 blks, inc 1 blk, make 2ch, *working across next scallop, inc 1 blk, work 6 blks, inc 1 blk, 2ch; rep from * 8 times more, then working across right scallop inc 1 blk, work 5 blks, turn.

5th row: 3ch, miss first tr, 1tr into each tr and each ch to end, turn. 94 blks worked over 94 blks.

Making Up

Each flower slightly overlapping the tips of the leaves, join them into two rectangles with a flower in each corner, 1 flower and 2 leaves on short sides and 7 flowers and 6 leaves on long sides. Sew onto fabric, then cut away fabric neatly and carefully under the crochet and make a small hem. Join the two rectangles together with another strip of flowers and leaves as illustrated.

TIP

Newly made stains of tea or coffee on cotton threads should be washed with soap and water; use bleach if possible. If the stains are old try and loosen them with glycerine before washing out.

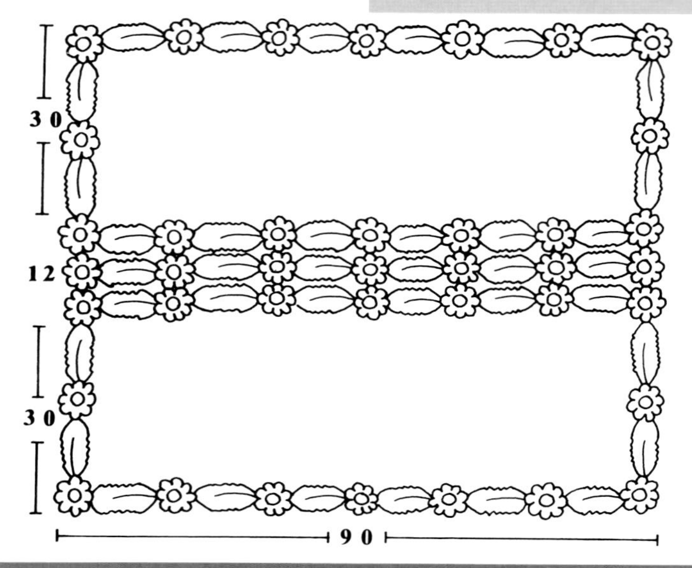

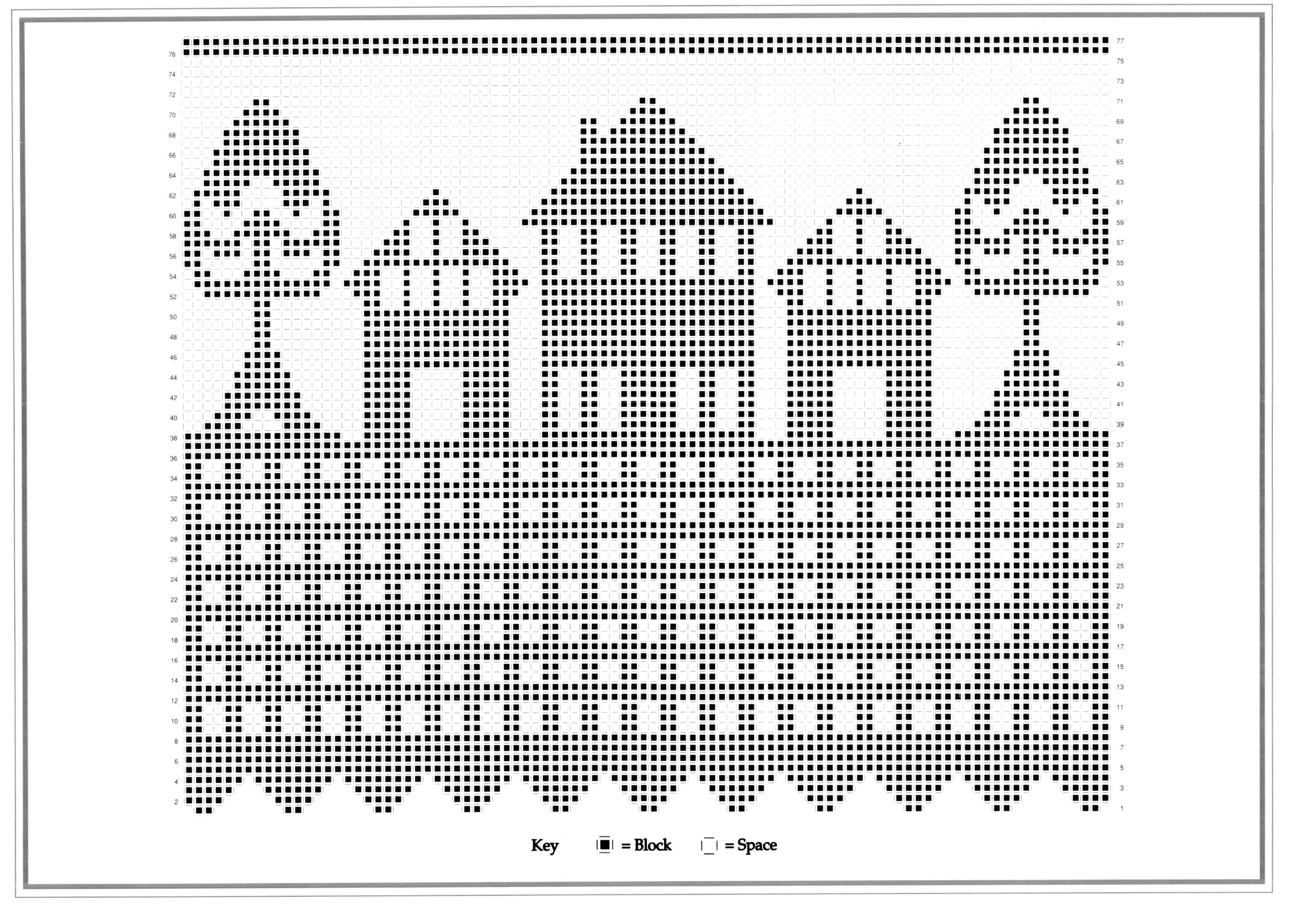
Key
= Block
= Space

9/10
GINGER
Mixed SPICES
THYME
BASIL
Oregano
Cinnamon

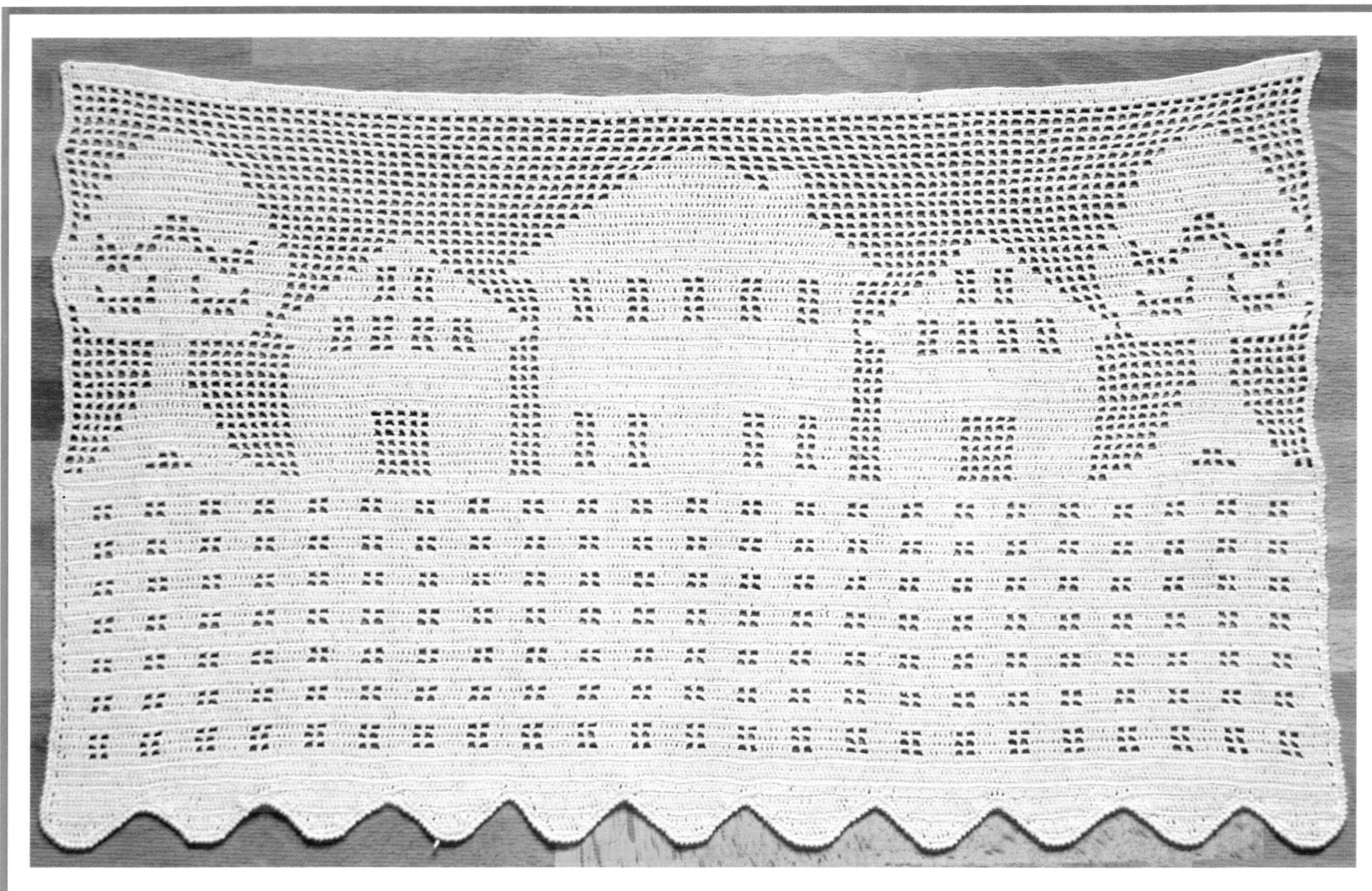

6th row: Work 94 blks over 94 blks.

Rep the last row twice more.

9th row: 3ch, miss first tr, 1tr into each of next 6tr (2 blks worked over 2 blks), *[2ch, miss 2tr, 1tr into next tr] twice (2 sps worked over 2 blks), 1tr into each of next 6tr; rep from * to end.

Continue in this way following chart to end.

Edging

Work 1 row of dc evenly down side edge, across scalloped edge and up left edge, **do not turn** and work a 2nd row of dc working from left to right. Fasten off.

TIP

It is advisable not to put crochet curtains in the washing machine. Wash them in barely warm water with normal washing detergent if the work is white, or a mild detergent if the fabric is coloured. Rinse in plenty of water and spread them out flat to dry. If they need ironing be careful not to distort them.

11

Motif for Hankerchief

✪✪✪✪

Materials

Coats Patons Opera No. 30 Crochet Cotton Shade 500 - 60 grams

0.75mm Milward Steel Crochet Hook

1 reel Sylko Sewing Thread

1 sewing needle

30cm x 30cm piece of fine white linen

Special Abbreviations

1 picot = make 3ch, sl st into first of these ch.

1 spoke = make 4ch, 1 picot, 4ch, sl st into st as indicated, then work 1dc into each of first 4ch, 1 picot and 1dc into each of next 4ch.

Main Piece

Wheels (Make 8)

Note: Following chart, join the wheels together with a htr while working, or with small hidden stitches later.

1st round Make 3ch and work 6dc into first of these ch, sl st into first dc.

2nd round: 1ch, work 2dc into each dc to end, sl st into first dc. 12dc.

3rd round: 1ch, [2dc into next dc, 1dc into next dc] 6 times, sl st into first dc. 18dc

4th round: 1ch, [2dc into next dc, 1dc into each of next 2dc] 6 times, sl st into first dc. 24dc.

5th round: 1ch, [1dc into next dc, 3ch, miss 1dc] 12 times, sl st into first dc. Fasten off.

Wheel with Spokes

Work the first 4 rounds as given for Wheels, fasten off then continue as follows:

Make 1 spoke into 1dc on wheel, 6ch, miss next dc on wheel, 1 spoke into next dc, 6ch, miss next dc, into next dc work [1 spoke, 6ch, 1 spoke], [6ch, miss next dc, 1 spoke into next dc] 3 times, 3ch, 1htr into each of 2 wheels as illustrated, 3ch, miss 1dc on wheel, [1 spoke into next dc, 6ch, miss 1dc] 3 times, into next dc work [1 spoke, 6ch, 1 spoke], [6ch, miss

1dc, 1 spoke into next dc] twice, 6ch, sl st into top of first spoke. Fasten off.

Linking Wheels

1st round: Make 2ch and work 3dc into 2nd ch from hook, sl st into first dc.

2nd round: 1ch, work 2dc into each of the 3dc, sl st into first dc, 6dc, then link up with the wheels with dtr or with spokes following the diagram.

Outer Edging

1st round: Rejoin yarn with a sl st into 6ch arch on wheel with spokes opposite 2 linked wheels and work [1tr, 5ch, 1tr] into arch, then continue round working ch, tr, dtr or spokes as illustrated to form an oval edging.

2nd round: 1ch, work 1dc into each ch and into each st to end, working 3dc into centre ch at each of the 2 points, sl st into first dc.

3rd and 4th rounds: 1ch, 1dc into each dc to end, working 3dc into each centre dc at each of the 2 points, sl st into first dc.

5th round: 5ch (count as 1tr, 2ch), miss 1dc, [1tr into next dc, 2ch, miss 1dc] rep from * to end, sl st into 3rd of 3ch at beg of round.

6th round: Sl st into first ch space, work [1dc, 1 picot, 1dc] into each ch space to end. Fasten off.

Making Up

Using small invisible stitches, sew motif to one corner of fabric. Carefully cut away any fabric under crochet motif and make a narrow hem. Work a narrow hemstitch all round remaining sides of handkerchief.

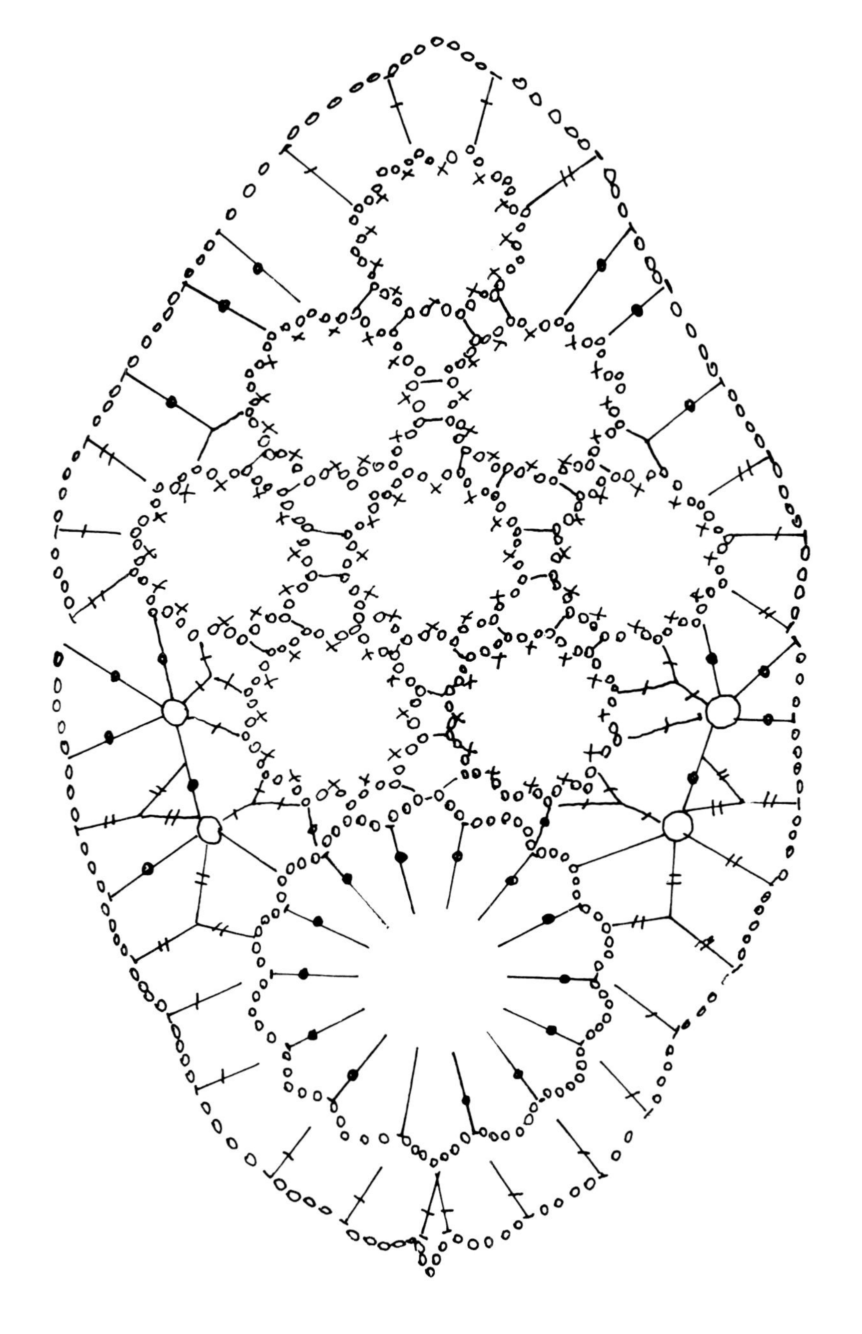

TIP

When fastening off, cut the thread to about 10 cm and pull it tightly through the last stitch on the hook.

11 - 14

12

Motif for Hankerchief

✪✪✪

Materials

Coats Patons Opera No. 30 Crochet Cotton Shade 500 - 60 grams

0.75mm Milward Steel Crochet Hook

1 reel Sylko Sewing Thread

1 sewing needle

30 cm x 30 cm fine white linen

Special Abbreviations

Picot = 3ch, sl st into first of these ch.

Ttr2tog = work 2ttr into ring until 1 loop of each ttr remains on hook, yo and through all 3 loops on hook.

Dtr4tog = work 2dtr into each of next 2 5ch arches until 1 loop of each dtr remains on hook, yo and through all 5 loops on hook.

Flower Motif (Make 2)

Make 12ch, sl st into first of these ch to form a ring.

1st round: 3ch (count as 1tr), work 23tr into ring, sl st into 3rd of 3ch at beg of round.

2nd round: 5ch (count as 1tr, 2ch), miss first 2tr, 1tr into next tr, 2ch, [miss 1tr, 1tr into next tr, 2ch] 11 times, sl st into 3rd of 5ch ag beg of round.

3rd round: 1ch, 1dc into same st as last sl st, 2ch, into first 2ch space work [1tr, 1dtr, 3ch, 1dtr, 1tr], 2ch, *1dc into next tr, 2ch, into next 2ch space work [1tr, 1dtr, 3ch, 1dtr, 1tr], 2ch; rep from * to end, sl st into first dc. 12 petals.

4th round: Sl st to centre 3ch arch of first petal, and work 1dc into arch, [5ch, 1dc into next arch] twice, 9ch (corner arch), 1dc into next arch; rep from * 3 times more, omitting 1dc at end of last rep, sl st into first dc.

5th round: 1ch, *work [3dc, 1 picot, 2dc, 1 picot, 3dc] into each of next 2 5ch arches, [5dc, 1 picot, 2dc, 1 picot, 5dc] into next corner arch; rep from * 3 times more, sl st into first dc. Fasten off.

Edging

1st row: With wrong side facing, rejoin yarn with a sl st between 2 corner picots and work 1dc, *[9ch, 1dc between 2 arches] 3 times, 9ch,

1dc between 2 picots of next corner arch; rep from * once more, turn.

★ **2nd row**: 1ch, into first arch work [3dc, 1 picot, 8dc], 11dc into each of next 2 arches, 6dc into next arch, turn.

3rd row: [9ch, 1dc into centre dc of next arch] 3 times, turn.

4th row: Work [3dc, 1 picot, 8dc] into first arch, 11dc into next arch, 6dc into next arch, turn.

5th row: [9ch, 1dc into centre dc of next arch] twice, turn.

6th row: [3dc, 1 picot, 8dc] into first arch, 6dc into next arch, turn.

7th row: 9ch, 1dc into centre dc of next arch, turn.

8th row: Work [3dc, 1 picot] 3 times and 3dc into 9ch arch, then continue as follows: [2dc, 1 picot, 3dc] into each of the next 3 arches, sl st into dc at beg of first row. **Do not** fasten off.

Work 2nd corner as follows: *[9ch, 1dc between 2 arches on 5th round] 3 times, 9ch, 1dc between 2 picots of next corner arch; rep from * once more, turn.

Complete as given for first corner from ★ to end. Fasten off ★★.

Square Motif (Make 2)

Make 10ch, sl st into first ch to form a ring.

1st round: Into ring work [1dc, 5ch, ttr2tog, 4ch, ttr2tog, 5ch] 4 times, sl st into first dc. Fasten off.

2nd round: Rejoin yarn with a sl st into a 4ch arch between 2 ttr2tog and work *[1tr, 5ch, 1tr] into 4ch arch (corner), 6ch, dtr4tog, 6ch; rep from * 3 times more, sl st into first tr.

3rd round: 1ch, work 1dc into same st as last sl st, 1dc into each st and each ch, working 3dc into centre ch at each corner, sl st into first dc.

4th round: 1ch, 1dc into each dc, working 3dc into centre dc at each corner, sl st into first dc.

5th round: 4ch (count as 1tr, 1ch), [miss next dc, 1ch, 1tr into next dc] twice, 1ch, miss next dc, *into next dc (corner dc) work [1tr, 1ch] 3 times, [miss 1dc, 1tr into next dc, 1ch] 11 times, miss 1dc; rep from * twice more, into last corner dc work [1tr, 1ch] 3 times, [miss 1dc, 1tr into next dc, 1ch] 8 times, sl st into 3rd of 3ch at beg of round. Fasten off.

Edging

1st row: With wrong side facing, rejoin yarn with a sl st into centre tr of a corner, work 1dc into tr, 9ch, miss 2tr, 1dc into next tr, [9ch, miss 3tr, 1dc into next tr] twice, 9ch, miss 2tr, 1tr into next tr (2nd corner), turn.

Complete as given for edging on flower motif from ★ to ★★.

With thread and needle, join the 4 motifs into a square as illustrated.

Making Up

Using small invisible stitches, sew square to one corner of fabric. Carefully cut away any fabric under crochet motif and make a narrow hem. Work a narrow hemstitch all round remaining sides of handkerchief.

TIP

If you stain your work with wine or fruit do not despair. Treat it as follows: cover the mark with fine salt, rub it in with a damp bar of soap and leave for several hours. Rinse thoroughly, then wash it in a diluted solution of bleach.

13

Motif for Hankerchief

✪✪✪

Materials

Coats Patons Opera No. 30 Crochet Cotton Shade 500 - 60 grams

0.75mm Milward Steel Crochet Hook

1 reel Sylko Sewing Thread

1 sewing needle

30cm x 30cm fine white linen

Special Abbreviations

Picot = 3ch, sl st into first of these ch.

Tr2tog = work 1tr into each of next 2 arches until 1 loop of each tr remains on hook, yo and through all 3 loops on hook.

Dtr3tog = working until 1 loop of each dtr remains on hook, work 1dtr into next dc as indicated, miss 1dc, 1dtr into next dc, miss 1dc, 1dtr into next dc, yo and through all 4 loops on hook.

Square Motifs (Make 2)

Make 6ch, sl st into first ch to form a ring.

1st round: 7ch (count as 1tr, 4ch), work 1tr into 5th ch from hook, into ring work [1tr, 4ch, 1tr into top of last tr worked] 7 times, sl st into 3rd of 7ch at beg of round.

2nd round: 9ch (count as 1tr, 6ch), work *1dc into 2nd ch from hook, 1htr into next ch, 1tr into next ch, 1dtr into each of next 2ch*, [1tr into next tr, 6ch, rep from * to *] 7 times, sl st into 3rd of 9ch at beg of round.

3rd round: 8ch (count as 1dtr, 4ch), 1dc into tip of triangle, 4ch, [1dtr into tr between 2 triangles, 4ch, 1dc into tip of next triangle, 4ch] 7 times, sl st into 4th of 8ch at beg of round.

4th round: 7ch (count as 1tr, 4ch), 1tr into 5th ch from hook, 4ch, 1tr into top of last tr worked, 1dc into next dc, 4ch, 1tr into last dc worked, 4ch, 1tr into last tr worked, 1tr into next dtr, [4ch, 1tr into last tr worked] twice, 1dc into next dc, 4ch, 1tr into last dc worked, 4ch, 1tr into last tr worked, 1tr into next dtr] 7 times, omitting 1dtr at end of last rep, sl st into 3rd of 7ch at beg of round.

5th round: 7ch, miss next 4ch arch, tr2tog, 4ch, into next tr (corner st) work [1tr, 2ch, 1dtr, 2ch, 1tr], 4ch, miss next 4ch arch, tr2tog, 4ch, *1tr into next tr, 4ch, miss 4ch arch, tr2tog, 4ch, into next tr (corner st) work [1tr, 2ch, 1dtr, 2ch, 1tr], 4ch, miss next 4ch arch, tr2tog; rep from * twice more, 4ch, sl st into 3rd of 7ch at beg of round.

6th round: Work 1dc into each ch and st to end, working 3dc into each corner dtr, sl st into first dc.

7th and 8th rounds Work 1dc into each dc and 3dc into each corner dc, sl st into first dc. Fasten off.

Centre Flower

Make 6ch, sl st into first ch to form a ring.

1st round: *Work 1dc into ring, 7ch, sl st into corner st of a square, then work over the 7ch as follows: 1dc into each of first 2ch, 1htr into each of next 3ch, 1dc into each of last 2ch, [1dc into ring, 8ch, work 1dc into 2nd ch from hook, 1dc into next ch, 1htr into each of next 3ch, 1dc into each of last 2ch] 3 times, rep from * once more working the joining sl st into corner st of 2nd square, sl st into first dc. Fasten off.

Fan

1st row: With right side facing, rejoin yarn with a sl st into 8th dc on square from joining st with flower, 6ch, into next tip on flower work [1tr, 3ch, 1tr], 5ch, 1dc into next tip, 5ch, [1tr, 3ch, 1tr] into next tip, 6ch, sl st into 8th dc from joining st with flower on 2nd square, turn.

2nd row: Sl st into next dc on square, work 7dc into first 6ch arch, 1dc into each tr, dc and ch to last arch, 7dc into last arch, sl st into next dc on square, turn.

3rd row Sl st into each of next 3dc on square, [3ch, miss 3dc, 1dtr into next dc] 3 times, [3ch, miss 2dc, 1dtr into next dc] 4 times, [3ch, miss 3dc, 1dtr into next dc] twice, 3ch, miss 2dc on square, sl st into next dc, turn.

4th row: Sl st into next dc on square, work 1dc into each ch and each dtr to end, sl st into next dc on square, turn.

5th row: Sl st into each of next 3dc on square, 3ch, miss 3dc, 1dtr into next dc, 2ch, miss 1dc, dtr3tog **missing 2dc between first 2dtr,** [1ch, 1dtr into same dc as last dtr of dtr3tog, 1ch, dtr3tog working first of these dtr into same st as last dtr] 5 times, 1ch, 1dtr into same st as last dtr of dtr3tog, 1ch, dtr3tog missing 2dc between 2nd and 3rd dtr, 2ch, 1dtr into next dc, 3ch, miss 2dc on square, sl st into next dc, turn.

6th row: Sl st into each of next 4dc on square, 1ch, 1tr into first 3ch arch, 1ch, 1tr into next dtr, 1ch, 1tr into next 2ch arch, 1ch, *1tr into next st, 1ch, 1tr into next ch space, 1ch; rep from * to last 2 arches, 1tr into 2ch arch, 1ch, 1tr into dtr, 1ch, 1tr into last 3ch arch, 1ch, miss 3dc on square, sl st into next dc, turn.

7th row: Sl st into next dc on square, work 1dc into each ch and each tr to end, sl st into next dc on square, turn.

8th row: Sl st into each of next 4dc on square, 3ch, miss 2dc, [1dtr into each of next 5dc, 2ch, 1 picot, 2ch, miss 4dc] 6 times, 1dtr into each of next 5dc, 3ch, miss 3dc on square, sl st into next dc, turn.

9th row: Sl st into each of next 4dc on square, 5ch, miss 1dtr, 1dtr into each of next 3dtr, 5ch, *miss 2dtr, 1dtr into each of next 3dtr; rep from * to end, 5ch, miss 3dc on square, sl st into next dc, turn.

10th row: Sl st into each of next 5dc on square, 4ch, miss 1dtr, into next dtr work [1dtr, 3 picots, 1dtr, *2ch, 1dc into next arch, 2ch, miss 1dtr, into next dtr work [1dtr, 3 picots, 1dtr]; rep from * to end, 4ch, sl st into corner dc on square. Fasten off.

Work 2nd fan in the same way on opposite side of flower and squares.

Making Up

Using small invisible stitches, sew motif to one corner of fabric. Carefully cut away any fabric under crochet motif and make a narrow hem. Work a narrow hemstitch all round remaining sides of hankerchief.

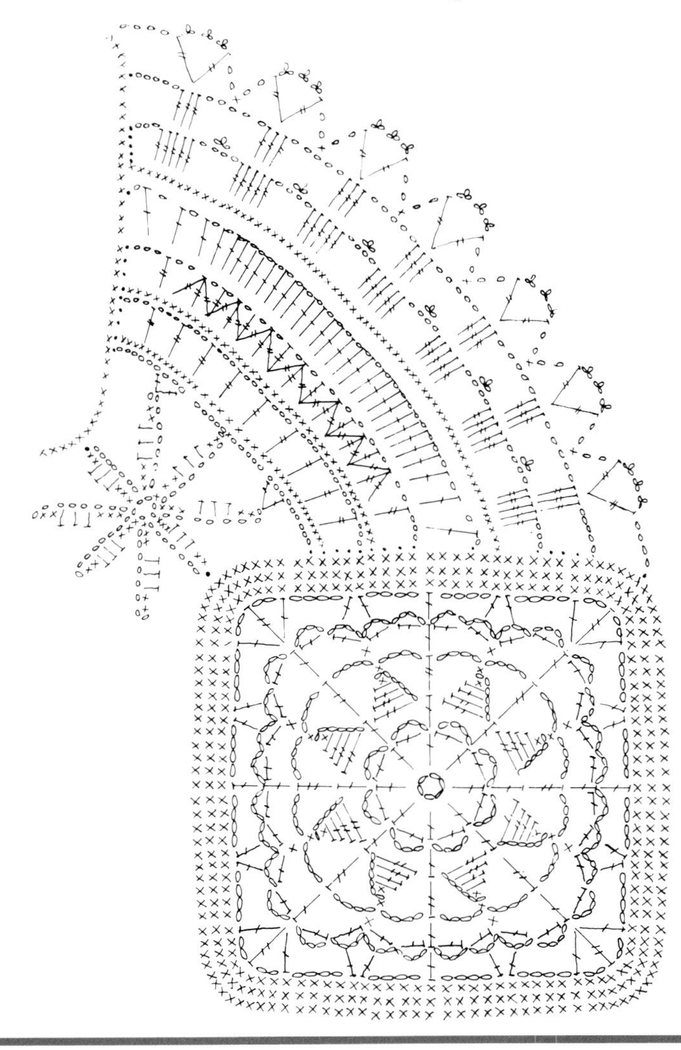

14

Motif for Hankerchief

✪✪✪

Materials

Coats Patons Opera No. 30 Crochet Cotton Shade 500 - 60 grams

0.75 Milward Steel Crochet Hook

1 reel Sylko Sewing Thread

1 sewing needle

30 cm x 30 cm fine white linen

Special Abbreviations

Tr3tog = work 1tr into each of next 3 dc (or 3tr into next arch) until 1 loop of each tr remains on hook, yo and through all 4 loops on hook.

Picot = 3ch, sl st into first of these ch.

To Make

Make 17ch, sl st into first ch to form a ring.

1st round: Work 36dc into ring, sl st into first dc.

2nd round: 3ch (count as 1tr), miss first dc, 1tr into each of next 2dc until 1 loop of each tr remains on hook, yo and through all 3 loops on hook (tr3tog at beg of round), 4ch, [tr3tog, 4ch] 11 times, sl st into 3rd of 3ch at beg of round.

3rd round: Sl st into first arch, *[tr3tog, 4ch, tr3tog] into next arch, [5ch, 1dc into next arch] twice, 5ch; rep from * 3 times more, sl st into first st.

4th round: Sl st into first arch, *[tr3tog, 5ch, tr3tog] into next arch, [5ch, 1dc into next arch] 3 times, 5ch; rep from * 3 times more, sl st into first st.

5th round: 4ch (count as 1dtr), 1dtr into each of next 2ch, *into next ch work [1dtr, 1 picot, 1dtr], 1dtr into each of next 20 sts (counting each ch as 1 st), turn and work corner as follows: 12ch, miss 9 dtr, sl st into next dtr, turn, work [1dc, 1htr, 1tr, 5dtr, 1 picot, 6dtr, 1 picot, 5dtr, 1tr,

1htr, 1dc] into 12ch arch, 1dtr into each of next 5 sts on 4th round, turn, [9ch, 1dc into next picot] twice, 9ch, miss 4dtr, sl st into next dtr, turn, work [1dc, 1htr, 1tr, 5dtr, 1 picot, 6dtr] into first arch, [6dtr, 1 picot, 6dtr, 1 picot, 6dtr] into next arch, [6dtr, 1 picot, 5dtr, 1tr, 1htr, 1dc] into 3rd arch, 1dtr into each of next 4 sts on 4th round; rep from * 3 times more omitting 3dtr at end of last rep, sl st into 4th ch at beg of round.

6th round: Sl st into each of next 3dtr, *[1dc into next picot, 11ch] twice, 1dc into next picot, 13ch (corner arch), [1dc into next picot, 11ch] twice; rep from * 3 times more, sl st into first dc.

7th round: Work 1dc into each dc and each ch to end, working 3dc into centre ch of each corner arch, sl st into first dc.

8th round: 6ch (count as 1dtr, 2ch), *[miss next 2dc, 1dtr into next dc, 2ch] 10 times, into next dc (corner dc) work [1dtr, 5ch, 1dtr], 2ch, [1dtr into next dc, 2ch, miss 2dc] 10 times, rep from * 3 times more, sl st into 4th of 6ch at beg of round.

9th round: Sl st into each of next 2ch and into next dtr, *[2dc into next arch, 1dc into next dc] 3 times, 1 picot, 2dc into next arch, 1dc into next dc, turn, 9ch, miss 5dc, sl st into next dc, turn, into 9ch arch just formed work [3dc, 1 picot, 2dc, 1 picot, 2dc, 1 picot, 2dc, 1 picot, 3dc]; rep from * to end working 1 arch as before over the 5dc at each corner, sl st into first dc. Fasten off.

Making Up

Using small invisible stitches, sew motif to one corner of fabric. Carefully cut away any fabric under crochet motif and make a narrow hem. Work a narrow hemstitch all round remaining sides of handkerchief.

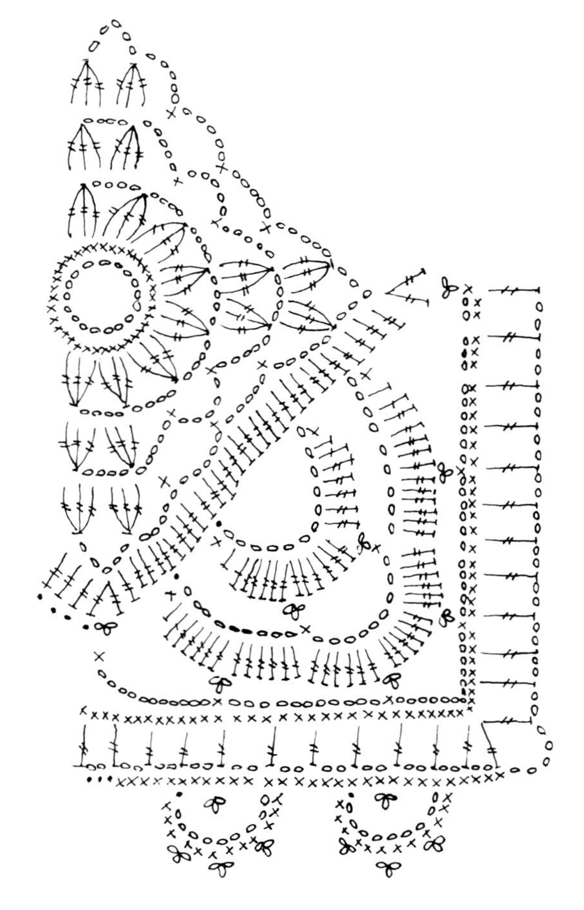

15

Scroll-edged Border for Tablecloth

✪✪✪

Materials

Coats Patons Opera Crochet Cotton No. 20 Shade 500 - 600 grams

1.00mm Milward Steel Crochet Hook

1 reel Sylko Sewing Thread

1 sewing needle

130 x 126 cm white linen

Size

The finished border is approximately 22 cm [8 3/4 ins] deep.

Special Abbreviations

Dc-bar with picot = work [6dc, 3ch (picot), 6dc] over the 5ch.

Tr-bar = work 9tr over the 5ch, then work 1 more tr until 2 loops remain on hook, work 1tr into each of next 2ch on 2nd strip until 1 loop of each tr remains on hook, yo and through all 4 loops on hook.

Tr3tog = work 1 tr into each of next 3 sts until 1 loop of each tr remains on hook, yo and through all 4 loops on hook.

Tr2tog: working until 1 loop of each tr remains on hook, work 1tr into same arch as last tr and 1tr into next arch, yo and through all 3 loops on hook.

Outer Section

Braid

First Strip: Make 4048ch, sl st into first ch to form a ring, then work 1 round as follows: 3ch (count as 1tr), 1tr into each of the following ch, sl st into 3rd of 3ch at beg of round. Fasten off.

Second Strip: Make 3904ch, sl st into first ch to form a ring, then work braid as follows: 3ch (count as 1tr), 1tr into each of next 2ch, 5ch, sl st into 1tr on first strip, then work dc-bar with picot, **[1tr into each of next 3ch, 5ch, miss 5tr on first strip, sl st into next tr, then work dc-bar with picot] twice, *[1tr into each of next 3ch, 5ch, miss 2tr on first strip, sl st into next tr, then work dc-bar with picot] 3 times, 1tr into each of next 3ch, 5ch, on first strip [miss 2tr, sl st into next tr, 3ch, miss 2tr, sl st into next tr], then work tr-bar, [1tr into each of next 3ch, 5ch, miss 2tr on first strip, sl st into next tr, then work dc-bar with picot] 4 times*, [1tr into each of next 6ch, 5tr, miss 2tr on first strip, sl st into next tr, then work dc-bar with picot] 6 times, rep from * to * once more, [1tr into each of next 3ch, 5ch, miss 5tr on first strip, sl st into next tr, then work dc-bar with picot] 4 times**, rep from ** to ** 3 times more, then **work corner** as follows: [1tr into each of next 3ch, 5ch, miss 5tr on first strip, sl st into next tr, then work dc-bar with picot] twice, rep from * to * once, [1tr into each of next 6ch, 5ch, miss 2tr on first strip, sl st into next tr, then work dc-bar with picot] 6 times, [1tr into each of next 3ch, 5ch, miss 2tr on first strip, sl st into next tr, then work dc-bar with picot] 8 times, [1tr into each of next 6ch, 5ch, miss 2tr on first strip, sl st into next tr, then work dc-bar with picot] 6 times, rep from * to * once, [1tr into each of next 3ch, 5ch, miss 5tr on 2nd strip, sl st into next tr, then work dc-bar with picot] 4 times, rep from ** to ** 8 times and continue in this way to end of round. Fasten off.

With right side facing, rejoin yarn to a tr on one side of braid, 3ch, miss first tr, 1tr into each tr to end, sl st into 3rd of 3ch. Fasten off.

Work 1 round of tr in the same way on the other side of braid.

Link

With wrong side facing and working inside a curve, rejoin yarn to tr level with the tr-bar of braid at right side of the curve and work as follows: make 41ch, sl st into the tr level with the tr-bar at opposite side of curve, turn, 2ch, miss 2tr on braid, sl st into next tr, 3ch, work 1tr into each of the first 20ch, 3tr into next ch, 1tr into each of last 20ch, miss 2tr on braid, sl st into next tr. Fasten off.

Small Star

Make 10ch, sl st into first ch to form a ring. With right side facing and working anti-clockwise in space between braid and link, continue as follows: 1dc into ring, 8ch, sl st into 21st tr on link, then work 12dc over the 8ch, 2dc into ring, 7ch, miss 6tr on link, sl st into next tr, then work 11dc over the 7ch, 2dc into ring, 6ch, miss 6tr on link, sl st into next tr, then work 10dc over the 6ch, 2dc into ring, 6ch, sl st into 7th tr on braid, then work 10dc over the 6ch, 2dc into ring, 7ch, miss 6tr on braid, sl st into next tr, then work 11dc over the 7ch, 2dc into ring, 8ch, miss 6tr on braid, sl st into next tr, then work 12dc over the 8ch, 2dc into ring, continue in this way working the 4 remaining rays symetrically and ending last ray with 1dc into ring, sl st into first dc. Fasten off.

Work 1 link and 1 small star in this way in each curve at either side of the undulating braid, **excepting** the 4 corners.

Second Section

Braid

First Strip: Make 3648ch and work as for First Strip of First Section.

Second Strip: Make 3720ch and work braid as given for Second Strip of First Section to corner, then **work corner** as follows: [1tr into each of next 3ch, 5ch, miss 5tr on 2nd strip, sl st into next tr, then work dc-bar with picot] twice, *[1tr into each of next 3ch, 5ch, miss 2tr on 2nd strip, sl st into next tr, then work dc-bar with picot] 4 times, 1tr into each of next 3ch, 5ch, on 2nd strip [miss 2tr, sl st into next tr, 3ch, miss 2tr, sl st into next tr], then work tr-bar, rep from * once more, [1tr into each of next 3ch, 5ch, miss 2tr on 2nd strip, sl st into next tr, then work dc-bar with picot] 4 times, [1tr into each of next 3ch, 5ch, miss 5tr on 2nd strip, sl st into next tr, then work dc-bar with picot] 4 times.

Complete to match First Section, including Links and Small Stars, and also working 1 link and 1 small star in each of the 2 curves at corners.

Intervalli di Quinta
Intervalli di Quarta

15

Place second section above first section as illustrated and join the curves and links where they touch with a few stitches.

Fill in each remaining space formed by the 2 sections and 2 links with a small star as before as illustrated.

Corner Motif

Link

With wrong side facing, rejoin yarn to tr level with first tr-bar of second section and make 25ch, sl st into tr level with tr-bar of first section, make 30ch, sl st into tr level with centre dc-bar with picot, 30ch, sl st into tr level with next tr-bar, 25ch, then sl st into tr level with second tr-bar of second section, turn, 2ch, miss 2tr, sl st into next tr, work 1tr into each of first 24ch, tr3tog (working into next ch, sl st and ch), [1tr into each of next 28ch, tr3tog] twice, 1tr into each of last 24ch, miss 2tr on braid, sl st into next tr. Fasten off.

Large Star

Make 10ch, sl st into first ch to form a ring. With right side facing and working anti-clockwise inside corner link, continue as follows: 1dc into ring, 13ch, work 1dc into 6th tr of link, 3ch, miss 1tr, 1dc into next tr, 1tr into each of the 13ch, 2dc into ring. Continue in this way, working 10 rays in all evenly spaced out as illustrated and ending with 1dc into ring, sl st into first dc. Fasten off.

Filet

With right side facing, rejoin yarn to 3rd free tr on first section, 2ch, 1dc into 3rd tr on link, [5ch, miss 3tr on link, 1dc into next tr] 6 times, 2ch, 1dc into 3rd free tr from the left on first section, 2ch, miss 3tr, 1dc into next tr, turn, 2ch, 1dc into 5ch arch, [5ch, 1dc into next 5ch arch] 5 times, 2ch, miss 3tr on first section, 1dc into next tr, 2ch, 1dc into next tr, turn, 2ch, 1dc into 5ch arch, [5ch, 1dc into next 5ch arch] 4 times, 2ch, miss 3tr on first section, 1dc into next tr, 2ch, miss 2tr, 1dc into next tr, turn, 2ch, 1dc into next arch, [2ch, miss 4tr on first section, 1dc into next tr, 2ch, 1dc into next arch] 3 times. Fasten off.

Work filet in 2nd space of corner in the same way, then in each of the 2 spaces of remaining 3 corners.

Leaves

With right side facing and working into space on the left between link and the two sections, rejoin yarn to 11th tr on link, 7ch, sl st into 11th tr from link on second section, then work 10dc over the 7ch, 9ch, miss 5tr on second section, sl st into next tr, then work 13dc over the 9ch, 9ch, sl st into 16th tr from link on first section, then work 13dc over the 9ch, 7ch, sl st into same tr on link as at beg. Fasten off.

Work a leaf on the right to match first leaf, then work these two leaves in each of the remaining 3 corners.

Outer Edging

1st round: With wrong side facing, rejoin yarn to 14th tr 1/3 of the way along one link and work 1dc into tr, *15ch, miss 10tr on braid, 1dc into next tr, [20ch, miss 12tr, 1dc into next tr] 3 times, 15ch, miss 13tr on next link, 1dc into next tr, 20ch, miss 15tr on link, 1dc into next tr, rep from * all round border **but** working 8 arches evenly spaced on each of the 4 corners, sl st into first dc, turn.

2nd round: 3ch, working tr2tog between each arch, work 20tr into each 15ch arch and 25tr into each 20ch arch, sl st into 3rd of 3ch at beg of round.

3rd round: 1ch, [1dc into each of next 5tr, 3ch (picot)] 3 times, 1tr into each of next 5tr, miss next st, [1dc into each of next 5tr, 3ch] 4 times, miss next st, 1dc into each of next 5tr, continue in this way working 3 picots separated by 5dc for each 20tr arch and 4 picots separated by 5dc for each 25tr arch, sl st into first dc. Fasten off.

Leaves

Work inside each of the **20tr arch** as follows: with right side facing, rejoin yarn to tr halfway along braid, 5ch, sl st into tr halfway along link, work 2dc over the 5ch, 5ch, sl st into base of 5th tr on arch, work 8dc over these 5ch, 2dc over the first 5ch stalk, [5ch, miss 4tr on arch, sl st into base of next tr, then work 8dc over these 5ch, 2dc over the first 5ch stalk] twice, sl st into same st as first sl st. Fasten off.

Inside each of the **25tr arch**, work as follows: with right side facing, rejoin yarn to centre tr on braid, 6ch, sl st into base of 10th tr on arch, then work 5dc over the 6ch, 3ch, miss 5tr, sl st into base of next tr, work 5dc over the 3ch, then 5 more dc over the initial 6ch, sl st into same st as first sl st. Fasten off.

Inner Braid

First Strip: Make 2088ch, sl st into first ch to form a ring, then work 1 round of tr as given for First Strip of First Section.

Second Strip: Make 2136ch, sl st into first ch to form a ring, then work braid as follows:

3ch, work 1tr into each of next 2ch, 5ch, sl st into a tr on first strip, then work dc-bar with picot, *1tr into each of next 3ch, 5ch, miss 2tr on first strip, sl st into next tr, then work dc-bar with picot, rep from * to * for first side until there are 170 dc-bars with picot, then **work corner** as follows: [1tr into each of next 6ch, 5ch, miss 2tr on first strip, sl st into next tr, then work dc-bar with picot] 4 times, tie a marker on tr level with 2nd of these dc-bars with picot. Rep from * 3 times more, sl st into 3rd of 3ch at beg of round. Fasten off.

With right side facing rejoin yarn to 3rd st from marker, 3ch, *work 1 tr into each tr to within 2tr of next marker, work 1tr into each of next 5tr until 1 loop of each tr remains on hook, yo and through all 6 loops on hook, rep from * 3 times more, sl st into 3rd of 3ch at beg of round. Fasten off.

With right side facing, rejoin yarn to tr on braid level with dc-bar in corner and work 1 round of tr. Fasten off.

Place inner braid above second section as illustrated, taking care that corner of inner braid faces centre of corners, and join curves and links where they touch with a few stitches.

Linking Leaves

With right side facing rejoin yarn with a sl st to tr on braid level with marker and work corner leaf as follows:

3ch, 1tr into same tr as last sl st, 8ch, sl st into tr halfway along link, then work 13dc over the 8ch, 16ch, sl st into corner formed by link and braid, and work 13dc over the 16ch, 8ch, sl st into other corner formed by link and braid, and work 13dc over the 8ch, work 13dc over the initial ch, sl st into 3rd of 3ch, 8ch, sl st into tr halfway along link, then work 13dc over the 8ch, sl st into 3rd of 3ch. Fasten off.

In spaces between link, inner braid and second section, work leaves as follows:

With right side facing, rejoin yarn to tr halfway on inner braid, 7ch, sl st into tr on link level with first ray of small star, then work 11dc over the 7ch, 7ch, sl st into tr level with next ray, then work 5dc over the 7ch, 3ch, sl st into 7th tr on braid from the link, then work 5dc over the 3ch, then continue with 6dc over the following ch, 7ch, miss 6tr on braid, sl st into next tr, then work 11dc on the 7ch, sl st into tr on inner braid.

Making Up

Cut out a 125cm square in the fabric and work a narrow hem all round. Pin crochet border evenly all round fabric and slip stitch in place.

TIP

While working crochet lace roll it up and keep it in place with pins. It will not get dirty and will remain flat as if it had been ironed.

16

Border in Filet Crochet

✪✪

Materials

Coats Patons Opera No. 20 Crochet Cotton Shade 500 - 100 grams

1.00mm Milward Steel Crochet Hook

1 reel Sylko Sewing Thread

1 sewing needle

20cm x 135cm piece of white linen

Size

The border is approximately 14 cm [5½ ins] deep.

Note

This border is worked lengthwise.

To Make

Make 105ch.

1st row: Work 1tr into 4th ch from hook, 1tr into each of next 2ch (1 blk) [2ch, miss 2ch, 1tr into next ch] 30 times (30 sps), 1tr into each of next 3ch (1 blk), 2ch, miss 2ch, 1tr into each of last 4ch (1 sp and 1 blk), turn. 34 squares.

2nd row : 3ch (count as 1tr), miss first tr, 1tr into each of next 3tr (1 blk worked over 1 blk at beg of row), 2ch, 1tr into each of next 4tr (1 sp worked over 1 sp and 1 blk over 1 blk), [2ch, 1tr into next tr] 24 times (24 sps worked over 24 sps), 2tr into next sp, 1tr into next tr (1 blk worked over 1 sp), [2ch, 1tr into next tr] 5 times (5 sps worked over 5 sps), 1tr into each of next 2tr, 1tr into next ch (1 blk worked over 1 blk at end of row), turn.

3rd row: 3ch, 1 blk, 5 sps, miss 2tr, 1tr into next tr (1 sp worked over 1 blk), 1 blk, 23 sps, 1 blk, 1 sp, 1 blk, turn.

Continue following chart on page 45 to 101th row inclusive, rep from 2nd row twice more, then work 1 row of sps. **Do not turn.**

16/17

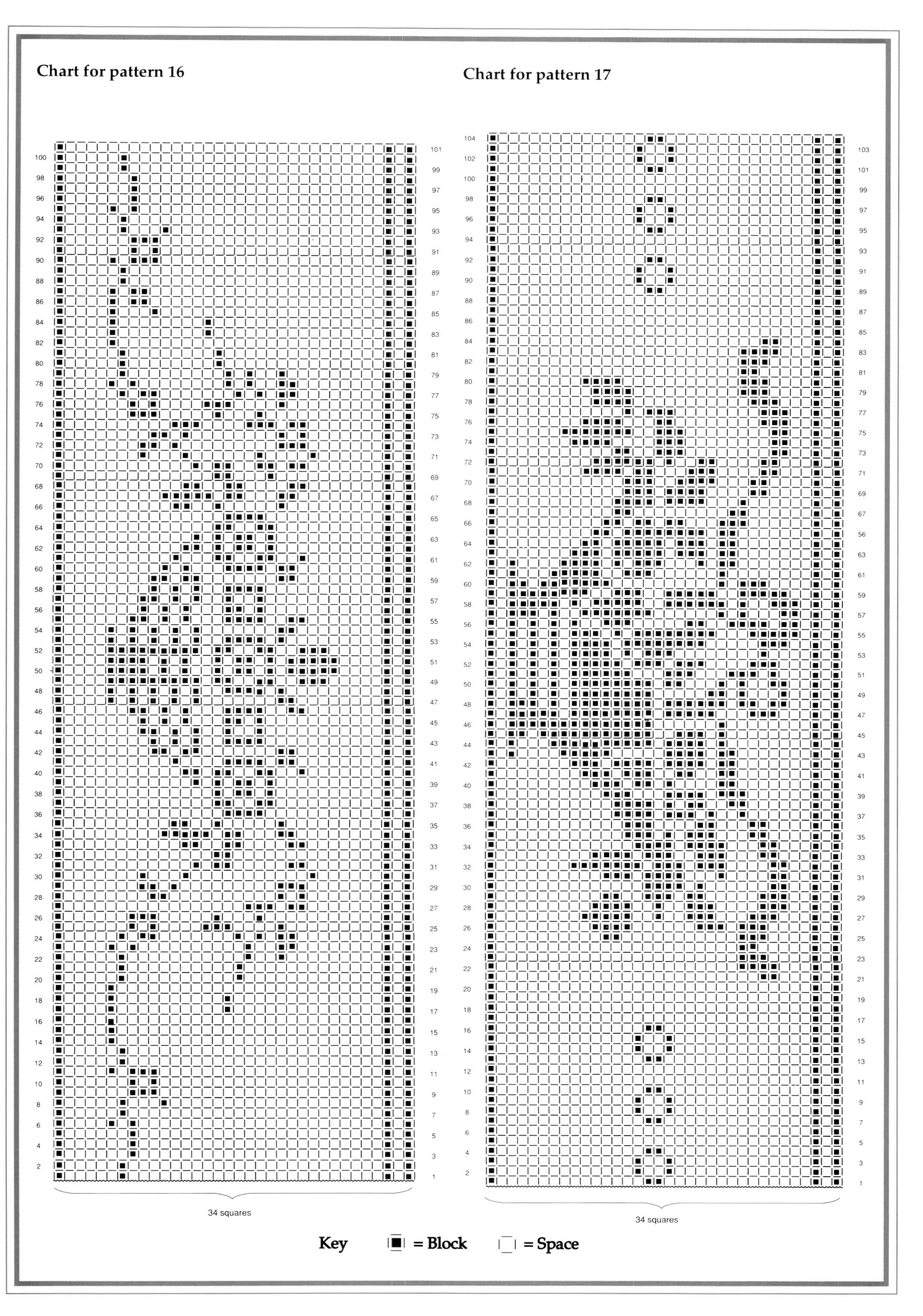
Chart for pattern 16
Chart for pattern 17
34 squares
34 squares
Key
= Block
= Space

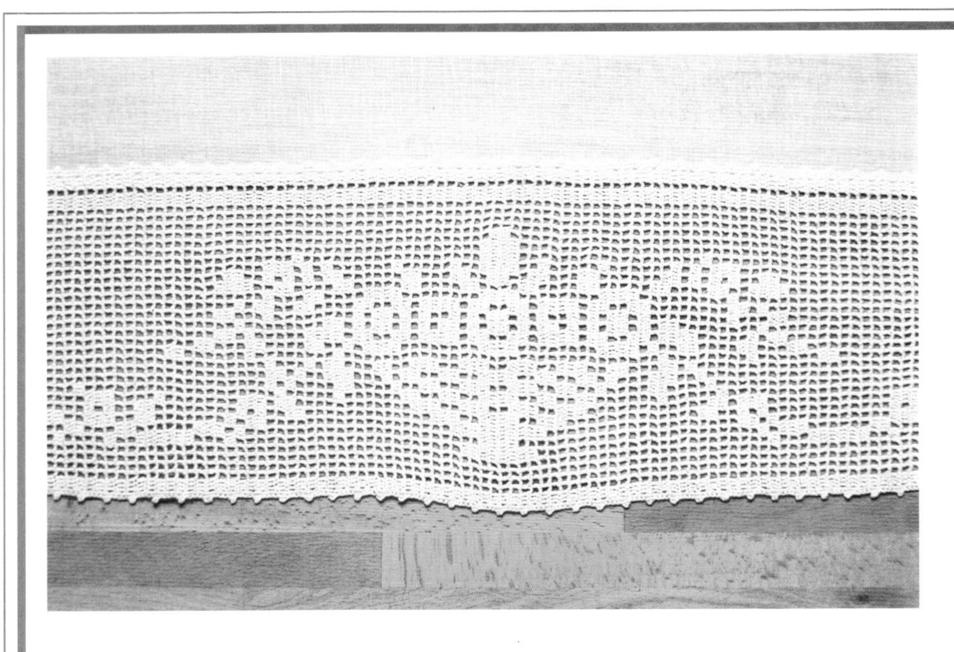

Edging

Work *5dc, 3ch (1 picot); rep from * evenly all round border, working [1dc, 1 picot, 1dc] into each corner st. Fasten off.

Making Up

Make a narrow hem all round fabric and sew border as illustrated.

> **TIP**
>
> After washing your work lay it out flat in its original shape on thick towel , fix it with stainless steel pins and leave it to dry.

17

Border in Filet Crochet

✪✪

Materials

Coats Patons Opera No. 20 Crochet Cotton Shade 500 - 100 grams

1.00mm Milward Steel Crochet Hook

1 reel Sylko Sewing Thread

1 sewing needle

20cm x 140cm piece of white linen

Size

The border is approximately 16 cm [6½ ins] deep.

Note

This border is worked lengthwise.

To Make

Make 105ch.

1st row: Work 1tr into 4th ch from hook, 1tr into each of next 2ch (1 blk), [2ch, miss 2ch, 1tr into next ch] 14 times (14 sps), 1tr into each of next 6ch (2 blks), [2ch, miss 2ch, 1tr into each of next 3ch] 14 times (14 sps), 1tr into each of next 3ch (1 blk), 2ch, miss 2ch, 1tr into each of last 4ch (1 sp and 1 blk), turn. 34 squares.

2nd row : 3ch (count as 1tr), miss first tr, 1tr into each of next 3tr (1 blk worked over 1 blk at beg of row), 2ch, 1tr into each of next 4tr (1 sp worked over 1 sp and 1 blk over 1 blk), [2ch, 1tr into next tr] 13 times (13 sps worked over 13 sps), 2tr into next sp, 1tr into next tr (1 blk worked over 1 sp), [2ch, 1tr into next tr] twice, (2 sps worked over 2 blks), [2ch, 1tr into next tr] 13 times (13 sps worked over 13 sps), 1tr into each of next 2tr, 1tr into next ch (1 blk worked over 1 blk at end of row), turn.

3rd row: 1 blk over 1 blk at beg of row, 13 sps, 1 blk, 2 sps, 1 blk, 13 sps, 1 blk, 1 sp, 1 blk, turn.

Continue following chart on page 45 to 104th row inclusive, then rep from 5th row twice more. **Do not turn**.

Edging

Work *5dc, 3ch (1 picot); rep from * evenly all round border, working [1dc, 1 picot, 1dc] into each corner st. Fasten off.

Making Up

Make a narrow hem all round fabric and sew border as illustrated.

18

Border with Flowers

✪✪✪✪

Materials

Coats Patons Opera No. 20 Crochet Cotton Shade 500 - 250 grams

1.00mm Milward Steel Crochet Hook

1 reel Sylko Sewing Thread

1 sewing needle

77cm x 77cm piece of white linen

Size

The border is approximately 13 cm [5¼ ins] deep.

Special Abbreviations

Ttr3tog = work 3ttr into ring until 1 loop of each ttr remains on hook, yo and through all 4 loops on hook. At beg of round replace first ttr by 5ch.

Dtr3tog = work 3dtr into dc until 1 loop of each dtr remains on hook, yo and through all 4 loops on hook.

Flowers (Make 76 - 18 for each side and 1 for each corner)

Make 13ch, sl st into first ch to form a ring.

1st round: Work [ttr3tog, 5ch] 10 times into ring, sl st into top of first ttr3tog. Fasten off.

Work remaining flowers in the same way but do not fasten off at end of last one.

2nd and joining row: Work 6dc into each of first 5 arches on last flower, [7ch, sl st into top of ttr3tog of next flower, 6dc into each of first 5 arches] 17 times, 7ch, sl st into top of ttr3tog on corner flower, work 6dc into each of next 7 arches; continue in this way until all the flowers have been linked together. Fasten off.

Outer Edging

★ With right side facing, rejoin yarn with a sl st into centre st of arch at left of a Flower above the ch link,

1ch, then working on linking ch: [miss 1ch, 1tr into next ch, 1ch] 3 times, 1dc into centre of corresponding arch of next flower, 3ch, 1dc into last dc of same dc arch, turn, 1ch, 1tr into dc, [1ch, 1tr into next tr] 3 times, 1ch, 1tr into first sl st, 1ch, 1dc into last dc of same arch of flower. Fasten off.

Rep from ★ to end **but** leaving 5 free arches on each of the corner flowers. **Do not** fasten off at end but turn and continue in rounds as follows:

1st round: Sl st into last dc worked, *[1ch, 1tr into next tr] 5 times, 1ch, 1tr into same st as last dc of filet worked on flower, [7ch, 1dtr between next 2 arches] twice, 7ch, 1tr into last dc worked on small filet; rep from * to end **but** working [7ch, 1dtr between 2 arches] 4 times on corner flower.

2nd round: Sl st into first ch sp and tr, 4ch (count as 1tr, 1ch), [1tr into next tr, 1ch] 3 times, 1tr into next tr, work 9dc into each of next 3 arches, *1tr into next tr, 1ch] 4 times, 1tr into next tr, 9dc into each of next 3 arches; rep from * to end, **but** working 9dc into each of the 5 arches in corners, end round with a sl st into 3rd of 4ch at beg of round.

3rd round: 4ch (count as 1tr, 1ch),[1tr into next tr, 1ch] 3 times, 1tr into next tr, **5ch, miss next arch of dc, into centre dc of next arch work [dtr3tog, 5ch] 4 times**, *1tr into next tr, [1ch, 1tr into next tr] 4 times, rep from ** to **; rep from * to end,**but** in the corners working [dtr3tog, 5ch] 4 times into 2nd arch of dc, 1dtr into centre dc of next arch, 5ch, and [dtr3tog, 5ch] 4 times into centre dc of next arch, end round with a sl st into 3rd of 4ch.

4th round: Sl st into next ch space and next tr, 4ch (count as 1tr, 1ch), 1tr into next tr, 1ch, 1tr into next tr, 6dc into each of next 6 arches, *miss 1tr, 1tr into next tr, [1ch, 1tr into next tr] twice, 6dc into each of next 6 arches; rep from * but working 6dc into each of the 10 arches at corners, end round with a sl st into * 3rd of 4ch.

5th round: 4ch, miss first tr, 1tr into next tr, 1ch, 1tr into next tr, **4ch, 1dtr between next 2 arches of dc, [5ch, 1dtr between last dc arch and next] 3 times, 4ch**, *1tr into next tr, [1ch, 1tr into next tr] twice, rep from ** to **; rep from * **but** working [5ch, 1dtr between last arch and next] 8 times at corners, end round with a sl st into 3rd of 4ch.

6th round: 4ch, miss first tr, 1tr into next tr, 1ch, 1tr into next tr, work 5dc into each 4ch arch and 7dc into each 5ch arch, *1tr into next tr, [1ch, 1tr into next tr] twice, 5dc into each 4ch arch and 7dc into each 5ch arch; rep from * to end, sl st into 3rd of 4ch.

7th round: 4ch, miss first tr, 1tr into next tr, 1ch, 1tr into next tr, 4ch,

18

1dtr between next 2 arches of dc, 5ch, 1dtr between last dc arch and next, 2ch, dtr3tog into centre dc on next arch, 2ch, 1dtr between last dc arch and next, 5ch, 1dtr between last dc arch and next, 4ch, *1tr into next tr, [1ch, 1tr into next tr] twice, rep from ** to **, rep from * **but** working [5ch, 1dtr between last dc arch and next] twice, 2ch, dtr3tog into centre dc on next arch, 2ch, 1dtr between last dc arch and next, [5ch, 1dtr between last dc arch and next] 4 times, 2ch, dtr3tog into centre dc on next arch, 2ch, 1dtr between last dc arch and next 5ch, 1dtr between last dc arch and next, end round with a sl st into 3rd of 4ch.

8th round: 4ch, miss first tr, 1tr into next tr, 1ch, 1tr into next tr, 5dc into next 4ch arch, 7dc into next 5ch arch, 3dc into 2ch arch, 1dc into top of dtr3tog, 2dc into 2ch arch, 7dc into 5ch arch, 5dc into 4ch arch, *1tr into next tr, [1ch, 1tr into next tr] twice, work 5dc into each 4ch arch, 7dc into each 5ch arch, 3dc into each 2ch arch and 1dc into top of dtr3tog; rep from * to end, sl st into 3rd of 4ch.

9th round: 3ch, miss first 2tr, 1dtr into next tr until 2 loops remain on hook, yo and through the 2 loops on hook (dtr2tog worked at beg of round), 1ch, [miss 1dc, 1dtr into next dc, 1ch] 6 times, into next dc work [1dtr, 1ch] 3 times, [miss 1dc, 1dtr into next dc, 1ch] 6 times, dtr2tog over next 3tr, continue in this way to end of round, working [1dtr, 1ch] 3 times into each dc above the dtr3tog, end round with a sl st into top of first dtr2tog.

10th round: Work *2dc into next ch space, [1dc, 3ch (picot), 1dc] into next ch space; rep from * but working [2dc, 3ch, 2dc] into each of the 2 spaces between the group of 3dtr above the dtr3tog, end round with a sl st into first dc. Fasten off.

Inner Edging

With right side facing, rejoin yarn with a sl st to last dc worked into arch at right of a flower, work 6dc into each 5ch arch on flower and work filet pattern between the flowers as before, continue in this way to end of round, sl st into first dc.

1st round: As 1st round of Outer Edging, **but** continuing filet pattern above corner flower as follows: *1ch, [1dc into centre dc on next arch, 1ch] 3 times.

2nd round: As 2nd round of Outer Edging, **but** into each corner work *1tr, [1ch, 1tr] 4 times and rep from * once.

3rd round: As 3rd round of Outer Edging, **but** in each corner work *1tr, [1ch, 1tr] 3 times and rep from * once, ending round with a sl st into first tr.

4th round: As 4th round of Outer Edging, **but** into each corner work [1tr, 1ch, 1tr] twice.

5th round: As 5th round of Outer Edging, **but** in each corner omit 1dtr and 4ch, and work 1dc between last arch and next and 1dc between the first 2 arches on next motif.

6th round: As 6th round of Outer Edging, **but** in each corner work 1dc into 3rd dtr3tog, 1dc into first dc on next arch, 1dc into last dc on first arch on next motif and 1dc into next dtr3tog.

7th and 8th rounds: As 7th and 8th rounds of Outer Edging, omitting filet pattern. Fasten off.

9th round: With right side facing, rejoin yarn with a sl st to a corner dc, *5ch, 1dtr into centre st of next arch, 5ch, 1ttr into centre of each of next 2 arches, 5ch, 1tr into next arch, 5ch, 1dc into next dc, rep from * to end, sl st into corner dc.

10th round: Work 1dc into each st and each ch to end.

11th round: 4ch (count as 1dtr), miss 3 sts, 1dtr into next st, *miss 3 sts, 1dtr into next st, 2ch, 1dtr into first of the 3 sts missed, 1dtr into next st; rep from * **but** working 1dtr, [miss 3sts, 1dtr] twice in each corner, sl st into 4th of 4ch.

12th round: Work [2dc, 3ch, 2dc] into each arch to end. Fasten off.

Making Up

Sew crochet neatly around fabric with invisible stitches, then make a narrow hem.

19

Hand Towel Border

✪✪

Materials

Coats Patons Opera No. 20 Crochet Cotton Shade 500 - 50 grams

1.00mm Milward Steel Crochet Hook

1 reel Sylko Sewing Thread

1 sewing needle

1 white linen hand towel

Special Abbreviations

1 shell = [2tr, 2ch, 2tr]. On following rows work shell into 2ch space of shell in previous row.

Tr3tog = work 1tr into each of next 3dc (or 3tr into next arch) until 1 loop of each tr remains on hook, yo and through all 4 loops on hook.

Picot = 3ch, sl st into first of these ch.

Inner Edging (Worked lengthways)

1st row: Make 14ch and work 1 shell into 6th ch from hook, 3ch, miss 3ch, [1dc, 1 picot, 1dc into next ch, 3ch, 1 shell into last ch, turn.

2nd row: 5ch, shell into first shell, 7ch, 1 shell into last shell, turn.

3rd row: 5ch, 1 shell into first shell, 3ch, into 3rd ch of 7ch arch work [1dc, 1 picot, 1dc], 3ch, 1 shell into last shell, turn.

Rep the last 2 rows for the required length, taking into account that 10 rows are needed for each Pineapple Motif. Fasten off.

Pineapple Motif

1st row: Working along side of edging, rejoin yarn to 2nd 5ch arch and work 1 shell into arch, 3tr into next 5ch arch, 6ch, 3tr into next 5ch arch, 1 shell into next 5ch arch, turn.

2nd row: 2ch, 1 shell into first shell, 2ch, 9tr into 6ch arch, 2ch, 1 shell into 2nd shell, turn.

3rd row: 2ch, 1 shell into first shell, 2ch, [1dc between next 2tr, 3ch] 7 times, 1dc between last 2tr, 2ch, 1 shell into 2nd shell, turn.

4th row: 2ch, 1 shell into first shell, [3ch, 1dc into next 3ch arch] 7 times, 3ch, 1 shell into 2nd shell, turn.

5th row: 2ch, 1 shell into first shell, 3ch, miss 1 arch, [1dc into next arch, 3ch] 6 times, 1 shell into 2nd shell, turn.

6th row: 2ch, 1 shell into first shell, 3ch, miss 1 arch, [1dc into next arch, 3ch] 5 times, 1 shell into 2nd shell, turn.

Work 4 more rows in this way, working 1 arch less in each of these rows.

11th row 2ch, 1 shell into each of the 2 shells, turn.

12th row: 2ch, 3tr into each of the 2 shells. Fasten off.

Work remaining Pineapple Motifs in the same way, leaving a 5ch arch free on inner edging between each one.

Outer Edging

1st row: Rejoin yarn with a sl st into first 5ch arch on inner edging, *3ch, [1dc into next 2ch arch on pineapple motif, 6ch] 5 times, 1dc into first tr at point of pineapple, 4ch, miss 4tr, 1dc into next tr, [6ch, 1dc into next 2ch arch] 5 times, 3ch, 1dc into 5ch arch on inner edging; rep from * to end, turn.

2nd row: 1ch, work 4dc into first 3ch arch, 9dc into each of next 5 arches, into next 4ch arch (point) work [3dc, 1 picot, 3dc], 9dc into each of next 5 arches, 4dc into last arch; rep from * to end **but at the same time** joining the centre dc of each of the first 2 arches with a sl st into centre dc of corresponding last 2 of previous pineapple. Fasten off.

Final Top Edging

1st row: Rejoin yarn with a sl st into 1st of starting ch on upper edging, 8ch (count as 1tr, 5ch), 1tr into next 5ch arch, *5ch, 1tr into next 5ch arch; rep from * to end, turn.

2nd row: 1ch, work 6dc into each 5ch arch to end, turn.

3rd row: 1ch, *1dc into next dc, 1 picot, miss 1dc; rep from * to last dc, 1dc into last dc. Fasten off.

Making Up

Using small invisible stitches, sew border to one edge of hand towel.

20

Hand Towel Border

✪✪

Materials

Coats Patons Opera No. 20 Crochet Cotton Shade 500 - 50 grams

1.00mm Milward Steel Crochet Hook

1 reel Sylko Sewing Thread

1 sewing needle

1 white linen hand towel

Special Abbreviations

1 shell = [2tr, 2ch, 2tr]. On following rows work shell into 2ch space of shell in previous row.

Tr2tog = work 1tr into each of next 2 sts as indicated until 1 loop of each tr remains on hook, yo and through all 3 loops on hook.

Picot = 3ch, sl st into first of these ch.

Inner Edging (Worked lengthways)

1st row: Make 12ch and work 1 shell into 6th ch from hook, 5ch, miss 5 ch,

1 shell into last ch, turn.

2nd row: 5ch, 1 shell into first shell, 5ch, miss 1 arch, 1dc into 3rd ch of next arch, 2ch, 1 shell into last shell, turn.

Rep the last row for the required length, taking into account that 18 rows are needed for each motif. Fasten off.

Motif

1st row: Working along side of edging, rejoin yarn with a sl st into top of tr before 5th 5ch arch, 7ch, 1dc into tr after same arch, 3ch, 1dc into next 5ch arch, turn.

2nd row (right side): Work 1 picot, 1tr into 7ch arch, *9ch, 1dtr into 5th ch from hook, [1dtr 2/3 down into stem of dtr just worked] 3 times, 3tr 2/3 down into stem of last dtr worked, 1dtr into **base** of each of the previous 4 dtr, 4ch, 1dc into each of remaining 4 of the 9ch, [1dc 1 picot, 1dc] into 7ch arch on Inner Edging*, rep from * 4 times more, 1dc into next 5ch arch on Inner Edging, 3ch, sl st into next 5ch arch, turn. 5 petals.

3rd row: Work 1dc into each of the 11 sts of each of the 5 petals, 1dc into next 5ch arch on Inner Edging, 3ch, 1dc into next 5ch arch, turn.

4th row: Work 1tr into first dc, *[1ch, miss 1dc, 1tr into next dc] twice, 1ch, [1tr, 1ch, 1tr] into next dc, 1ch, 1tr into next dc, 1ch, miss 1dc, 1tr into next dc, 1ch, miss 1dc, tr2tog over next 2dc*, rep from * to end, omitting tr2tog at end of last rep, 1tr into last dc, sl st into next 5ch arch on Inner Edging, 3ch, sl st into next 5ch arch, turn.

5th row: Work 1tr into first ch space, *1ch, [1tr into next space, 1ch] twice, [1tr, 1ch, 1tr] into next space, [1ch, 1tr into next space] twice, 1ch, tr2tog over next 2 spaces; rep from * to end omitting tr2tog at end of last rep, work 1tr into last ch space, sl st into next 5ch arch of Inner Edging, turn.

6th row: 3ch, miss first ch space, *2tr into next space, 2 picots, 2tr into next space, [2tr, 2 picots, 2tr] into next space, 2tr into next space, 2 picots, 2tr into next space, 1tr into each of next 2 spaces*, rep from * to end, omitting 1tr at end of last rep. Fasten off.

Work remaining motifs in the same way.

Upper Edging

1st row: With right side facing, rejoin yarn with a sl st into first 5ch arch of Inner Edging and work on other side as follows: 8ch (count as 1tr, 5ch), *1tr into next 5ch arch, 5ch] rep from * to end, placing last tr into top of last tr, turn.

2nd row: 1ch, work 6dc into each 5ch arch to end, turn.

3rd row: 1ch, 1dc into first dc, *3ch, 1tr into first of these ch, miss 2dc, 1dc into next dc; rep from * to end. Fasten off.

Making Up

Using small invisible stitches, sew border to one edge of hand towel.

TIP

The crochet hook you work with must be perfectly smooth and the correct size for the thread. It should also be flat in the middle of the handle so that it can be held firmly without twisting your fingers.

19/20

21

Hand Towel Border

✪✪✪

Materials

Coats Patons Opera No. 20 Crochet Cotton Shade 500 - 50 grams

1.00mm Milward Steel Crochet Hook

1 reel Sylko Sewing Thread

1 sewing needle

1 linen hand towel

Special Abbreviations

1 picot = 3ch, sl st into first of these ch.

Tr2tog = work 1tr into each of 2 picots as indicated until 1 loop of each tr remains on hook, yo and through all 3 loops on hook.

Quintr2tog = work 1quintr into each of 2 picots as indicated until 1 loop of each quintr remains on hook, yo and through all 3 loops on hook.

Motifs

Make 5ch, sl st into first ch to form a ring.

1st round: Work [1dc into ring, 5ch] 8 times, sl st into first dc.

2nd round: Sl st into each of first 2ch of first arch, 1dc into same arch, *12ch, work 1dc into 2nd ch from hook, 1dc into each of next 10ch, 1dc into same arch as last dc, 3ch, 1dc into next arch, rep from * 7 times more omitting last dc at end of last rep, sl st into first dc.

3rd round: Working around each bar, work as follows: Sl st into each of first 2ch on first bar, *1dc into each of next 9ch, 2ch, 1dc at top of bar, 2ch, 1dc into each of next 9dc on other side of bar, 3ch, miss first 2ch of next bar, rep from * 7 times more, sl st into first dc.

4th round: Sl st into each of next 2dc on first bar, *1dc into each of next 6dc, [1dc, 2ch, 1dc] into next 2ch arch, 1dc into next dc, [1dc, 2ch, 1dc] into next 2ch arch, 1dc into each of next 6dc, 3ch, miss next 2dc on next bar, rep from * 7 times more, sl st into first dc.

5th round: Sl st into each of next 2dc on first bar, *1dc into each of next 4dc, [1dc 2ch, 1dc] into 2ch arch, 1dc into each of next 3dc, [1dc, 2ch, 1dc] into next 2ch arch, 1dc into each of next 4dc, 4ch, miss next 2dc on next bar, rep from * 7 times more, sl st into first dc.

6th round: Sl st into each of next 2dc on first bar, *1dc into each of next 2dc, [1dc, 2ch, 1dc] into next 2ch arch, 1dc into each of next 5dc, [1dc, 2ch, 1dc] into next 2ch arch, 1dc into each of next 2dc, 5ch, miss next 2dc on next bar, rep from * 7 times more, sl st into first dc.

Turning at each end of rows, continue as follows:

1st row: Sl st to first 2ch arch, 7ch (count as 1tr, 4ch), miss 3dc, 1tr into next dc, 4ch, 1tr into next 2ch arch, *14ch, work 1dc into 2nd ch from hook, 1dc into each of next 8ch, 4ch, 1tr into next 2ch arch, 4ch, miss 3dc, 1tr into next dc, 4ch, 1tr into next 2ch arch, rep from * 4 times more, turn.

2nd row: 3ch (count as 1tr), *2tr into next 4ch arch, 3ch, 2tr into next arch, 5ch, miss 2dc on bar, 1dc into each of next 7dc, 2ch, 1dc at top of bar, 2ch, 1dc into each of next 7ch, 5ch, miss next arch; rep from * 5 times more, 2tr into next arch, 3ch, 2tr into next arch, 1tr into 3rd of 7ch at beg of previous row, turn.

3rd row: Sl st into each of first 2tr, 3ch, *2tr into next arch, 3ch, 2tr into next arch, 4ch, miss 2dc on bar, 1dc into each of next 4dc, [1dc, 2ch, 1dc] into next 2ch arch, 1dc into next dc, [1dc, 2ch, 1dc] into next 2ch arch, 1dc into each of next 4dc, 3ch, 2tr into next arch, 3ch; rep from * 5 times more, 2tr into next arch, miss 1tr, 1tr into next tr, turn.

4th row: *[3ch, 2tr into next arch] twice, 3ch, miss 2dc on bar, 1dc into each of next 2dc, [1dc, 2ch, 1dc] into next 2ch arch, 1dc into each of next 3dc, [1dc, 2ch, 1dc] into next 2ch arch, 1dc into each of next 2dc, [3ch, 2tr into next arch] twice; rep from * 5 times more, 3ch, miss 1tr, 1dc into next tr, turn.

Final round: *[2ch, 1 picot, 2ch, 1dc into next arch] 3 times, [2ch, 1 picot,

2ch, miss 1dc, 1dc into next dc] twice, [2ch, 1 picot, 2ch, 1dc into next arch] 4 times; rep from * 5 times more, 5ch, 1dtr into next tr on 2nd row, 5ch, 1ttr into 2ch arch of bar at beg of 1st row until 2 loops remain on hook, 1dtr into first 2ch arch of next bar until 3 loops remain on hook, yo and through all 3 loops on hook, 5ch, 1dtr into centre dc at top of same bar, 5ch, 1dtr in next 2ch arch of same bar until 2 loops remain on hook, 1ttr into first 2ch arch of next bar until 3 loops remain on hook, yo and through all 3 loops on hook, 5ch, 1dtr into tr on 2nd row 5ch, sl st into dc at end of 4th row. Fasten off.

Work required number of motifs in the same way, joining them on last round as illustrated by working [1ch, sl st into picot of corresponding previous bar, 1ch] in place of the picot.

Upper Edging

1st row: Rejoin yarn into 3rd picot before last on first motif, 4ch, 1tr into next picot, 4ch, 1dc into next picot, [4ch, 2tr into next arch] 6 times, 4ch, 1dc into next picot, 4ch, tr2tog over next 2 picots, 4ch, quintr2tog over last picot worked into and next picot of next motif, 4ch, dtr2tog working first st into last picot worked into and next picot, continue in this way to end of row, turn.

2nd row: 1ch, 1dc into each st and 4dc into each 4ch arch to end, turn.

3rd row: 4ch (count as 1tr, 1ch), miss first 2dc, 1tr into next dc, *1ch, miss 1dc, 1tr into next dc; rep from * to end, turn.

5th row: 1ch, 1dc into first tr, 1 picot, *1dc into next arch, 1 picot; rep from * to end, 1dc into 3rd of 3ch at beg of previous row. Fasten off.

Making Up

Using small invisible stitches, sew border to one edge of hand towel.

TIP

When you need to join a fresh ball of yarn onto a finished one try to do it at the end of a row to avoid ugly knots in the middle of your work. Pull the new thread through the top of the last stitch, then hold the two ends behind the last row and cover them in as you work the next.

— ♦ —

22

Border in Filet Crochet

✪✪

Materials

Coats Patons Opera No. 20 Crochet Cotton Shade 500 - 50 grams

1.00mm Milward Steel Crochet Hook

1 reel Sylko Sewing Thread

1 sewing needle

105cm x 40cm piece of white linen

Size

The border is approximately 16 cm [6½ ins] deep.

Special Abbreviation

1 picot = make 3ch, sl st into first of these ch.

Note

The border is worked lengthwise.

To Make

Make 75ch.

1st row: Work 1tr into 4th ch from hook, 1tr into each of next 2ch (1 blk), 2ch, miss 2ch, 1tr into next ch (1 sp), 1tr into each of next 15ch (5 blks), [2ch, miss 2ch, 1tr into next ch] 16 times (16 sps), 1tr into each of last 3ch (1 blk), turn. 24 squares.

2nd row: Inc 1 blk, 1tr into each of next 3tr (1 blk worked over 1 blk), [2ch, 1tr into next tr] 3 times (3 sps worked over 3 sps), [2tr into next sp, 1tr into next tr] 6 times (6 blks worked over 6 sps), [2ch, 1tr into next tr] 7 times (7 sps worked over 7 sps), 2ch, miss 2tr, 1tr into each of next 13tr (1 sp worked over 1 blk and 4 blks over 4 blks), 2ch, 1tr into each of next 2tr, 1tr into next ch (1 blk worked over 1 blk at end of row), turn.

3rd row: 3ch (count as 1tr), 1tr into each of next 3tr (1 blk worked over 1 blk at beg of row), 1 sp, 4 blks, 7 sps, 4 blks, 2 sps, 1 blk, 4 sps, 1 blk, turn.

EXTRA PUR
100%
MARSEILLE
EXTRA PUR
100%
MARSEILLE

21/22

Continue following chart to end (80 rows). Rep these 80 rows for the length required. Fasten off.

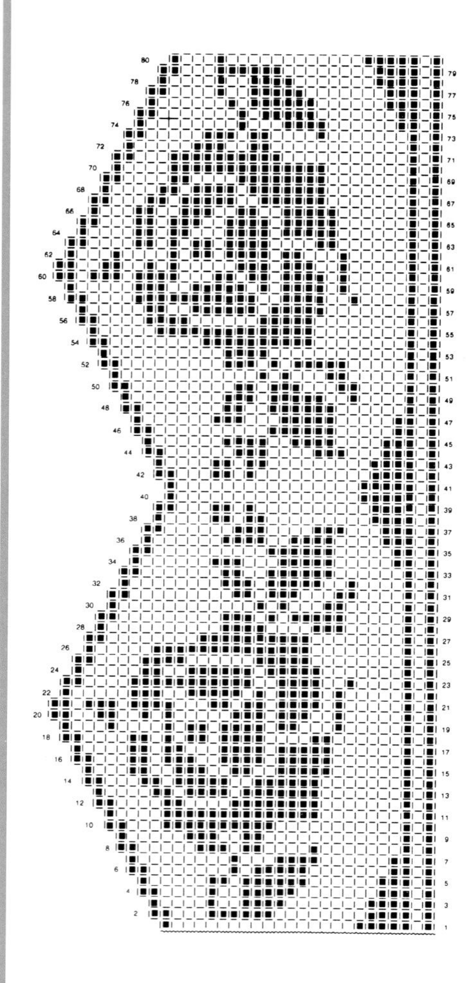

Key ■ = Block □ = Space

Edging

Rejoin yarn to first starting ch and work *5dc, 1 picot, rep from * evenly along up right side edge, top and left side edge, then continue in dc along lower edge working the picot at each outer corner, sl st into first dc. Fasten off.

Making Up

Make a narrow hem all round fabric and sew border as illustrated.

23

Border

✪✪✪

Materials

Coats Patons Musica No. 8 Crochet Cotton Shade 500 - 50 grams

1.25 Milward Steel Crochet Hook

Size

The border is approximately 16.5 cm [6 3/4 ins] deep.

Rings

First Ring

Make 10ch, sl st into first ch to form a ring.

1st round: 3ch (count as 1tr), work 19tr into ring, sl st into 3rd of 3ch at beg of round ★ .

2nd round: 4ch (count as 1tr, 1ch), miss next tr, **working into back loop only** of each tr, work [1tr into next tr, 1ch] 19 times, sl st into 3rd of 3ch at beg of round. Fasten off.

2nd Ring

Work as given for First Ring to ★ .

2nd round: 4ch (count as 1tr, 1ch), miss next tr, **working into back loop only** of each tr, work [1tr into next tr, 1ch] 16 times, 1tr into next tr, sl st into a ch space on previous ring, 1tr into next tr, 1ch, 1tr into next tr, sl st into next ch space of previous ring, sl st into 3rd of 3ch at beg of round. Fasten off.

Work 20 more rings in this way, joining them to previous ring as before, leaving 7 spaces free on either side of links.

First Point

1st row: With wrong side facing, rejoin yarn to 2nd free ch space of first ring before link with next ring, 1dc into space, *2ch, miss 1 space on next ring, 1dc into next space, [2ch, miss 1 space, 1dc into next space] twice; rep from * 5 times more, 2ch, miss 1 space on next ring, 1dc into next space, turn.

2nd row: 3ch, *2tr into 2ch space, 2ch; rep from * to end, turn.

Rep the last row until 2 groups of 2tr remain. Fasten off.

Second Point

1st row: With wrong side facing rejoin yarn to 4th free ch space on ring after dc of first row of first point, 1dc into ch space, *4ch, miss 1 space on next ring, 1dc into next space, [4ch, miss 1 space, 1dc into next space] twice; rep from * 5 times more, 4ch, miss 1 space on next ring, 1dc into next space, turn.

2nd row: 1ch, work 5dc into each 4ch arches to end, turn.

3rd row: Sl st into each of first 3dc, *4ch, 1dc into centre dc on next arch; rep from * to end, turn.

Rep the last 2 rows until one 5dc arch remains. Fasten off.

Third Point

With wrong side facing rejoin yarn to 4th free ch space on ring after dc of first row of second point, 1dc into space, then complete point as given for first point.

Work 37 more rings joining them together as before and to the edges of the points as illustrated, thus having 6 rings on each of the 2 outside edges, 1 at each point, 1 between the points and 5 along each inner edge of points.

Upper Edging

With wrong side facing rejoin yarn to 8th free ch space on first ring before link with 2nd ring, 1dc into ch space, then work as given for first row of second point to end.

2nd row: 1ch, 1dc into first dc, work 5dc into each 4ch arch to end, 1dc into last dc, turn.

3rd row: 5ch (count as 1tr, 2ch), miss first 3dc, 1dc into next dc, *5ch, miss 4dc, 1dc into next dc; rep from * to last 3dc, 2ch, 1tr into last dc, turn.

4th row: 1ch, 1dc into first tr, 3dc into first 2ch arch, *7dc into next 5ch arch; rep from * to end, 3dc into last 2ch arch, 1dc into 3rd of 5ch at beg of previous row, turn.

5th row: 1ch, 1dc into first dc, *5ch, miss 6dc, 1dc into next dc; rep from * to end, turn.

6th row: 1ch, 1dc into first dc, *7dc into next 5ch arch; rep from * to end, 1dc into last dc, turn.

7th row: 5ch, miss first 4dc, 1dc into next dc, *5ch, miss 6dc, 1dc into next dc; rep from * to last 4dc, 2ch, 1tr into last dc.

8th row: As 4th row.

9th row: As 5th row **but** working 4ch only between each dc.

Continue in rounds as follows:

1st round (right side): Work 1dc into each ch and each dc, then continue down side edge as follows: work in dc evenly along edge of upper edging to first ring, then work [1htr, 2ch] into each of the ch spaces on rings around each point, but omitting the 2ch on each of the 3 rings between points, then work up other edge as for first, sl st into first dc.

2nd round: Work *1dc into each of next 3dc, 3ch; rep from * along top edge, then continue as follows: work [1dc, 3ch, 1dc] into each 2ch spaces to end, sl st into first dc. Fasten off.

— ♦ —

24

Border with Flowers

Materials

Coats Patons Opera No. 20 Crochet Cotton Shade 500 - 50 grams

1.00mm Milward Steel Crochet Hook

Size

The border is approximately 11 cm [4½ ins] deep.

Flowers (Make 9)

Centre Petal

Make 5ch, sl st into first ch to form a ring.

1st round: Work 10dc into the ring, sl st into first dc.

Continue in rows as follows:

1st row: [5ch, miss 1dc, 1dc into next dc] twice, turn.

2nd row: 7ch, 1dc into next arch, 5ch, [1dc, 5ch, 1tr] into next arch, turn.

3rd row: [5ch, 1dc into next arch] twice, 5ch, [1dc, 4ch, 1tr] into next arch, turn.

4th row: [5ch, 1dc into next arch] 3 times, 5ch, [1dc, 4ch, 1tr] into next arch, turn.

5th row: [5ch, 1dc into next arch] 3 times, 1tr into next arch, turn.

6th row: 5ch, 1dc into next arch, 4ch, 1tr into next arch. Fasten off.

Second Petal

Rejoin yarn to top of left side edge of Centre Petal and work 13dc along side edge of petal, sl st into dc on ring, turn.

2nd row (wrong side): 1ch, work 1dc into each of first 2dc, 1htr into next htr, 1tr into each of next 10 dc, turn.

3rd row: 3ch (count as 1tr), miss first tr, 1tr into each of next 10tr, 1htr into next htr, 1dc into each of next 2dc, turn.

4th row: 1ch, 1dc into each of next 13 sts, then work in dc along top of petal, sl st into side of centre petal. Fasten off.

Third Petal

With right side facing, rejoin yarn to last dc worked into on ring at right of Centre Petal, work 12dc along side edge of centre petal to tr at top corner, 1dc into tr, turn.

23 - 25

2nd row: 3ch (count as 1tr), miss first dc, 1tr into each of next 9dc, 1htr into next dc, 1dc into each of last 2 dc, turn.

3rd row: 1dc into each of first 2dc, 1htr into next htr, 1tr into each of next 10tr, turn.

4th row: 1ch, 1dc into each of next 13 sts, sl st into next dc on ring, turn.

5th row: Working into **back loop only** of each dc, sl st into each of next 13dc, work in dc along top of petal then along top edge of centre petal to next side edge, then working into **back loop only** of each dc, sl st into each dc along top and side edge of second petal, 1dc into same dc on ring as last dc, turn.

Calyx

1st row: 3ch, work 4tr into ring between the 2 side petals, turn.

2nd row: 3ch, miss first tr, work 1tr into each of next 3tr until 1 loop of each remains on hook, yo and through all 4 loops on hook, 1tr into next tr. Fasten off.

With right side facing, work 1 row of dc all round calyx. Fasten off.

Buds (Make 20)

Centre Petal

Make 8ch, sl st into first ch to form a ring.

1st row: 7ch, 1dc into ring, 5ch, 1tr into ring, turn.

2nd row: 7ch, 1dc into next arch, 5ch, [1dc, 3ch, 1tr] into next arch, turn.

3rd row: [5ch, 1dc into next arch] twice, 3ch, 1tr into next arch, turn.

4th row: 5ch, 1dc into next arch. Fasten off.

Second Petal

1st row: Rejoin yarn into ring and work 9dc along side of centre petal, turn.

2nd row: 3ch (count as 1tr), 1tr into first dc, 1tr into each of next 6dc, 1htr into each of last 2dc, turn.

3rd row: 1ch, 1dc into each of first 2htr, 1htr into each of next 2tr, 1tr into each of next 5tr, 1tr into next ch. Fasten off.

Third Petal

Rejoin yarn to top side of centre petal and work to match Second Petal **do not** fasten off at end but work 1dc into ring, turn and work 1 row of dc all round third petal, top of centre petal and down second petal ending with a dc into ring. Fasten off.

Leaves (Make 62)

1st round: Make 12ch, work 1dc into 2nd ch from hook, 1dc into next ch, 1htr into each of next 2ch, 1tr into each of next 3ch, 1htr into each of next 2ch, 1dc into next ch, 3dc into last ch, then continue along other side of ch as follows: miss first ch, 1dc into each of next 9ch, 2dc into next ch, sl st into first dc.

2nd round: Work 1dc into each of first 11 sts, 3dc into next dc, 1dc into each of next 11dc, 3dc into last dc, sl st into first dc. Fasten off.

Petals (Make 2)

1st row: Make 14ch, sl st into 5th ch from hook, 3ch, miss 1ch, sl st into next ch, 2ch, miss 1ch, 1htr into next ch, turn.

2nd row: 5ch, 1dc into next arch, 2ch, 1htr into next arch, turn.

Continue as follows: 5ch, 1dc into next arch, sl st to starting ch, [1dc into next ch, 3ch, miss 1ch] twice, 1tr into next ch, turn, 5ch, 1dc into next arch, 2ch, 1htr into next arch, turn, 5ch, 1dc into next arch, 3dc into next arch, 6ch, sl st into first of these ch, work 10dc into ring just made, 5dc into next arch, 1dc into each of next starting ch, 7ch, sl st into 2nd of these ch, work 10dc into ring just made, then continuing on other side work in dc into each of next 5 arches, sl st into first dc. Fasten off.

Stems

For each stem work as follows:

1st row: Make 4ch, work 1dc into 2nd ch from hook, 1dc into each of next 3 dc, turn.

2nd row: 1ch, 1dc into each of the 3dc, turn.

Rep the last row for the required length for each stem. Fasten off.

Upper Edging

Make a starting ch of the required length for the Border (the chain should be of a multiple of 3 sts plus 1).

1st row: Work 1dc into 2nd ch from hook, 1dc into each ch to end, turn.

2nd row: 3ch (count as 1 tr), miss first dc, 1tr into each dc to end, turn.

3rd row: 1ch, 1dc into each of first 3dc, *3ch (picot), 1dc into each of next 3dc; rep from * to end.

Making Up

Copy the design, enlarged, onto a tracing cloth and firmly tack all the motifs onto it following the design. With needle and embroidery thread, work the corded links. Sew motifs together where necessary with small invisible stitches.

25

Border with Triangles

✪✪✪

Materials

Coats Patons Opera No. 20 Crochet Cotton Shade 500 - 50 grams

1.00mm Milward Steel Crochet Hook

Size

The border is approximataly 14cm [5½ ins] deep.

Special Abbreviations

1 picot = 3 ch, sl st into first of these ch.

Tr3tog = working until 1 loop of each tr remains on hook, work 1tr into side of same triangle as before, 1tr between the 2 triangles and 1tr into corresponding row on side of next triangle, yo and through all 4 loops on hook.

Triangles

★ Top Row Triangles

First Triangle: **1st row**: Make 24ch, work 1dc into 2nd ch from hook, 1dc into each ch to end, turn.

2nd row: 1ch, miss first dc, 1dc into each dc to end, turn.

Rep the last row until 2dc remain (21 rows worked). Fasten off.

Second and Joining Triangles: Sl st into last of the starting ch of First Triangle, then make 24ch, turn.

Work Triangle as before **at the same time** joining it to first as follows:

At the end of the 6th row (17 dc remain), **do not turn** but make 6ch, sl st into 6th row of previous triangle, turn. Over the last 6ch work 2dc and [1 picot, 2dc] 3 times, then continue working on 2nd Triangle to end of the 12th row (11 dc remain), **do not turn** but make 5ch, 1dc into centre picot of previous arch between the two triangles, 5ch, sl st into 12th row of previous triangle, turn. Work 2dc and [1 picot, 2dc] 3 times into each of the 5ch arches, then continue working on 2nd Triangle to the end of the 18th row (5 dc remain), **do not turn** but make 5ch, 1dc into centre picot of first arch, 5ch, 1dc into centre picot of 2nd arch, 5ch, sl st into 18th row of previous triangle, turn. Work over each of the 3 arches as before, then complete Triangle.

Work a third Triangle joining it to the 2nd as before.

Second Row Triangles

First Triangle: Rejoin yarn with a sl st to point of First Triangle on previous row of triangles, make 23ch and sl st to point of next triangle. Work a Triangle as before.

Work a Second Triangle, joining it to the previous triangle as before.

Last Triangle

Rejoin yarn and work as for First Triangle on second row.

Rep from ★ the number of times required to obtain the correct length for the Border, **but** do not fasten off at end.

Edging

1st round: Work 5ch (count as 1tr, 1ch), [1tr, 2ch, 1tr] into point, then continuing along first side work [2ch, 1tr] 25 times evenly to inner corner between 2 triangles, 2ch,

tr3tog into corner, [2ch, 1tr] 25 times evenly along side of next triangle, [2ch, 3tr] at point of same triangle, continue in this way to top right-hand corner of last triangle, then continue along top edge as follows: 1tr into next dc, 2ch, miss 2dc; rep from * to other top corner, then work down side edge of first triangle as before, sl st into 3rd of 5ch at beg of round.

2nd round: Work *2dc into each of next 2 arches, 1 picot; rep from * to end of round, sl st into first dc. Fasten off.

Flower

Work between each Triangle as follows:

Stem

Rejoin yarn with a sl st into first picot at right of inner corner, 4ch, sl st into corresponding picot on other triangle, turn and work 4dc into the 4ch arch, turn.

Next row: 1dc, work 1dc into each of the 4dc, turn.

Rep the last row 26 times more, **at the same time** do not turn at end of the 11th of these rows **but** work 1tr into 2nd free picot of triangle, turn and work 1dc into each of the 4dc, then work 1tr into corresponding picot on other triangle. Fasten off.

Small Leaf

1st round: Make 23 ch and work 1dc into 2nd ch from hook, *1dc into next ch, 1htr into each of next 2ch, 1tr into each of next 14ch, 1 htr into next 2ch, 1dc into next ch*, 3dc into last ch (tip of leaf), then continuing on other side of starting ch, miss first ch, then rep from * to * once more, 2dc into last ch, sl st into first dc.

2nd round: Work 1dc into each of first 22 sts, 1dc into next dc (tip of leaf), 1dtr into 5th free picot on side of triangle, 1dc into each of next 11 sts on leaf, sl st into 2nd free picot from picot worked into, 1dc into each of last 12 sts, 1htr into side of stem just above the dtr. Fasten off.

Work a second Small Leaf to match between other side of stem and next triangle.

Large Leaf

Make 23ch and work 1st round as given for Small Leaf.

2nd round: Work as 2nd round of Small Leaf **but** omitting the joining sts and working 3dc into centre dc of each tip.

3rd round: Working **into back loop only** of each dc, work 1sl st into each dc **at the same time** joining tip of leaf by working 1dtr into 3rd free picot from last picot worked into on side of triangle and halfway along side edge work 1tr into tip of small leaf, sl st into first dc at end of stem. Fasten off.

Work a second Large Leaf to match first, working a sl st into tip of first Large Leaf before fastening off.

Bud

1st row of arches: With wrong side facing, sl st into 4th st on right Large Leaf from link with other leaf, 5ch, sl st into corresponding st on other leaf, turn and work 2dc and [1 picot 2dc] 3 times into the 5ch arch, sl st into same st as last sl st on leaf, turn

2nd row of arches: Sl st into each of next 3 sts on leaf, 5ch, 1dc into centre picot on previous arch, 5ch, miss 2 sts on other leaf, sl st into next st, turn and work 2dc and [1 picot, 2dc] 3 times into each of the 2 arches, sl st into same st as last sl st on leaf, turn.

3rd row of arches: Sl st into each of next 3 sts on leaf, 5ch, [1dc into centre picot of next arch, 5ch] twice, miss 2 sts on other leaf, sl st into next st, turn and work 2dc and [1 picot 2dc] 3 times into each of the 3 arches, sl st into same st as last sl st on leaf, turn.

4th row of arches: Sl st into each of next 3 sts on leaf, 5ch, [1dc into centre picot of next arch, 5ch] twice, miss 2 sts on other leaf, sl st into next st, turn and sl st into each of next 5ch, 2dc and [1 picot, 2dc] 3 times into each of next 2 arches. Fasten off.

5th row of arches: With wrong side facing rejoin yarn to centre picot of first arch, 5ch, sl st into centre picot of next arch, turn and work 2dc and [1 picot, 2dc] 3 times into 5ch arch, sl st into same picot as sl st at beg of arch. Fasten off.

Lower Edging

1st row: With wrong side facing, rejoin yarn with a sl st into 2nd picot from picot at point of first triangle, 6ch, 1dtr into tip of first large leaf, 9ch, 1tr into first 5ch arch of bud, 9ch, 1tr into next picot of bud, 9ch, 1dc into centre picot at point of bud, 9ch, miss next picot on bud, 1tr into next picot, 9ch, 1tr into 5ch arch on bud, 9ch, 1dtr into tip of next large leaf, 6ch, 1dc into 2nd picot before point of next triangle, turn.

2nd row: Work 1dc into each st and into each ch to end, 3ch, sl st into next picot towards point of triangle, turn.

3rd row: *1ch, miss 1dc, 1tr into next dc; rep from * to end, sl st into next picot on leaf, turn.

4th row: Work 1dc into each ch and each tr to end, turn.

5th row: 1ch, 1dc into first dc, *5ch, miss 4dc, 1dc into next dc; rep from * to end, turn.

6th row: Work 2dc and [1 picot, 2dc] 3 times into each 5ch arch. Fasten off.

TIP

When working in the round, the starting ring can often turn out too loose or too tight. In this case, instead of working the base chain stitches, wind the thread twice round the forefinger of your left hand, making a small ring. Work the first round inserting the hook directly into this ring. When finished, pull the end of the thread until it is the right size.

1098 Antioch is finally captured on 2 June.

Holy Lance discovered by Peter Bartholomew on 15 June.

On June 28 Crusaders defeat Kerbogha, who had been besieging the city since its capture.

1099 Jerusalem falls to Crusaders on 17 July. Two weeks later Urban II dies before hearing of the victory.

1112 St Bernard joins Cistercian Order.

1118 Year cited by William of Tyre as the foundation of the Templars.

1119 Battle of Ager Sanguinis (Field of Blood).

1120 Year now believed by many historians to be the actual date of the Order's foundation. Templars receive their first ecclesiastical recognition at the Council of Nablus in January.

Fulk V, Count of Anjou, joins Templars as an associate member.

1125 Hugh of Champagne joins the Templars after abdicating his lands to his nephew Theobald.

Battle of Azaz.

1127 William of Tyre is born.

1128 Earliest date given for Bernard's *De Laude Novae Militiae*.

1129 The Templars are granted their Rule of Order at the Council of Troyes.

1130 Templars participate in the Siege of Damascus, but are defeated.

1131 Baldwin II dies on 31 August and is succeeded by Fulk of Anjou.

1135 Templars make their first recorded loan to Petre Desde.

1136 Hugues de Payens dies on 24 May and is succeeded by Robert de Craon.

1137 Cressing donated to Templars by Matilda, daughter of Eustace of Boulogne.

Louis VII becomes King of France.

1139 Pope Innocent II pens *Omne datum optimum*, which grants the Templars special privileges.

1140 According to Dr Nicholson

1144

1146

...ave.

1148 Templars finance Louis VII to continue his crusade.

Siege of Damascus is a failure. Second Crusade comes to an effective close.

1149 Raymond of Antioch is killed by Saladin's uncle at the Battle of Inab.

1150 Baldwin III gives Gaza to the Templars.

1152 Everard des Barres resigns as Master and is succeeded by Bernard de Tremeley.

1153 Bernard of Clairvaux dies. Andrew Montbard becomes Master of the Order on the death of Bernard de Tremeley.

In the Battle of Ascalon, the Templars assist in capturing the port city.

1169 Saladin succeeds his uncle Shirkuh as Vizier of Egypt.

1170 Saladin attacks Templar fortress at Daron.

Thomas Becket is murdered in Canterbury Cathedral on 29 December. Henry II sends money to the Templars for a new crusade as part of his penance.

1171 Philip de Milly resigns as Master and returns to secular life.

1173 Saladin attacks Kerak of Moab under order from Nur ad-Dīn.

Gerard de Ridefort has a falling out with Raymond of Tripoli.

1174 Nur ad-Dīn dies at Damascus on 15 May.

King Amalric I dies of dysentery on 11 July, leaving his thirteen-year-old son Baldwin as heir.

continued inside the back cover

NOBLY BORN

NOBLY BORN

An Illustrated History of the Knights Templar

STEPHEN DAFOE

Lewis Masonic

Above: **A modern depiction of a Templar ship sailing off for points unknown prior to the arrests of their brethren in France.** *Stephen McKim*

Frontispiece: **King Richard I during the Battle of Arsuf fought on 7 September 1191. Despite the Hospitallers' impetuously breaking ranks, leading to the mêlée shown here, the Christians emerged victorious in their battle against Saladin.** *ClipArt.com*

First published 2007
ISBN (10) 0 85318 280 9
ISBN (13) 978 0 85318 280 1

Published by Lewis Masonic
an imprint of Ian Allan Publishing Ltd, Hersham, Surrey KT12 4RG.
Printed in England by Ian Allan Printing Ltd, Hersham, Surrey KT12 4RG
Code: 0709/B2

Visit the Lewis Masonic website at www.lewismasonic.com

Contents

Acknowledgements

This book is dedicated to Christian Tourenne, Gordon Napier and Christine Leddon who have helped steer me from the path of historical speculation back to the path of historical fact.

There are two names on the cover of this book which share relatively equal billing. The first is that of the Knights Templar, the subject of this book; the latter is my own, the writer of this book. While some of you may have purchased the book because of the subject, the author or perhaps a combination of the two, there are many other names hidden in the margins, whose assistance was necessary for this book to be a reality.

First and foremost, I must thank my wife Bonnie, who throughout the entire time that I was working on *Nobly Born* remained understanding of the fact that I seldom emerged from my office. And when I did, it was not to ask how her day had been.

On a professional level, I must thank my agent Fiona Spencer Thomas for presenting the proposal to Lewis Masonic and my editor Jay Slater for making the bridge between writer and editor strong and easy to cross. I'd also like to thank Matt Keefe, Malcolm Preskett and Matthew Wharmby for their efforts in proofing and designing the book.

To Dr. Robert Cooper, author of *The Rosslyn Hoax*, my sincerest thanks for his willingness to preview the book and write the foreword for the same.

Although it has often been said that one cannot judge a book by its cover, a book's cover design is an important aspect of the marketing of any book. To this end, I am eternally grateful to Stephen McKim who provided the cover graphic for Nobly Born as well as several of its interior images. Stephen is a multi-talented digital artist who provided no less than a dozen images, which were presented as possible cover designs. I'm also grateful to Gordon Napier, a man who is equally comfortable as an author or as an artist. Gordon, who has written two books on the Templars, provided three wonderful original drawings depicting the arms and armour of the knights and sergeants who made up the Knights Templar. In so doing he has provided the reader of *Nobly Born* with a picture that is truly worth a thousand words. My thanks must also go to Gordon for his photos of Templar locations as well as Mira Vogel, Simon Brighton and Linda Berthelsen for permitting me to reprint theirs.

Lastly, I'd like to thank the hundreds of authors who have written books on the Templars over the past two hundred years that have presented fiction as fact. For had they not muddied the waters of history with fanciful notions, there would be no need for a book like *Nobly Born* to help tip the balance back to reality.

Foreword

THE MASON'S PERSPECTIVE
A Word From Robert L D Cooper

Over the course of the last twenty years or so, a large number of books have been published which comment on Freemasonry and associated subjects. What is noticeable in respect of such books is that very few of them are written by Freemasons. This has created the curious situation whereby Freemasons are being 'educated' about Freemasonry by people who are not Freemasons! This most unusual situation arises for a number of reasons, not least because there is no central 'Masonic educational authority' (or any other central authority for that matter) that publishes, or oversees material produced about Freemasonry. Masonic authors have little choice therefore but to enter the world of commercial publishing, where the reading public has no guidance as to what is authoritative Masonic writing and what is not. Unfortunately, non-Masonic authors have a long head-start over Masonic authors. This as perhaps due to the naive belief held by Freemasons that members of the public were not interested in an organisation of which they were not members. This belief was certainly widespread twenty years or more ago when non-Masons first began to write about Freemasonry. This belief is still commonly held.

Fortunately, this situation is beginning to change with the publication of some good quality writing by Freemasons about Freemasonry and subjects which have come to be associated with the modern Order. This process has become more apparent in the last few years, and this book, *Nobly Born*, is an example of that process. Although not a book about Freemasonry *per se*, it is about a subject with which many will be familiar – the Religious and Military Order of the Poor Soldiers of Christ and Solomon's Temple, more commonly known as the Knights Templar. The reason why many people who are interested in Freemasonry are also interested in this apparently completely unconnected subject is due, in the main, to the work of popular non-Masonic authors who have strongly and repeatedly claimed (and produced 'evidence') that there is at least a link, if not a direct lineal descent, from the medieval Order of Knights Templar, to modern Freemasonry. I have argued elsewhere, as a Freemason, quite the opposite of this claim and consider that this is also part of the new process of Freemasons writing work about the Order of which they are members.

Much of what has been written about the Knights Templar, and the alleged links with Freemasonry is wildly speculative and is not substantiated by credible evidence. Other less popular books are solidly based and a use verified source material. Here then lies the crux of this preface. Much speculative work on Freemasonry and the Knights Templar is easy to read and seems, at first glance, to be based on sound historical technique. Other work, although well written and well researched, is simply not as 'sexy' as the other type and so are not so appealing. How then is one to judge what is good and what is not so good? One way is to strike a balance between these two approaches is by providing a well written book with a light touch and Stephen Dafoe's work presented here is an excellent starting point for anyone (Freemason and non-Mason alike) interested in the medieval Order of Knights Templar.

Robert L D Cooper
August 2007

Author's Introduction

'The lunatic is all idée fixe, and whatever he comes across confirms his lunacy. You can tell him by the liberties he takes with common sense, by his flashes of inspiration, and by the fact that sooner or later he brings up the Templars.'

Jacobo Belbo in Umberto Eco's *Foucault's Pendulum*

Why another book on the Templars?

LIKE any book, the one that you now hold in your hands, began with a proposal – an outline of what the book would be about, an explanation of why the author felt the book was necessary and an analysis of its market potential. What follows is an extract of the proposal sent to my publisher, detailing my intentions for *Nobly Born*:

> 'There have been a number of books on the Templars in recent months, but what would seem to be missing are books that concentrate on the actual history of the order, which is no less interesting than the speculative material and fictional accounts that have dominated the marketplace in recent years.'

Indeed, there have been a number of books written in the last decade which have introduced a variety of theories about the Templars and what they were up to during the two centuries of their existence. Some of these books have presented plausible theories put forth from a serious and sincere study of the extant primary source materials on the Order, or from a re-evaluation of the same.

However, some authors have put forward theories on the Templars that would make Umberto Eco's delirious study of the subject read as if penned by an Oxford professor in comparison. To believe the words of alternative historians (as they prefer to be called), one would have to accept that the Templars did nothing with their time other than dig for treasure and to conceal items of wealth and beauty. These writers suggest that the Templars hoarded every holy relic and priceless manuscript they could, subsequently burying them beneath Rosslyn Chapel. And, of course, the chapel was built by the Templars to house these relics themselves. From the Ark of the Covenant to the severed and mummified head of Jesus Christ, the Templars had it all.

With their suspended form of logic, these authors have expressed their points-of-view to present a one-sided story. Their particular style of writing and narrative will in one chapter present a concept as a possibility, turning this to a likelihood in a subsequent chapter, and finally to established fact, without any further evidence having been introduced, as if repetition were itself proof. However, the authors cannot be held entirely to blame, for they earn their money through royalties, and royalties are only earned if books sell. Such writers for hire are often contracted to write books on current market trends, which are generated by the public.

One book that inspired publishers to release a plethora of rip-offs and imitations was Dan Brown's bestseller, *The Da Vinci Code*. Brown's novel – which should be applauded for no other reason than attracting adults to read – is a work of fiction, but one that claims be based on fact. Although the Templars do not play any major role in Brown's book or the motion picture, the story of them being guardians of the secret knowledge in which Mary Magdalene was Christ's wife and bore him children, has prompted publishers to buy almost anything connected with the Templars.

Garway, Herefordshire on the Welsh Border was home to the Templars from the late 12th century. The predominant feature of the property is the tower of St Michael's Church.
Photo Simon Brighton

It is a scenario I know all too well. When my tent was firmly pitched in the 'alternative historian' camp over ten years ago, I co-authored two books which have been republished in recent years on the resurgence of interest in the Knights Templar. While this interest in the Templars has led to the publication of a number of non-fiction books that could easily find readership amongst those who enjoy fantasy novels, it has also given rise to a number of works of outright fiction on the Templars, or works which use the Order as a plot device. Just as *The Da Vinci Code* has been accepted by many as fact rather than fiction, many of these new works have likewise been accepted as a true depiction of the Templars by a reading public who may no longer be able to discern the difference. As Napoleon Bonaparte once said, 'What is history but a fable agreed upon?' Therefore, as soon as one author devises a theory involving the Templars, another will seize upon it until eventually, by means of continual retelling, fiction becomes 'fact'.

This brings us full circle to the need for a book such as *Nobly Born*. There have been many credible books on the Templars over the years, many of which I have used as source material during research for this book. However, many of the best books on the subject are written by academics and published by university presses. Consequently, they are out of reach of the average reader, who perhaps cannot invest the time to devour a 1000 page tome, nor wade through the copious footnotes and references that are a necessary part of such works.

However, I believe that footnotes are an essential part of any credible book on an historical subject and have provided my fair share of them in *Nobly Born*. Those of us who have studied the Poor Knights of Christ and the Temple of Solomon are indebted to historians such as the late Sir Steven Runciman, as well as current historians such as Helen Nicholson, Malcolm Barber, Alain Demurger and Christopher Tyerman who continue to provide us with a wealth of credible materials to draw from. However, as much as we may not care to admit it, we are also indebted to modern authors of popular fiction such as Dan Brown and Jack Whyte, who have crafted fascinating novels, which have brought the Knights Templar to a readership who were previously unfamiliar with the Order.

Many readers versed in popular fiction who purchased this book may have no other familiarity with the Order than the fictional accounts they have read in novels such as Brown's. As such, *Nobly Born* is not so much a book about the Knights Templar as it is a book about the world in which they existed. Much time is spent in the first section of this book chronicling the events that led to the formation of the Order, and other sections deal with people who never even wore a red cross on a white mantle. It is my belief that one cannot truly understand the Templars unless they appreciate the complex era of the Crusades, for it was in this world of nobly born Christians and Muslims that the Templars existed.

The political intrigues, infighting and unusual alliances, which would turn enemy to ally and vice versa at the drop of a hat, were realities which the Order had to adapt to meet in order to survive. Although *Nobly Born* covers a time some 700 years before the present, it is not so much a book of history as a mirror through which we can see what little has changed in the seven centuries that have passed since the end of the Templars' story.

On the 700th anniversary of the arrest of the Templars in France, it is my sincerest hope that this humble addition to the annals of literature on the Knights Templar will serve to separate fact from fiction and, in so doing, offer a fitting tribute to the memory of an Order which occupied a prominent place in the medieval landscape for nearly two centuries.

Stephen Dafoe
13 October 2006
On the evening of the
699th anniversary of the
arrest of the Templars

Abraham prepares to sacrifice his son Isaac. It is from this rock that Muslims believe the prophet Muhammad ascended to heaven.
ClipArt.com

The Changing Tide

'If I forget thee, O Jerusalem, let my right hand forget her cunning.'

Psalm 137: 5

Right: **King David captured the city of Jebus from the Jebusites in 1004 BC.** *ClipArt.com*

In AD 638, after a siege that had lasted two years, Caliph Umar ibn al-Khattab found himself standing on the Temple Mount in Jerusalem, the third holiest city in Islam. By his side, was Sophronius, the Byzantine Patriarch of Jerusalem, who had personally surrendered the city to the Muslim caliph earlier that day. For the Byzantine Christians, the capture of Jerusalem marked the end of their decade-long control over the city,[1] while for the Muslims, the conquest of the Holy City was the beginning of a reign that would last more than four and a half centuries. For Jerusalem itself, it was yet another conquest in a long history of occupations, which had seen the city change hands many times since it was liberated from the Jebusites more than a millennium and a half earlier.

In the year 1004 BC, King David accomplished what previous warriors had been unable to do. The city of Jerusalem was not large, measuring only about 380 metres from north to south and about 120 metres from east to west. However, it was perched on a mountain ridge and had thick walls built to a 'V' shape, which the citizens considered to be impenetrable.[2] According to the later Jewish historian Flavius Josephus, the Jebusites were so confident in the strength of their fortifications that they put their blind and maimed on the ramparts of the city to taunt and mock the king, arguing that even their weakest citizens could hold back his army.[3] David was not amused and laid siege to the city, conquering the lower section in a short period of time; the citadel, however, proved more difficult. The king saw an opportunity to take Jebus (as Jerusalem was then named) by sending his men through channels that supplied the city with water. Determined to emerge victorious, David offered command of his army to whoever could emerge from the gullies below to take control of the citadel.[4] Many warriors rushed forwards, Joab being the first to emerge from the water shaft into the heart of the city, taking the Jebusites by surprise and was consequently promoted to commander of the conquering army.

After capturing Jebus, David rebuilt the city and named it 'The City of David', joining the captured citadel to the lower city and enclosing the entire area with a wall.[5] David allowed the Jebusites who had surrendered to remain and made an alliance with Hiram, King of Tyre, who provided labour and materials to build a royal palace. It was the beauty of David's palace that inspired the king to build a temple to house the Ark of the Covenant, which he had

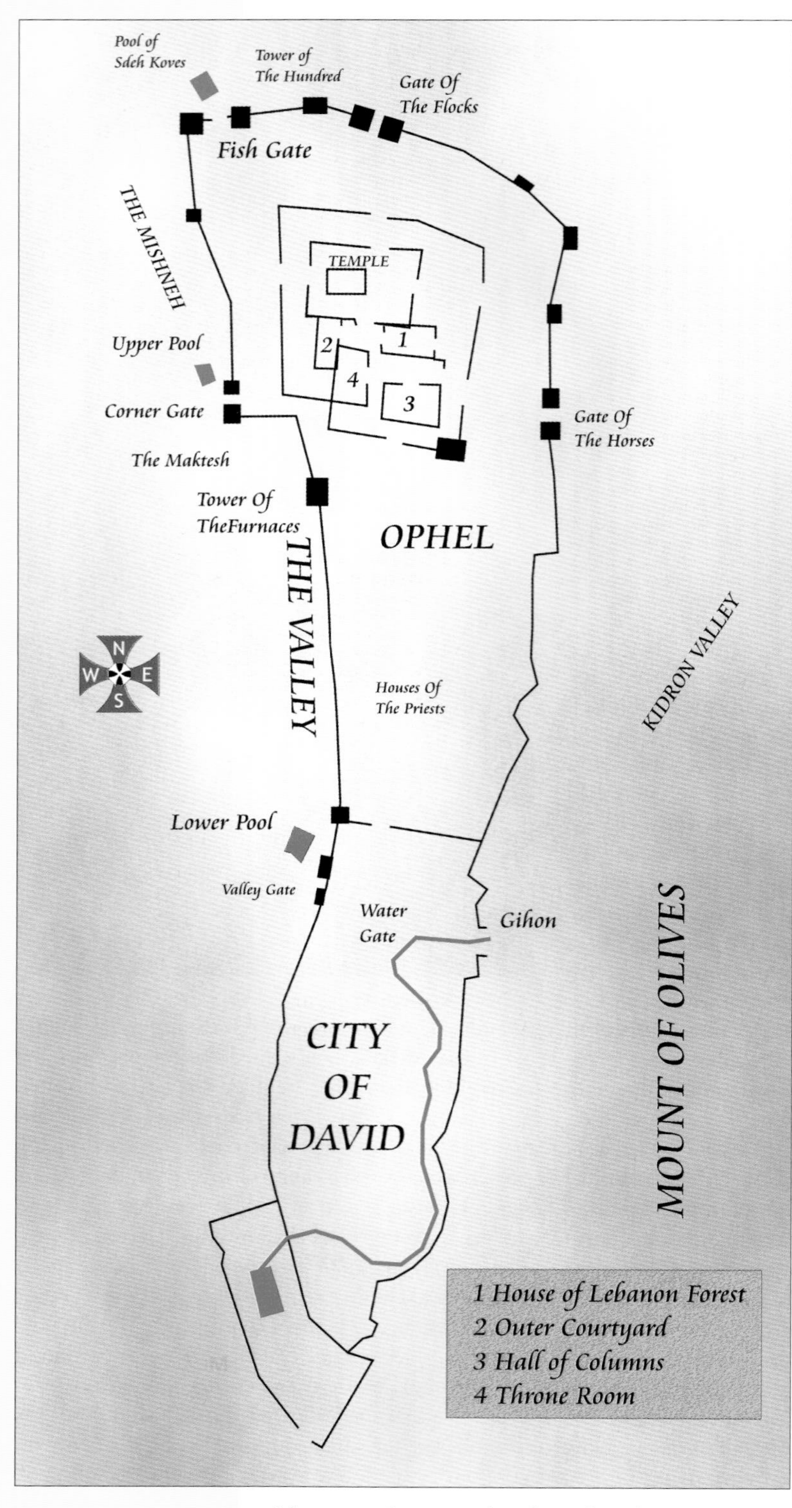

After capturing Jerusalem from the Jebusites, David fortified and expanded the area, renaming it the City of David. *Author*

brought to the recently captured city.[6] However, David had fought in many wars and his hands were stained with the blood of his enemies. The king therefore, was not thought a proper choice for the building of such a sacred temple. The prophet Nathan told David that the task of building the temple should fall to his son Solomon. It did not, however, stop the king from paving the way for his successor.

According to biblical tradition, David ordered Joab to conduct a census of his citizens to ascertain how many fighting men were in the kingdom. Jewish law required that whenever a census was conducted a sum of one half-shekel was to be paid to God's service for each citizen who had been numbered. David did not comply with Hebrew law and was informed by the prophets that God had decreed that the king could choose one of three punishments for his disobedience: three months of defeat at the hands of his enemies, seven years of famine or three days of plague. David chose the plague believing it better to be killed by God than at the hands of his enemies. Following the plague, which the Bible records as having killed 70,000 people, David was instructed to build an altar and offer a sacrifice at the threshing floor of Araunah (Ornan) the Jebusite.[7] Although Araunah offered the threshing floor to David as a gift, the king insisted on paying for it and gave him a sum of 50 shekels.

This threshing floor was not merely a location for the Jebusites to process their wheat; it was also sacred to them. To the Jews also, this was the very spot where Abraham had been willing to offer his son Isaac as a sacrifice to God, and where the patriarch Jacob had his vision of angels ascending into heaven on a ladder. It would be on this holy rock that Solomon would build his famed temple, known to the Jews as the First Temple.

But for the Muslim caliph who took control of the city some 1700 years later, the sacred rock held additional significance. For here, according to the faith of Islam, was the very spot where the Prophet Muhammad, like Jacob's angels, had ascended into heaven. The Holy Koran tells how Allah 'transported his servant by night from the sacred temple of Mecca to the farther temple of Jerusalem'.[8] Islamic tradition would later claim that Muhammad and Archangel Gabriel journeyed from the sacred Kaaba at Mecca to Jerusalem on a winged steed called el Buraq.[9] At Jerusalem, Muhammad led Abraham, Moses, Jesus and other prophets in prayer before mounting the steed and flying through the seven heavens to meet Allah, who gave the prophet instructions for the Muslim people.

To Caliph Umar, the story of the prophet's night journey, known as the Isra and Miraj, was not some

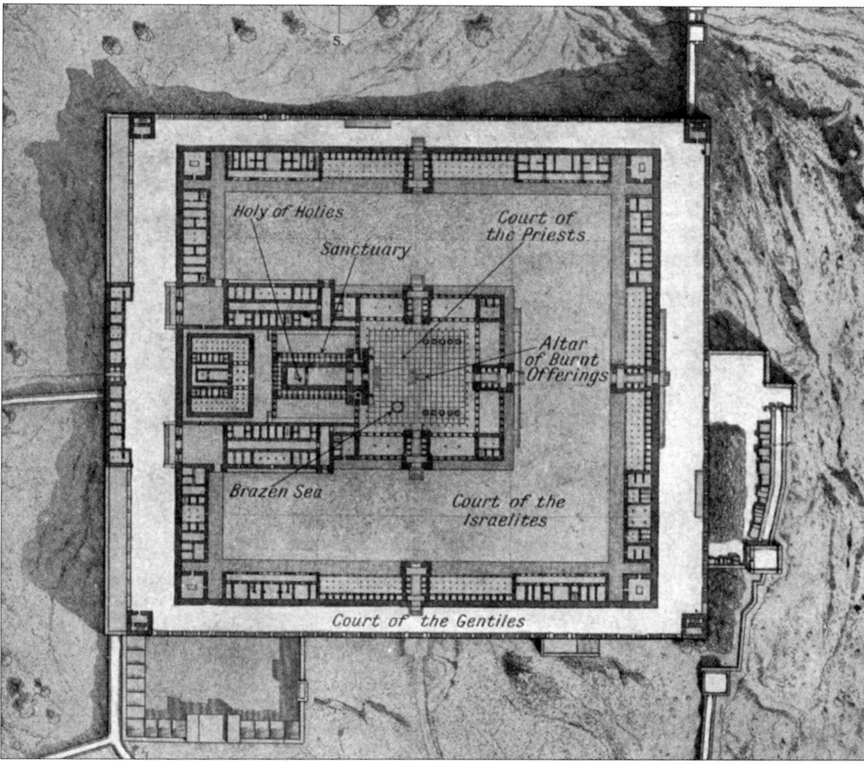

religious tradition that had been passed down from generation to generation but rather it was a near current event. Although Muhammad was the prophet of Umar's religion, he was also one of his closest friends, a friend who had died only six years previously.[10] The Isra and Miraj was therefore not some ancient happening, but an event that Umar believed took place less than two decades earlier.

But as Umar stood looking at the place sacred to his faith, as well as the faiths of Judaism and Christianity, he found not a place of reverence but a place of refuse. According to Islamic tradition, the Temple Mount area was being used by the Byzantine Christians as a place to dump their rubbish.[11] In some accounts of the story, the caliph, angered at the Byzantines' desecration of the sacred spot, made the patriarch crawl through filth on his hands and knees. In other versions, Umar cleared the area himself. Regardless, Umar did erect a temporary mosque on the Temple Mount so that Muslims had a place to offer their prayers to Allah.

Although erroneously referred to as the Mosque of Umar, the present day Dome of the Rock was not actually built by Umar, but by Abd al-Malik, who completed construction of the mosque in AD 691, almost a half-century after Umar's death. Almost a decade later in AD 705, al-Malik's son, al-Walid, completed a second mosque on the southern end of the Temple Mount, where it is believed Umar had erected the original wooden mosque after capturing the city. This new mosque was called al-Masjid al-Aqsa or 'The Farthest Mosque' after the words found in Sura 17:1 of the Holy Koran relating to the prophet's night journey.

In addition to constructing new mosques, the Muslims allowed existing religious buildings such as the Church of the Holy Sepulchre, which many believe was the inspiration for the Dome of the Rock,

Above left: **A romantic depiction of the dedication of Solomon's Temple, built on the site chosen by Solomon's father David.** *ClipArt.com*

Above right: **Nineteenth-century depiction of the layout and position of the Temple of Solomon on the Temple Mount at Jerusalem.** *ClipArt.com*

Left: **Islamic depiction of the Prophet Muhammad's night journey known in Islam as the Isra and Miraj.** *ClipArt.com*

Above left:
The Kaaba in Mecca is the holiest place in Islam. It is from here that Muslims believe the prophet Muhammad began his night journey.
ClipArt.com

Above upper right:
Erroneously referred to as the Mosque of Omar, the Dome of the Rock was actually built by Caliph Abd al-Malik and completed in AD 691.
ClipArt.com

Above lower right:
Interior of the Dome of the Rock.
ClipArt.com

to remain. In fact, the Church of the Holy Sepulchre remained a Christian church throughout the Muslim reign of Jerusalem until Caliph al-Hakim tore the building down in 1009. Following this, and up until al-Hakim's death in 1021, Christians were not permitted to return to the site, let alone rebuild it.

However, such acts of religious intolerance were almost unknown in the early history of Islam. When Umar had captured the city in AD 638, he allowed the Jews – who had been expelled by the Byzantine Christians in AD 614 – to return to the city sacred to their faith. What was unique about Islam was that Christians, Jews and even Zoroastrians were considered to be 'al al-kitab'. Although this Arabic term has often been translated in English as 'people of the book', a more correct interpretation would be 'followers of an earlier revelation'.[12] Regardless of the exact translation, whenever the Muslims conquered a new territory, they allowed the 'dhimmis', or protected subjects who remained, to practice their own faith, so long as the Koran tolerated the faith.[13] Although Christ was not considered to be divine, Muslims regarded him as an important prophet, and a similar respect extended to the Jewish prophets and patriarchs.

Under al-Walid's rule, the Muslims continued their conquests, expanding into North Africa, and by AD 711 were successful in establishing a strong foothold in Spain.[14] In less than a century since the prophet Muhammad had received his revelations, Islam had spread from the Arabian Peninsula to the Iberian Peninsula. This was, however, the limit of their western expansion. In October of AD 732, a Muslim army under Abdul Rahman Al Ghafiqi, was defeated by Charles Martel at the Battle of Tours (also know as the Battle of Poitiers, but not to be confused with a much later, unrelated battle of the same name). Although Western Christendom would battle the Muslims in the Iberian Peninsula for many years, it would be another three centuries before they would battle them in the East.

During this time, Muslims continued to fight amongst themselves in a power struggle that was political rather than religious in nature. However, amid the internal conflicts, Muslims continued to conquer land held by the Byzantine Christians, which further weakened the empire's eastern frontiers.

The Battle of Manzikert

In the last decade of the tenth century, the Seljuks – a nomadic tribe from Central Asia – converted to Islam.[15] By the middle of the eleventh century, under the leadership of Sultan Alp Arslan, the Seljuks had succeeded in gaining full control of Armenia.[16] In 1067, the Byzantine Emperor Constantine X died, which left his young son Michael, as heir to the throne. Needing a strong leader to act as regent for her son, the Byzantine empress Eudocia married the commander of the Byzantine army, Romanus Diogenes, who was crowned emperor.

Romanus had a difficult task before him in fighting the Seljuks, for his predecessor had significantly reduced the Byzantine army.[17] In fact, when Romanus came to power, the Byzantine army consisted mostly of unreliable foreign mercenary troops. Even the commander of his army, Andronicus Ducas, was a man whom the emperor could not entirely count on. Ducas was the nephew of the former emperor and, like many members of his family, had a deep hatred for the new emperor.[18]

However, wishing to regain some security on his eastern frontier, Romanus led his army into the region in August of 1071 determined to regain occupied Byzantine land. Part of the army was sent to besiege Akhlât, while Romanus and the rest of the army moved on to besiege Manzikert near Lake Van in present day Turkey.[19]

The Sultan Alp-Arslan, learning of the Byzantines' movements, moved to meet the army head on at Manzikert. This manoeuvre forced Romanus to withdraw towards Akhlât in the hopes of regrouping with the army he had sent there. However, the emperor found no assistance in that direction, for the mercenary troops had defected to the other side the night before.[20] Ducas and his men added to the treachery by fleeing the field and returned to Constantinople, leaving Romanus to his fate. While the Byzantines waited for support that would never arrive, Alp Arslan and his army descended on them and delivered them a crushing defeat, capturing the emperor in the process.

The Byzantine defeat at Manzikert was a devastating one, not only for the loss of men and the capture of the emperor, but also for the loss of territory.[21] The empire continued to shrink and within a decade of the Battle of Manzikert, the Seljuk Turks had established such a presence in the region that Turkish nomads felt secure enough to travel throughout Anatolia with their flocks.[22] Within another decade, the Seljuk Empire extended to within 160 kilometres of Constantinople and Byzantium. Powerless to stop the Turkish advances in what was left of their empire, the Byzantines sought the help of their Western Christian

Charles Martel defeated al Ghafiqi at the Battle of Poitiers on 10 October AD 732.
ClipArt.com

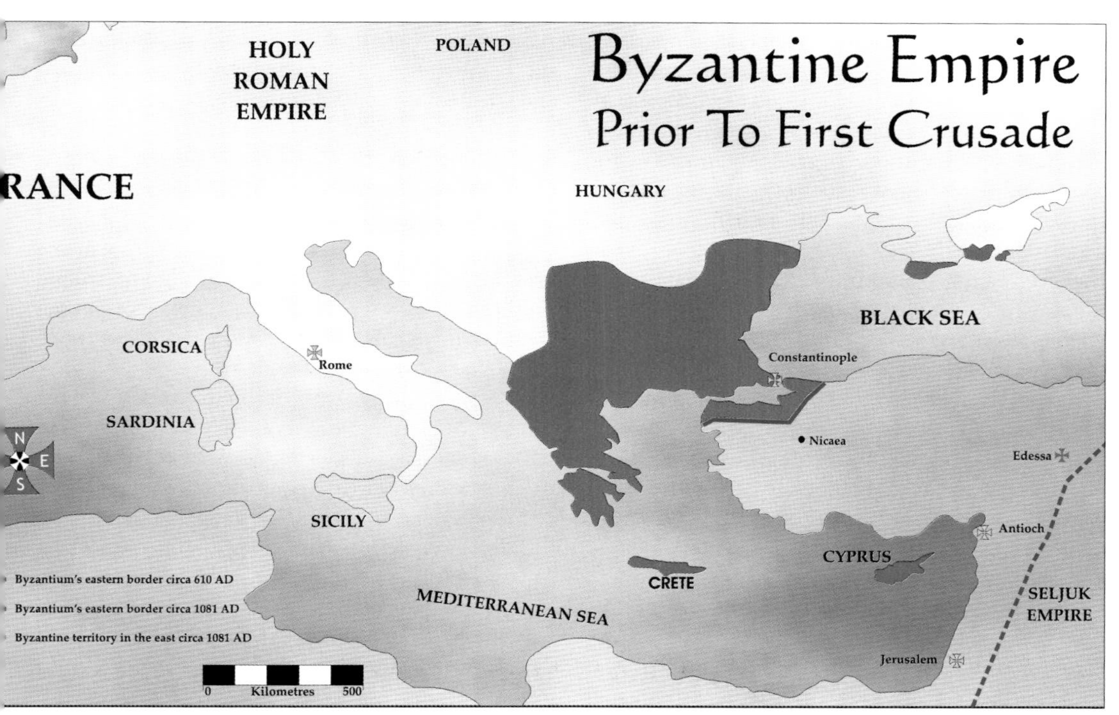

Within a decade of the Byzantine defeat at the Battle of Manzikert in AD 1071, the empire, which had once extended as far south as Jerusalem, would be driven back to within 160 kilometres of its capital Constantinople.
Author

brethren by appealing to the pope. However, help was not immediately forthcoming as Western Christendom was still then recovering from its own power struggles, having suffered loyalties divided between a pope supported by the church, and an anti-pope backed by the Holy Roman Emperor.

The Man Who Launched the Crusades

Otto de Lagery, who would be crowned Pope Urban II, was born in AD 1042 near Châtillon-sur-Marne in the province of Champagne.[23] Although born into a noble and knightly family, Otto was not a first-born son, and like many young men in medieval Europe, family inheritances were out of reach. As such, these nobly born second and third sons often entered the church, and Otto was no exception. He first studied at the Cathedral of Rheims under his uncle Bruno, who would go on to establish the Carthusian Order. Despite having a bright future ahead of him, Otto abandoned Rheims to become a monk at Cluny. He was eventually made prior of the abbey, and it was in this capacity that he was sent to Rome early in the reign of Pope Gregory VII.

Gregory was considered to be one of the greatest of the reforming popes and was involved in the lay investiture controversy, the cause of which was an argument over who would have control the appointment of church officials: the papacy or the Holy Roman Emperor. Prior to these reforms, secular authorities appointed church officials (and on occasion ecclesiastical offices) such as abbots and bishops, and these offices were often bought with land and promises of loyalty. Simony, as the practice was called, was frowned on by the papacy, but highly prized by the secular rulers who used it as a source of income and fealty. What made matters complicated for the papacy was that, under the existing system, the Holy Roman Emperor was the one who appointed the pope.

Some years before Gregory became pope, the church decided to wrestle control of investitures from the emperor, and did so in 1059 when the College of Cardinals was created. This was at a time when the current Holy Roman Emperor, Henry IV, was nine years of age. Of course, by the time Gregory came to power as pope in 1073, Henry was no longer a child, he was a powerful man and one not afraid to confront the church. He sent Gregory a letter, in which he accused him of being a false monk and refused to accept him as pope. But Gregory was also a man who was not afraid to go up against the king and excommunicated Henry in 1076.[24] This standoff between the Holy See and the Holy Empire did not stop Gregory from pushing his reforms and surrounding himself with men who would assist him in accomplishing his goals. To that end, Pope Gregory saw in Otto de Lagery, a trusted advisor who was of great help in the church reforms in which Gregory was engaged.

In 1078, Gregory made Otto Cardinal Bishop of Ostia,[25] and from 1082 until 1085, Otto served as legate, his chief duty being to go to France and Germany to enforce the new laws of the Holy Church. In the midst of his term as legate, Otto was captured en route to Rome and imprisoned by Henry. Although his imprisonment was brief, by the time Otto finally returned to Rome, his mentor Gregory VII was dead and a new pope had been elected: Victor III.

Upon Victor's death in the autumn of 1087, a meeting was called at Terracina, where all concerned were informed that Otto was the man suggested by both Gregory and Victor to be their successor. On 12 March 1088, the nobly born Otto de Lagery was elected pope,[26] took the name Urban II, and immediately began to campaign to ensure that those bishops and princes who had shown loyalty to the reforms of Gregory VII would continue to do so.

However, Urban's papacy was not as simple as merely following the reforms laid down by his mentor. Like his predecessor, he was unable to take the throne in Rome as it was under the control of Emperor Henry who had his own pope, Clement III (Guibert of Ravenna), installed there. As such, he spent the first eight months of his papacy in exile. It was only after a three-day battle between Urban and Clement's troops, that the anti-pope was driven from Rome and Urban was permitted to enter Rome for the first time. The stay would prove to be short-lived, and in the autumn of 1089, Henry, having succeeded in a campaign in northern Italy, had Clement III placed back in Rome. Urban spent the next three years of his papacy wandering around southern Italy, where he held a number of church councils and did his best to perform his duties as pope from outside the walls of Rome.

Urban was finally able to sit on the papal throne as a result of simony, the very sin which Gregorian reforms, enthusiastically supported by Urban, had tried to stamp out. In 1094, six years after Urban had been elected, the governor of the Lateran palace, the principal residence of the popes, offered to sell the palace to Urban. The pope, virtually penniless due to his years in exile, received the funds for the purchase from Gregory of Vendôme, a French abbot, whom Urban made Cardinal Deacon of Sta Prisca in return for his support.

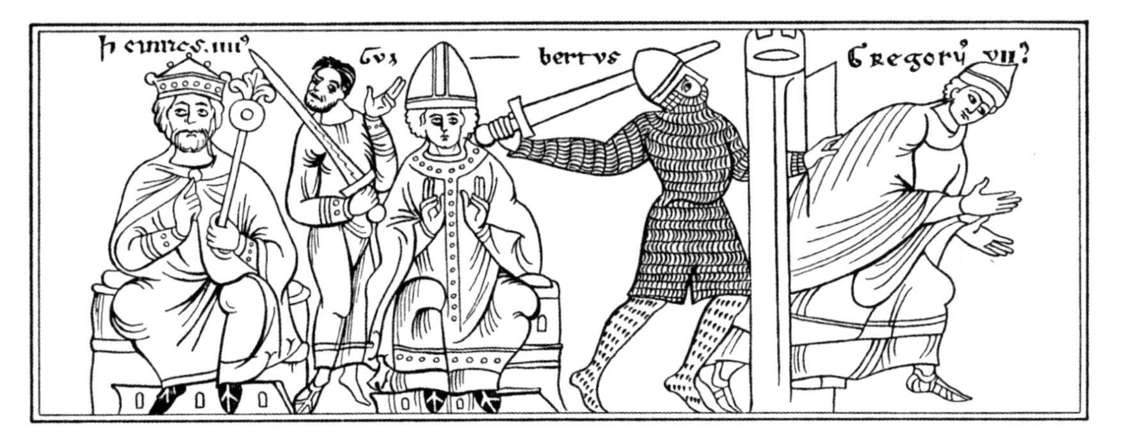

Pope Gregory VII is chased from Rome by Holy Roman Emperor Henry IV and his anti-pope Clement III in this medieval engraving.
ClipArt.com

The Council of Piacenza

After a rocky start to his papacy, Urban was prepared to move forwards with matters and to instil upon the Christian mind that he was the man in charge. In the spring of 1095, Urban held a council at Piacenza in northern Italy. As synods went, it was a routine affair, though affairs were precisely what Urban II was faced with. In attendance, were representatives of King Philip I of France who hoped to reverse their monarch's excommunication, issued by Archbishop Hugh of Lyons. Philip had illegally divorced his wife Bertha in order to marry Bertrade de Montfort, the wife of Fulk IV of Anjou. Both Philip and Hugh had been called to Piacenza, but neither made an appearance at the council. This prompted the pope to suspend the archbishop from his position and to give Philip until Pentecost to straighten out his affairs, both figuratively and literally.

While the intimate private lives of the Catholic faithful may have added a little spice to an otherwise dull gathering, it was not the only business that aroused interest. The Byzantine emperor, Alexius I Comnenus, who had come to power a decade after the Battle of Manzikert, had sent representatives to the council as well. Although Alexius had been excommunicated by Gregory VII, Urban saw fit to remove the excommunication upon being elected pope seven years earlier. This lifted a long-standing barrier between Eastern and Western churches, and once again, the two compass points of Christendom were on friendly terms.

The purpose of the Eastern Church's presence at Piacenza was to request the assistance of the West in stemming the rising tide of Islam that was threatening their faith.[27] In addition to making the pope aware of Byzantium's situation, Alexius also wanted to remind his Western co-religionists that Jerusalem was still in the hands of the infidels. That alone, should be sufficient reason for the West to be concerned.

Although Urban took no formal action upon the matter at Piacenza, word of the Eastern Christians' plight swept through Europe, and by the time Urban arrived in France in the Autumn of 1095, Jerusalem was on the minds of the people. For four months prior, Urban had been touring Europe, stopping to meet with the movers and shakers of Christendom in Province, Languedoc, Burgundy and even at his beloved Cluny Abbey, where he had lived as a monk some years earlier.[28]

The Council of Clermont

In November of 1095, Urban II called for a larger synod to be held in the town of Clermont in Auvergne province. The council was attended by 13 archbishops, 82 bishops and a large number of abbots and other ecclesiastics[29] who had gathered at the Church of Notre-Dame du Port to continue the papal decrees against simony, secular investitures of church officials and clerical marriages. Additionally, Philip of France, who had been given an opportunity to straighten out his affairs, failed to do so and was formally excommunicated for adultery. However, the most interesting decision of the council (given the fact that this was also the council that launched the Crusade) was the desire to uphold the 'Treuga Dei' or Truce of God. Although the truce had been introduced in France a century earlier, it was the first of thirty decrees issued by the Council of Clermont.

Feudalism had given rise to infighting among Christians, especially of the knightly and noble classes, and the Truce of God was designed to put an end to this. The truce prohibited fighting from sunset on Wednesday until sunrise on Monday for the nobility; women, churchmen, labourers and merchants were

Pope Urban preaches the First Crusade on 27 November 1095. His speech would prompt thousands of Christians to travel to the Holy Land to liberate Jerusalem from Muslim control. *ClipArt.com*

forbidden to engage in conflicts at all times. However, if the pope were unwilling to countenance fighting between Christians, he would soon offer them an opportunity to direct their hostilities towards a common foe.

Deus Lo Volt

With ecclesiastical business out of the way, the council turned its attention to the matter of how to deal with the problem in the East. Because of the time he had spent touring Europe, word had spread that Urban planned to make a statement at the end of the council. Although history does not record precisely how many were in attendance that day, it is generally agreed to have been in the thousands – so many in fact, that proceedings were moved from the church to a field. On 27 November 1095, Pope Urban II, standing at a podium erected in the field, addressed the multitudes of abbots, priests, nobles and peasants who had gathered to hear him speak.

There are at least five surviving versions of the speech given that day, which was the speech which first moved Western Christendom to take up the sword and the cross. Although several of the accounts were written by men who were actually in attendance, it is almost certain that all were written from the later perspective of the Christian's victory at Jerusalem in 1099. Among the first hand accounts is that of Fulcher of Chartres who was not only present at the Council of Clermont, but also participated in and chronicled the First Crusade. As such, his may be regarded as being the most reliable. Fulcher quotes Urban:

> 'They [the Muslims] have killed and captured many, and have destroyed the churches and devastated the empire. If you permit them to continue thus for awhile with impurity, the faithful of God will be much more widely attacked by them. On this account I, or rather the Lord, beseech you as Christ's heralds to publish this everywhere and to persuade all people of whatever rank, foot-soldiers and knights, poor and rich, to carry aid promptly to those Christians and to destroy that vile race from the lands of our friends. I say this to those who are present, it is meant also for those who are absent. Moreover, Christ commands it.'[30]

Another chronicler of the First Crusade was Robert the Monk. Unlike Fulcher of Chartres, Robert did not go on crusade, however it is generally agreed that he was in attendance when Urban spoke. Robert's account of Urban's speech contains language intended to shock the reader:

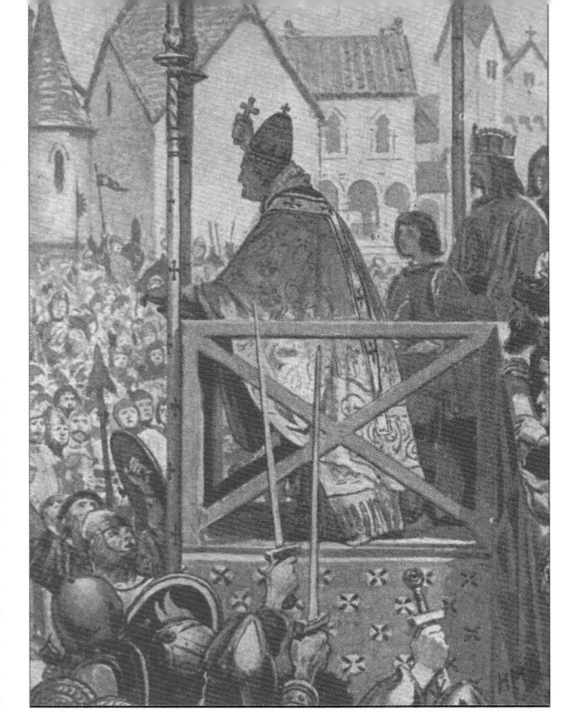

> 'From the confines of Jerusalem and the city of Constantinople a horrible tale has gone forth and very frequently has been brought to our ears, namely, that a race from the kingdom of the Persians, an accursed race, a race utterly alienated from God, a generation forsooth which has not directed its heart and has not entrusted its spirit to God, has invaded the lands of those Christians and has depopulated them by the sword, pillage and fire; it has led away a part of the captives into its own country, and a part it has destroyed by cruel tortures; it has either entirely destroyed the churches of God or appropriated them for the rites of its own religion. They destroy the altars, after having defiled them with their uncleanness. They circumcise the Christians, and the blood of the circumcision they either spread upon the altars or pour into the vases of the baptismal font. When they wish to torture people by a base death, they perforate their navels, and dragging forth the extremity of the intestines, bind it to a stake; then with flogging they lead the victim around until the viscera having gushed forth the victim falls prostrate upon the ground. Others they bind to a post and pierce with arrows. Others they compel to extend their necks and then, attacking them with naked swords, attempt to cut through the neck with a single blow. What shall I say of the abominable rape of the women? To speak of it is worse than to be silent. The kingdom of the Greeks is now dismembered by them and

> deprived of territory so vast in extent that it can not be traversed in a march of two months. On whom therefore is the labour of avenging these wrongs and of recovering this territory incumbent, if not upon you? You, upon whom above other nations God has conferred remarkable glory in arms, great courage, bodily activity, and strength to humble the hairy scalp of those who resist you.'[31]

That Urban would refer to the French as a nation favoured by God should come as no surprise. Although he sat upon a throne in Rome, Urban was still very much a French nobleman at heart. But if his French sympathies and tongue were not enough to move his countrymen to war, the pope offered another incentive to those who would take up the cross. In a letter written to the crusaders in December of 1095, Urban wrote:

> 'Grieving with pious concern at this calamity [the situation in the east], we visited the regions of Gaul [Western Europe] and devoted ourselves largely to urging the princes of the land and their subjects to free the churches of the East. We solemnly enjoined upon them at the council of Auvergne such an undertaking, as a preparation for the remission of all their sins.'[32]

This plenary indulgence was offered to all who would make the journey for the sake of devotion alone and the pope vowed to treat the personal property and landholdings of those who took the cross as sacred and under the protection of the Church. And of those who may give their lives for the cause of Christ, Fulcher of Chartres adds to his account of Urban's speech: 'All who die by the way, whether by land or by sea, or in battle against the pagans, shall have immediate remission of sins. This I grant them through the power of God with which I am invested.'[34]

Legend has it that the Christian faithful, whipped into a religious frenzy at the sound of Urban's voice, rose together in but a single voice in response to his words 'Deus Lo Volt' or 'God Wills It'. In his book *God's War*, Christopher Tyerman, a fellow in history at Hertford College and a lecturer in Medieval History at New College, Oxford, suggests that priests in the audience may have initiated the chanting.[34] Tyerman paints an interesting portrait of the Clermont speech as a kind of ritual, in which the chanting of 'Deus Lo Volt' involved those in attendance in the ceremony, which the author convincingly equates to a church mass. However, Urban's speech was the first time that his concept of Holy War was presented in a public setting, [35] and as such, those in attendance could not have known that they were expected to take up the cross. To set the tone and example, Adhémar, Bishop of Le Puy, who would lead the crusade in Urban's stead, was the first to pin on a woollen cross that had been prepared ahead of time. He was not the only one to do so, as the crowds are said to have clamoured to take up the cross of their saviour as they chanted the mantra of the day: 'Deus Lo Volt'.

They were three simple words, which made warriors out of peasants, widows out of wives and would change the landscape of the Near East for nearly two centuries.

References for chapter 1

1 Jerusalem was recaptured from the Persians in AD 628 by Byzantine Emperor Heraclius. The Persians had taken it in AD 614.

2 Potok, Chaim, *Wanderings*. p. 147

3 Maier, Paul L., Josephus, *The Essential Writings* op. cit. 122-123

4 Ibid p.123

5 Ibid p.123

6 Ibid p.125

7 2 Samuel 24

8 Sale, George, *The Koran: A Verbatim Reprint*. p.206 Surah 17: 1. Other translations do not specify Jerusalem. Rodwell's 1876 translation reads 'the temple that is more remote,' while Palmer's 1880 translation reads 'from the Sacred Mosque to the Remote Mosque.' The Arabic for farthest mosque is al-Masjid al-Aqsa.

9 Comay, Joan, *The Temple of Jerusalem*. p. 207 The first indication in Islamic writing of Muhammad being carried on the winged steed is derived from the Hadith, which was published in the 9th century.

10 Armstrong, Karen, *Islam: A Short History*. p. 202. Umar became the second caliph after Muhammad's death and it was under him that the Arabs began their wars of conquest.

11 Comay op. cit. p. 209

12 Armstrong op. cit. p. 203.

13 Ibid. p. 204

14 Ibid p. 50

15 Ibid. p. xxi

16 Runciman, Steven, *A History of the Crusades V. 1*. p. 50

17 Ibid p. 51

18 Ibid p. 51

19 Catherwood, Christopher, *A Brief History of the Middle East*. p. 96

20 Runciman op. cit. p. 51

21 Concurrent with the Empire's loss of land on their eastern frontier, they were also losing ground on their western front. In the same year, Byzantium's last fortress in Italy was taken by the Normans of Sicily.

22 Armstrong op. cit. p. 95

23 Coulombe, Charles, *A History of the Popes*. p. 223

24 Tyerman, Christopher, *God's War*. p. 7

25 Coulombe op. cit. p. 223

26 Ibid p. 223

27 Tyerman op. cit. p. 61

28 Ibid p. 63

29 Ibid p. p. 62

30 Urban II (1088-1099): Speech at Council of Clermont, 1095. Five versions of the Speech – Medieval Sourcebook http://www.fordham.edu/halsall/source/urban2-5vers.html

31 Ibid.

32 Ibid.

33 Ibid.

34 Tyerman, Op. Cit. p. 65

35 Ibid. p. 64

Godfrey de Bouillon, one of the leaders of the First Crusade is depicted in this heroic interpretation showing the Jerusalem or Crusader's Cross.
Author

Holy Land, Holy War

'Si vis pacem, para bellum'
('If you want peace, prepare for war.')

Publius Flavius Vegetius
Renatus (AD 360 – AD 400)

Right: **Peter discusses the crusade with Pope Urban II in this nineteenth-century illustration. Some contemporary chronicles claim that Peter had been east prior to the First Crusade.**
ClipArt.com

URBAN's speech had prompted many Westerners to put their lives on hold to take up the cause of Christendom's defence. But the journey east would take considerable planning, at least for the nobly born members of society. There were supplies to buy, armies to equip, and most importantly, the nobles required people to look after their estates in their absence. However, for the ignoble majority of Frankish society, there was no property to find custodians for, no money to buy supplies or hire soldiers with and no real reason to delay leaving. To many of those preparing to leave, Jerusalem was a land flowing with milk and honey,[1] while their towns and villages offered them nothing more than further years of feudal servitude.

While the princes of Europe were assembling their armies, the first crusaders left for the Holy Land, led not by a broad-shouldered knight mounted on a powerful warhorse, but by a small, ugly man[2] riding a donkey. His name was Peter the Hermit and his ability to motivate the common man was without peer. One of the chroniclers who actually met him was Guibert de Nogent, who said of Peter's influence:

> 'By his wonderful authority he restored everywhere peace and concord, in place of discord. For in whatever he did or said it seemed as if there was something divine, especially when the hairs were snatched from his mule for relics.' [3]

In her book *The Alexiad*, Anna Comnena, the daughter of the Byzantine emperor Alexius Comnenus, wrote that Peter had previously been to the East and was alarmed by what he saw. Upon his return to the West, he began preaching a crusade to garner support to return again.[4] Although other chroniclers such as William of Tyre and Albert of Aix also painted an important role for Peter the Hermit, it is generally believed that he did not begin preaching the crusade until after the Council of Clermont. Whatever his personal motivations or experience may have been, he was successful in rousing support among the peasantry.

The People's Crusade

ALTHOUGH it is impossible to know exactly how many followers Peter was able to attract, Steven Runciman, in his *History of the Crusades*, suggests that the number was probably in the neighbourhood of 20,000.[5] The vast majority of these would have been non-combatants: wives and children of the simple peasants who had taken up the cross. Even those who were prepared to fight were little more than foot soldiers whose only experience in battle would have been the obligatory military service they owed to their landlords. There were, of course, some knights drawn into Peter's crusade earlier on and among these were Walter de Poissy and his four nephews.[6]

Peter the Hermit is seen talking to his followers and Walter's soldiers in this nineteenth-century illustration by Edouard Zier depicting the legendary but failed People's Crusade. *ClipArt.com*

As the rabble that was Peter's army made their way east, they stopped in Cologne, where Peter hoped to garner further support from the Germans. De Poissy's nephew, nicknamed Walter the Penniless, was unwilling to wait for Peter to gain further recruits and set off with his men on 12 April. By May, Walter and his party arrived in Hungary where King Colomon granted permission for the army to pass through his realm. However, when the party reached the eastern frontier at Semlin, a handful of Walter's men stayed behind, while the bulk of the army crossed the River Save into Belgrade. The men who remained behind attacked a bazaar, which resulted in them being beaten by the Hungarians who stripped them of their clothing and gear, and sent them across the river naked.[7] Meanwhile in Belgrade, Walter had attempted to get supplies for his army but was denied, which prompted his men to pillage the countryside. During the battle that followed many of their number were killed.

When Peter's army arrived at Semlin in late June, they found the armour of those who had been stripped hanging from the city walls as a warning to bandits. Despite the warning, violence once again ensued, with a dispute over a pair of shoes.[8] When all was said and done, 4000 Hungarians had been killed, property destroyed and provisions for the army had been taken by plunder. Fearing reprisals from King Colomon, the army moved quickly into Belgrade, but their passage across the Save was met with resistance leading to another battle which cost even more lives.[9] When they had finally fought their way into Belgrade, the army pillaged the city and then set fire to it.

Those who survived pressed on, arriving at Nish a week later, where food and supplies were requested. Hostages were taken in exchange for the provisions as an assurance that the crusaders would move on. When the crusaders set off for Sofia the next morning, some Germans at the rear of the army set fire to some mills which once again led to fighting and the loss of more peasant crusaders.[10]

When the remnants of Peter's army had reached Sofia, it was met by an envoy from Constantinople who kept the crusaders on a tight leash to ensure that no further pillaging or violence occurred. For the first time since leaving Hungary, the army moved forwards without incident. Prior to arriving at Constantinople on 1 August, Peter received word from Emperor Alexius that the sins of his army had been forgiven due to the punishment they had already received along the way.[11] However the warning implicit in the emperor's reprieve must have fallen upon deaf ears, for the crusaders pillaged the countryside upon their arrival outside Constantinople, even going so far as to strip the lead from church roofs.

Alexius was not impressed with the rabble that made up Peter's army, nor that of Walter, who arrived a few weeks earlier. The emperor felt that if they made any attempt to battle the Turks, they would suffer a crushing defeat. Although he urged Peter to wait for the arrival of the main crusading armies before engaging the Muslims, he also realised that he needed to keep them moving. Therefore on 6 August, the crusaders marched across the Bosphorus. Despite the emperor's advice, the crusaders pillaged the countryside as they had throughout their journey. Anna Comnena wrote of the barbaric actions of part of Peter's army who ravaged the area around Nicaea:

> 'For they dismembered some of the children and fixed others on wooden spits and roasted them at the fire, and on persons advanced in age they inflicted every kind of torture. But when the inhabitants of Nicaea became aware of these doings, they threw open their gates and marched out upon them, and after a violent conflict had taken place they had to dash back inside their citadel as the Normans fought so bravely. And thus the latter recovered all the booty and returned to Helenopolis [Civetot].' [12]

Whether or not the army actually engaged in the atrocities described by Anna, they did manage to capture substantial booty, which made the Germans jealous. By the end of September, the Germans, looking for spoils of their own, set out beyond Nicaea and captured the castle of Xerigordon. By the month's end, the Turks, unable to recapture the castle, had taken control of the well that supplied it and the Germans were forced to drink their own urine to survive.[13] Within eight days, the castle surrendered to the Muslims. Those who converted to Islam were

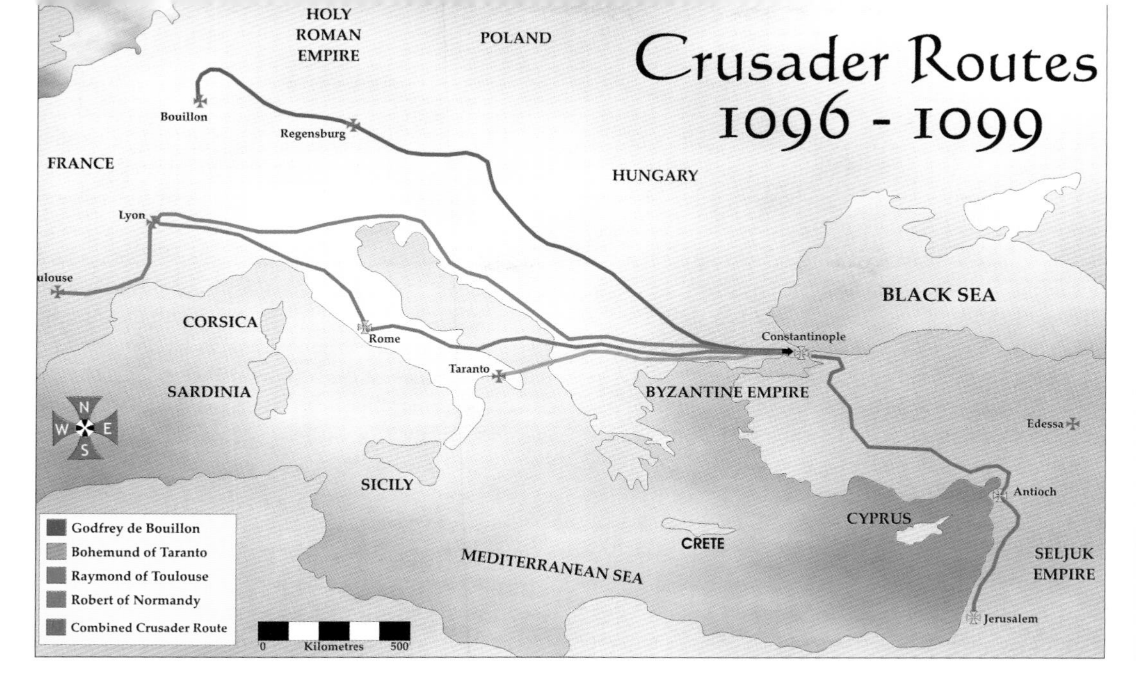

When the four main crusader armies left in the late summer and early fall of 1096, they did not all take the same route to the rallying point of Constantinople.
Author

taken captive, while those who held firm in their faith were executed.

Kilij Arslan, the Seljuk sultan of Rüm, sent spies into the crusader camp at Civetot to inform them that the Germans had captured Nicaea and were splitting the booty among the soldiers. The ruse was designed to draw the remaining crusaders into a trap and although the crusading army soon learnt the truth of the Germans' fate, the camp was divided as to what to do next. Peter was in Constantinople and Walter was determined to await his return. However, others felt that inactivity was equal to cowardice and insisted on marching forwards immediately.

On 21 October 1096, the entire crusader army set out for Turkish territory. Three miles outside of camp, the Turks were lying in ambush in a wooded area. As the crusaders passed by, the Turks launched a volley of arrows that caught the Christians unaware. Those who survived this initial onslaught fled back to camp, pursued by the Turks, who slaughtered combatant and non-combatant alike. Few survived and the majority of those who did were taken away as slaves.[14]

Six months after it had begun, the People's Crusade was over, having never accomplished its goal of freeing Jerusalem from the hands of the infidel.

The German Crusade

Others would follow the trail left by Peter the Hermit and his disastrous peasants' crusade. One such army was the German Crusade of Count Emrich of Leisingen, a minor lord from the Rhineland. Emrich was able to attract a good number of nobly born Germans to his cause. However, unlike the peasants who had rushed off to fight on foreign shores, Emrich saw Christ's enemies a little closer to home.

Soon after Urban had called the crusade, the German Jews became fearful of persecution and petitioned Emperor Henry IV for assistance. In response, the German emperor wrote to his vassals requesting that they protect the Jews in their regions. Emrich ignored the emperor's request, and after launching his crusade in May of 1096, launched an attack on the Jewish community at Spier where twelve were killed for refusing to convert to Christianity.[15]

By mid-May, Emrich and his troops arrived at Worms, where a rumour was spread that the local Jews had recently drowned a Christian in a well and were using the contaminated water to poison other wells. This was sufficient to rouse the townspeople who were not particularly fond of the Jews to begin with, and soon every Jew that fell into their hands was put to an immediate death. The bishop at Worms, heeding Henry's directive, took many Jews into his home, but Emrich and his men broke down the door and killed another five hundred men, women and children.[16]

Within five days of the massacre at Worms, Emrich and his men were outside the city of Mainz, where the Archbishop had barred the city's gates. But word of the count's approach had raised the citizens of Mainz against the Jews, and amid the turmoil, a Christian was killed. This prompted those inside the city to open the gates to Emrich and his men who finished the job the city's incensed Christians had already begun. Although the Jews paid a considerable amount of money to Emrich to spare their lives,[17] the count and his men set fire to the Archbishop's palace where many had sought refuge. Those who fled the burning building were offered the choice of conversion or death. Although a few saved themselves by renouncing their faith, most were put to the sword. Solomon bar Sampson, writing a generation after the barbarous events, told of how the Jews took their own lives and those of their families rather than let the crusaders kill them:

> 'The women there girded their loins with strength and slew their sons and their daughters and then themselves. Many men, too, plucked up courage and killed their wives, their sons, their infants. The tender and delicate mother slaughtered the babe she had played with, all of them; men and women arose and slaughtered one another.'[18]

The massacre continued for two days, and when Emrich left, there were 1000 Jewish corpses lying in the streets of Mainz.[19]

At Cologne, the Jews had sufficient notice of Emrich's approach to seek proper shelter. The streets had already experienced anti-Jewish rioting when Peter's army had stopped by two months earlier and they did not want to experience more of the same. Their hiding was successful; although Emrich set fire to the local synagogue, the body count in Cologne was minimal by comparison to his earlier massacres. Satisfied that he had taken sufficient revenge on the Jews for having killed Christ, Emrich left the Rhineland for Hungary. Meanwhile, some of his army whose thirst for Semitic blood was yet to be sated set off for the Moselle Valley to purge the region of its Jews.[20]

When the main contingent of Emrich's army arrived in Hungary in late June, King Colomon refused to allow them passage through the country due to his previous experience with crusaders. However, Emrich was better prepared than the peasant rabble that had passed through some months earlier and fought the Hungarians for six weeks. Emrich's army laid siege to the fortress of Wieselburg but when word arrived that the Hungarian king was returning with reinforcements, the army's discipline disintegrated and the garrison's defenders were able to destroy the Germans. Utterly routed by the Hungarians, Emrich and a few knights managed to escape and return to their homelands.

Once again the crusaders had failed.

The Prince's Crusade

When Pope Urban II called the crusade, he knew that it would take time to prepare for war, if the war was to be won. As such, he had set the date of departure for mid-August of the following year and, although the leaders of the First Crusade left on or close to that date, they did not leave as one cohesive force. Nor did they all take the same route to arrive at the rallying point of Constantinople.

The first to leave was Hugh, Count of Vermandois, who was the younger brother of the French king excommunicated by Urban for adultery at the Council of Clermont. He set out in late August and was joined by a number of knights who had survived Emrich's earlier debacle.[21] Hugh preceded his arrival in Constantinople with a peculiar letter to the Byzantines, outlining how he expected to be treated once there:

> 'Know, O Emperor that I am the king of kings and the greatest of those under heaven; and it behoves you to meet and treat me on arrival with all pomp and in a manner worthy of my nobility.'[22]

Upon his arrival, Hugh was indeed treated with the greatest of Byzantine hospitality, but kept on a close leash, so much so that many in Hugh's party regarded him as a prisoner.[23] Alexius had learnt a great deal about the Westerners from his previous experience with Peter's army and was convinced that the crusaders, despite their apparent religious zeal, were intent on carving out an empire of their own in the East.[24] While the emperor had no problem with the idea, he wanted to make sure that their empire did not consist of the same land that had once constituted his own! As such, he had Hugh swear an oath that he would return recaptured land to Byzantium and it would be a policy he would try to enforce with those who followed.

The next army to arrive from the West was that of Godfrey de Bouillon, Duke of Lower Lorraine, who was a descendent of Charlemagne[25] – a pedigree that certainly added to his status both before and after the crusade. Godfrey was accompanied by his two brothers: Eustace and Baldwin, and their cousin Baldwin of Le Bourg. Like Hugh's army, Godfrey's party had left in late August, but approached the East by way of Hungary, as the previous failed expeditions had done.

Hugh of Vermandois was sent to invite Godfrey to meet the emperor and take the same oath to which he had sworn. Godfrey declined, wanting instead to wait for the remaining Crusaders to arrive, but the emperor preferred to keep the massive armies of his Western allies on the move, crossing the Bosphorus to prevent a build-up of troops so close to his own capital.

Alexius attempted to cut off the food supply, hoping it would urge Godfrey to swear his oath and move on, but the tactic only led to more pillaging. The standoff culminated in Godfrey attacking the city. Alexius sent out messengers to tell Godfrey that he could leave without taking the oath, but his men attacked the messengers before they could speak. Alexius had had enough and sent out enough soldiers to teach the Westerners a lesson. Soon after, Godfrey conceded defeat, took the oath and was transported across the Bosphorus with his army.

Three days later, another crusader army arrived at Constantinople under Bohemund of Taranto and his nephew Tancred. Like the crusaders before him, Bohemund was asked to take the oath and did so without hesitation, but added that he wished to be made commander of the Imperial troops in Asia.[26] The emperor politely declined the request, but did not rule out the possibility, although he had no intention of ever granting him the post. On 26 April, Bohemund's army was transported across the Bosphorus. However, Tancred and his cousin, Roger of Salerno, slipped through at night to avoid swearing the oath their uncle had taken.

The next to arrive was Raymond IV, Count of Toulouse, whose army arrived at Constantinople the same day that Bohemund's had left. Of all the leaders of the crusade, Raymond was the only one who had met with the pope to discuss the matter. He was also an experienced crusader, having fought against the Muslims of Spain[27] on numerous occasions. Bishop Adhémar of Le Puy, who had been assigned by Urban to accompany the crusaders, was in Raymond's party, which had left the West in October of 1096.[28] However, the bishop had been wounded during the journey and stayed behind at Thessalonica, thus was not with Raymond's army upon their arrival at Constantinople.

Like the others, Raymond was asked to meet with the emperor and take an oath, which he refused to do; largely due to the absence of Adhémar, and his own resentment of Bohemund of Taranto, whose appointment as commander of the armies in Asia must then have seemed a possibility. Raymond eventually swore a somewhat altered oath to honour the emperor's life and see that neither his men nor himself compromised the emperor's interests.[29] Alexius accepted and when Adhémar and the rest of his army arrived, Raymond crossed the Bosphorus.

The last of the crusader armies to depart for the East was that of Robert, Duke of Normandy: the oldest son of William the Conqueror and the brother of King William II. Robert was accompanied by his brother-in-law, Stephen, Count of Blois, and Robert, Count of Flanders. With the majority of the crusaders having already departed Constantinople by the time of Robert's arrival, Alexius was less cautious than he had been in his admittance of previous groups and entertained this last party for two weeks before sending them to join the others across the Bosphorus.

The Campaign in Asia

It is difficult to determine the size of the army assembled on Asia's western frontier. Medieval chroniclers had a tendency to record figures for effect more than accuracy. Certainly when chroniclers like Albert of Aix wrote that the crusaders numbered in the hundreds of thousands, their intent was to impress upon their readers that the number was large. Runciman, by examining the varying accounts of individual battles, arrived at a figure of approximately 4,500 cavalry and 30,000 infantry when the armies were combined.[30]

As before, this was not one cohesive force, but several individual armies, each with their own agenda and motives for being on crusade. The leaders of the crusade were as suspicious of their co-religionists as they were the enemies of their faith. Even the rival factions who had made up Peter's crusade had fought with one another over the spoils of war and the campaign ultimately came to an end because of it. The leaders of the First Crusade proper, for all their existing wealth in Europe, were no less attracted by the glitter of gold than their pauper predecessors. However, despite their rivalries and infighting, they would succeed where the others had failed, scoring their first victory at the very same place where the previous expedition met its demise, Nicaea.

The medieval chapel of Saint Michel d'Aiguilhe was built in AD 962 on a volcanic formation that rises 83 metres above the valley at Le Puy-en-Velay in the Auvergne district of France. It was here that Adhémar Le Puy, the papal legate selected by Pope Urban II to accompany the crusaders in 1096, held his bishopric.
istockPhoto.com Peter Banks

The Capture of Nicaea

The town of Nicaea lay on the shores of Lake Ascanius and was the capital of Kilij Arslan's sultanate. It was in this very location that the Nicean Creed had been established more than seven centuries earlier in AD 325[31] and the town had been part of the Byzantine Empire until the Turks captured it in 1077. But now the time had come to take it back.

Timing was certainly on the crusaders' side when they set out to capture the city. Arslan anticipated that this new army of Westerners were no more formidable than the untrained peasants he had slaughtered some months earlier. Arslan set off to deal with more important matters, leaving his wife and children behind at Nicaea.[32]

Godfrey de Bouillon, Bohemund of Taranto, Raymond, Count of Toulouse and Robert, Duke of Normandy are shown in this nineteenth century illustration. Despite the unity of this romantic depiction, the crusade leaders seldom acted in harmony. *ClipArt.com*

Godfrey de Bouillon and Bohemund of Taranto began the siege on 14 May, and were joined by Raymond of Toulouse and the other crusaders two days later. Upon his arrival, Raymond spread his army out along the southern wall of the city, and when the first of the Turkish relief troops arrived it was Raymond's men who fought against them. However, these were clearly not the same calibre of soldier that the Turks had battled before, and the relief force withdrew to wait for the rest of Arslan's men. When the sultan and his men arrived on 21 May, they resumed their attacks but were once again repelled by the crusaders.

Although the crusaders had been successful in fending off the Turkish advances, they were having difficulty breaking down the walls of Nicaea. To add to the problem, the Turks behind the walls were receiving fresh supplies and soldiers from across the lake. The crusaders appealed to Alexius for support in halting the shipments and the emperor responded by providing a small flotilla of boats. Raymond d'Aguiliers, who accompanied Raymond of Toulouse on crusade, wrote of how the arrival of the Byzantine ships prompted the Turks to capitulate:

'At length the city, terrified with fear, was compelled to surrender. One reason was that the ships of the Emperor which had been dragged over the land were let down into the lake. They therefore gave themselves up to the Emperor, since they now expected no further aid and saw the army of the Franks increasing daily, while they were cut off from their forces.' [33]

On 19 June, the crusaders awoke to find the emperor's banner flowing from the city's towers. Nicaea had surrendered the previous evening and the emperor's men had entered through the lakeside gates.[34] Alexius had recaptured some of his land, and in exchange for their support, the soldiers were fed a meal of fine food while the barons were presented with gold and silver taken from Kilij Arslan's treasury. In exchange for the gifts, those who had yet to take the oath were requested to do so, and Tancred, after a great deal of protesting, finally complied.

A German medieval illustration of the Siege of Nicaea in AD 1097. This was the Franks' first victory in the Near East. *ClipArt.com*

The Battle of Dorylaeum

Two weeks after the capture of Nicaea and nearly a year after the crusaders had left their homes in Europe, the Western armies were more than 1000 kilometres from Jerusalem, but the crusaders were optimistic after their first victory. That optimism would be raised even higher in the battle that lay ahead.

After being repelled at Nicaea, Kilij Arslan retreated eastwards to procure additional troops.[35] Once he had acquired sufficient manpower, Arslan hastened westwards to the Dogorgon Valley at Dorylaeum, where he hoped to ambush the crusaders as he had with Peter's army. On 1 July, Arslan launched his attack on Bohemund's army who had made camp nearby the night before. They quickly surrounded the crusaders, who did their best to fight back against the seemingly endless stream of Muslim archers.

However, Arslan had once again underestimated the Westerners, for he had failed to encircle their entire number. By noon, Godfrey, Hugh and Raymond's armies had arrived and merged with Bohemund's men to launch a counter assault. The Muslim forces were little match for the heavy charge of the Western cavalry. If they hoped to retreat towards the southern hills, their hopes were dashed for Adhémar of Le Puy and a number of French knights were staring down on them from the crest of the hills. In fact, Bishop Adhémar had employed guides to take him through the mountains, specifically to prevent such a retreat.[36]

The Turks, sensing imminent defeat, fled the field of battle leaving their tents and treasures behind. Although the Christians had suffered many casualties, the Battle of Dorylaeum was another great victory over their Muslim enemies. It would be almost four months before they began their next military campaign, and in the interim, the first of the Crusader States was established at Edessa under Godfrey's brother, Baldwin, who seized power not by the sharpness of his sword, but by the sharpness of mind.[37]

Siege of Antioch

Thus far the crusaders' battles had been short. The Turks at Dorylaeum had been sent fleeing in less than a day while Nicaea surrendered within a month. Antioch, however, would not fall so easily and the crusaders would find themselves outside her 40 kilometre long walls for seven months.

Although Antioch and Jerusalem had fallen into Muslim hands in AD 638, the Byzantines recaptured Antioch in AD 969. The city remained in Byzantine hands until the Seljuk Turks seized it in 1085, and despite being controlled by Muslim forces, the majority of its inhabitants were a combination of Syrian, Greek and Armenian Christians.[38] When the crusaders arrived at the city gates, the governor of the city, Yaghi Siyan, had the Christian Patriarch of Antioch imprisoned and many of the leading Christians expelled from the city. The Arab chronicler Ibn al Athir wrote of how Siyan expelled the Christians through deception:

> 'When Yaghi Siyan, the rule of Antioch, heard of their approach, he was not sure how the Christian people of the city would react, so he made the Muslims go outside the city on their own to dig trenches, and the next day sent the Christians out alone to continue the task.
> When they were ready to return home at the end of the day he refused to allow them.' [39]

The crusader siege of Antioch began on 21 October 1097 and dragged on for months as the crusaders fought constantly to gain control of the city with little success. As the winter months advanced, the crusaders' food supplies dwindled and parties were sent further and further from the camp in search of provisions. During the harsh winter, many died and with them, hope, prompting scores to desert the cause. Among them was Peter the Hermit, who had travelled with the Franks when they left Constantinople.[40] Peter was soon brought back to camp along with William the Carpenter, who had accompanied him on his desertion and original crusade in 1096. Due to his reputation, Peter was forgiven but William received a harsh lecture from Bohemund.

In February, the crusaders were faced with the departure of the Byzantine general Taticius who had accompanied them so far as an imperial advisor. Anna Comnena believed that Taticius's departure was due not to cowardice, but because Bohemund had told him that there was a plot to kill him. She wrote that Bohemund had hoped to remove the general from the picture to prevent Taticius from taking the city on behalf of his emperor.[41] She was probably right, because soon after Taticius left, Bohemund threatened to leave unless he was allowed to keep the city once it was captured.

In early March, an English fleet arrived at St Simeon from Constantinople with supplies for building a siege engine. Due to a lack of trust within the crusader camp, Bohemund and Raymond had both escorted the supplies back to Antioch, but were ambushed by the Turks on their return, losing the load as they fled.[42] However, the raiders faced the same problem when they tried to secure the supplies for themselves and soon found themselves under attack. The princes united in their efforts and massacred the raiders, taking the English supplies and booty from the slaughtered Turks. By mid-March, the supplies had been put to good use in finishing the construction of a fortress to guard the approach to a fortified bridge, further strengthening the siege.

A month later, the crusaders received assistance from an unexpected quarter when a Fatimid embassy from Egypt arrived hoping to form an alliance with the Christians. The Seljuk Turks had captured Jerusalem from the Fatimids a generation earlier, therefore the Christians and Egyptians shared a common enemy. The embassy even offered the Christians access to Jerusalem so long as the Fatimids were permitted to take control of the city itself – the crusaders could keep the lands to the north while the Fatimids would occupy the lands to the south. The Franks treated the embassy courteously, and although the Fatimids left for their homeland two weeks later laden with gifts, a formal agreement with the Christians was not secured.

The Battle of Dorylaeum, fought on 1 July 1097, was a victory for the crusaders – an impression of the battle by the famous nineteenth-century engraver Gustave Doré. *ClipArt.com*

Although the crusaders had successfully repelled a number of attempts to break their siege of Antioch, they would meet their largest opposing force in May of 1098, when Kerbogha, the atabeg of Mosul, through several alliances with his Muslim neighbours, assembled a massive army to march on the Christians. Fortunately for the crusaders, Kerbogha attempted to take Edessa from Baldwin of Bolougne so as to remove it as a later threat once he had captured Antioch for himself. The three weeks Kerbogha spent trying to capture Edessa gave the Franks opportunity for a cunning attempt to capture the city.

At some point, Bohemund had made contact with an Armenian convert to Islam named Firouz, who had risen to a lofty station in Yaghi Siyan's government. But Firouz was not happy with his current situation – his governor had fined him for hoarding grain, and in his desire to get even, he made an agreement with Bohemund to sell the city.[43] Although it is not known precisely when Bohemund made the arrangement, he kept it a secret until the time was right, preferring to seed the camp with fear of the danger they faced from Kerbogha's army. Of course, his real intention was to make his forthcoming capture of the city seem to be an even greater victory than it was. His propaganda worked, and such was the fear the Christians felt of Kerbogha that for the second time the crusaders faced an exodus of men deserting the army. This time, they deserted in such numbers that any attempt to stop them was futile.

Antioch fell to the Seljuk Turks a decade before Urban called the First Crusade. The city's walls would prove a significant challenge for the crusader armies. *ClipArt.com*

Among the first to flee was Stephen of Blois who, of all the nobly born Franks who ventured east, was probably the most reluctant to be there in the first place. He had little choice: he was married to the daughter of William the Conqueror and she ruled the household. Only two months previously he had written to his domineering wife informing her of the progress of the siege and boasting of his own importance in the campaign:

> 'God, however, fought for us, His faithful, against them. For on that day, fighting in the strength that God gives, we conquered them and killed an innumerable multitude – God continually fighting for us – and we also carried back to the army more than two hundred of their heads, in order that the people might rejoice on that account.'[44]

But now, instead of carrying a Muslim's severed head with pride, he was hanging his own in shame as he fled Antioch accompanied by a large contingent of French knights. If only Stephen waited a few hours longer he would have had fodder to pen another flowery letter to his wife, for the time had come for Bohemund to make his move.

At sunset, Bohemund left Antioch with a number of his knights under the pretence of setting off to meet Kerbogha's army. In the middle of the night the army returned, set up ladders where Firouz was waiting and sixty Franks breached the city that they had previously spent several months trying to capture by force. Within a short time, the crusaders had secured two more towers followed by the Gate of St George and the Gate of the Bridge. The gates were flung wide open allowing the Franks the victory they had long been waiting for. Raymond d'Aguiliers, who was an eyewitness to the event, wrote of what followed next:

> 'How great were the spoils captured in Antioch it is impossible for us to say, except that you may believe as much as you wish, and then add to it. Moreover, we cannot say how many Turks and Saracens then perished; it is, furthermore, cruel to explain by what diverse and various deaths they died.'[45]

Although Antioch was once again in Christian hands, the crusaders soon found themselves defending its walls. Within two days of capturing the city, Kerbogha's army had finally arrived outside the gates of Antioch – the besiegers were now the besieged. And while the Muslim leader found Antioch every bit as impregnable as the crusaders had, the Franks were now inside a city filled with rotting corpses and devoid of fresh food. Their only hope of salvation would be the arrival of Alexius and his troops. However, as the emperor moved towards Antioch, he met up with a fleeing Stephen of Blois who told him that he believed the Franks had been annihilated by the Turks. Realising that it would be futile to march on so large an army, the emperor abandoned his plans and returned to Constantinople.[46]

The Holy Lance

On 10 June, with Antioch still under siege from the Muslims, a poorly dressed and dishevelled peasant named Peter Bartholomew demanded an audience with Count Raymond of Toulouse and Adhémar of Le Puy. The story Peter told the nobly born Franks defied belief. Over the past few months, St Andrew had come to him in a series of visions informing him of the exact location of one of Christendom's most sacred relics, the spear that had pierced Christ's side. And what was even more unbelievable was that the Holy Lance was buried in the Cathedral of Antioch.

Adhémar, despite his religious office, was sceptical of the peasant's claims. Adhémar had seen a relic purported to be the Holy Lance in Constantinople, and whether or not he believed it to be the real article, he certainly believed Peter to be a man of unreliable character.[47] But Raymond, despite his age and experience, was more easily impressed and vowed to search for the relic in five days' time.

There were others who reported seeing visions. Among them was Stephen of Valence, who claimed to have seen Christ who had told him that in five days time he would send support, if the Franks would repent their sinful ways. It is entirely possible that the visions, if they occurred at all, were little more than hallucinations brought on by starvation. However, on 14 June, a meteor was seen shooting through the sky which seemed to fall on the Turkish camp. The crusaders took it as a favourable omen.[48]

The next morning Peter was accompanied to St Peter's Cathedral by a party of twelve men, among them the Count of Toulouse, William, the Bishop of Orange and Raymond d'Aguiliers. The floor of the cathedral was excavated throughout the day with no results. The count, who wanted to believe the claims, left disappointed. Raymond d'Aguiliers, who was present, wrote of the discovery that was made after the count had left and the reaction to the same:

> 'The youth who had spoken of the Lance [Peter], however, upon seeing us worn out, disrobed and, taking off his shoes, descended into the pit in his shirt, earnestly entreating us to pray to God to give us His Lance for the comfort and victory of His people. At length, the Lord was minded through the grace of His mercy to show us His Lance. And I, who have written this, kissed it when the point alone had as yet appeared above ground. What great joy and exultation then filled the city I cannot describe.'[49]

Although Raymond was among those who accepted the authenticity of the found relic, Adhémar was content in his original view that Peter was a fraud. Nonetheless, the crusaders seemed to be reinvigorated with the discovery of this sacred relic. On 28 June, the gates of Antioch opened as Raymond d'Aguiliers, carrying the Holy Lance aloft, led the crusaders out of the city to their final battle with Kerbogha's army. As the crusaders advanced, many claimed to see a vision on the hill of a number of white mounted knights displaying white banners, which they were convinced, was led by St George himself.[50]

Turks began to leave the field in ever increasing numbers. The departure led to panic, which led to even greater numbers retreating. Kerbogha, realising that he and his men were all that was left to face the crusaders, fled the field as well. Although some must have believed that they had overcome the Muslims by the power of the Holy Lance and St George's army of ghosts, the reality was that many of the armies that had accompanied Kerbogha betrayed him in the final hours (for had they succeeded in overcoming the Franks, their own holdings would be compromised by Kerbogha's increased power). Despite the body count on both sides of the field, Antioch was captured not by martial prowess but by political intrigue. Even when the city was secured, such politicking continued, and the leaders of the crusade fought over who should have ultimate control.[51]

Doré's impression of the siege of Antioch. It took the crusaders nearly eight months to capture the city from the Muslims. *ClipArt.com*

References for chapter 2

1 Exodus 3:8 refers to the Holy Land as a land flowing with milk and honey.

2 Payne, Robert, *The Crusades*. p. 39

3 Peter the Hermit and the Popular Crusade: Collected Accounts, Medieval Sourcebook http://www.fordham.edu/halsall/source/peterhermit.html

4 Anna Comnena: The Alexiad: Complete Text, Medieval Sourcebook http://www.fordham.edu/halsall/basis/AnnaComnena-Alexiad00.html#BOOK%20X

5 Runciman, Steven, *A History of the Crusades Vol. I*. p. 281

6 Payne op. cit. p. 39. The nephews were named Walter, William, Matthew and Simon.

7 Runciman op. cit. p. 102

8 Ibid p. 103

9 Ibid p. 104

10 Ibid p. 105

11 Ibid p. 106

12 Comnena op. cit.

13 Runciman op. cit. p. 108

14 Ibid p. 109 Runciman mentions that another 3000 were able to take refuge in an old castle that was abandoned by the sea.

15 Ibid p. 114. In addition to the twelve killed, one woman committed suicide.

16 Ibid p. 114

17 Ibid p. 114

18 Solomon bar Samson: The Crusaders in Mainz, 27 May 1096, Medieval Sourcebook http://www.fordham.edu/halsall/source/1096jews-mainz.html

19 Ibid p. 115

20 Ibid p. 115

21 Ibid p. 119

22 Comnena op. cit.

23 Runciman op. cit. p. 120

24 Ibid p. 120

25 Ibid p. 121

26 Ibid p. 131

27 Ibid p. 132

28 Ibid p. 132

29 Ibid p. 136

30 Ibid p. 280

31 The Council of Nicaea was held in AD 325 by Roman Emperor Constantine. It was at this council that the Nicaean Creed, which defined the divinity of Christ, was established.

32 Runciman op. cit. p. 147

33 Raymond d'Aguiliers, The Siege and Capture of Nicea: Collected Accounts, Medieval Sourcebook http://www.fordham.edu/halsall/source/cde-nicea.html

34 Runciman op. cit. pp. 149-150

35 Ibid p. 153

36 Ibid p. 154

37 When the bulk of the crusaders moved south towards Antioch, Baldwin of Bolougne went east to Edessa. There he convinced Thoros, the lord of Edessa, to adopt him as a son. A short time later Thoros was assassinated and Baldwin took control of Edessa, proclaiming himself count.

38 Runciman op. cit. p. 177

39 Gabrieli, Francesco, *Arab Historians of the Crusades*. p. 5

40 Runciman op. cit. p. 185

41 Comnena op. cit.

42 Runciman op. cit. p. 188

43 Ibid p. 192 Gabrieli op. cit. p. 6 Ibn al Athir records the man as being a cuirass maker who was in command of a tower over the river, who was bribed by the Franks.

44 Stephen Count of Blois, Dana C. Munro, Letters of the Crusaders, *Translations and Reprints from the Original Sources of European History*, Vol 1:4 Medieval Sourcebook http://www.fordham.edu/halsall/source/cde-letters.html

45 *Raymond d'Aguiliers* Historia francorum qui ceperint Jerusalem, Medieval Sourcebook http://www.fordham.edu/halsall/source/raymond-cde.html

46 Runciman op. cit pp. 191-192

47 Ibid p. 201

48 Ibid p. 202

49 Raymond d'Aguiliers op. cit.

50 Runciman op. cit p. 205

51 Ibid p. 189

Defender of the Holy Sepulchre

'He was just, he avoided evil, he was trustworthy and dependable in his undertakings. He scorned the vanities of the world, a quality rare in that age and especially among men of the military profession. He was assiduous in prayer and pious works, renowned for his liberality, graciously affable, civil, and merciful. His whole life was commendable and pleasing to God.' [1]

William of Tyre on the character of Godfrey de Bouillon

A romantic depiction of the crusaders seeing Jerusalem for the first time as they crest the Judean Hills. *ClipArt.com*

No sooner had the crusaders defeated one enemy than they were assaulted by a new one. However, this enemy could not be seen advancing over the horizon as Kerbogha's armies had. In July, the crusaders were hit by an epidemic, probably typhoid brought on by the lack of sanitary conditions in the recently captured city. On 1 August, the epidemic took the life of Adhémar of Le Puy, who had played so vital a role in the Battle of Dorylaeum a year earlier. The loss of Urban's papal legate was not only a spiritual loss for the crusaders, but a political one as well. Adhémar had been able to mediate between the quarrelling princes, and now that he was dead, there was no one left to stop them from pursuing their own ambitions.

Chief among these was Bohemund, who had secured the capture of the city through his cunning. Bohemund wanted Antioch for himself and argued that since Alexius had abandoned the crusaders when they needed him most, any claim he had to the city was forfeited. Raymond, however, felt that his vow was sacred and the city should be returned to the Byzantine emperor as promised. But Raymond may not have been as altruistic as he seemed, for he still held parts of the city himself.[2] The bickering between the princes prompted the troops to force the two men to form a truce, and in November they set out to capture Ma'arrat, which fell on 11 December. But the two princes quarrelled over control of the town, which dissolved the month old truce. By now, the troops had had enough of the bickering – they wanted to move on to Jerusalem and, to force Raymond's hand, they began tearing Ma'arrat to the ground.

On 13 January, Raymond, barefoot and penitent, began the march towards the Holy City surrounded by priests who offered their prayers.[3] As Ma'arrat burned behind them, their reputation as ruthless conquerors became infamous. Raymond, accompanied by Tancred and Robert of Normandy, passed through the region and were granted safe passage and assistance from the local rulers in exchange for their own safety and protection of their towns and villages. However, not all were free of crusader molestation. Although the emir of Tripoli had offered Raymond similar terms to his co-religionists further north, the count chose to besiege his town of Arqah, northeast of his capital.

On 14 March, Robert of Flanders and Godfrey de Bouilllon joined the crusaders, but as was the case whenever the princes united, internal conflicts soon arose and the Franks were quarrelling with each other. It was at this time that Peter Bartholomew began to lose any credibility he had with the crusaders, but the loss of esteem had as much to do with his association with Raymond as the lack of belief in his increasingly strange prophecies. His latest had occurred on 5 April when Christ and St Peter and St Andrew told him that he must launch an immediate assault on Arqah.[4] Naturally, the timing was rather convenient for the siege had not been going well and Raymond was the only prince who wanted to continue the struggle.

Ordeal by Fire

Finally fed up with the pauper's claims, Peter was confronted and told that Adhémar had never believed his claims about the Holy Lance. Once again the crusaders were divided, as many came to Peter's defence. Chief among his supporters was Raymond d'Aguiliers who had kissed the tip of the lance when it was embedded in the ground and reminded the crusaders of the fact. Another priest, Peter of Desiderius, defended Raymond and defamed the papal legate in the process when he announced that Adhémar had come to him in a vision – he was told that doubters would burn in hell for believing that the sacred relic was a fake, a fate Adhémar himself confessed to be currently suffering.[5] Others were soon reporting their own visions until Peter demanded to prove the relic's authenticity by taking a trial by fire. On Good Friday he got what he had asked for. Clothed in nothing but a tunic and clutching the lance, Peter emerged from the flames horribly burned and died twelve days later as a result of his wounds. Although the lance had been discredited, it didn't stop Raymond – who still put stock in its authenticity – from hanging on to it, just in case. It would be almost another month before Raymond was convinced to lift the siege, and on 13 May 1099, the crusaders continued south towards Tripoli.

After capturing Antioch in the summer of 1098, the crusader princes spent the next several months arguing over what should be done with the city. *ClipArt.com*

There were many crusaders who doubted the authenticity of the Holy Lance discovered by Peter Bartholomew at Antioch. To prove its authenticity, Peter underwent an ordeal by fire, shown in this illustration by Gustave Doré. *ClipArt.com*

The Fatimid Embassy

Around this time another embassy of Fatimids approached the crusaders hoping to come to terms over Jerusalem, although the terms were not as favourable as before. There was good reason. While the epidemic had been devastating the Franks in July of 1098, the Fatimids had been attacking Jerusalem. In fact, the crusaders' defeat over Kerbogha at Antioch had indirectly assisted the Fatimids in taking the city from his Ortoqid allies. [6] The Fatimids now offered the Franks limited access to the Holy City, providing that pilgrims came unarmed. Once again the offer was declined. It became apparent to the crusaders that Jerusalem must be captured at all costs, especially considering that once the Fatimid embassy returned to Cairo, an army would be dispatched to thwart their move on the Holy City. Christopher Tyerman, in his book *God's War*, suggests that this was a turning point in the campaign:

'Social and political reality in Syria and Palestine had revealed to the Westerners that, with the fracturing of the Byzantine alliance, there was no fraternal Christian ruling class in church or state to whom the Holy Places could be entrusted. This subtle but profound shift from a war of liberation to one of occupation represented a portentous development in Urban II's schemes, one forged by the experience of the campaign.' [7]

It had taken the crusaders six months to travel from Antioch to Tripoli. However, renewed with fanatical zeal, the crusaders covered the remaining 360 kilometres in just over three weeks. Leaving Tripoli on 16 May, the crusaders negotiated treaties and procured safe passage down the coastline, with minor resistance encountered at Sidon. The crusaders turned east at Arsuf (where an important battle would be fought against the Muslims 92 years later) and marched on to Ramla where they found the town evacuated. The crusaders paused for a few days before pressing on to Qubeiba, 16 kilometres from their goal. From here the crusaders spread out through the Judean hills capturing small villages along the way.

The Siege of Jerusalem

When the Franks had left their homes in the summer and fall of 1096, there had been as many as 35,000 crusaders between the four armies. However on 7 June 1099 when they crested the Judean hills and saw the Holy City for the first time, their number had been reduced to 14,000.[8] For every kilometre, as the crow flies, the crusaders had lost six men.[9] Of course, not all had been killed in battle; others died of starvation or thirst, or the epidemic that struck the Franks at Antioch while huge numbers had deserted the crusade or joined Bohemund in Antioch or Baldwin at Edessa. What remains important is that less than half of those who had set out to seize Jerusalem from the Muslims were now left to complete the job.

This would be no easy task, for the city's defence had been left in the hands of its Fatimid governor, Iftikhar ad-Dawla. Like Antioch's governor, Yaghi Siyān, Iftikhar had expelled the Christians from the city, lest they assist their co-religionists. Additionally, he rounded up the flocks to deprive the crusaders of food, poisoned the wells to deprive them of water and cut down trees that could be used to build a siege tower. In the event that the crusaders would bring their own equipment, Iftikhar had filled his towers with hay and cotton to absorb the shock of their mangonels.[10]

On 12 June, the Franks made a pilgrimage to the Mount of Olives, where Christ had once walked. Here they met a hermit who told them that if they attacked the city at once and had faith in God, He would deliver the city into their hands. Despite the crusaders' protestations that they did not have the siege engines necessary to accomplish the task, the hermit persisted in his admonishment. On 13 June, the Franks began an assault on the city walls with the few ladders in their possession. Their feeble attempts to gain access over the ramparts were easily repelled by the Fatimids and the crusaders drew back to their encampments demoralised.

What is important to understand is that despite the crusaders being united in their zeal to capture Jerusalem, they were still divided over how to accomplish the task. Raymond of Toulouse had initially deployed on the Western Wall and Tower of David area, but ultimately moved to the south, along the Zion Gate. Meanwhile Godfrey, Tancred and the two Roberts had set up camps to the north and from there planned their assaults. Although this has often been portrayed as attacking the city on multiple fronts, the division of the armies was as much Frankish disunity as it was military strategy.

The crusaders under Godfrey de Bouillon were able to gain entry into the city by way of a siege tower, which was wheeled close to the city's northern wall. *ClipArt.com*

On 17 June, the armies received assistance in the form of a fleet of Christian ships that made port at Jaffa. The vessels arrived loaded with the materials necessary to build the siege towers and mangonels needed to besiege the city. However, even with this windfall, the crusaders acted in divided fashion, each making their own arrangements and paying the skilled craftsmen out of their own pockets.[11]

As the towers were being erected, the crusaders began to argue over a number of matters including who should get to keep Bethlehem which had been captured by Tancred on 6 June, and who would rule over Jerusalem once it was captured. The secular authorities and clergy were divided on the matter. The clergy argued that a secular ruler should not rule Christ's birthplace; no man should wear a crown of gold in the city where Christ had worn a crown of thorns.

On 6 July, Adhémar, the dead papal legate, once again visited Peter Desiderius in a vision. He told the priest that if the crusaders repented of their sinful ways and conducted a barefoot march in penance around the city, Jerusalem would be theirs in nine days.[12] Given the fact that the city did fall nine days later, it is likely that the specific details of Peter's vision were apocryphal embellishments. However, this doesn't mean that Peter did not believe that his vision was real, or that he wasn't able to convince others of the same, and on 8 July, the Franks, led by priests carrying holy relics including the discredited Holy Lance, marched around the city walls mimicking the biblical account of the fall of Jericho. It was one of the few acts of unity since their arrival a month earlier.

Although the circumambulation failed to tear the city's walls apart as it had in Jericho, it did serve to bring the rival factions together in their religious

In this map we see the positions of the four crusader armies on 14-15 July 1099, when the final assault on the city got under way.
Author

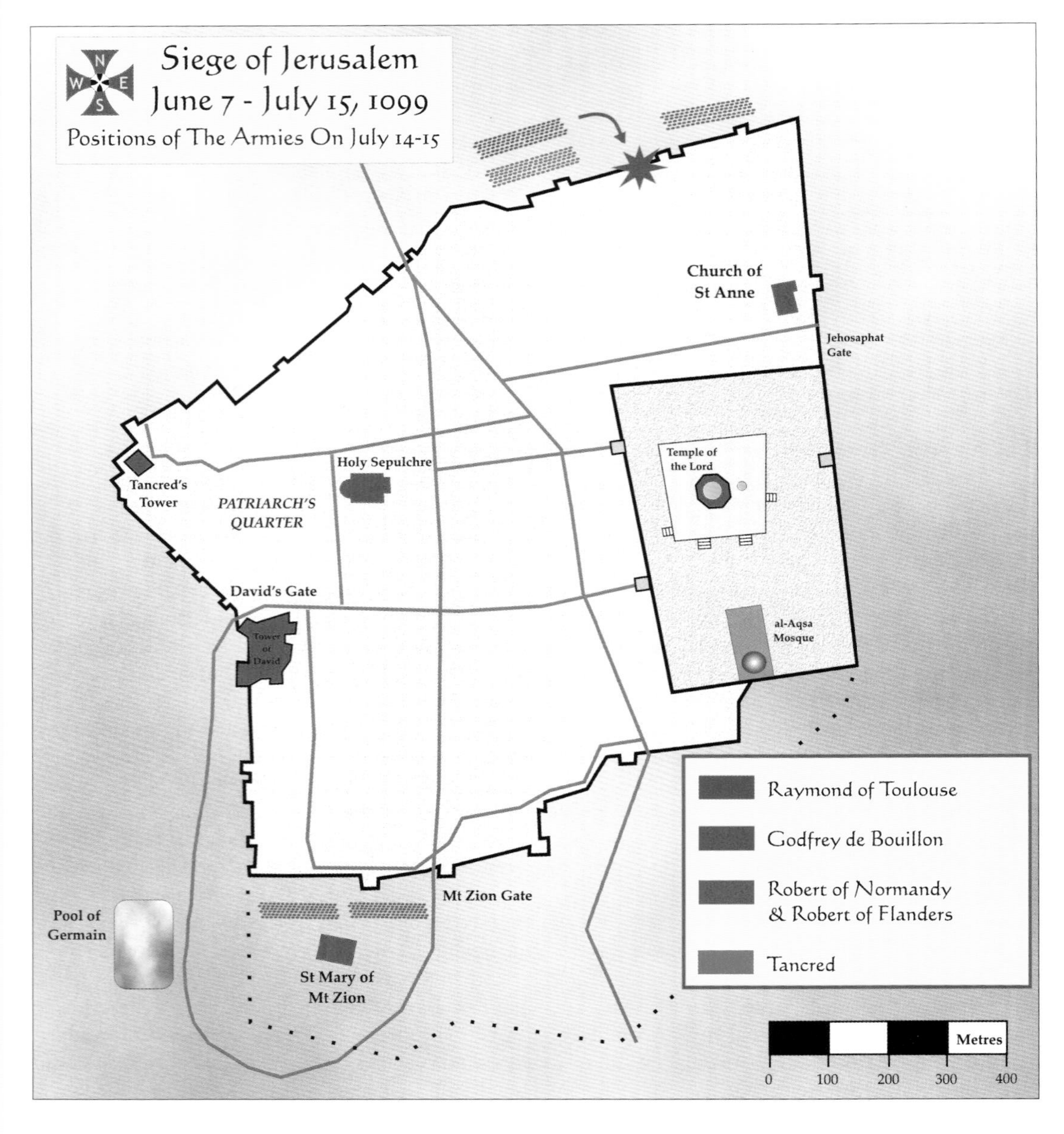

zeal. After being addressed on the Mount of Olives by Raymond d'Aguiliers, Arnulf de Choques and Peter the Hermit, the crusaders continued to operate from separate areas; this time it was for strategic purposes. On 13 July, Raymond and his men began in earnest their assault on the walls near the Zion Gate to the south, while Godfrey, Tancred and the two Roberts continued to attack the northern walls of the city.

In the early morning hours of 15 July, Godfrey's tower was close enough to be effective, and by midday was against the city wall. Planks were thrown across to the ramparts and the crusaders were able to enter the city. Although Godfrey de Bouillon is often credited with being the first to enter the city, two brothers from Tournai named Engelbert and Ludolf preceded him. However, the duke was not far behind the brothers as they stormed the city, followed by Bohemund's nephew Tancred.[13] Soon the city's gates were opened and the crusaders flooded through.

Seeing that the city's defences had been shattered, the Muslims fled to the Temple Mount area where their predecessors had erected the Dome of the Rock and the al Aqsa Mosque in the years that followed the Muslim conquest of Jerusalem in AD 638. It was here, at the very spot where the prophet Muhammad had

Tancred, upon entering the city, plundered the Dome of the Rock *(centre)* before moving on to the al Aqsa Mosque *(far right)* where many of the city's Muslims had fled. *ClipArt.com*

made his night journey, that the Muslims met their end. Tancred pursued the Muslims and plundered the Dome of the Rock of its valuables before turning his attentions to the al Aqsa Mosque, where many had taken refuge.

Tancred offered to spare their lives if they would surrender and soon his banner was flying over the mosque. Meanwhile, Raymond pursued Iftikhar to the Tower of David. The governor also offered to surrender the fortified tower and a considerable amount of booty if Raymond would spare his life and those of his personal bodyguards. The count agreed and Iftikhar and his men were permitted to leave the city. Others were not so lucky. Even those in the al Aqsa who had surrendered the mosque for their lives were cut down the next day by a group of crusaders who ignored Tancred's banner flying overhead. Even the city's Jews who had sought shelter in their synagogue were killed when the Franks set the temple ablaze, as Emrich of Leisingen had done in Germany three years earlier.

Every man, woman and child the crusaders came across was slaughtered, and had the Christians not been expelled from the city before the siege, it is possible that they too would have been among the dead. Perhaps the most gruesome of the contemporary accounts of the massacre is that of Raymond d'Aguiliers who described the carnage thus:

> 'Piles of heads, hands, and feet were to be seen in the streets of the city. It was necessary to pick one's way over the bodies of men and horses. But these were small matters compared to what happened at the Temple of Solomon, [al Aqsa] a place where religious services are ordinarily chanted. What happened there? If I tell the truth, it will exceed your powers of belief. So let it suffice to say this much, at least, that in the Temple and porch of Solomon, men rode in blood up to their knees and bridle reins.' [14]

Although his sea of blood was most certainly a poetic exaggeration intended to shock his reader, d'Aguiliers nonetheless went on to endorse the slaughter:

> 'Indeed, it was a just and splendid judgment of God that this place should be filled with the blood of the unbelievers, since it had suffered so long from their blasphemies.' [15]

Jerusalem had been captured, its Muslim and Jewish inhabitants slaughtered and its treasures divided between the princes who had come east to rescue the city. It had taken the Franks three years to liberate Jerusalem but it took more than a fortnight for the news of its capture to travel westwards. Unfortunately, Pope Urban II, who had called the Crusade, died on 29 July 1099.

Advocatus Sancti Sepulchri

When Urban's legate, Adhémar of Le Puy, died in 1098, so too did any of the plans he may have had for the government of Jerusalem. It is likely that, as papal legate, he envisioned an ecclesiastic state run by a patriarch. However, both the bishop and the pope were dead and the immediate problem at hand was deciding who should rule the city for news had arrived that the Egyptian army was on the march.

Above and below: **Iftikhar, the governor of the city, fled to the Tower of David when the city capitulated. It was here that he offered to surrender the citadel to Raymond of Toulouse in exchange for his life.** *ClipArt.com*

A nineteenth-century depiction of Godfrey de Bouillon as Defender of the Holy Sepulchre. The crusade leader did not wish to be called king in Christ's Holy City. *Author*

As the corpses of the dead were being burned, the crusade's leaders held a council to determine who should rule, but again there was disagreement. The clergy felt that before any discussion could be had over electing a secular ruler, the matter of who would serve as patriarch must be settled. Most of the legitimate contenders for the position were now dead, killed either in battle or in illness. The rival factions felt that those suggested to assume the position were a plot put forth by the other side, and as a result, they decided to elect the secular first.

Of the princes who had left the east in 1096, only four now remained – Bohemund had got his way and taken up residence in Antioch, while Baldwin of Bolougne had staked his own claim at Edessa. Of those who remained, both Roberts and Godfrey's brother Eustace, wanted to return to their homes. This left Raymond, Tancred and Godfrey as the viable contenders for the throne although Tancred had few supporters.

The discussions went on for several days, but ultimately the crown was offered to Raymond of

Toulouse who declined it on the basis that he had no desire to be king in Christ's city. Once again, as was the case in Antioch, Raymond's motives may have been less altruistic, less pious than they seemed. The reasons for his refusal were doubted in Runciman's time[16] and current historians like Tyerman believe that the refusal was a political manoeuvre.[17] Whatever his motivations for refusing the crown, it was offered to Godfrey de Bouillon, who, although initially expressing his unwillingness, accepted on the condition that he not be called king, but rather Advocatus Sancti Sepulchri or Defender of the Holy Sepulchre. Of course, the difference in nomenclature did not change the fact that he was in every sense of the word elected as the first Christian King of Jerusalem.

In the months and years that followed, the Christians would spread out from Jerusalem, Edessa and Antioch taking additional lands – some by conquest, some by surrender and others by the political intrigues that had accompanied them east. Despite their nobly born lineage, the crusader princes had proven that they were every bit as common and human as their ignobly born co-religionists. They had quarrelled amongst themselves throughout the journey east and had failed to hold the discipline of their troops in combat. In less than a generation after the Frank's arrival in the east, there would spring from the Holy City a new knighthood that would attempt to change it all.

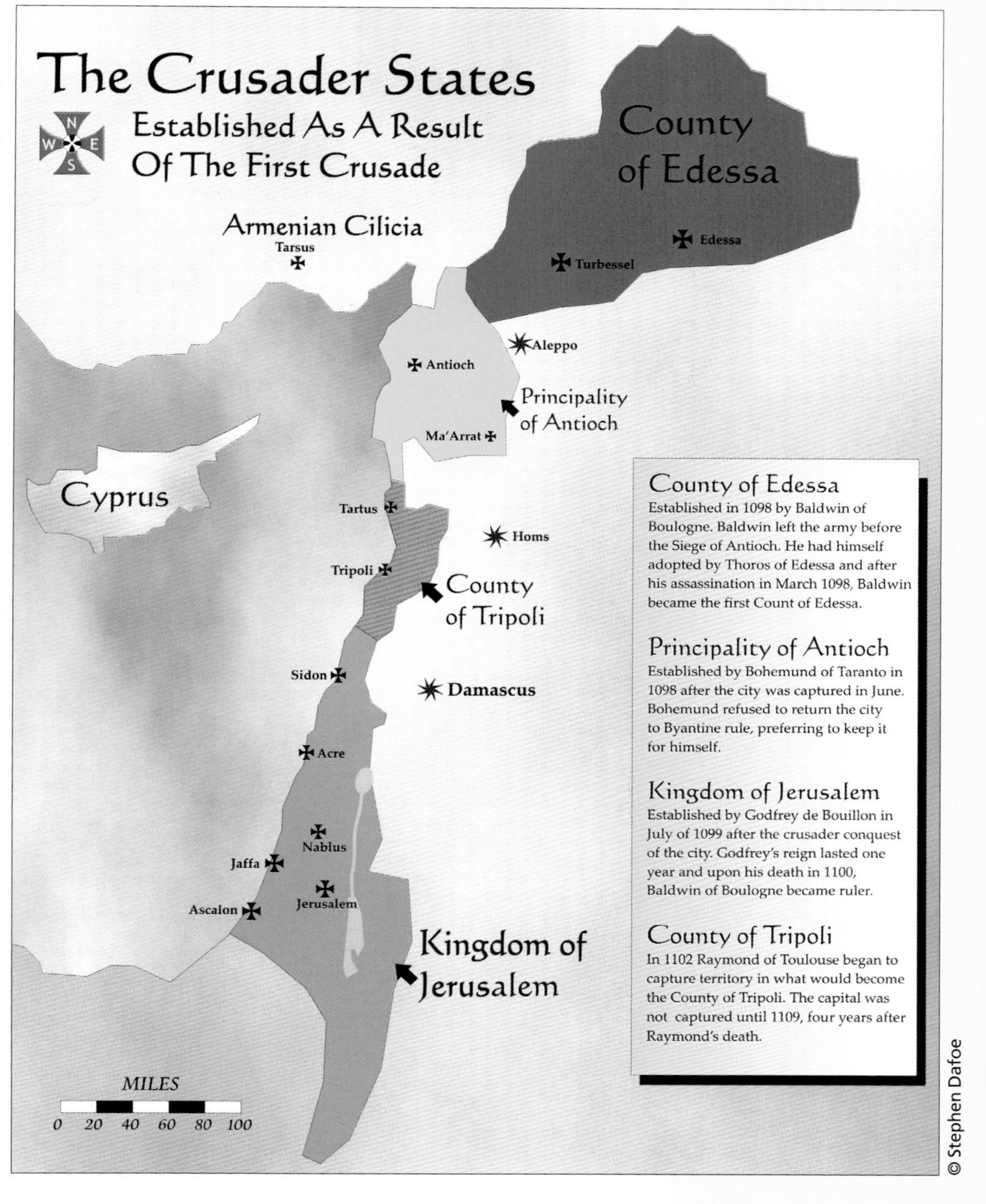

References for chapter 3

1 William of Tyre, Historia rerum in partibus transmarinis gestarum, Medieval Sourcebook http://www.fordham.edu/halsall/source/tyre-godfrey.html

2 Tyerman, Christopher, *God's War: A New History of the Crusades*. p. 149

3 Ibid. p. 150

4 Runciman, Steven, *A History of the Crusades Vol. 1*. p. 226

5 Ibid. p. 226

6 Tyerman op. cit. p. 149

7 Ibid. p. 152

8 Tyerman op. cit. p. 153, Billings, Malcolm, *The Cross and the Crescent*. p. 60 Tyerman suggests 14,000, while Billings suggests that there may have been as many as 15,000.

9 The distance between Paris and Jerusalem is 3,336 kilometres. Given that the crusaders lost approximately 20,000, we arrive at a loss of six men for every kilometre.

10 Runciman op. cit. p. 232

11 Tyerman op. cit. p. 155 Tyerman indicates that Raymond paid his own way while the northerners operated from a common fund.

12 Runciman op. cit. p. 235

13 Tyerman op. cit. p. 157

14 Raymond d'Aguiliers Historia francorum qui ceperint Jerusalem, Medieval Sourcebook http://www.fordham.edu/halsall/source/raymond-cde.html

15 Ibid.

16 Runciman op. cit. pp.241-242 Runciman was writing in the late 1940s and early 1950s.

17 Tyerman op. cit. pp. 159-160

This eighteenth-century French illustration entitled The First Templars
is a romantic depiction of the humble origins of the Order, when it was alleged
that they were so poor they had to share one horse.
Author

A New Kind of Knighthood

'This is, I say, a new kind of knighthood and one unknown to the ages gone by. It ceaselessly wages a twofold war both against flesh and blood and against a spiritual army of evil in the heavens.'

Bernard de Clairvaux, *De Laude Novae Militiae*

Little is known of the early years of the Templars. The order, unlike many religious institutions of the era, kept no records of its early years – at least none that have survived. Therefore, in order to understand the origins of this, the greatest of the military orders, we must put together the bits and pieces that lie scattered on the table of medieval history, sorting through the personal biases, apocryphal accounts and outright fabrications in order to get to the bottom of the story of the beginnings of the Knights Templar.

Much of what has come to be the accepted account of the origins of the order was written more than a half century after the Templars began in Jerusalem and was penned by William of Tyre, a man who had a clear distaste for what he perceived the order had become in his day. William, Archbishop of Tyre, is one of three chroniclers, writing in the latter half of the twelfth century who rendered an account of the early days of the Templars: the other two being Michael the Syrian, Jacobite Patriarch of Antioch and Walter Map, Archdeacon of Oxford, who was also clerk in the court of King Henry II of England. Of the three, William's account, despite his personal bias and factual errors, is generally accepted to be the most reliable of the accounts.

The Chronicling Cleric

William was part of the second generation of children born in the recently formed Kingdom of Jerusalem and historians place his birth somewhere between the years 1127 and 1130. As such, the Templars came into existence before William's birth although he would have encountered members of the order while growing up in Jerusalem where he was educated. Like many men in the medieval era, William entered the church at a young age and was versed in Greek and Latin.[1] It is said that he also spoke Arabic, which is evident from the manuscripts he wrote on the history of the Muslims, but his comprehension of the language was probably due to the geographical proximity to Arabic-speaking populations, rather than formal education.

By the mid-twelfth century, the borders between East and West began to blur. The Franks, particularly those of the second and subsequent generations born in the East, had adapted Eastern dress and customs. A common practice among many Christians in the east – and a tradition that the Templars would be charged with by later writers – was really just a matter of the Franks embracing the 'When in Rome, do as the Romans do' philosophy.

Around the year 1146, William left the Levant for Europe to continue his education and spent two decades studying under some of the greatest scholars in Christendom in Paris and Bologna.[2] Upon his return to the Holy Land in 1165, he first became a cleric at Acre, and in 1167, performed the marriage sacraments of Amalric I, King of Jerusalem, and Maria Comnena, the niece of Byzantine emperor Manuel Comnenus. In 1168, as Archdeacon of Tyre, he would

The Temple Mount at Jerusalem viewed from the east. The al Aqsa Mosque on the left is where the Templars were granted quarters by King Baldwin II after their formation in 1119-1120. The building was believed to be the Temple of Solomon and it was from this connection that the Order became known as Templars.
iStockPhoto.com Luis Alvarez

assist both Amalric and Manuel in a diplomatic mission to form an alliance between the Kingdom of Jerusalem and the Byzantine Empire for a joint campaign against Egypt. After a trip to Rome in 1169 – in order to address some personal trouble brought his way by a fellow cleric[3] – William returned to the Holy Land where he became the tutor of Amalric's son, who would later be crowned Baldwin IV, the Leper King. In fact, it was during William's tenure as court tutor that he discovered the future king suffered from leprosy, although the disease did not fully manifest until the lad reached puberty.

It was around this time that the cleric turned his attentions to recording a history of the Kingdom of Jerusalem, entitled *Historia rerum in partibus transmarinis gestarum* or 'History of Deeds Done Beyond the Sea'. It is from this account that the traditional history of the founding of the Knights Templar is derived.

William's Account

> 'In this same year [1118], certain noble men of knightly rank, religious men, devoted to God and fearing him, bound themselves to Christ's service in the hands of the Lord Patriarch. They promised to live in perpetuity as regular canons, without possessions, under vows of chastity and obedience. Their foremost leaders were the venerable Hugh of Payens and Geoffrey of St Omer. Since they had no church nor any fixed abode, the king, gave them for a time a dwelling place in the south wing of the palace, near the Lord's Temple. The canons of the Lord's Temple gave them, under certain conditions, a square near the palace which the canons possessed. This the knights used as a drill field. The Lord King and his noblemen and also the Lord Patriarch and the prelates of the church gave them benefices from their domains, some for a limited time and some in perpetuity. These were to provide the knights with food and clothing. Their primary duty, one which was enjoined upon them by the Lord Patriarch and the other bishops for the remission of sins, was that of protecting the roads and routes against the attacks of robbers and brigands. This they did especially in order to safeguard pilgrims.'[4]

And so we have the traditional story of the beginnings of the order. A group of knights of noble birth led by Hugues de Payens and Geoffrey de St Omer took upon themselves the vows of chastity, poverty and obedience and further vowed to defend the pilgrims who were en route to see the sacred shrines of Christendom. Being poor and virtuous knights with no place to call home, the King of Jerusalem, Baldwin II,[5] gave them part of his palace, which was in the al-Aqsa Mosque as well as other areas of the Temple Mount as a base of operations.

The cleric also tells us in his account that the Templars wore secular clothing and 'used such garments as the people, for their soul's salvation, gave them.' [6] Additionally we are told that by the end of their ninth year there were only nine knights. What is interesting in this account is that nowhere does he specify that there were nine knights who founded the order, only that by the end of their ninth year, there were nine of their number.

Michael's Account

WHEREAS William's account of events is unclear as to whether the order had nine knights at its conception or that number after the first nine years, it is in stark contrast to another late twelfth century chronicler, Michael the Syrian. In Michael's account of the foundation of the Templars, there were thirty-one knights:

> 'At the beginning of the reign of King Baldwin II, a Frank came from Rome to pray at Jerusalem. He had made a vow never to return to his own country, but to take holy orders, after having assisted the king in war for three years, he and the thirty knights who accompanied him, and to terminate their lives in Jerusalem. When the king and his nobles saw that they were renowned in battle, and had been of great use to the city during their three years of service, he advised this man to serve in the militia, together with those attached to him, instead of taking holy orders, to work towards saving his soul, and to protect those places against thieves.
>
> 'Now this man, whose name was Hough de Payen, accepted this advice; the thirty knights who accompanied him joined him. The king gave them the house of Solomon for their residence, and some villages for their maintenance. The Patriarch also gave them some villages of the Church.' [7]

Although discredited as unreliable by historians, Michael's account does contain an element of authenticity as it answers a few questions many have had about the Templars' early days. For example, if the Templars were charged with protecting the pilgrim routes from 'robbers and brigands' as both accounts seem to indicate, how was this a tenable proposition with nine or fewer knights? And if there were but nine knights, why would Baldwin II give the al-Aqsa Mosque – which was then the royal palace and believed by the crusaders to be the Temple of Solomon – for their use?

Despite the actual events being impossible to verify, it would appear that Michael's account of thirty-one knights is the more believable. A small number by today's military standards, it is important to realise that in the year following the First Crusade, there were an estimated three hundred knights and three hundred foot soldiers in the Jerusalem area.[8] This is because many of the knights who fought for the victory of Jerusalem had returned home with the spoils of war once victory had been achieved. Although new settlers – including knights and other military men – visited the Holy Land during the years between 1099 and the start of the Templars some two decades later, many lived in the more populated areas along the coast, leaving Jerusalem relatively unpopulated and unprotected. Baldwin II could not be ignorant of this deficiency in his military defences and, as we will look at in due course, would have welcomed thirty well-trained knights and their capable leader.

Walter's Account

IN LIGHT of the previous two accounts, Walter Map – a man who was the farthest removed in terms of geography and time – gives an account that could be mistaken for an Arthurian romance. Walter does not number the founders at thirty-one or nine. His account of events would state that the task of protecting the pilgrims was a one-man show. Well, at least initially …

Walter, who has been accused, and with good reason, of letting a good yarn pervert history, tells of a lone Burgundian knight named Paganus, who was troubled by routine attacks upon pilgrims at a horse-pool near to the city of Jerusalem.[9] Paganus guarded against the bandits on his own until their numbers were too great for him to deal with. Thereafter, he approached the canons of the Temple of the Lord for assistance, acquiring a hall as a base of operations from which he could recruit more knights to help the cause.

Although Walter's account is almost certainly a work of fiction, there is an interesting kernel in his naming of the central character. The Latin word 'Paganus', despite any immediate parallels to the modern word pagan, had the much simpler meaning of countryman, peasant or civilian. This is compelling because Hugues de Payens, who is undisputedly recognised as the founder of the Templars, was a Burgundian nobleman and knight, certainly not a peasant or civilian. However, Walter may have been alluding to his vow of poverty in choosing to refer to him as Paganus or peasant. Speculation as to Walter's intentions aside, it may have been a matter of spelling as no two accounts are inclined to spell the title of the founding father of the Templar Order the same way.

Payens, Payen, Pedanis, Pedano and even Paganus are to be found among the variations used over the years. What we do know for certain is that Hugues, by whatever name he was then known, was born in 1070 in the village of Château de Payns, which is located near Troyes, a city that would play a prominent role in the early years of the Order.

Other Accounts

WITH regards to the Templars' early years, the task of understanding the three accounts would be problematic, because as divergent as they are, none provide any great detail, their bare bones glossed and tainted with romantic notions. Fortunately there are other primary sources of information, written much closer to the time of the actual events, which provide us with some additional insights.

The first of these comes from a charter written between the spring of 1130 and the spring of 1131 by Simon, Bishop of Noyons, documenting a donation granted to Hugh, Master of the Knights of the Temple. In the preamble, Simon wishes the order the strength to persevere in 'the life of the religious order you have entered'. The Bishop of Noyons writes further:

> 'We give thanks to God, because through his mercy he has recovered the order which had perished. For we know that three orders have been instituted by God in the Church, the order of prayers, of defenders and of workers. The other orders were in decline while the order of defenders had almost completely perished. But God the Father and our Lord Jesus Christ, God's Son, had mercy on His Church. Through the infusion of the Holy Spirit in our hearts, in these most recent times He deigned to repair the lost order.' [10]

While this statement may, at first glance, seem to indicate that the Templars had existed in some prior form and had recently been restored, it is important to note that what Simon was referring to by the 'three orders' was a natural division in society that existed at that time. At the top of the chain, at least to the clergy, was the order of prayers – the churchmen who looked after ecclesiastical matters, which were the hub around which the medieval world turned. Next to the order of prayers was the order of defenders, or those who fought. This was the nobly born aristocracy of medieval Europe, who with sword and horse were charged with defending the interests of their liege lord and protecting the weak and poor who were under his care. Last was the order of workers. As the peasant class made up the bulk of society and owed their fealty to the nobility, it was unsurprising that they would be the workers. However, the context in which all of this is placed is within the context of religion. The church was the central rallying point for the medieval community, however, the nobility were probably the least likely to honour their part. As such, Simon is commending the Templars for restoring this decline and for setting an example for other knights to follow.

The next written information on the early years of the Templars was recorded between 1135 and 1137 by Simon de St Bertin, a monk from the St Omer area. In *Gesta Abbatum Sancti Bertini Sithensium*, Simon puts forth the notion that the founding members of the Templars were soldiers from the First Crusade who had stayed behind rather than returning to Europe as most had done. In writing about the events following the crowning of Godfrey de Bouillon, the St Bertin monk tells us:

> 'While he was reigning magnificently, some had decided not to return to the shadows of the world after suffering such dangers for God's sake. On the advice of the princes of God's army they vowed themselves to God's Temple under this rule: they would renounce the world, give up personal goods, free themselves to pursue purity, and lead a communal life wearing a poor habit, only using arms to defend the land against the attacks of the insurgent pagans when necessity demanded.' [11]

However, Simon was not alone in the suggestion that the original Templars were crusaders. Otto, the Bishop of Freising, writing sometime between 1143 and 1147 in his work, *Chronicon*, stated that during the time of the Investiture controversy (see chapter 1), certain knights who realised that they wore their sword belts for a more noble purpose headed for Jerusalem on crusade, where they formed a new type of knighthood dedicated to bearing arms against Christ's enemies:

> 'Around this time, while the kingdom of the Romans was divided in civil and parricidal war caused by a desire for domination, others, despising what they had for Christ's sake, and realising that they did not bear the belt of knighthood without good reason, headed for Jerusalem. And there they began a new type of knighthood. Thus they bear arms against the enemies of Christ's cross, so that continually carrying the mortification of the cross on their bodies; they might appear to be in life and lifestyle not knights but monks.' [12]

Although the Templars may have appeared as monks rather than knights, they accommodated both aspects of society, which is what made them so unique. In a letter to Pope Eugenius III, Anselm, Bishop of Havelburg, describes the dual nature of the Templars in 1145:

> 'They [The Templars] cut themselves off from superfluity and costly clothes, prepared to defend the glorious Sepulchre of the Lord against the incursions of the Saracens. At home peaceful, out of doors strenuous warriors; at home obedient to the discipline of a religious rule, out of doors conforming to military discipline; at home instructed in holy silence, out of doors undaunted by the clash and attack of battle; and, to sum up briefly, they perform everything they are ordered to do, indoors and out of doors, in simple obedience.' [13]

Anselm's praise for the Templars and the words he chose to describe the knighthood to the pope were nothing new. Much of what he wrote had been lifted directly from another influential churchman, Bernard of Clairvaux, a man who may have had as much to do with the Templars' success as Hugues de Payens himself – perhaps even more.

Saint Bernard

BERNARD, who was canonised in 1174 and made a doctor of the Church in 1830, was born into a noble family in 1090 at Fontaines, which is just outside the old Burgundian capitol of Dijon. Bernard's father was a knight by the name of Tescelin and his mother was a woman named Aleth, who was from the Montbard family.[14] In fact, Aleth's younger brother was Andrew de Montbard, believed to be one of the founders of the Templars and certainly a later Master of the order (which would make Bernard his nephew despite the fact that he was much older than Andrew).[15] Like the early years of the Templars, we know little of Bernard's early life, and like the Templars' story, his is also coloured with fanciful myths.

What we do know is that, unlike his father, Bernard did not become a knight and entered the religious life at around eight years of age. He first attended school at St Vorles at Châtillon-sur-Seine, where Tescelin owned property, allowing the family to visit Bernard often. Although his nobly born family accepted Bernard's education at St Voles, the decision to enter a monastic life was opposed. However, the young man prevailed, and in 1112, Bernard – along with thirty-two other young men who also sought the ascetic life – entered the newly formed Citeaux Abbey, birthplace of the Cistercian Order.[16] Within three years of joining the Cistercians, Stephen Harding, the abbot of Citeaux, sent Bernard to form a new abbey at Ville-sous-la-Ferté.

It is interesting to note a parallel between the account of Bernard's early career in the Cistercian order and Michael the Syrian's explanation of the early career of the Templars: a single man, accompanied by thirty-some others enter a new vocation and after a three year period of service, proceed to bigger and better things.

The connection is probably pure coincidence, though, given the fact that Michael's account was written well after Bernard and the Templars had risen to fame in Christendom, and given Bernard's influence upon the success of the Order, there may have been an underlying allegory. Speculations aside, the request to form this new abbey had come from Count Hugh of Champagne,[17] a man who was Hugues de Payens's liege lord and who himself joined the Templars in 1125. Although the land provided by the count was a virtual swamp, Bernard chose to call the new abbey Clairvaux or 'clear valley' and remained its abbot until his death in 1153.

The Cistercian abbot Bernard of Clairvaux was the nephew of Andrew Montbard who is believed to be one of the original members of the Knights Templar. Bernard was one of the Order's greatest patrons.
ClipArt.com

During his time as abbot of Clairvaux, Bernard probably spent more time away from his abbey than within its walls. This is because the Cistercian abbot had become a mover and shaker within Christendom. Bernard reformed and expanded his Cistercian Order, wrote sermons and even penned a letter to Pope Eugenius III entitled 'De Consideratione' which was a guidebook of sorts on how popes should conduct themselves. As such, it is no surprise that Bernard is often referred to as the second pope. Equally unsurprising is that he wrote a letter to his friend Hugues de Payens that set in motion a chain of events which saw the Templars explode in both numbers and notoriety.

In Praise of the New Knighthood

OF THE primary sources available on the Templars (along with the Templars' *Rule of Order*), Bernard's *De laude novae militae* – meaning 'In Praise of the New Knighthood' and written sometime between 1128 and 1138 – is one of the most valuable in terms of providing us with a picture of the early days of the Order and how they differed from what had existed before them. The document was intended to serve a dual purpose: praising and encouraging the Templars and serving as a recruitment flyer. However, regardless of the personal motivations behind Bernard's exhortation of the fledgling Order, the letter, a response to Hughes's third request for endorsement, served to inform Christendom of this new knighthood.

Bernard referred to the Templars as 'a new kind of knighthood' because their method of fighting was twofold. First, like secular knights, they waged war against flesh and blood. Second, and far more important to the Cistercian abbot, the Templars waged war against 'a spiritual army of evil in the heavens'. Taken separately, Bernard regarded neither type of warfare as particularly worthy of his highest praise, for the world was full of both knights and monks who waged war in their own way. It was the combination of the two that set Bernard to write a letter praising the Templars:

> 'But when one sees a man powerfully girding himself with both swords and nobly marking his belt, who would not consider it worthy of all wonder, the more so since it has been hitherto unknown? He is truly a fearless knight and secure on every side, for his soul is protected by the armour of faith just as his body is protected by armour of steel. He is thus doubly armed and need fear neither demons nor men.'[18]

Bernard's words echo the theme behind Pope Urban's speech at Clermont several decades earlier – the knight who fought and killed in the name of Christ was not committing murder, nor was he engaging in evil. Indeed, as the Cistercian abbot wrote: 'the knights of Christ may safely fight the battles of their Lord, fearing neither sin if they smite the enemy, nor danger at their own death; since to inflict death or to die for Christ is no sin, but rather, an abundant claim to glory.'[19] Like the twofold nature of the Templars themselves, Bernard saw a dual-purpose gain in fighting the enemies of Christ; they made a gain for Christ when one of His enemies fell on the battlefield and Christ gained when they themselves died in battle. To Bernard, the Lord was more concerned with losing one of His believers than one of His non-believers and would deal with the death of each accordingly.

Combining the best attributes of the contemplative and active lifestyle, Bernard wrote of the dichotomy that existed in the Templars, marvelling that this new knighthood appeared gentler than lambs and yet were fiercer than lions. In fact, the abbot was unsure as to whether they should be styled as monks or soldiers. Bernard concluded that it was best to recognise them as both for they lacked neither the meek nature of monks or the military strength of the warrior class. But regardless of the appellation used to describe the Templars, Bernard saw them as the hand picked troops of God chosen by the deity to wage war against the infidel.

Bernard believed that this new form of knighthood was a stark contrast from the secular knighthood of the day, and he spared no feelings in condemning the latter for their ways. In typical fashion, the Cistercian abbot used words to their full advantage, referring to the new knights as a *militia* or knighthood and to the secular knights as *malicia* or evil.[20] But beyond his clever play on words, Bernard directly charged the secular knight with vanity: horses were covered with silk, armour adorned with all manner of coloured rags, they painted their shields, decorated their saddles and their remaining accoutrements were encrusted with gold, silver and precious jewels. To Bernard, these were not the trappings of a warrior, but rather the accessories of a woman. If anything, he saw the secular knight of his day as anything but masculine. Their long flowing hair and flowing tunics were, to Bernard, the very antithesis of what a knight should be. By contrast, the Templars, by their very Rule of Order, were to keep their hair well tonsured.

Bernard described knights as requiring three attributes: 'He must guard his person with strength, shrewdness and care; he must be free in his movements, and he must be quick to draw his sword.'[21] The Templars possessed these attributes in abundant supply. Even when this new knighthood was not on the field of battle, their free time was not truly their own. Idleness was viewed by the Templars as a waste of valuable time and games of dice and chess as well as idle gossip and unrestrained laughter were prohibited.

This illustration of a twelfth-century European knight depicts the slightly effeminate accoutrements that Bernard criticised them for in his 'In Praise of the New Knighthood'. *ClipArt.com*

The Agnus Dei or Lamb of God was one of the most commonly used symbols by the Templars; however, it was far from exclusive to the Order. Shown here are a variety of representations of the Christian icon representing Christ from non-Templar sources. *ClipArt.com*

Hugh of St Victor, shown here reading to his fellow monks at the Abbey of St Victor in Paris, is the most likely candidate to have authored the Letter to the Knights of Christ in the Temple at Jerusalem, which was penned to boost their sagging morale. ***Author***

These means of passing time were shunned in favour of repairing armour, mending their humble and donated clothing and making sure that things were set to order so that they may be ready at a moment's notice to do the bidding of their superior.

In pointing out the lifestyle of the knights of Christ, Bernard does so to shame those knights who, according to the abbot, were 'fighting for the devil rather than for God.'[22] Indeed, the manner in which the Templars lived was a stark contrast from the lifestyle that the nobly born secular knight was accustomed to. Although secular knights – especially those who had come on crusade – usually owed their fealty to a lord or baron, the Templars were far more restricted in what they could and could not do. They came and went at the call of their superior, ate what he provided them, wore what he gave them to wear and, above all, lived together without the company of women. Unlike the secular knight, whose noble birth may elevate his station in life, the Templar knights had no such distinction among them, although they were, for the most part, nobly born also. This lifestyle, which we will look at in full detail in another chapter, was not to everyone's taste and morale was said to be low at times.

Hugh are You?

The state of low morale was addressed in another letter of encouragement to the Templars, written sometime between 1119 and 1135. However, unlike *De laude novae militae*, the authorship of the *Letter to the Knights of Christ in the Temple at Jerusalem*, remains somewhat of a mystery as it was signed simply Hugh Peccator or Hugh the Sinner. What is clear about the document is that it was intended to reassure the Templars of their mission and to boost troop morale, which had been sagging.

Those outside the Order had been telling the Templars that their mission did not meet with God's favour, that fighting as Christians was not allowed, and rather than battling the enemies of Christ, the Templars ought to love them. The Templars were further told that the path to salvation could only be achieved through the contemplative life, and that if they wished to see heaven, they ought to lay down their swords and shields and join a regular monastic order. This situation caused many of the fledgling Templars to feel that Christendom had forgotten them – they believed that prayers and donations of support were few.

The writer defends the active life of the Order and informs the reader that each man has a calling from God and that it is his duty to heed that calling. He draws a metaphor that each part of the body has a separate function and if all served the same purpose, the body would die:

> 'See, brothers, if all the parts of the body had the same duties, the body could not survive. Listen to what the Apostle says: "If the foot should say, 'I am not an eye, therefore I am not part of the body,' isn't it still part of the body?"'[23]

He then goes on to lay the blame for the decline in morale at the foot of the devil, arguing that because the devil cannot tempt the Order to drunkenness and other worldly vices, he had taken another route by casting doubts in their minds. Although we can gain more knowledge of the early Templars from the content and purpose of the letter than as to who

Above: **The Church of the Holy Sepulchre in Jerusalem is, according to the Chronicle of Ernoul and Bernard the Treasurer, the origin point for the Knights Templar.** *iStockPhoto.com Claudia Dewald*

Right: **Although many have suggested that the dome depicted on the Templars' seal is that of the Dome of the Rock, it is in fact that of the Holy Sepulchre. The seal above is a Templar seal, while the one below is a non-Templar seal depicting the Holy Sepulchre.** *ClipArt.com*

actually wrote it, there are two candidates behind the 'Hugh Peccator' pseudonym. Like many aspects of the Templars' story, there is little agreement among historians as to which one, if either, was the actual author of the letter. The most widely accepted candidate is Hugues de Payens himself: certainly if troop morale was low, it would be expected that he would take action to improve it. However, the style and content of the letter makes de Payens a less credible contender.[24]

The second candidate is Hugh of St Victor who joined the Augustinian Abbey of St Victor in Paris in 1115 and became head of the abbey's school in 1133. Although he is not the most favoured contender as 'Hugh Peccator', the fact that the manuscript is headed with the words 'Prologus, magistri hugonis de sancto victore' (prologue, teacher Hugh of St Victor) strongly indicates that he was the author of the letter.[25] But what may be greater interest is that the Abbey of St Victor provided the canons (clergy) of the Order of the Holy Sepulchre with their rule. It is towards the Order of the Holy Sepulchre that a final account of the early days of the Templars points.

Ernoul's Chronicle

Written after the Battle of Hattin in 1187, (see chapter 14) *The Chronicle of Ernoul and Bernard the Treasurer*[26] presents us with more bits and pieces from which to examine the Templars' beginnings. The writer tells us that when the crusaders had conquered Jerusalem, a great number of knights stayed behind to attach themselves to the Church of the Holy Sepulchre,[27] and more were to dedicate themselves to the cause. Among those who had adopted a pious life at the sacred shrine were a number of knights who recognised that although they served God and obeyed a priest, they no longer took up arms – something the area was in need of. So they decided amongst themselves to elect, with their prior's permission, one of their number to serve as Master and to lead them into battle when and if the need arose:

> 'At that time Baldwin was king. So they came to him and said: 'Lord, advise us for God's sake. We have decided to make one of us a master who may lead us in battle to help the country.' The king was delighted with this, and said that he would willingly advise them and aid them.'[28]

The account goes on to state that the king summoned the Patriarch of Jerusalem, bishops, archbishops and barons of the country to discuss the proposal. It was agreed that the idea was a sound one and the prior of the Holy Sepulchre was persuaded to release the knights from their allegiance to him. After being released from obedience to the Holy Sepulchre, the new knighthood was granted quarters in the Temple of Solomon (al-Aqsa Mosque) from which the order derived their name. What is particularly interesting about this account is that the Templars as well as the Knights Hospitallers followed the liturgy of the Church of the Holy Sepulchre. Additionally, the obverse of the Grand Master's seal depicted the dome of the Holy Sepulchre.[29]

Sorting Through the Pieces

Thus far in our examination of the early years of the Templars, we have encountered nine sources that can be considered contemporary. Although some were written many years after the Templars' conception, all accounts were by people who were alive when the order still existed. Little seems to have changed in the nine centuries that have passed, for modern authors are no closer in agreement over the details than the contemporary chroniclers were. As divergent as the various accounts would appear, there are areas in which the authors agree. By examining these areas alongside what we know of the times from other sources, we may piece together a plausible account of the Templars' origins.

The principle area where the nine primary accounts are synoptic is in their description of the purpose and need of the Templars as a force to protect the sacred shrines of Christendom and the pilgrims who would venture to see them. Although the crusaders had succeeded in eliminating the Muslims within Jerusalem, they had, despite capturing considerable territory, not defeated them entirely. While the Crusader States of Edessa, Antioch and Tripoli were established before or soon after the fall of Jerusalem and were relatively safe places for the Christian faithful to congregate, the roads between them were dangerous. Pilgrims were often attacked in areas where they would gather to take water. A Russian Abbot named Daniel, writing of his journey to Galilee during his pilgrimage to the Holy Land in 1106, tells of his feelings in passing the town of Bashan:

> 'And this place is very dreadful and dangerous. Seven rivers flow from this town of Bashan and great reeds grow along these rivers and many tall palm trees stand about the town like a dense forest. This place is terrible and difficult of access for here live fierce pagan Saracens who attack travellers at the fords on these rivers.'[30]

The Russian abbot was not exaggerating about the perilous situation that existed outside the city walls, for fifteen years later, an event occurred which may have been the catalyst for the formation of the Templars. At Easter in the year 1119, a large group of travellers who had been on a Lenten pilgrimage, were travelling along the road between Jerusalem and the River Jordan after a visit to the Church of the Holy Sepulchre. As pious travellers, they had undergone a period of Lenten fasting combined with travelling in a climate that they were no doubt unaccustomed to and unprepared for. Weak, tired and unarmed, the 700 Christian pilgrims were no match for a band of Muslims from Tyre and Ascalon who saw fit to attack them. Three hundred of the pilgrims were slain and another 60 were carried off as slaves along with the possessions of those who had been killed.[31] Although King Baldwin dispatched a group of knights to the scene, they arrived too late to rescue the captured pilgrims,[32] and one can only imagine the reaction of the residents of Jerusalem when the knights returned to the city with the grave news. Both the King and the Patriarch were said to be stricken with grief over the carnage. But as great a loss as the slaughter of 300 pilgrims was, another massacre a few months later would fuel the unstable landscape of the Crusader States further.

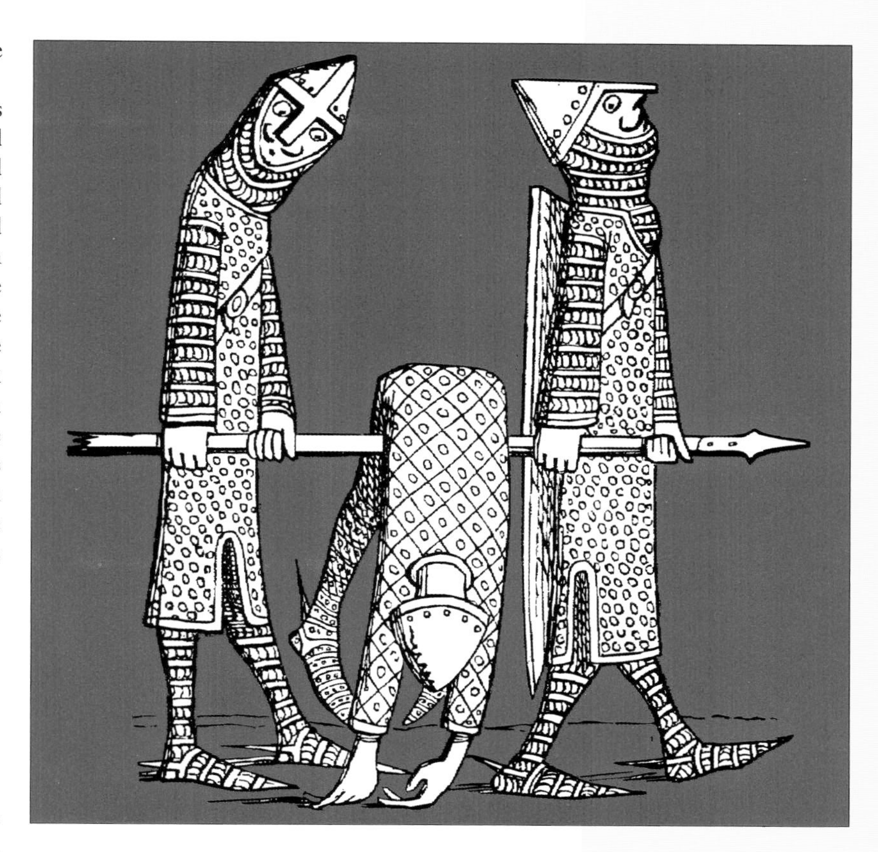

This medieval illustration depicts two knights carrying a fallen comrade from the field of battle on his lance. The continual loss of fighting men was a problem that threatened the security of the Crusader States throughout their existence.
ClipArt.com

The Field Of Blood

When Bohemund of Taranto died in 1111, his nephew Tancred became regent. When Tancred died a year later, the regency passed to his cousin, Roger of Salerno, who had come east with Bohemund and Tancred during the First Crusade. By 1115 it was Roger's desire to add Aleppo to his principality. In 1119, his truce with Aleppo finally expired and he decided to act upon his desires to conquer the city.[33] However, word of his intentions reached the ears of Ilghazi, the Emir of Mardin, who assembled a large army to march against him. Roger had called upon Baldwin II of Jerusalem and Pons, Count of Tripoli, for assistance and the two Latin rulers assembled all the troops they could spare – about two hundred and fifty knights between them.[34] Despite being urged to wait for the king's reinforcements, Roger decided to move on regardless and set out to take his prize.

On 27 June, his army of about seven hundred knights and four thousand foot soldiers – mostly consisting of Turcopoles recruited from the area – made camp in a narrow gorge between two mountains at al-Balat, fifteen miles south of Aleppo. Roger assumed that he would have the element of surprise in

Charles du Fresne du Cange (1610-1688) is the man responsible for the widely-publicised list of founding members of the Knights Templar.

his favour, but Ilghazi's army, which far outnumbered Roger's, was well on the march and had surrounded the Christians on every side. The Muslims attacked the next morning, and although Roger knew that sheer numbers would overwhelm them, his men fought valiantly against the enemy. For a time, the crusaders seemed to be gaining ground, but the Muslims counterattacked, slaughtering all except 140 men who were taken prisoner. Among those who lost their life that day at the Battle of Ager Sanguinis (Latin for the Field of Blood) was Roger, who was beheaded at the foot of the large golden crucifix the crusaders had brought with them from the basilica of Antioch. Ilghazi paraded Roger's head, along with the survivors of the Antiochan army, through the streets of Aleppo to the cheers of its residents. Those who survived must have wished for the quick death that had befallen their comrades, for the emir tortured them before finally taking their lives.

For whatever reason, Ilghazi failed to press on to Antioch, which was now depleted of its defences. Having learned of Roger's death and the slaughter of the Antiochan army, and anticipating that Ilghazi would attempt to besiege the city, Baldwin and Pons moved on to Antioch preparing for a battle that never came. With Roger dead and Bohemund's legitimate heir Bohemund II too young to rule his principality, Baldwin II took on the role of its regent, further taxing the resources of his own kingdom.

The Need Arises

Those who lived in Jerusalem were already afraid to venture outside the city walls without an armed escort, and the tragedy at Easter and the massacre in June would have done little to change their minds. What made matters worse was the fact that Jerusalem was inland and was not as popular a location for settlement as the coastal cities of Acre and Tyre. Writing of the time of King Baldwin I, the successor of Godfrey de Bouillon as King of Jerusalem, William of Tyre, paints the following account:

> 'At this time the king realised with great concern that the Holy City, beloved of God, was almost destitute of inhabitants. There were not enough people to carry on the necessary undertakings of the realm. Indeed there were scarcely enough to protect the entrances to the city and to defend the walls and towers against sudden hostile attacks.'[35]

William's claims are certainly supported by the small numbers that Baldwin and Pons were able to spare in 1119 to support Roger of Salerno. In reviewing the situation in the Latin States, especially in the City of Jerusalem, we see that the need for an organised military force was indeed a logical and necessary objective, if for no other reason to give the perception that Jerusalem was a secure place for Western Christians to settle and visit. As such, King Baldwin II would surely have welcomed an offer of assistance from a group of knights. The question that remains is who were these knights and just how many of them were there?

The Founding Fathers

Many modern books dealing with the Knights Templar – in keeping with William of Tyre's assertion that there were nine members of the order at the time of the Council of Troyes (see chapter six) – list the names of nine men believed to be the founders of the order. This list of names seems to have originated with Charles du Fresne du Cange (1610-1688) who was, among other things, a historian specialising in Byzantine and medieval history. Du Cange wrote a book entitled *Les familles d'outre-mer*, (published in 1869 long after his death) in which he lists the founders as Hugues de Payens, Godefroid de Saint-Omer, Andre de Montbard, Geoffrey Bisol, Payen de Montdesir, Archambaud de Saint-Aignan, Gundomar, Godefroy and Roral.[36] However, none of the contemporary accounts we have dealt with heretofore provide us with any names other than Hugues de Payens and Geoffrey de St Omer.[37] Andrew (or Andre) de Montbard served as Master in 1153 and Payen de Montdidier (Montdesir) served as Master of the Order in France, so it is likely that both were also involved in the early days of the Order. As to the others, however, especially the three whom are only recorded by their Christian names, little can be said with any degree of certainty.

What also remains uncertain is whether or not the original members were veterans of the First Crusade. Modern historians seem split down the middle with respect to this question, although many of the contemporary accounts indicate the Templars were involved in the victory of the First Crusade, having either taken up residence in the area or joined with the Order of the Holy Sepulchre as the Chronicle of Ernoul and Bernard the Treasurer suggests.

With respect to Hugues de Payens, some authors have suggested that the founder of the Templars may have joined the First Crusade after the death of his wife. That said, any mention of Hugues having a wife would appear to be based on the idea that he was married to Katherine de St Clair which is unfounded; yet another popular assertion found in more 'popular' works and quite possibly based upon a prominent Scottish tradition.[38] Other more credible historians suggest that he may have first arrived to the Holy Land in 1114 with his lord, Hugh de Champagne.[39]

It is known that Hugh, who would cast aside his nobility and family to become a Templar, visited Jerusalem on three occasions: 1104-1108, 1114 and 1125.[40] It was on his final visit to the Levant that he joined the Order after having divorced his wife and disinheriting his son, whom he claimed was never his to begin with. But Hugh was not the only nobly born Frank to join the Templars ranks; Fulk V, Count of Anjou, also became a Templar for a short period of time when he made pilgrimage to the Holy Land in 1120 and later paid an annual allowance to the order. If the list of nine founding members was correct, the addition of Fulk V as an associate member in 1120 and Hugh de Champagne as a full member in 1125, would seem to be sufficient evidence to discredit William of Tyre's assertion that by the end of their ninth year, the Templars had but nine members.

In fact, in studying the primary accounts, it seems more and more likely that the first Templars were either veterans of the First Crusade or knights who had come east in the years that followed, or perhaps a combination of both. Certainly it seems possible if not probable that their number were greater than the nine knights in nine years, which Barber suggests carries a suspicious symmetry.[41]

Nailing Down The Date

The next area in which historians disagree is the actual date the Templars came into existence. William of Tyre's date of 1118 has long been accepted and modern-day Masonic Knights Templar derive their calendar year, which they refer to as 'Anno Ordinis', upon it. But other than William's account, the majority of the primary sources do not specify a year, instead simply referring to the Templars' official sanctioning as having occurred during the reign of King Baldwin II. As Baldwin II was crowned King of Jerusalem at Easter, 1118, following the death of Baldwin I, it is possible that William was correct.

But in recent years, Templar historians have begun to discredit this date and have suggested that the Templars were founded in 1119 or 1120. Malcolm Barber, arguably one of the world's foremost authorities on the Templars (using primary source documents as a point of calculation), dates the formation of the Order as being sometime between 14 January and 13 September 1120.[42]

What we do know is the Templars first received ecclesiastical recognition at the Council of Nablus, held in January of 1120.[43] Although not a church council per se, it was nonetheless called by Baldwin II and Warmund, Patriarch of Jerusalem, to deal with a number of secular and religious matters confronting the kingdom at the time. As we have seen, the Kingdom of Jerusalem was not the utopia that some chronicles wished people to believe; times were hard, threats from enemies were great, citizens lived in constant fear and the ability to deal with problems were limited by a lack of manpower. In fact, concurrent with the Council of Nablus, Warmund and Gerard, Prior of the Holy Sepulchre, had written to the Archbishop of Compostella urging him to send both money and men to help the eastern cause.[44]

Of the twenty-five canons[45] that came out of the council, one is particularly interesting in light of the Templars' dual role as warriors and monks. The Truce of God, which we looked at earlier, prohibited clerics from fighting at any time; however, canon twenty penned at the Council of Nablus states that a monk should not be held guilty if he takes up the sword and shield in defence. Simply put, the kingdom needed all the muscle they could muster. But what is interesting in this canon is that it seems to be in keeping with the account of the crusaders who had attached themselves to the Order of the Holy Sepulchre found in *The Chronicle of Ernoul and Bernard the Treasurer*:

> 'We have left our lands and our loved ones, and have come here to raise [sic] up and exalt the law of God. So we rest here eating and drinking and spending, without doing any work. We do not perform any deed of arms either, although this country has need of that. We obey a priest, and so we do no labour of arms. Let us take advice, and with our prior's permission we shall make one of us our master, who may lead us in battle when necessary.'[46]

Krac des Chevaliers in present-day Syria was an important castle during the crusader era and is located east of Tripoli. Although the location had been a fortress before the First Crusade, it was given to the Hospitallers in the 1140s, who expanded it into the largest of the crusader fortresses in the Levant. *ClipArt.com*

A Possible Origin of the Knights Templar Compiled from Contemporary Sources

After the conquest of Jerusalem, the crusading armies left the Holy City, taking with them the spoils of war. Other knights, remembering that the purpose of the crusade was as much a matter of pilgrimage and dedication to God as it was a war of liberation, vowed to stay in the Holy Land, perhaps taking their lead from Godfrey de Bouillon who refused to be king in a city where Christ was crucified, choosing the title Advocatus Sancti Sepulchri, or Defender of the Holy Sepulchre, instead. The knights attached themselves to the Church of the Holy Sepulchre that worked in tandem with the Knights Hospitaller, who began as an Amalfitan hospital for poor pilgrims and had been in operation near to the Sepulchre since 1080. Perhaps having witnessed enough spilt blood over several years of hacking their way east, these knights had given up their knightly vocation and taken up the contemplative life.

Although their Muslim enemies has been driven out of the city and the Crusader States, they had not been forced out of the Holy Land, and many of their number were as dedicated to taking it back as the crusaders were to keeping it. Over the years, the security of the region declined. After the massacre of seven hundred pilgrims at Easter 1119 and the Battle of Ager Sanguinis in June of the same year, the former knights, now living the ascetic life, began to question their decision. Perhaps some of their number had already served with both the cross and sword as it was not unknown for priests to take up arms when the need arose as they had done at the Battle of the Field of Blood.

At some point, Hugues de Payens – who may have first arrived to the Holy Land with the crusaders or with his lord, Hugh, Count of Champagne – got the idea that a man could serve two masters and lead an active and contemplative life. He spoke to his fellow knights, chief among them Geoffrey St Omer, who also may have been a veteran of the crusade, and together they arranged for a number of knights to support the idea. They approached Baldwin II who was in desperate need of assistance in defending the Kingdom of Jerusalem, the Principality of Antioch and other Crusader States from the Muslims, who came closer to his walls every day. Baldwin was thrilled with the idea and after consulting with the Patriarch of Jerusalem and other ecclesiastics and barons of the country, approached the Prior of the Church of the Holy Sepulchre, asking that he free the former knights of their allegiance. The prior accepted the request and granted his charges their freedoms and blessings.

The council of Nablus was held in January 1120, where the new knighthood was first given its ecclesiastic recognition. As they were no longer attached to the Holy Sepulchre, Baldwin II granted them part of the al-Aqsa Mosque, which served as the royal palace and was believed to be the Temple of Solomon itself. From this base of operations, the knights began to take up their dual role as a monastic and military order that would patrol the roads surrounding the kingdom, protecting the pilgrims in the process and acting as a deterrent against further incursions on Baldwin's turf.

Although the Order had been recognised and was supported by king and patriarch, they largely relied on donations and wore simple clothing provided to them for their use having taken vows of poverty, chastity and obedience. There were some within the city, however, who did not approve of this new style of knight, believing that it was wrong for a Christian to take up arms. Rumours and accusations travelled the kingdom, which sapped the fledgling order of its esprit de corps. Eventually, letters praising the Templars were written and the order slowly began to grow and prosper.

It is towards this rise in power that we now turn our attentions.

References for chapter 4

1 Catholic Encyclopedia 1912 edition William of Tyre – www.newadvent.org/cathen/15639a.htm – 5 January 2007

2 In William of Tyre's *History* he provides a biographical chapter on his time in Europe. This chapter was excluded from some editions and translations, but was discovered in the Vatican Library and included in a 1962 edition of the book. William lists Master Bernard the Breton, Master Peter Helias, Master Ivo of Chartres, Gilbert Porée, bishop of Poiters among his teachers. The account indicates he studied in Paris and Bologna.

3 William went to Rome in 1169 to answer charges brought against him by Frederick de la Roche, the archbishop of Tyre. While the nature of the charges are unknown, it is speculated that it may have had something to do with the amount of money he was receiving as archdeacon.

4 William of Tyre: The Foundation of the Order of Knights Templar – Medieval Sourcebook – www.fordham.edu/halsall/source/tyre-templars.html – Professor James Brundage translation.

5 Baldwin II was Godfrey's cousin Baldwin of Le Bourg who became the second count of Edessa after Baldwin of Bolougne succeeded his brother Godfrey as King of Jerusalem taking the name Baldwin I.

6 William of Tyre op. cit.

7 Burman, Edward, *The Templars: Knights of God.* pp. 19-20.

8 Nicholson, Helen, *The Knights Templar: A New History*. p. 17.

9 Barber, Malcolm, *The New Knighthood*. p. 7.

10 Nicholson, Helen – Contemporary reactions to the foundation of the Templars – www.deremilitari.org/resources/sources/templars1.htm

11 Ibid.

12 Ibid.

13 Ibid.

14 Meadows, Dennis, *A Saint and a Half*. p. 92.

15 Barber, op. cit. p. 71. Andre de Montbard was the sixth son of Bernard, Lord of Montbard and Humberge of Ricey.

16 Meadows, op. cit. p. 100

17 Tobin, Stephen, *The Cistercians*. p. 53

18 Bernard of Clairvaux, in Praise of the New Knighthood www.theorb.net/encyclop/religion/monastic/bernard.html

19 Ibid.

20 Nicholson – op. cit. p. 26.

21 Bernard of Clairvaux op. cit.

22 Ibid.

23 Nicholson, Helen – Letter to the Knights of Christ in the Temple at Jerusalem – www.the-orb.net/encyclop/religion/monastic/hughssin.html. In this section the author, possibly Hugues de Payens or Hugh de St Victor, is quoting from I *Corinthians* 12:15. This is one of many scriptural references used in the document to support and defend the Templars' lifestyle and mission.

24 Barber op. cit p. 42.

25 Ibid. It is interesting to note that Barber mentions the prologue tying Hugh de St Victor to the letter, however, Nicholson makes no mention of it in her book, *The Knights Templar: A New History*. In Nicholson's book she states that the Latin used in the letter is of too poor a quality for a theologian and yet of too good a quality for a knight.

26 *The Chronicle of Ernoul and Bernard the Treasurer* was edited by L. de Mas Latrie in 1871 and is likely to have been based on a French version of William of Tyre's book. The Ernoul mentioned in the title is generally believed to be a squire named Ernoul who was part of the company who travelled with Balian of Ibelin, a major figure in the history of Jerusalem. Balian of Ibelin was the central character in Ridley Scott's film *Kingdom of Heaven* (2005) about the loss of Jerusalem to Saladin in 1187. Bernard was the treasurer of Corbie Abbey in France.

27 The Temple of the Holy Sepulchre or Church of the Holy Sepulchre is one of the most sacred sites in Christendom and is believed to be the very spot where Christ's body was placed after the crucifixion. The shrine was built by Constantine the Great sometime around AD 325, but damaged by the Persians in 614 when they captured Jerusalem. It was restored in 630 by Emperor Heraclius and remained a Christian church when the Muslims took control of Jerusalem until it was destroyed in 1009 by al-Hakin bin-Amir Allah. The church was rebuilt in 1048 and completely reconstructed sometime in the mid-twelfth century.

28 Nicholson, Contemporary reactions to the foundation of the Templars op. cit.

29 Nicholson, *The Knights Templar*. p. 29

30 Barber op. cit p. 6

31 Burman op. cit. p. 19. Burman attributes the story to the work of Albert of Aix. And other credible historians such as Malcolm Barber recount the story with Barber attributing it to Albert of Aachen's (Aix) *Hiistoria Hierosolymitana*.

32 Barber op. cit pp. 9-10.

33 Oldenbourg, Zoe, *The Crusades*. p. 248

34 Ibid. p. 251

35 Burman, op. cit. p. 17.

36 Burman op. cit. p. 21. This listing is likely taken from *Les familles d'outre-mer* published by M. E. – G. Rey in *Documents inédits de l'histoire de France* in 1869. The spellings used are those of Burman's book.

37 A letter from Baldwin II does make mention of an Andreum and Gundemarum and the roster from the Council of Troyes lists several Templars in attendance. It is likely that Du Cange cobbled together his list of nine knights from a combination of the primary sources and the Council of Troyes documents.

38 Lord, Evelyn, *The Knights Templar in Britain*. p. 4. Although Lord and many other authors mention Hugues being married to Katherine or Catherine Sinclair or St Clair, however, Thierry Leroy in his book Hugues de Payns, Chevalier Champenois makes the claim that de Payens married Elizabeth de Chappes in 1107 and left her in 1114. This would be in keeping with the suggestion that Hugues came to the Levant with lord Hugh, Count of Champagne, in the same year.

39 Read, Piers Paul, *The Templars*. p. 91.

40 Tyerman, Christopher, *God's War: A New History of the Crusades*. p. 253.

41 Barber op. cit. p. 10.

42 Ibid p. 9. Barber indicates that a charitable grant issued to Hugues de Payens from Thierry, Count of Flanders, and dated 13 September 1128 mentions the grant was given in the Order's ninth year, which would make the year of foundation 1120.

43 Ibid. p. 9

44 Ibid. p. 9

45 The 25 canons of the Council of Nablus largely dealt with such matters as church tithes, adultery and bigamy, homosexuality, sexual relationships between Muslims and Latins, the prohibition of Muslims dressing like Christians and theft. It was believed by the organisers of the council that the problems confronting the kingdom were due to the sins of its population.

46 Nicholson – Contemporary reactions op. cit.

The members of the 1867 Jerusalem Survey Team.
***Standing:* Jerius, Dragoman to the British Consulate.**
***Seated left to right:* Lieutenant Charles Warren, R.E., Bishop Joseph Barclay, Corporal Henry Phillips.**
***Reclining:* Mr Frederick W. Eaton**
Palestine Exploration Fund

Templars on the Mount

'If you would be a real seeker after truth, it is necessary that at least once in your life you doubt, as far as possible, all things.'

Rene Descartes

Right: **The Ark of the Covenant is but one of a number of sacred objects that modern authors have claimed the Templars found beneath the Temple Mount.**

If we were to base our ideas about the Templars solely upon the many books written over the last decade, it would appear that the wealth and power that the Templars enjoyed throughout the bulk of their existence happened overnight. Such sudden fortune was as rare then as it is now, and so the Templars' meteoric rise from poverty and humility to wealth and power must, according to the authors of many currents books, be due to some vast conspiracy.

The problem with this argument is twofold. First, as we will see over the next several chapters, the Templars' rise to power was not overnight. Nor was it particularly meteoric, although its demise was swift. Second, as with the subject of the Templars' formative years, no two authors can seem to agree on what the conspiracy was. One author will tell you that the Templars found the Ark of the Covenant; another that they found the mummified head of Jesus Christ; one group of writers will tell you that they found the secret writings of Jesus, another that the Templars had learned the secret that Jesus was married with children.

Regardless of what the Templars are alleged to have found during those first nine years, the majority of the 'alternative historians' are utterly convinced that their discovery as a result of digging beneath the Temple Mount made them rich and powerful.[1] Of course, many of these authors seem to overlook the fact that the knights, whether they were nine or ninety in number, would have been under the watchful eye of the King of Jerusalem, especially as the city could come under attack at any moment. The central hub around which the excavation theories spin is the belief that the Templars were never engaged in their stated purpose in protecting pilgrims and must instead have been occupied by some other, secret business. Some say there is no evidence that the Templars were ever engaged in the protection of pilgrims. However, as we have seen in the previous chapter, the early days of the Templars were not chronicled until much later, when the Order had become noteworthy.

The lack of documented cases of Templars swooping pilgrims from the hands of their Saracen enemies does not prove that they were not involved in such activities any more than it proves they must have been doing something else. As we have seen previously, the security situation in the east was a precarious one. Although the Templars are not specifically mentioned by name there were many skirmishes and battles during the first nine years of the Templars' existence.

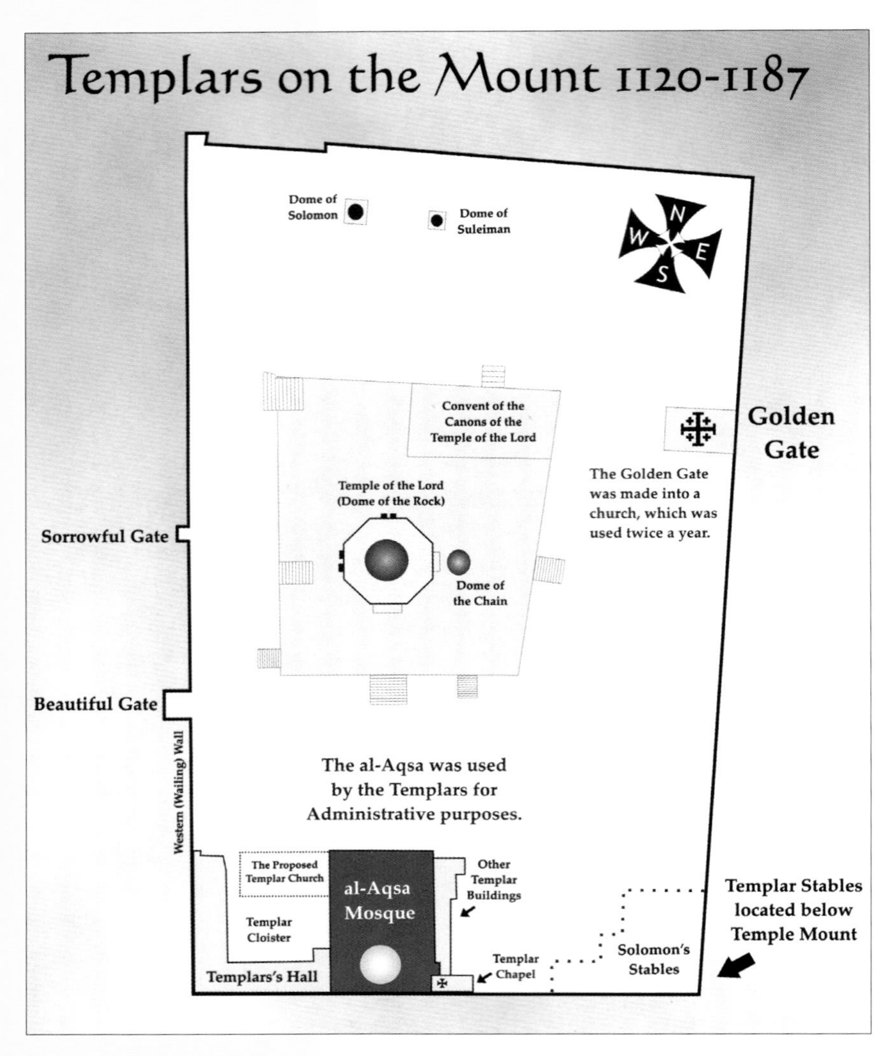

Diagram depicting the Templars's headquarters on the Templar Mount from their formation in 1120 until the loss of the city in 1187. *Author*

In 1120, almost as soon as King Baldwin had returned from Antioch following the Battle of Auger Sanguinis and the later stalemate campaigns, Bulag, governor of Athareb under Ilghazi, marched into Antiochan territory. Continuing the Muslim advance, Ilghazi marched on Edessa but the Franks thwarted both advances.[2] The following spring, Toghtekin, who had played a role in the Field of Blood, launched an extensive raid on Galilee thinking that Baldwin was still occupied with northern conflicts. Baldwin and his army countered Toghtekin that summer when they crossed the Jordan and destroyed their fort at Jerash.[3]

Matters continued to be militant over the next few years with the capture of Joscelin, Count of Edessa in 1122, which spread Baldwin's administrative resources even thinner. In fact, it was on a return trip from Edessa in the spring of 1123, during which he had secured the government of the county, that Baldwin himself would be captured and imprisoned until 1124. Other battles during those formative years included the siege of Tyre in 1124 and the Battle of Azaz in 1125, which depleted soldiers on both sides of the battle. While the Templars may not have been involved in all of these military campaigns, there is no reason to assume that while their co-religionists were working with sword and lance, the fledgling Templars stayed home to work with pick and shovel. However, many modern day authors, seemingly oblivious to the state of affairs that was the Latin East, would have us believe otherwise.

The source upon which many authors base their treasure hunting suppositions is generally the same – an archaeological dig conducted in the Victorian Era during which 'conclusive proof was found' linking the Templars to the subterranean passages beneath the Temple Mount. But before we can examine what the Templars were up to below the Temple Mount, it is wise to first have an understanding of their relationship and connection to the area in the first place.

The Base of Operations

From the time of their first ecclesiastical recognition at the Council of Nablus in 1120, until the loss of Jerusalem after the Battle of Hattin in 1187, the Templars based their headquarters in the Levant on the Temple Mount in Jerusalem. Baldwin II had granted the Order a portion of the al-Aqsa Mosque, which had served the king and his predecessors as a royal palace since the capture of the city in 1099. Although we do not know precisely when, we do know that at some point during the 1120s – possibly after his release from captivity – Baldwin abandoned the al-Aqsa Mosque and constructed a new palace next to the Citadel of Jerusalem or Tower of David, located on the western side of the city overlooking the route to Jaffa.[4] From this point on the Templars seem to have made full use of the area granted them, and over the next five decades, the Order expanded the buildings on the southern section of the Temple Mount considerably. We are fortunate to be left with several contemporary accounts of the Templars' presence there, which provide us with some indication of their activities and the scale to which they evolved.

The first account comes from Usama ibn Munqidh, emir of Shaizar, who had visited Jerusalem in 1138 in order to negotiate a pact between Fulk, King of Jerusalem, and the governor of Damascus against Zengi, governor of Aleppo.[5] At the time, the Kingdom of Jerusalem was on fairly friendly terms with their Muslim neighbours to the northeast.

Usama was an interesting figure in Arab history – a man who has been labelled an unscrupulous political intriguer,[6] but who was certainly well acquainted with key players among both the Franks and the Arabs. And, like the Templars, Usama was willing to make alliances when it would bring broader benefit. Usama was a member of the Munqidhites, a small dynasty that lived in constant fear of being absorbed by more powerful dynasties. This made the Munqidhites amenable to working with the Franks and theyhad done so as far back as the First Crusade. This tolerance was for sake of convenience, however, and Usama had no love for the Franks since he had seen his father's property compromised by the Christian incursions into Antioch, and had even battled alongside Ilghazi and Toghtekin at the Battle of Ager Sanguinis in 1119.[7]

A well-known account of his visit, in addition to placing the Templars in the al-Aqsa, gives an interesting example of the widely held belief that the Templars were tolerant of Muslim ways:

> 'When I was in Jerusalem I used to go to the Masjid al-Aqsa, beside which is a small oratory which the Franks have made into a church. Whenever I went into the mosque, which was in the hands of the Templars who were friends of mine, they would put the little oratory at my disposal, so that I could say my prayers there. One day I had gone in to say the Allah akhbar and risen to begin my prayers, when a Frank threw himself on me from behind, lifted me up and turned me so that I was facing east. 'That is the way to pray!' he said. Some Templars at once intervened, seized the man and took him out of my way, while I resumed my prayer.'[8]

Usama's story continues where the Frank interrupted his prayers once again and was finally thrown out by the Templars. They apologised to the Muslim, informing him that the Frank had just arrived from the west and had yet to learn of eastern ways. This unwillingness of western immigrants to adopt and learn new customs was often counterproductive to the policies established in Outremer. Such attitudes were probably more prevalent in the church among the western born Patriarchs whom were seldom in favour of any agreement with the infidels.[9] While Usama's story is indeed an interesting one, many authors have taken the liberty to use it as an indicator that the Templars had become as tolerant of the Muslim faith as to actually embrace it themselves; however, times of war can make for strange alliances, as history has shown. When taken in context and bearing in mind the purpose of Usama's visit to Jerusalem, it shows that this tolerance was seldom anything other than political positioning.

The al Aqsa Mosque on the Templar Mount served as the Templars headquarters in the East from their formation in 1120 until the loss of Jerusalem in 1187.
Author

But there is a small element of Usama's account that provides us with an insight into what their expansion of the Temple Mount may have been like in the late 1130s when he made his visit. For he tells us that beside the al-Aqsa was 'a small oratory which the Franks have made into a church.' By this early stage in the Templars' story, it seems that the Order had not made any major expansion from the area they had been gifted by their patrons seventeen years earlier. As we will see, this situation did not remain this way for long – several decades later the Templars had made plans to expand upon their church considerably.

The most detailed account of the Templars' presence on the Temple Mount comes to us by way of a German pilgrim named Theodoricus who visited the area around 1172 and wrote of his experiences in *Libellus de locis sanctis*. Theodoricus states that south of the Dome of the Rock was the al-Aqsa Mosque, which he referred to as the Palace of Solomon, comparing its oblong shape and domed roof to that of a church.

> 'This [the al-Aqsa] and all its neighbouring buildings have come into the possession of the Templar soldiers. They are garrisoned in these and other buildings belonging to them. And with stores of arms, clothing and food, they are always ready to guard the province and defend it.'[10]

Later in his account, the pilgrim documents that on the western side of the al-Aqsa, the Templars built a new house, which was far beyond the normal building constructed in the area. Theodoricus states that if he described its dimensions, he feared his account would not be believed. In describing the other buildings the pilgrim tells us:

> 'There [on the western side of al-Aqsa] indeed they have constructed a new palace, just as on the other side they have the old one. There too have

they founded on the edge of the outer court a new church of magnificent size and workmanship.' [11]

The church, which the Templars had began laying the foundations for at the time of Theodoricus's visit, was never completed. However, the size and scope of the proposed structure certainly would have been impressive – it was to run from the northern edge of the al-Aqsa, westward towards the edge of the Temple Mount area and would have enclosed a large section of the southern area occupied by the order.[12] However, there was another foundation which caught the interest of the pilgrim Theodoricus, and which has led to much speculation on the Templars and what they were up to in those early years.

The area known in crusader times as Solomon's Stables is today the Al Musalla Al Marwani Mosque. These photos, taken long before the rededication in 1996, show what the area would have looked like when the Templars stabled their horses there. *ClipArt.com*

Solomon's Stables

Below the south-eastern corner of the Temple Mount lies the Al-Musalla Al-Marwani, a mosque and prayer hall said to be large enough to accommodate 10,000 Muslim faithful (rededicated in 1996 after some major renovations.) During the crusader period, the subterranean area was referred to as Solomon's Stables. Although the arches that make up Solomon's Stables are below ground, they were constructed to elevate and level the area during the time of Herod the Great who expanded the southern section of the Temple Mount. Essentially, Herod filled in the existing walls with dirt, placed the arches on top of the levelled ground and built on top of the arches. As such, Solomon's Stables are believed to be a Herodian and not Solomonic construction, although many Muslim historians date the construction to the eighth century Umayyad period.

During his visit to the Holy Land in 1172, Theodoricus visited the stables and told of their size in his account:

> 'Below them [the Templars] they have stables once erected by King Solomon. They are next to the Palace, and their structure is remarkably complex. They are erected with vaults, arches and roofs of many varieties, and according to our estimation we should bear witness that they will hold ten thousand horses with their grooms. A single shot from a cross-bow would hardly reach from one end of this building to the other, either in length or breadth.' [13]

The pilgrim was probably exaggerating his claim, for an earlier visitor to the subterranean area in describing its volume, suggested that it would hold 2000 horses or 1500 camels.[14] Regardless of its capacity as a stable, the area measures 30 metres from east to west and 60 metres from north to south, scaling to a summit of nine metres overhead. Although the area is off-limits to non-Muslims today, it wasn't always the case and during the latter half of the nineteenth century was part of an important archaeological survey conducted at Jerusalem.

Warren and Company

Charles Warren, who is best known as having served as the head of the Metropolitan Police during the Jack the Ripper case, went to the Holy Land in 1867 as part of the Palestine Exploration Fund, a London-based organisation which is still in existence today. Warren, who was 27 years old at the time, was a military man having joined the Royal Corps of Engineers a decade earlier in 1857, and as such had the necessary skills to undertake the task, though problems still remained. When he arrived at the port of Jaffa on 15 February 1867, the customhouse authorities were convinced that his equipment consisted of war materials and he had to procure a voucher from the vice-consul ensuring that the materials were peaceful and unlikely to detonate.[15] Even after receiving clearance from the officials, his first attempt to excavate along the Sanctuary wall was halted for fear that his efforts would bring down the walls.[16] The Explorations at Jerusalem (1867-1870) was the first major undertaking of the new organisation and Warren was charged with the task of investigating the site of the Temple, the fortification lines of the ancient city, positioning the Fortress Antonia[17] and the City of David as well as investigating the authenticity of the Holy Sepulchre.

In addition to the topographical studies, Warren and company also conducted extensive exploration of the ancient water systems. Among the discoveries made by Warren and his team was the shaft that King David's army was believed to have used when they captured Jerusalem from the Jebusites as well as many other aqueducts, wells and cisterns. But it is one of Warren's colleagues whom several authors claim made a discovery which has served as a launching point endless speculation on the secret activities of the Knights Templar during their first decade of activity.

Charles Wilson, a contemporary of Warren, received a commission with the Royal Engineers in 1855, two years before his colleague. A well-

Top left: **The Golden Gate, shown from below the Temple Mount along the Eastern Wall, is one of several areas around Jerusalem that Charles Warren examined in Victorian times.** *ClipArt.com*

Top right: **Charles Warren, shown examining a shaft in this nineteenth-century engraving, made extensive explorations of Jerusalem and its environs during the 1867 Palestine Exploration Fund's project.** *Author's collection*

respected archaeologist, Wilson would go on to be awarded the Diploma of the International Geographical Congress in 1871 in recognition of his efforts in archaeological work. In 1864, a year before the Palestine Exploration Fund was formed, Wilson was in the area as part of an ordnance survey of Jerusalem. The purpose of this earlier mission, in addition to creating a topographical map of the city, was to do some groundwork for the improvement of Jerusalem's then polluted water supply. Either during the ordnance survey of 1864 or the Explorations at Jerusalem, Wilson is said to have discovered a number of artefacts that comprised the tip of a spear and the hilt of a sword as well as some spurs and a cross made of lead.

There is no question that either the ordnance survey of 1864 or the Excavations at Jerusalem conducted by the Palestine Exploration Fund between the years of 1867–1870 occurred, for the events are well-documented complete with photographic and cartographic evidence. However, the alleged discovery of Templar artefacts is far less substantiated and the Palestine Exploration Fund has no knowledge of them.[18] If the artefacts found in the shafts below the Temple Mount date to the time of the Templars, how can we with any certainty claim they were Templar in origin? The armour and weapons used by the first Templars were no different than those used by the crusaders who had captured the city of Jerusalem two decades before. In fact, armour remained the same from the Battle of Hastings in 1066 until the mid-thirteenth century when plate armour was widely used. So while it is possible that the alleged findings may have been Templar in origin, it is a far stretch from crediting a pair of old spurs as the Holy Grail, although it has not stopped many modern authors making such a claim.

In the book, *The Second Messiah*, authors Christopher Knight and Robert Lomas make the following statement regarding the alleged artefacts and the Warren excavations:

> 'In 1894, almost eight hundred years after the Templars had begun digging under the ruined Temple of Jerusalem, its secret depths were probed again, this time by a British army contingent led by Lieutenant Charles Wilson of the Royal Engineers. They found nothing of the treasures concealed by the Jerusalem Church, but in the tunnels cut centuries earlier they found part of a Templar sword, a spur, the remains of a lance and a small Templar cross. All of these artefacts are now in the keeping of Robert Brydon, the Templar archivist for Scotland, whose grandfather was a friend of a certain Captain Parker who took part in this and other later expeditions to excavate beneath the site of Herod's Temple. In a letter to Robert Brydon's grandfather, written in 1912, Parker tells of finding a secret chamber beneath Temple Mount with a passage that emerged out in the Mosque of Omer [Dome of the Rock.] On breaking through into the mosque, the British army officer had to run for his life from irate priests and worshippers.'[19]

The fundamental problem with this passage is that the man they are referring to is Captain Montague Parker who was not born until 1878, more than a decade after

Some of the actual archaeological materials discovered during Warren's expedition to Jerusalem, which were well publicised in the pages of Harper's New Monthly Magazine. *Author's collection*

Warren and Wilson first explored Jerusalem. Therefore the suggestion that Parker was part of the Warren and Wilson expeditions is not only absurd, it is utterly impossible.[20] Parker's expedition did not occur for another four decades and was of a different purpose than the academic surveys of the Palestine Exploration Fund.

The Parker Expedition

The impetus behind Parker's expedition and exploration of the Temple Mount in the years between 1909 and 1911 was the work of a Swedish philosopher and eccentric named Valter Henrik Juvelius who believed that he had deciphered a coded passage in the Book of Ezekiel, which disclosed the location of Solomon's Treasure.[21] Juvelius was convinced that the location of the treasure was the area examined forty years earlier by Warren and company, and spent a considerable period of time attempting to raise the necessary funding for the trip, promising his proposed backers a share of his future fortunes.[22] Unable to secure backers for the trip, Juvelius made the acquaintance of Montague Parker who had served as Captain of the Grenadier Guards during the Second Boer War (1899-1902). Excited by the opportunity to jump into another adventure, Parker accomplished what Juvelius had been unable to do: raising the required funds for the expedition. As the son of the Earl of Morey, Parker undoubtedly had contacts that Juvelius could only dream of.

In the early days of the expedition, Parker arrived in Constantinople where he tried to obtain permission for the exploration from Turkish officials, but had not realised that the Ottoman Empire had strict policies on their antiquities – in short, what was discovered there, stayed there.[23] However, this did not deter the young Englishman, who decided to bribe a couple of officials in order for the expedition to proceed. At the suggestion of a Danish psychic hired by Juvelius, Parker had one of Warren's tunnels reopened after nearly half a century in the hope that it would lead to their treasure.

Unfortunately for Parker, his men were not the only ones exploring the area. American and European archaeologists were suspicious of the veil of secrecy Parker had drawn around his activities and were offended at the lack of protocol in how these 'archaeologists' handled their dig.[24] In fact, the only member of Parker's party who was a trained archaeologist was a Dominican monk named Père Louis Hugues Vincent who was hired to assist the team but was not informed of the true nature of Parker's quest. Despite complaints to the Turkish Governor, little came of it and Parker continued with his work until the winter rain made it impossible to proceed.

The spurious nature of Parker's explorations is confirmed by a passage in the 1909 edition of the Palestine Exploration Fund's Quarterly Statement:

> 'Sensational reports have, from time to time, during the last few months, appeared in the London and provincial press relating to works of excavation which have been conducted by an English party of amateurs on Ophel. The operations have been carried on, with much secrecy, in and about the aqueduct discovered by Sir Charles Warren; and their object is locally supposed to be to find the Royal Treasures of David. It is believed that no result of value has been attained; but the work is in no way connected with the Palestine Exploration Fund, nor, so far as we can ascertain, does there appear to be with the party any trained archaeologist. By the last reports the work is suspended.'[25]

The work did not remain suspended for long. Returning to the area in the summer of 1910, Parker found that his officials had left for Constantinople, displeased that they did not receive their promised reward. Also, Parker learnt that his team had been given until the end of summer the following year to finish their project.[26] In an attempt to meet the deadline, he set his crews to work day and night despite the return of heavy rains. Parker had found a new official to bribe: a man named Azmey Bey who was paid $25,000 to allow Parker's men on the Temple Mount. Disguised as Arabs, Parker and his crew were led onto the Temple Mount at night when no one was around. Here, once again at the suggestion of Juvelius's psychic, they excavated in the south-eastern corner of Solomon's Stables. However, a week of nightly clandestine effort bore no fruit and the treasure hunters soon turned their attention to other areas, which would prove their undoing.

On 17 April 1911, once again disguised as Arabs, Parker and company entered the Dome of the Rock. They decided to examine a cavern beneath the sacred rock, where Muslims believe Mohammed had made his journey to heaven and the Jews believe Abraham had been willing to sacrifice his son Isaac at God's command. The crew lowered themselves into the natural cavern below the sacred rock and excitedly hacked their way towards the treasure they felt was waiting for them to discover. However, to their misfortune, an attendant of the mosque had decided to sleep on the Temple Mount that evening and woke to find an Englishman with pickaxe in hand.

Although Parker and his accomplices managed to escape, the attempted desecration of Islam's third most sacred site by non-Muslims led to accusations that the English treasure hunters found and stole what they were looking for. The accusations turned to rumours, which then led to a riot in the streets of Jerusalem and some serious trouble for Azmey Bey who had arranged access to the Temple Mount. Amid the chaos and confusion, Turkish officials detained Parker for questioning. Parker convinced the authorities to continue their discussion aboard his yacht, which he was allowed to board ahead of the officials. Of course, by the time they arrived to discuss matters further, Parker had long since pulled anchor and set off to sea.[27]

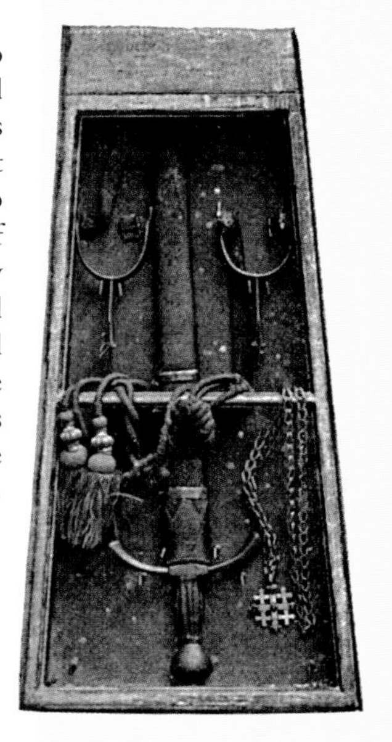

This display case is said to contain the sword and spurs of Godfrey de Bouillon. However, like many alleged relics, its authenticity is highly suspect. *ClipArt.com*

Separating Fact from Fiction

WHAT is interesting about Knight and Lomas's account are that the two expeditions, which could not be more opposite in purpose or approach, are interwoven in the course of their text as if they were a continuation of the same operation. It's as if the authors were unable to discern the difference between a legitimate and well-documented archaeological expedition by trained engineers and a clandestine expedition conducted by a bunch of amateur treasure hunters. This would seem to be the case, for in their first book, *The Hiram Key*, the authors make the following claim:

> 'We found further evidence that the Templars had been involved in digging for something under the ruins of Herod's Temple in the writings of Lieutenant Charles Wilson of the Royal Engineers who led an archaeological expedition to Jerusalem at the turn of the century.'[28]

Once again, there is a problem with the claim, especially where Wilson's involvement is concerned. Although he served as the Chairman of the Palestine Exploration Fund from 1901 until his death in 1905, Wilson would have last visited the east in the late 1800s. During the years 1886 and 1894, Wilson was listed as director of the Ordnance Survey of Ireland, and until his retirement in 1898, served as Director General of Military Education – therefore it was unlikely that he was involved in any expeditions at the

A collection of crusader era artefacts in the possession of Robert Brydon, whose grandfather received them from Montague Parker prior to the First World War. Although several authors have claimed the items to be Templar in origin and therefore proof that the Order excavated below the Temple Mount, the owner of the collection makes no such claims himself. *Robert Brydon*

turn of the century. To offer the authors the benefit of the doubt, there is a possible reason for confusing the two expeditions. In 1876, Warren published an account of his work with the Palestine Exploration Fund entitled *Underground Jerusalem*. This book was followed by another which was written in 1911 by Père Louis Hugues Vincent who had worked with Parker titled *Underground Jerusalem: Discoveries on the Hill of Ophel (1909-1911)*. As neither book is listed in Knight and Lomas's bibliography, we have no way of knowing if the authors were aware of either publication.[29] However, one book that the authors did use for reference material was Graham Hancock's *The Sign and the Seal*, which, to the author's credit, clearly distinguishes between the two expeditions and their purpose, going so far as to refer to Parker as a lunatic.[30] As Hancock spends several pages discussing and distinguishing between the two expeditions, one is left to wonder how Knight and Lomas could have possibly confused them.

Sadly, Knight and Lomas are not alone in making such claims about Templar excavations and discoveries; nor are they alone in using the same alleged Templar artefacts to support their claims. In his book, *The Head of God*, Dr. Keith Laidler states:

> 'These remains are currently held in Scotland by a relative of Captain Wilson, Robert Bryden [sic]. I spoke with Mr. Bryden [sic] at length about the finds, and he confirmed that the remains do exist. They have been dated to the twelfth century and comprise a spearhead, spurs, a sword hilt, and most telling of all, a leaden cross pattee, the symbol of the Templars.' [31]

The author offers this material as one of three incontrovertible facts – the other two being documentary evidence that treasure was hidden below the Temple Mount and the existence of manmade tunnels.[32] He then goes on to tell us:

> 'Taken together, this makes the argument that the Templars found a treasure of some sort during the early years of their formation, extremely persuasive.' [33]

But can we conclude that these artefacts were Templar in origin? Robert Brydon, the owner of said items, was quite prepared to contest the notion.[34] Brydon confirmed that the pieces had belonged to his grandfather who had received them from a man named Parker before the First World War. However, this gentlemanly Scottish septuagenarian was quick to point out that although the pieces were clearly medieval in origin and of the type likely to have been used by the Templars, there was no way to positively identify them as being Templar in origin.[35] In fact, Brydon said that Parker's letter – which makes absolutely no mention of Warren or Wilson – merely implied that they were Templar in origin. Brydon quoted the words of his grandfather's letter from memory: 'These are relics of our Brethren of former days.'

Although many authors have regarded the artefacts as treasured items, Brydon referred to them as archaeological detritus[36] equating them to something found at 'the end of a rubbish tip.' Brydon said that had there been any real historical value to the pieces, they would have been placed in a museum; however, his grandfather wanted to acknowledge Parker's gesture and placed them in a tasteful display as a gesture of his own. The items have been part of his family's collection and have never been placed in a museum, although they were placed on display at Rosslyn Chapel for about five years.

There also would seem to be some discrepancy in the assertion that Brydon was a Templar archivist. While his grandfather was a member of a neo-

Templar Order, Brydon regards himself as nothing more than the archivist of his grandfather's collection, which contains some artefacts from his grandfather's Order. Thus far we have established three things. First, in the years between their formation and the loss of Jerusalem in 1187, the Templars had amassed enough wealth and power to build their headquarters into an impressive complex successfully serving the administrative, military and religious needs of the Order. Second, the idea that this wealth came from secret excavations beneath the Temple Mount is based on some medieval artefacts claimed to be Templar in origin. And third, and perhaps most importantly, the man who owns the artefacts and knows of their origin (while open to the possibility that they might have belonged to the Templars) makes no such claims himself, despite the number of authors who wish to state otherwise.

What remains is to tell the story of how the Templars came to their position of wealth and power during the first half-century of their existence. By examining the story from contemporary accounts and documents, we can perhaps, once and for all, cast the notion that the Templars' wealth came from a secret discovery back into the non-existent excavation pit from which it came.

References for chapter 5

1 There have been a large number of books written over the years making claims about Templar excavations – many of these have been written in the late 1990s and early 2000s. Among the suggestions of Templar discoveries have been The Ark of the Covenant in *The Sign and the Seal* by Graham Hancock and *Templar Gold* by Patrick Byrne. Additionally, the bloodline of Jesus story, which originated with *The Holy Blood and the Holy Grail* by Michael Baigent, Richard Leigh and Henry Lincoln, has spawned an entire library of books following similar lines. Perhaps the most bizarre suggestion is that the Templars found the severed and mummified head of Jesus Christ. This theory was put forth by Dr. Keith Laidler in his 1998 book *The Head of God.*

2 Runciman, Steven, *The Crusades*. V. 2 p. 158

3 Ibid. p. 159.

4 Barber, Malcolm, *The New Knighthood*. p. 90.

5 Read, Piers Paul, *The Templars*. p. 130

6 Gabrieli, Francesco, *Arab Historians of the Crusades*. p. xxviii

7 Oldenbourg, Zoe *The Crusades*. p. 503

8 Gabrieli op. cit. pp. 79-80

9 Runciman op. cit. p. 320

10 Gabrieli op. cit. pp. 92-93. This would seem to indicate that by the time of Theodoricus's visit, the al-Aqsa Mosque served as an administrative building for the Order.

11 Ibid. p. 93

12 Ibid. p. 194

13 Ibid. p. 93

14 Barber op. cit. p. 94.

15 Abbott, Lyman, The Recovery of Jerusalem, *Harper's New Monthly Magazine* Volume XLIII June to November 1871. p. 198.

16 Ibid. p. 198.

17 The Fortress Antonia was a Herodian construct located on the northwest corner of the Temple Mount, named after Marc Antony and was a reconstruction of a previous fortress called the Baris by Josephus and referred to as the tower of Birah in Nehemiah 2:8.

18 In an e-mail correspondence of 17 January 2007, Felicity Cobbing, an executive of the PEF stated: *'I do not recall any of the objects you describe being connected to either Charles Wilson's survey for the Ordnance Survey in 1864 (not the PEF – we were founded in 1865), or with Charles Warren's PEF explorations beneath the Temple mount 1867-1870.'*

19 Knight, Christopher and Robert Lomas, *The Second Messiah*. p. 22.
In addition to the comments contained in the text on the factual inaccuracy of the author's claims, Knight and Lomas were also incorrect in dating the Wilson/Warren expedition as occurring in 1894. According to The Palestine Exploration Foundation's website, the organisation engaged in several explorations of the Levant; Excavations in Jerusalem (1867-1870) under the leadership of Charles Warren and Henry Birtles, The Survey of Western Palestine (1871-1878) under Claude R. Conder and Horatio H. Kitchener and Excavations at Tell el-Hesi (1890-1893) under Sir William Flinders Petrie and Frederick J. Bliss. They also conducted The Wilderness of Zin Archaeological Survey (1913-1914) under Sir Leonard Woolley and T. E. Lawrence (Lawrence of Arabia). Nowhere is there any mention of Montague Parker as having been involved in any of the expeditions.

20 Although Parker was deceased when Wilson and Warren took part in explorations at Jerusalem, there was a man named Henry Spencer Wilson, who joined the Royal Engineers in 1856, who took part in the expeditions. It is possible that Knight and Lomas were confused by the similar sounding names.

21 Silberman, Neil Asher – In Search of Solomon's Treasure – Biblical Archaeology Society – http://members.bib-arch.org/nph-proxy.pl/000000A/http/www.basarchive.org/bswbSearch.asp=3fPubID=3dBSBA&Volume=3d6&Issue=3d4&ArticleID=3d3&UserID=3d0&

22 Ibid. Silberman indicates that Juvelius estimated the value of the treasure at $200 million dollars.

23 Ibid.

24 Ibid.

25 *1909 Quarterly Statement of the Palestine Exploration Fund.* p. 3.

26 Silberman, op. cit.

27 Ibid.

28 Knight and Lomas, *The Hiram Key*. p. 38.

29 No mention of either book is listed in the bibliography of *The Second Messiah* and the previous book *The Hiram Key* provided no bibliography at all. However, they do reference a work entitled Excavations at Jerusalem, which they cite as being written by Warren. This may actually be a book entitled *The Recovery of Jerusalem: A Narrative of Exploration and Discovery in the City and the Holy Land* published in 1871, the year after the Palestine Exploration Fund's Explorations of Jerusalem project. But as we have seen the PEF has no knowledge of the alleged findings in connection with either Wilson or Warren.

30 Hancock, Graham *The Sign and the Seal*. p. 397. Hancock, in quoting Hebrew University archaeologist Gabby Barkai, one of his research sources, states that Parker was not an archaeologist but a 'lunatic.'

31 Laidler, Keith, *The Head of God*. p. 178.

32 Ibid. p. 178

33 Ibid. p. 178.

34 I telephoned Robert Brydon on 2 February 2007 after having made contact with him via Dr Karen Ralls, author of *The Templars and the Grail.* Mr Brydon, upon learning that I was writing a book about the Templars and interested in his artefacts, was a little standoffish having dealt with several authors in the past, whom he asserted didn't listen to what he had told them.

35 Brydon's exact words were *'You couldn't say they were Templar at all.'*

36 In archaeology detritus is debris or materials left behind when sand or clay begins to erode.

A modern interpretation of a medieval illustration depicting a crusader battle.
Author

Friends in High Places

'We who were once Westerners are now Easterners,
a Roman or a Frenchman in this country
becomes a Galilean or a Palestinian.'

Fulcher of Chartres

WHEN American playwright John Guare wrote his 1990 play *Six Degrees of Separation*, he certainly did not have the Templars or the medieval world in mind. However, the premise of the play, which was made into a movie a few years later, is based on the concept that any person in the world can be linked to any other person in the world by a chain of no more than six others: Mr. Smith knows Mr. Jones, who once rented a flat from Mrs. Carlington, who is the cousin of Mr. Webster and so on. It is certain that this theory of interconnectedness, although unknown to the medieval world, was as real in the twelfth century as it is today.

Throughout the formative years of the Templars, we see an interconnection of many of the key players. For example, Bernard, the first abbot of Clairvaux Abbey, was the nephew of Andrew de Montbard, who was one of the early, if not founding, members of the Order. Bernard, in turn, would not have founded his new abbey if Hugh, Count of Champagne, had not granted land to the Cistercians and requested that they build on it. Hugh, in turn, was a powerful count who had Hugues de Payens, the founder of the Templar Order, as one of his vassals. While this may read as a conspiracy involving the early movers and shakers of the Templar Order, it boils down to what and whom you know. It is this type of interaction, which the business world calls networking, which helped get the Templars moving on the road to wealth and power. But before looking at the series of events that would lead to an increase in the Templars' power and wealth, it is important to learn of the early patrons and members of the Order.

The Temporary Templar

THE first influential westerner to join the Templars' ranks was Fulk V, Count of Anjou, who joined the Order while on pilgrimage to the Holy Land in 1120. Fulk was born between 1089 and 1092 and would have been in his early thirties when he became involved with the Templars. He was the son of Fulk IV of Anjou and Bertrade de Montfort, who deserted her husband and took up with the King of France, Philip I. The reader will recall that this adulterous relationship had been discussed at both the Council of Piacenza and the Council of Clermont where Pope Urban II excommunicated Philip for adultery for not setting his business in order as he had been instructed to.

Upon the death of Fulk IV in 1109, his son became Count of Anjou, and a year later married Eremburge of La Flèche, the heiress of Maine, who bore him four children. Unlike Hugh de Champagne who would join the Order in 1125, Fulk was not of single status when he joined the Templars. For those familiar with the Templars' story, this could be considered to be an error, as it is well known that the Templars took a vow of chastity. While it is certainly true that brother knights were not allowed to marry, it is important to realise that the Order accepted married men. These *Fratres conjugate*, or married brothers, were provided for in the original Latin Rule of the Order, which

This diagram shows the interconnection between several key players in the early days of the Knights Templar as outlined in this chapter.
Author

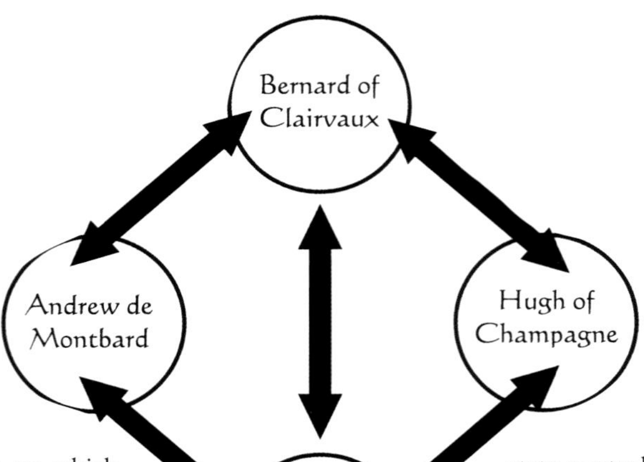

outlined the conditions on which they could be admitted. They were not permitted to wear the white habit of the knights, and if the Fratre conjugati should die before his wife, a portion of his estate was to be given to the Templars, the rest to the widow for her future support.[1] However, these rules were penned some years after Fulk made his pilgrimage to Jerusalem and it would appear that he was a short term or associate member. The Templars did permit men to join the Order for a fixed period of time, and it is under these two conditions that Fulk V was a Templar.

Although his time with the Order may have been brief, he continued to support the Templars upon his return to Europe by granting them an annual allowance of thirty pounds.[2] As we will see in due course, it would not be his final involvement with the Templars nor with the Kingdom of Jerusalem.

Hugh, Count of Champagne

ANOTHER nobly born Frank who would be influential in the early years of the Templar Order was Hugh de Champagne who had served as Count of Champagne from 1093 until he joined the Templars in 1125. Champagne is an historic province located in the north-eastern region of France and was originally referred to by the Latin name Campania, which means plain. The flat land of the region was perfect for the production of wine of a particularly good quality, which is universally known by the name of the province. Although Champagne-Ardenne is a part of France, the county of Champagne did not become part of the Crown Territories until the year 1314. At that time Louis Hutin, the son of Philip IV – the man who had Jacques de Molay, the last Master of the Templars, executed – was crowned King Louis X of France. From 1305 until his coronation, Louis had been the count of Champagne, and upon taking the throne of France, he brought the region under state control. But 221 years earlier, Champagne had been under the control of Hugh who inherited the title after the death of his older brother Eudes. Although some authors have suggested that Hugh had participated in the First Crusade,[3] there seems to be no evidence to support the theory that he travelled to the Holy Land any earlier than 1104, five years after the capture of the Jerusalem.[4] In fact, Hugh made several trips to Outremer, in 1104, 1114 and 1125 when he took the Templar vows.[5]

As discussed earlier, Hugh was not a happy man. He believed that his wife had been unfaithful and had doubts if his oldest son was the product of his loins.[6] This notion seems to be credible because during his visits to the east in 1114, Hugh received a letter from Ivo, Bishop of Chartres, in which the cleric was critical of the count for abandoning his wife and transferring his loyalties to the knights of Christ and their gospel of knighthood.[7] Although some have used this letter as an indication that the Templars were created before 1119, Dr. Helen Nicholson proposes that the Bishop was probably suggesting that the count had taken crusading vows as part of his pilgrimage or he had joined one of the many knightly confraternities, which began in the century before the First Crusade.[8]

By 1125, Hugh had divorced his wife and disowned his eldest son, transferring his holdings to his nephew Theobald, who had been Count of Blois since 1102 and became Theobald II, Count of Champagne. Free from his familial bonds, the former count was now able to join the Templar Order taking orders from a man who had previously been his vassal.

Upon hearing of his new vocation, Bernard – who had built Clairvaux Abbey on lands donated by Hugh a decade earlier – wrote a letter to his friend and patron. Although the Cistercian abbot was disappointed that Hugh had not joined his Cistercian Order, he was pleased that he had decided to serve God. Bernard told his friend: 'If for God's cause you have turned from count to knight and from rich to poor, we congratulate you on your advancement. For this is the work of God's right hand.'[9] These words of encouragement would be the first of many to be penned by the Cistercian abbot.

The Man Who Would Be King

At the start of the Templars' evolution, the situation in the east was fairly grim in terms of manpower. Little had changed since the crushing defeat at the Battle of Ager Sanguinis in 1119. Although two more battles (Azaz in June 1125 and Tell al-Shaqab in January 1126) had been victories for the Latin States, Baldwin's forces must have been greatly depleted.[10] The king had wanted to address the military weakness that existed in the kingdom. The death of his long-time adversary, Toghtekin, in February of 1128 was certainly much welcome news and opened up an opportunity for the king to march on Damascus. But he'd first need some fresh troops to do so.

By this period, Baldwin was nearly sixty years old, a man tired of three decades of piques and quarrels with his allies, constant warfare with his enemies and the humiliation of twice being their captive.[11] Adding to the king's problems, his queen, Morphia, had born him four daughters, but no male heir. His two youngest, Hodierna and Joveta, were children and he had wed his second oldest daughter Alice to Bohemund II, the Prince of Antioch, in 1126. This left his eldest daughter Melisende as heir to the kingdom, but in order to secure her privileges in accordance with feudal law, he would need to find her a suitable husband.[12]

Although the Kingdom of Jerusalem did not owe any particular fealty to the Kingdom of France, Baldwin did not hesitate to broach the matter with King Louis VI, allowing him to find a suitable husband for his daughter. One name was recommended to the King of Jerusalem: Fulk of Anjou, a widower after has wife Eremburge had died in 1126. There was little doubt that Fulk was the man for the job – he was acquainted with the Holy Land having been on a pilgrimage in 1120, he was powerful and wealthy as well as accustomed to the art of war and diplomacy of peace. Fulk's reputation was well known in the west as he had successfully gone up against both the kings of France and England and fought alongside Louis VI against the German Emperor.[13]

To persuade Fulk to take his daughter's hand in marriage, Baldwin sent William de Bures, Prince of Galilee and Guy de Brisebarre, Lord of Beirut, to negotiate.[14] The idea of a royal marriage would certainly have been an appealing one. Prior to his departure for the Levant, Fulk would witness the marriage of his eldest son Geoffrey to Matilda, the daughter of Henry I of England – a union that would start the Plantagenet Dynasty.[15] As such, Fulk knew that his marriage to Baldwin's eldest daughter would one day assure him a kingdom. While Fulk's son Geoffrey, who, at 15, was to marry a woman 12 years his senior,[16] Fulk was taking a bride 16 years his junior.

As powerful and wealthy as he may have been, Fulk was a short, fat and redheaded man in his forties, and as such, hardly the visually appealing mate that a young Melisende at 24 had probably hoped for. However, she agreed to the arranged marriage, if only out of political necessity. But like his father before him, Fulk would find that he was married to a woman who loved another man.[17]

Henry I, King of England from 1100 to 1135 was the younger son of William the Conqueror. Henry's daughter Matilda married Fulk of Anjou's son Geoffrey. *ClipArt.com*

Of Mace and Men

At the same time when William de Bures and Guty de Brisebarre were in talks with Fulk, Baldwin also sent Hugues de Payens west in search of fresh recruits for his proposed campaign against Damascus. Although de Payens is last recorded at Acre in 1125, it is likely that he sailed with the king's embassy in the fall of 1127. Both de Payens and de Bures are recorded at Le Mans in April of 1128.[18] The two are also listed as having attended a ceremony on 31 May in which Fulk took the cross and Barber theorises that de Payens may have attended the marriage of Geoffrey and Matilda on 17 June.[19] Although we have no way of knowing for certain, it is possible that it was at this wedding that Hugues made the acquaintance of King Henry I of England, for in that year Henry, assisted Hugues in achieving the purpose of his journey west. The Anglo-Saxon Chronicle provides us with an account:

> 'Hugo of the Templars came from Jerusalem to the king in Normandy; the king received him with much honour, gave him much treasure in gold and silver, and afterwards sent him to England, where he was received by all good men; all gave him treasure, in Scotland also, and sent by him much property all in gold and silver. He summoned folk out of Jerusalem, and then with him went so many folk as never before nor since the first journey in pope Urban's day, though it availed little. He said that a full war was set between the Christians and the heathen; when they came thither it was naught but lying, and thus wretchedly were all those folks afflicted.'[20]

Geoffrey of Anjou, the son of Fulk of Anjou who replaced Baldwin II as King of Jerusalem. Geoffrey was the father of the Plantagenet Dynasty. *ClipArt.com*

These donations, which were granted in 1128, were not the first nor would they be the last. Baldwin himself had granted the new order his property in Flanders,[21] and in 1127, Theobald, Hugh de Champagne's successor as Count, granted to the Order a house, grange and meadow along with a tenement of forty-six hectares of land at Barbonne near Sézanne.[22] Theobald also granted his vassals the permission to gift the Templars from their lands so long as it did not conflict with the count's interests. Other donations included much needed horses and armour. While we cannot be certain if all of these donations were specifically earmarked for the Templars – or if they were, at least in part, intended for Baldwin's proposed campaign against Damascus – we can be reasonably sure that the bulk of donations were gifted by nobly born Europeans who were not able to take up the cross as Hugues and his companions in the Latin East had done.

The Council of Troyes

King Baldwin's dual purpose mission had so far been a success. William de Bures and Guy de Brisebarre had convinced Fulk to return east and wed the king's daughter, and Hugues had been successful in recruiting both men and means for the Eastern cause. But the best was yet to come when Hugues and several of his fellow knights attended a council held in their Master's old stamping grounds of Troyes, which was hosted by Hugh de Champagne's nephew, Theobald. It was at this Council of Troyes that the Order received papal acceptance as well as its Rule.

Whether or not Hugues and his comrades had gone to Europe looking for a Rule to guide the new Order is a matter of disagreement among historians. The French historian Desmond Seward makes the claim that until the Order met Bernard they did not see themselves as a religious organisation, but rather merely a voluntary band of knights. In fact, the author suggests that at the time of their trip to Europe, the fledgling group was on the verge of disbanding, having been unable to attract many recruits to their cause.[23] However, other information points to the idea that the desire for papal recognition and favour had been planted as early as 1126. In a letter from King Baldwin to Bernard of Clairvaux, the king tells the Cistercian abbot:

> 'The Templar Brothers whom God has raised up for the defence of our province and to whom he has accorded special protection, desire to obtain apostolic approval and also a Rule to govern their lives.'[24]

There is some reason to suspect that this letter may be a forgery as the reference to Templar Brothers, or 'Fratres Templari' in its Latin form, is not in keeping with the supposed date of the letter. Nicholson argues that until 1140 the Order was not referred to as Templars, but rather as 'Milites Templi Salomonis' or Knights of the Temple of Solomon.[25] Regardless of the authenticity of the letter, what remains important is that the Order, by whatever name it was then known, did receive papal approval and a Rule of Order at the Council of Troyes that was held in January of 1129.[26] Attendance at the council included a veritable who's who of Christendom. The council was presided over by the papal legate: Matthew du Remois, Cardinal-Bishop of Albano (who was supported by the archbishops of Rheims and Sens), ten bishops and seven abbots including Stephen Harding of Citeaux and Bernard of Clairvaux.[27] In addition to Hugues, the Templars were represented in the persons of Geoffrey de St Omer, Archambaud de St Armand, Geoffrey Bisot, Payen de Montdidier and a knight named Roland.[28]

The proceedings began with Hugues explaining to the council the nature and purpose of his new Order. Like regular canons they attended to the offices of the choir, but being required for outside military service, they could not always fulfil the obligation and would recite a set number of paternosters. Also separating the Order from the regular canons, Hugues's Order permitted servants and one horse per knight. They ate a communal meal, had no contact with women and wore the simple clothing that was given to them by their patrons and supporters.[29]

After Hugues completed his address to the council, the Rule of Order penned by Bernard was presented and recorded by a clerk named Jean Michael. Although the similarity to the Cistercian Rule of Order shows that Bernard's hand was clearly at play, the matters were discussed in infinite detail by those in attendance who accepted or rejected clauses as they saw fit. By the end of the council, the seventy-two clauses of the final draft of the original Latin Rule, although Bernard's brainchild, was very much a work by committee.

With both papal approval and a Rule of Order in hand, Hugues and his companions probably accompanied Fulk when he returned to the Levant in the spring of 1129. As such, it is possible that Hugues had the opportunity to witness the marriage of his old colleague and his king's daughter Melisende on 2 June 1129.

The Siege of Damascus

HUGUES returned to Outremer with an estimated three hundred fresh recruits hungry for action and Baldwin's campaign against Damascus would afford them the opportunity. This was to be the first major campaign in which the Templars were involved in and one of only two mentioned by William of Tyre prior to the Second Crusade. The second was a minor skirmish in Hebron in 1139 where Odo de Montfaucon, a prominent Templar, lost his life.[30]

Following the death of Toghtekin in 1128, Damascus fell under the control of his son Buri, but the period was one of religious turmoil that bordered on civil war.[31] It is possible that Baldwin, who had a reputation as a careful strategist, saw a weakness in the enemy that did not exist or was perhaps urged into battle by the zeal of his new son-in-law. Despite the strong morale of his forces and the influx of fresh and eager troops, the plan to invade Damascus was an ambitious one. The lands west of the Jordan were hostile to the Christians and if a victory could be secured, it would require an army larger than the Franks possessed to even hold the area.[32] However, Baldwin ignored such statistics, and in November 1129 launched his campaign, assisted by the armies of Joscelin of Edessa, Pons of Tripoli and Bohemund of Antioch.[33]

Although Buri was every part as capable a military man as his father, the crusaders pressed hard against the Muslims, and despite heavy losses, were making headway in their siege against Damascus when a violent storm struck.[34] The heavy rains thinned the blood of those who fell in battle as well as seriously limiting the Franks' ability to continue the fight. Unable to navigate the sea of mud that the battlefield had become, Baldwin withdrew, having been bested not by his enemies but by Mother Nature.

The end result of Hugues's journey west in search of fresh recruits was for the founder of the Templars to survey their dead lying in the muddy, blood-soaked battlefield around Damascus, their lives cut short by an enemy whose tactics and methods were different from anything they had been accustomed to. Although it would not be the last time the Templars drew their swords against their enemies, it would be the last time Baldwin drew his.

Betrayal in the Family

A FEW months after the defeat at Damascus, Baldwin's son-in-law, Bohemund of Antioch, was struck by the desire to address his principality's decline in power in the Armenian Kingdom of Cilicia. In February of 1130, Bohemund and a small force travelled up the river Jihan towards Anazarbus. Although he expected some resistance from the Armenians, he did not anticipate that Leo I of Armenia would enter into an alliance with the Danishmend Turks to thwart them.[35] As Bohemund marched along the river, the Danishmend Turks descended upon his army and slaughtered them. Had the Turks recognised the Prince of Antioch, they might have spared his life preferring to hold him for ransom; like many of his soldiers, the prince was decapitated.

The head of the slain prince was taken to the Danishmend emir who had it embalmed and sent to the Caliph as a gift.

St-Urbain, in Troyes was built in the second half of the thirteenth century by Pope Urban IV. It was in this city that the Council of Troyes was held in 1129, which gave the Templars their Rule of Order. *Author's collection*

The news of Bohemund's death created a mixed reaction in Antioch. As he was well liked by his people, they were in shock at the death of their prince. Bohemund's widow would seem to have had less concern for her dead husband and orphaned daughter Constance than for her own sovereignty. The matter of her control over Antioch was not as clear-cut as it would have been if Alice were a man. The principality required a warrior to lead them, and like her sister Melisende, Alice might have been forced to marry a man she did not love in order to achieve this. Such a prospect did not suit the princess and she decided to take matters into her own hands by making a deal with the devil. She dispatched a messenger to Zengi, the atabeg of Aleppo, offering her two-year-old daughter's hand in marriage to a Muslim prince if she was allowed to remain sovereign of Antioch until her death.[36]

By this time, Baldwin had heard of his son-in-law's death and set out northward for Antioch. Along the way his party captured the messenger on route to Aleppo, and after questioning him, discovered of his daughter's treacherous plans. Baldwin is said to have flown into a fit of rage, and in a true case of shooting the messenger, had Alice's horseman hanged on the spot.[37] Anticipating her father's arrival and his reaction should he discover her plans, Alice had barred the gates to the city, but some in the principality whose loyalties were with the king made sure that some of the city's gates were left open in case he should arrive.

When Baldwin and company arrived, Alice locked herself in the citadel. She may have been willing to

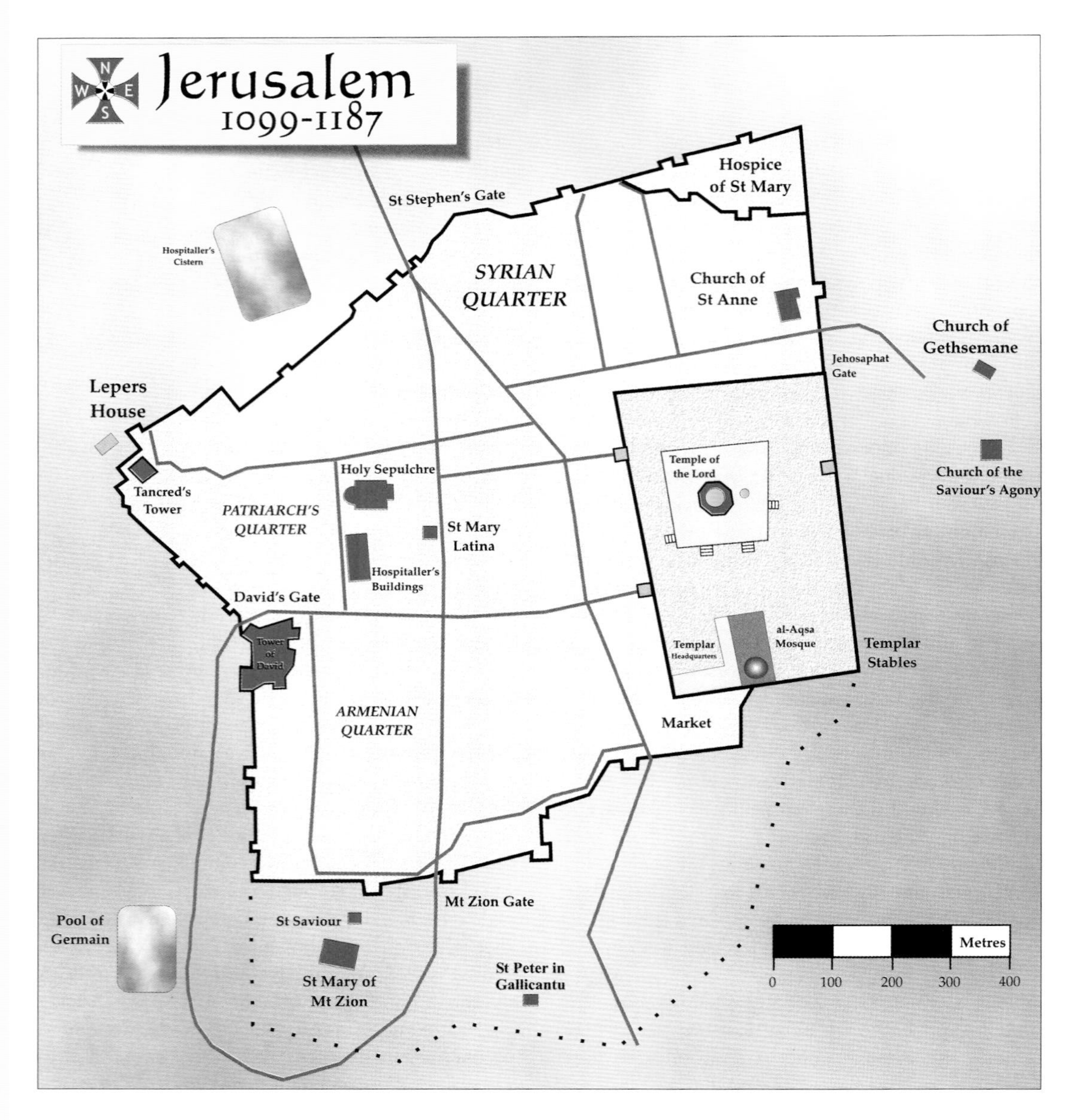

Diagram depicting the city of Jerusalem as it would have been during the reign of the later kings of Jerusalem.

betray her father but was not willing to lead her army against him – and it is doubtful that her men would have followed her orders if she had. Alice threw herself to her father's feet pleading for mercy, and unwilling to execute his own child, Baldwin had her deposed. Alice was forbidden from ever having power in Antioch but her father allowed her to hold power in Lattakeih and Jabala, which were part of her wedding dowry from Bohemund.[38]

The Death of Baldwin II

For the second time in his life Baldwin became regent of Antioch securing it for his granddaughter Constance.

On his return to Jerusalem, the king must have been a broken man. Perhaps the treachery of his own flesh and blood accelerated his demise, for within a few short months, the king developed an illness from which he never recovered. In August of 1131, knowing that his death was imminent, the king asked to be moved from the royal palace to the patriarch's palace that he could die as close to Calvary as possible. He had always been a pious man and legends told that his knees were calloused from so much time at prayer.[39] As death drew ever closer, Baldwin summoned the nobly born members of his kingdom and Melisende and Fulk who came with their one-year-old son Baldwin. From his bed, he abdicated the throne transferring power of the kingdom to his daughter and son-in-law and asked those present to accept them as sovereigns of the kingdom.[40] With this passing of the torch, the Templars had seen the sovereignty of their kingdom move from the head of their first patron to the head of their first associate member. As soon as Baldwin had abdicated the throne he was presented with a monk's robe and admitted as a canon of the Holy Sepulchre. As such, Baldwin's life ended in the very Order from which the Templars may have originated a little more than a decade earlier.

Upon his death, on 31 August 1131, he was buried in the Church of the Holy Sepulchre alongside his kinsman and predecessors, Baldwin I and Godfrey de Bouillon. 32 years had passed since Baldwin had assisted in wrestling the Holy Land from the hands of the infidels, and with his death, the reign of the original Crusader kings came abruptly to a close. Writing a few years prior to Baldwin's death, Fulcher of Chartres – who had also heard firsthand of Urban's call to go east and who had now been in the Levant for more than a generation – wrote of the differences that existed between West and East:

> 'We who were once Westerners are now Easterners, a Roman or a Frenchman in this country becomes a Galilean or a Palestinian. He who was of Rheims of Chartres has become a citizen of Tyre or Antioch. For we have already forgotten the lands of our birth, which are unknown to many of us and never mentioned among us.
>
> 'Some already possess homes and households and tenants by inheritance. Some have taken wives not only of their own people but of Syrians and Armenians or Saracens who have been granted the grace of baptism ... Those who were poor in the West, God has made rich in the East. Those who had little money there have innumerable bezants here and a man who did not have even a house in the West now possesses a city. Why return to the West when there is an Orient like this?'[41]

This opulent lifestyle embraced by Fulcher of Chartres was vastly different from the austere and restrictive lifestyle laid out for the Templars in their Rule of Order.

References for chapter 6

1 Upton-Ward, Judith, *The Templar Rule*. p. 36.

2 Nicholson op. cit p. 26.

3 Ralls, Karen, *The Templars and the Grail*. p. 36. Dr. Ralls states in reference to Hugues de Payens, 'He is said to be a vassal of Hugh I, whose court was centred at Troyes and who we know took part in the First Crusade.' However, she does not indicate a source for the claim and other historians, most notably Malcolm Barber and Helen Nicholson, make no mention of the idea that Hugh went to the east prior to 1104.

4 Nicholson, Helen, *The Knights Templar*. p. 22. This date is also given by Piers Paul Read in his book *The Templars*. p. 91.

5 Ibid. p. 22. Read seems to disagree with Nicholson on this claiming that Hugh returned to Europe in 1108, presumably having spent four years in the east.

6 Read, Piers Paul, *The Templars*. p. 91

7 Nicholson op. cit. p. 22

8 Ibid. p. 22. Nicholson suggests that the confraternities were groups of knights bound together for mutual support.

9 Tobin, Stephen, *The Cistercians*. p. 65.

10 Seward, Desmond, *Monks of War*. p. 31.

11 Oldenbourg, Zoe, *The Crusades*. p. 263

12 Ibid. p. 264.

13 Ibid. pp. 264-265

14 Barber, Malcolm, *The New Knighthood*. p. 11

15 Runciman, Steven, *The Crusades V. 2*. p.178

16 Geoffrey is believed to have been born in 1113 and Matilda in 1101, which would place their ages at 15 and 27 respectively in 1128.

17 Oldenbourg op. cit. pp. 304-305. Shortly after Fulk's reign as King of Jerusalem began (1131) Melisende was involved in a relationship with her childhood friend and second cousin Hugh de Puiset, the son of Hugh I, Count of Jaffa. The affair ended after Hugh was charged with treason and having failed to appear in his defence was condemned in absentia. However, he was granted a pardon on the condition that he leave Outremer immediately and return to Europe. While waiting for a ship to arrive to take him west, he was stabbed by a knight, whom many believed had been hired by Fulk. Although Fulk had the murderer tortured, it is not known if Melisende was ever able to accept that he had nothing to do with her lover's death.

18 Barber op. cit p. 12.

19 Ibid. p. 13. Although some historians date the wedding of Matilda and Geoffrey as occurring in 1127, both Malcolm Barber and Christopher Tyerman date the marriage as having happened in 1128.

20 Savage, Anne, *The Anglo-Saxon Chronicles*. p. 262. The number of recruits listed in the Anglo Saxon chronicles is clearly an exaggeration as it is estimated that Hugues returned east with 300 recruits.

21 Nicholson op. cit. p. 33.

22 Barber op. cit p. 13.

23 Seward op. cit. p. 31.

24 Burman, Edward, *The Templars Knights of God*. pp. 22-23.

25 Nicholson op. cit. pp. 28-29.

26 Like William of Tyre's date of 1118 for the formation of the Templars, the date of the Council of Troyes is traditionally believed to have taken place in 1128 or even 1127. However, recent interpretations of primary source materials now place the date in 1129. One of the reasons for the later date is the fact that council documents refer to Stephen de Chartres as the Patriarch of Jerusalem. As Warmund de Picquigny did not die until July of 1128, the Council must therefore have taken place in January of 1129.

27 The attendance of Bernard at the Council of Troyes is agreed upon by virtually every major historian with the singular exception of Desmond Seward who claims that Bernard sent the Rule to the council but did not attend in person. As the author does not cite a source for the claim there is no way to tell the origin of the notion, which is contrary to the majority of authors.

28 Burman op. cit. p. 101. It is likely that the roster of attendance at the Council of Troyes was the basis for Du Cange's list of founding members.

29 Barber op. cit pp. 14-15.

30 Ibid. p. 35.

31 Oldenbourg op. cit. p. 265.

32 Ibid. pp. 262-263.

33 Payne, Robert, *The Crusades*. p. 134.

34 Ibid. p. 134.

35 Runciman op. cit. p. 182.

36 Payne op. cit p. 135.

37 Runciman op. cit. p. 184.

38 Runciman ibid. p. 184.

39 Payne op. cit. p. 128.

40 Runciman op. cit pp. 184-185.

41 Payne Ibid. p. 138.

The Templar Life

'Above all things, whosoever would be a knight of Christ, choosing such holy orders, you in your profession of faith must unite pure diligence and firm perseverance, which is so worthy and so holy, and is known to be so noble, that if it is preserved untainted for ever, you will deserve to keep company with the martyrs who gave their souls for Jesus Christ.'

Prologue to the *Primitive Rule of the Templars*

A Templar initiate is received into the Order in this nineteenth-century romantic painting. The ceremony of reception was described in detail in the Templar Rule, but would later be misinterpreted after the arrests of 1307. *Author's collection*

Life for the men who joined the ranks of the Poor Knights of Christ was vastly different from what many of them had been accustomed to. The Order of the Temple was a religious one and embraced a lifestyle that matched its holy mission. But before we examine in detail the new life and vocation that these nobly born sons of Europe embraced, we should be aware of the life from whence they came.

The Templars were born in an era of feudalism, which had developed in Northern France and eventually spread throughout Europe, taking different forms as it spread.[1] In the medieval era there were two ways to occupy land apart from conquering it: by possession and by tenure. Possession of land was traditionally the God-given right of kings who owned the land that made up their domains. However, land could also be held by tenure whereby the king would grant tracts of land, called fiefs, to the kingdom's barons and church magnates who were essentially tenants of the king.[2] There was a price to be paid for this granting of land and that was to render military service to the king by providing a set number of knights. In order to obtain these knights, the barons would sublet parcels of their lands to the knights who would add another link in the chain of fealty. It is through such an arrangement that Hugues de Payens owed his loyalty to Hugh, Count de Champagne, until the count gave his land to his nephew in order to join the Templars. This arrangement of land for service was referred to under the system as a knight's fee or 'seigneuri' from which comes the word 'seigneur' or lord.

Under the feudal system, at least in Northern France, anyone who held less than a knight's fee was referred to as a sergeant. The term was originally used to describe a foot soldier, but by the twelfth century, the word referred to regular and mounted troops who were not of the knightly class.[3] This was certainly the case with the Templars, as we will see in our chapter on the hierarchal statutes of the Order. Knights who were granted lands by their barons would, in turn, often divide their land holdings into farms or manors. The peasants who were permitted to work the lands were obligated to provide the lord either produce or military service in exchange. Under the system, the knights could assemble a retinue of crudely armed soldiers like those who followed Peter the Hermit. The soldiers would leave their lands to fulfil their obligation to the barons who would fulfil their obligations to the king who owned all the land.

The land for arms arrangement was not continual. Although the land usage was granted all year round, those who held it were only required to provide forty days of military service without pay whether it be in times of war or peace. During peace times, military service may have consisted of taking a rotation at the royal garrison or to act as a guard when the king travelled. However, if the kingdom were at war, service would often extend well beyond the required forty day period and the army was often paid for the additional periods of service.[4] But it was during times of peace that feudal society was perhaps most problematic. The knightly class, with little else to do with their time, often fought amongst themselves – a situation confirmed by Pope Urban's reiteration of the Truce of God at the Council of Clermont in 1095. However, as we shall soon see, this was not to be a problem for the knights who became Templars due to the lack of free time in their daily lives.

Illustration depicting two knights on a single horse, based on Matthew of Paris' interpretation of the Templar seal. Despite the common symbolism of the design, the Templar Rule actually forbade the knights from riding two to a horse. *Author*

The Templar Rule

We are fortunate to be able to paint a portrait of the day-to-day life of the Templars from the Rule of Order they left behind. Although there are no original manuscripts remaining – the originals possibly having been destroyed at the time of the Templars' arrests – we are fortuitous to have three extant manuscripts to work from: those of Paris, Rome and Dijon. Of the three, Dijon is the oldest, dating back to the early thirteenth century, while those of Rome and Paris appear to date from the late thirteenth and early fourteenth centuries respectively.[5] Although the Templar Rule was originally crafted at the Council of Troyes in 1129, it did not remain limited to the original seventy-two clauses. Over a period of approximately 150 years it, like the Order it was intended to govern, expanded. The version we are left with today consists of six hundred and eighty-six clauses broken into several parts: the Primitive or Latin Rule penned by St Bernard, the Hierarchal Statutes (which were probably added at some point between 1165 and the Fall of Jerusalem in 1187), a section on Penances, Conventual Life, The Holding of Ordinary Chapters, Further Details on Penances and an appendix on the ceremony of Reception into the Order.

While we can place great reliance on this primary source in examining the life of the Templars, it is important to consider that the Rule tells us of how Templar life was intended to be, not how it always was. Like all sets of rules, the Templars were certain to have bent them on occasion and even disobeyed them at times. This is confirmed in the part of the Rule dealing with further details on penances. This section, written between 1257 and 1268, reiterates the earlier infractions and penances but adds concrete examples of instances where Templars had broken the rules and punishments they had received for their transgressions. However, as these infractions and adjustments were certainly the exception to the rule, the 686 clauses give us an authoritative account of Templar life and how it evolved as the Order evolved.

A Day in the Life

In his secular life, the knight may have had the luxury to sleep in as late as he pleased; however, a Templar had no such luxury. Like his Brethren, he would be woken by the ringing of a bell announcing 'Matins' – the first of the canonical hours or offices observed by the Order of which he was now a member. The sun had not even begun to rise when the Matins bell rung at four in the morning. He would rise from his bed, which consisted of a mattress, one bolster and a blanket. Without hesitation, he would put on his hose, fasten his cloak and take up his habit. The hood of his habit was to be worn over his head when he entered the chapel to take part in the service.[6]

While he was in the chapel, the Templar was to remain silent except when reciting the twenty-six paternosters (Lord's Prayer). He was required to recite thirteen for the Matins of the Virgin Mary and an additional thirteen for the day.[7] These would be the first of many prayers he would recite during the course of his day. When the office of Matins was complete, the Templar left the chapel in silence to where the horses were stabled. Although many Masters' seals depict two knights on a single mount, the Templars were forbidden to ride in this fashion.[8] There have been various suggestions as to the background of the seal ranging from a visual interpretation of Christ's words 'For where two or three are gathered together in my name, there am I in the midst of them'[9] to ridiculous claims that the two knights on one horse symbolised the institutionalised homosexuality that was practised in the Order. The most likely interpretation is that the seal was simply a homage to the poor conditions which existed at the Order's foundation under Hugues de Payens and Geoffrey de St Omer, although it is doubtful that conditions were so bad that knights had to share a horse. In fact, we find a different story presented in the Primitive Rule of 1129:

> 'Each knight brother may have three horses and no more without the permission of the Master, because of the great poverty which exists at the present time in the house of God and of the Temple of Solomon. To each knight brother we grant three horses and one squire, and if that squire willingly serves charity, the brother should not beat him for any sin he commits.'[10]

In the middle of the night, the knight was required to inspect his three horses and equipment. If repairs were necessary, it was the knight's responsibility or he would arrange it so that his squire could finish the work; however, all discussions with his squire were to be done so quietly.[11] The Templar Rule shows a great emphasis on silence and many clauses make reference to it. The Templars believed that too much talk was a sin and all idle words and bursts of laughter were prohibited.

After ensuring that his equipment was in a state of readiness, the knight was permitted to return to his bed. However, before sleeping, he was required to say one paternoster in case he had sinned between Matins and his mattress. But he did not sleep for long. The knight's slumber was to be interrupted by a bell that announced prime: the second of the canonical hours observed by the Order. As in the routine established a few hours earlier, he would dress and make his way in silence to the chapel. This time, the hood on his mantle was to be worn around his neck.

The dressing of the knight was only partial as the Rule required that he would 'at all times sleep dressed in shirt and breeches and shoes and belts'.[12] The clause also required that the area where he slept was to remain lit until morning. Although this requirement of sleeping fully clothed and with lights burning has been portrayed by some writers as peculiar to the Templars, it was a common practice in many monastic orders. In the Rule of St Benedict written in AD 530:

> 'A candle shall always be burning in that same cell until early in the morning. They [the monks] shall sleep clothed, and girt with belts or with ropes; and they shall not have their knives at their sides while they sleep, lest perchance in a dream they should wound the sleepers.'[13]

Fully clothed and wiping the sleep from his eyes, the Templar would arrive at the chapel at 6am for prime where he was to listen to the entire office and take part in the Mass which followed. This process was repeated for terce at 9am and sext at midday.[14] The canonical hours, which the Templars faithfully observed, may seem odd to modern readers and those who are not familiar with the Catholic faith. The hours of daylight and night-time were divided into 12 portions – as a result, in the summer, the hours of daylight would be longer than the hours of night and the situation would reverse during the winter months.[15]

In between the religious hours, the Templar was to keep himself busy. He was to follow whatever orders the Master or Commander might give him and these orders were always to be answered with the words 'on behalf of God'.[16] However, if the knight could not complete the order or did not know how to do it, he could request that the Master assign the task to another brother. If his superiors had no orders for the brother, he was to tend to his horses and equipment. If his equipment were found in good order, the Templar was to tend to small productive tasks such as making tent pegs and posts to ensure that 'The Enemy [Satan] does not find him lazy, for the Enemy assails more boldly and more willingly with evil desires and vain thoughts and mean words, a lazy man than he does one whom he finds busy in good work.'[17]

With the morning's religious services and required work assignments completed, he could now partake of a meal with his brethren in the refectory or dining hall. For the Templars at Jerusalem, the palace or al-Aqsa Mosque served as their refectory. Like so many other aspects of the Templars' lives, the communal meal was to be eaten in silence and sign language was to be used where necessary. For example, if a brother wanted bread, he would make a circle with two fingers and a thumb. If he sucked his finger, he wanted milk and by licking his finger, he was requesting honey.[18] However, the Primitive Rule made allowances for men who were not familiar with the sign language, and in such instances, requests were to be made quietly. Such allowances shows that the learning of the protocol of the Order took a period of time to be understood; certainly, a newly admitted member could not be expected to know all of the peculiar aspects of his new life immediately upon being received into the Order.

Meals were served in two sittings: the first for the knights and the second for the sergeants. Of course, before either class of Templar was to take nourishment, it was important that he had attended prime, terce and sext. More importantly, he was required to recite the sixty paternosters each day on behalf of his brethren and benefactors, both living and dead.[19] The meal would begin with the priest giving the blessing after which the Templars would stand and recite yet another paternoster before sitting to eat. During the meal, a clerk would read the holy lesson from the scriptures, through which the knight would remain silent. The Templars ate in pairs sharing a bowl between them[20] with whatever food was served to them. Meat was served three times per week, as it was believed that too much flesh corrupted the body. When meat was distributed to the brethren, it was important that the food be distributed as fairly as possible – the Rule goes as far as to instruct the Commander of the Victuals to make sure that neither two good cuts nor two bad cuts were served together.[21] On Fridays, Lenten food, such as fish and vegetables, was served to the Brethren whereas the Order was served a variety of vegetable dishes and bread on other weekdays. None were to leave the table until the priest had finished, and when they were

The Templar Rule prohibited members of the order from engaging in hunting and falconry. *ClipArt.com*

permitted to rise, they were to go to the chapel to give thanks for the meal they had received, remaining silent until they had done so. Although time was short after lunch and the return to the chapel for nones at 3:00 pm, the knight was expected to continue his working duties but was not to leave until the bell was rung.[22]

Checking his horses and equipment was part of the afternoon routine. Throughout all facets of Templar Rule, great emphasis is placed on the equestrian nature of the Order. The knight is admonished to 'zealously take care of his equipment and horses'. As we will see when we examine the military aspect of the Order, the cavalry was the backbone of the Templars' military strategy and great care was to be taken with the horses. Being permitted three horses to his care, he was not to favour one over another and the Rule is explicit that no horse should be fed a greater ration of food than another so that any one horse suffered because of it.[23] Although the knight was allowed to ride his mount for pleasure, he was not to run his horse without it resting previously or to gallop without permission. But above all, he was not permitted at any time to run his horse impetuously against another person nor to wager upon the outcome.

Although it is often said that gambling was forbidden to the Templars, the Rule seems to indicate otherwise. We are told that the Templar was permitted to wager against another brother with their crossbows up to no more than ten pieces of candle. In fact, many games that would have been common in the knight's secular life were forbidden to him in his new vocation. He was denied playing chess, backgammon and eschaçons but forbot and marelles were permitted.[24] Although we have no information on what these approved games were, they would appear to have been a board game played with tent pegs.

When the bell rang for nones at 3.00 pm and vespers at dusk, the process was repeated with the Templars returning to the chapel to hear the offices of the church. The Rule did allow for a few brethren to skip these services. If the baker had his hands in dough, or the blacksmith had an iron in the fire or was shoeing a horse, he was allowed to stay behind but was required to go to the chapel as soon as he was finished. Once vespers had been attended to, the knights returned to the refectory for the evening meal.

Unlike his secular life, the knight's day was not done with the eating of supper. Soon the chapel bell would ring calling him to compline, the last of the canonical hours he was to observe. Prior to the service, the knight would partake in a communal drink with his brethren. This drink consisted of water or diluted wine, the decision on which was to be offered was at the discretion of the Master of the Order. If wine was offered it was not to be taken to excess. Once he had heard compline, the knight was required to once again check in on his horse and equipment before turning in for the night where he could enjoy a few hours sleep before the bell rang once again, calling him to Matins.

Of course, there were times and circumstances where the Templar would be away on the business of his house and unable to attend the offices of the church. This did not, however, free him from his religious duties and the Rule is explicit on what was expected of him:

> 'And each brother should know that, if he is not in a place where he may hear the hours, each one should say for each of those hours named below the paternoster as many times as is given below, that is to say for prime, terce, sext, nones and compline. For each hour fourteen paternosters: seven times for the hours of Our Lady, and seven times for the hours of the day. And the hours of Our Lady should always be said and heard standing; and those of the day may always be said and heard seated.
>
> 'And for vespers each one should say the paternoster eighteen times: nine times for those of Our Lady, and nine times for those of the day.'[25]

But the religious observances were not the only differences between the new life and the secular life found in the Rule. They were not permitted to wear pointed shoes or shoes with laces. Pointed shoes were a fashion statement among the nobility of the twelfth century, so the prohibition against them was largely a matter of breaking any secular habits the knights may have had. Likewise, the Templars were prohibited from having their hair or robes too long for similar reasons: a trend among secular knights which Bernard of Clairvaux so eloquently criticised in *De Laude Novae Militiae*. Additionally, the knight was prohibited from hunting and falconry and was not to accompany someone who did, although an exception was made in the hunting of lions which could be deemed to have been part of his mission of protecting pilgrims. The Rule is clear in making the distinction:

> 'This above prohibition of hunting is by no means intended to include the lion, for he comes encircling and searching for what he can devour, his hands against every man and every man's hand against him.'[26]

The writers of the Rule seem to have had a similar disdain towards women which was not uncommon in the religious orders of the day:

> 'The company of women is a dangerous thing, for by it the old devil has led many from the

> straight path of Paradise. Henceforth, let not the ladies be admitted as sisters into the house of the Temple; that is why very dear brothers, henceforth it is not fitting to follow this custom, that the flower of chastity is always maintained among you.'[27]

This passage of the Rule has caused some confusion among researchers, as it seems to indicate that in the early years, before the Rule had been drafted, the Order had admitted women among their ranks. While we will probably never learn if this was the case or not, it is known that the Order had at least one nunnery in its later years.[28] But the Rule went further on the matter of women. Not only were they not to be admitted into the Order, they were to be avoided as much as possible and a Templar was not even permitted to kiss his own mother.[29] This prohibition was a serious matter and the knight who violated this or any of the Orders rules could find serious consequences awaiting him.

Chapter Meetings

Outside of being at war, the weekly chapter meeting was one of the few places the Templar could find a little spice in his otherwise mundane existence. For here, the members would gather to deal with the business of the Order, particularly the transgressions of the brethren. These meetings were for members of the Order alone and associate members were barred from the closed doors of the chapter meeting.[30]The utmost secrecy was to be kept on matters discussed in the chapter meeting and a brother who disclosed chapter business to anyone, including another brother of the Order, could find himself barred from future meetings and the Order itself. A great deal was made of this secrecy during the trials that followed the Templars' arrest in 1307, but it was a similar conduct to that of other monastic institutions of the medieval era. Unlike other monastic Orders such as the Cistercians, the Templars did not always have buildings set aside specifically for the purpose of holding chapter meetings and would use whatever building was practical, often the chapel.[31]

The meeting would begin with the Templars entering the building and crossing themselves in the name of the Father, the Son and the Holy Spirit. They were to remove their cloth cap and coif, but if a brother was bald, he could leave his coif on.[32] Before taking his seat in the chapter he was to recite one paternoster. At this point, the brother in charge of the meeting would say, 'Good lord brothers, stand up and pray to Our Lord that He today sends His holy grace among us,' and the brethren would stand up once again for yet another paternoster, which was followed by a prayer from the chaplain.[33] The prayers were always followed by a sermon, and once the sermon began, no brother was permitted to move from his seat, nor leave the building for any reason without permission. With the prerequisite religious observances out of the way, the matter of dealing with the business of the Order could commence.

Brethren who believed they had sinned or violated the Rule of the Order would rise and come before the brother in charge stating, 'Good lord, I plead for mercy to God and Our Lady and to you and the brothers, for I have failed in this way,' after which he would recount the details of his failings.[34] Any brother present at the chapter meeting who believed he had committed a similar sin was required to join the confessed brother and plead the same mercy. Of course, not all brethren were willing to admit their faults and the Rule made provisions for another brother to accuse others of their crimes.[35] However, these accusations were not to be for trivial matters nor based on hearsay evidence. Rather, the brother making the accusation must have firsthand knowledge of the crime.

Those making accusations would stand when permission was given to call the brother he wished to accuse by name. The accused would stand and come before the brother in charge of the meeting. There was no finger pointing or name calling in the matter; rather the accuser was cautioned to deliver his accusation calmly by stating to the accused, 'Good brother, plead for mercy for such-and-such a thing,' after which he would recount the fault he believed the accused to be guilty of. The accused brother was then expected to kneel and plead mercy in the same fashion, which those who voluntarily confessed had done. However, if he believed he was not at fault, he was to say so in as delicate a manner of speech as he had been accused. It was a serious violation of the Rule for a brother to falsely accuse another brother. Indeed, no brother could accuse another of anything unless it was done in front of a member of the Order.

If there was a witness other than the accuser, they were not to be called by name in open chapter. Rather, the accusing brother was to inform the one in charge that there was a brother or brethren who knew of the matter. The brother in charge would then ask if any brother present knew of the matter. If no brother stepped forward, the brother in charge would ask twice more. If the brethren still did not come forward, the accuser would then be instructed to call them forward by name, at which time they would be obligated to tell what they knew.

Once the accusations or confessions were made, the brother in charge would request the offending brother or brethren to leave the chapter meeting so that the community may weigh the matter and mete out any penance that the transgression warranted. It was important that the information presented be weighed against the brother's previous behaviour.[36] In this way, a brother who had led a good life and who was charged with a minor infraction would be given a lighter penance than one who had regularly shown contempt for the Rule. Once the community had discussed the matter, the brother was allowed to return to the chapter meeting. There, the brother who was in charge of the meeting would inform him of the decision of the community. He did not, however, disclose which brethren had spoken for or against the punishment.

Penances

THERE were several ways in which the Templars dealt with members who had violated the Rule and punishment depended on the severity of the brother's infraction. What makes the Rule such a valuable document for understanding the Templars is how matters are dealt with in its several parts. For example, the writers of the Primitive Rule make reference to faults and serious faults and simply state that punishment should fit the severity of the sin.[37] However, in the section on Penances, which seems to be contemporary with the Hierarchal Statutes (1165-1187),[38] the penances had evolved into a fairly clear-cut form. By the time of the section on further details of penances, written between 1257 and 1268, the document had evolved to include not only a clear-cut explanation of infractions and penalties, but examples of past violations and how they were dealt with. The purpose in this later section was twofold: to explain the penalties and to provide the brethren with some guidelines in passing judgment based on past experiences.

The harshest penalty a brother could face was that of expulsion and the Rule lists several offences that would result in being thrown out of the Temple forever: simony, sodomy, conspiracy, heresy, theft, desertion (either from the Order or the field of battle) and killing or causing a Christian to be killed. Of these, sodomy was not initially in the listing and was added in the section dealing with chapter meetings. The choice of wording shows the utter contempt the order had for the practice:

> 'The fourth [grounds for expulsion] is if a brother is tainted with the filthy, stinking sin of sodomy, which is so filthy and so stinking and so repugnant that it should not be named.'[39]

Although the Templars would be accused of homosexual practices at the trials, there seems to be little evidence to support that there was ever anything other than a few isolated cases. Historian Helen Nicholson, in examining more than nine hundred trial testimonies, found only three admissions of homosexuality, which might be deemed as credible.[40] Indeed, the only truly authenticated instance of homosexuality is found in the Rule itself. The Rule tells that the incident happened at Château Pélerin and that the matter was regarded as so horrific that it was not even brought before the chapter. Instead, the brethren were thrown in prison. However, one escaped and joined the Saracens, one was killed while trying to escape and the third remained in prison for many years.[41]

Another example of Templar justice comes to us from the same section of the Rule and shows that before expelling a brother, the Templars wanted to first ensure that the secular world knew how harshly they dealt with those members who violated their duties. The story is told of three Templars who killed a number of Christian merchants at Antioch. When brought before the Commander they were asked why they would do such a thing, to which the murderers replied that sin had made them commit the crime. They were, of course, expelled from the Order, but were first stripped and flogged through the streets of Antioch, Tripoli, Tyre and Acre, crying 'See here the justice which the house exacts from its wicked men.'[42] The three men were given life sentences and died in prison at Château Pélerin. Like much of the Templar way of life, ceremony and ritual was important and expulsion was no different.

Although expulsion did not always include imprisonment, it was simply not a case of the expelled brother being given his walking papers and freedom to return to his secular life; rather, the expelled brother was to join a stricter order. After recounting the daily life of a Templar and the examples of how offending brethren were dealt with, it is hard to imagine that an order stricter than the Templars could exist. However, the Rule dictated that an expelled brother should redeem himself in one of the non-military orders such as that of St Benedict or St Augustine. It didn't matter which order the expelled brother enrolled in so long as it had a strict rule and he was not permitted to join the Hospitallers by mutual agreement, nor could he join the Order of St Lazarus unless he was a leper. If the expelled brother decided this was not to his liking, he would find himself imprisoned until he had changed his mind.[43]

The second punishment that a Templar could face was the loss of his habit. The white habit, or mantle of the knight, was his badge of honour and what set him apart from those around him. Having their habit taken away would be the Templar equivalent to a police officer being asked to turn in their badge. The penance of losing the habit generally lasted for a year plus one day, although it could be restored in a shorter period of time.

The list of offences that could result in a loss of habit is considerably longer than those for expulsion. This indicates that, although it was a harsh penalty, was to be meted out for crimes that could be redeemed in the eyes of the Order. Among the 34 infractions listed which could result in the habit being pulled from his back were striking a brother or any Christian, sexual relations with a woman, falsely accusing a brother of something he could be expelled for, falsely accusing himself in order to be expelled, threatening to join the Saracens, lowering the Templar banner in battle, killing, wounding or losing a slave or horse and refusing food to a travelling brother.

However, there was far more to this penance than merely losing the mantle of the Order. During the year and a day that the penance was to be served, the brother was to stand outside the closed doors of the chapter meeting and was required to sleep in the hospital, where, if he were ill, would be cared for. If he was well enough to work, he was to work with the slaves. When it was time to eat, he was permitted to join the brethren in the refectory, but no table awaited him. Instead, he was to eat on the floor and serious penalties awaited any brother who allowed him to do otherwise. On Mondays, Wednesdays and Fridays, he was to fast and eat nothing other than bread and water. But of all the additional punishment that came with the loss of habit, Sundays were perhaps the worst. For on this day, the penitent brother was to come before the chapel for corporal punishment, which was delivered with a whip or belt.[44]

Although a brother who had lost his habit could be restored to the comfort of the white mantle, any aspirations of career advancement were effectively over, for he was henceforth barred from ever carrying the purse of seal of the Master or the banner of the Order. Likewise, he would never be permitted to hold the office of Commander of Knights or even offer his advice in chapter on matters of discipline.[45]

The Rule also outlines a string of lesser penances meted out in cases where a brother would have lost his habit, but was permitted to keep it 'for love of God'. These penances would be served for a period ranging from one to three days per week for as long as the chapter saw fit. During this time the brother would be required to do menial work such as working in the kitchen cleaning bowls or peeling garlic and chives.

As we have seen, the day-to-day life of the Templar was quite different from the chivalric notion many people have about these white-mantled warriors of God. Life was routine, restrictive and vastly different from the secular life from which they came. Unlike their previous life, the Templar was no longer master of his own affairs, and if he made any attempt to act in such a fashion, he would find himself facing the strictest of disciplinary actions. Indeed, his life as a relatively free agent who owed forty days of the year to his landlord had been replaced by life in an Order that demanded his unwavering servitude all year round.

Despite its demanding and often unforgiving adherence to the Rule, the Order was in many ways a democratic society, and the Templar who was nobly born could soon find himself rising through the ranks of his new Order.

***References for chapter* 7**

1 Wise, Terence, *Medieval Warfare*. p. 5.

2 Ibid. p. 2.

3 Ibid. pp. 3-4.

4 Ibid. p. 5.

5 Upton-Ward, Judith, *The Templar Rule*. p. 11. These three manuscripts were used by Henri de Curzon to compile his 1886 edition and it is from de Curzon's edition that Upton-Ward used in her English translation.

6 Ibid. p. 82 § 281.

7 Ibid. p. 82 § 282.

8 Ibid. p. 104 § 379. The reason for this rule is not 100 per cent clear, but as it comes in a clause on caring for horses, it seems likely that the concern of two knights on one horse is probably related to not harming the animal.

9 KJV Matthew 18:20.

10 Upton-Ward op. cit. p.32 § 51.

11 Ibid. p.82 § 283.

12 Ibid. p.25 § 21.

13 The Rule of St Benedict c. 530 – Medieval Sourcebook – http://www.fordham.edu/halsall/source/rul-benedict.html. Accessed 27 January 2007.

14 Upton-Ward op. cit. p. 83 § 284.

15 Nicholson, Helen, *The Knights Templar: A New History*. p. 138.

16 Upton-Ward op. cit. p. 88 § 313.

17 Ibid. p. 83 § 285.

18 Ibid. p. 25.

19 Ibid. p. 83 § 286.

20 Ibid. p. 26 § 26.

21 Ibid. p. 102 § 372.

22 Ibid. p. 86 § 300.

23 Ibid. p. 90 § 319.

24 Ibid. p. 89 § 317.

25 Ibid. p. 86 § 306.

26 Ibid. p. 33 § 56. This seems also to be a play on 1 Peter 5:8, which says, '*Be sober, be vigilant; because your adversary the devil, as a roaring lion, walketh about, seeking whom he may devour*.'

27 Ibid. p. 36 § 70.

28 Nicholson op. cit. p. 131. Nicholson tells that in 1272 a nunnery was given to the Order by Bishop Eberhard of Worms and that following the dissolution of the Templars the nunnery was transferred to the Hospitallers.

29 Upton-Ward op. cit. Ibid. p. 36 § 71.

30 Nicholson op. cit. p. 137.

31 Ibid. 137.

32 Upton-Ward op. cit. p. 106 § 386.

33 It is important to note that it was not until 1139 that the order was permitted to have its own priests after Pope Innocent II issued the bull, Omne datum optimum (see Chapter nine).

34 Upton-Ward op. cit. p. 106 § 389.

35 Ibid p. 108 § 400.

36 Ibid p. 111 § 414.

37 Ibid p. 30 § 45-46.

38 Ibid p. 14.

39 Ibid p. 112 § 418.

40 Nicholson, op. cit. p. 140.

41 Upton-Ward op. cit. p. 148 § 573.

42 Ibid. p. 144 § 554.

43 Barber, Malcolm, *The New Knighthood*. p. 220.

44 Upton-Ward op. cit. p. 132 § 502.

45 Ibid p. 126 § 478.

Masters of the Temple

1119 – 1314

Throughout the nearly two centuries that the Knights Templar were active in the Holy Land, a number of men served the Order as Master of the Temple. While historians generally agree on who these men were, there is often a difference of opinion as to the exact dates that they served as Master. The following list is one of several chronologies of Templar Masters.

Hugues de Payens	1119 - 1136
Robert de Craon	1136 - 1149
Everard des Barres	1149 - 1152
Bernard de Tremeley	1152/3 - 1153
Andrew de Montbard	1154 - 1156
Bertrand de Blancfort	1156 - 1169
Philip de Milly	1169 - 1171
Odo de St Amand	1171 - 1179
Arnold de Torroja	1181 - 1184
Gerard de Ridefort	1185 - 1189
Robert de Sablé	1191 - 1192/3
Gilbert Erail	1194 - 1200
Philip de Plessis	1201 - 1209
William de Chartres	1210 - 1218/9
Peter de Montaigu	1219 - 1230/2
Armand de Périgord	1232 - 1244
Richard de Bures	1244 - 1247 *
William de Sonnac	1247 - 1250
Reginald de Vichiers	1250 - 1256
Thomas Bérard	1256 - 1273
William de Beaujeu	1273 - 1291
Theobald Gaudin	1291 - 1292/3
Jacques de Molay	1293 - 1314

Author

The Templar Hierarchy

'The strongest is never strong enough to be always the master, unless he transforms strength into right, and obedience into duty.'

Jean Jacques Rousseau

JUST as it would take the newly admitted knight a while to properly learn the many rules and regulations he swore to uphold, it would also require some time to understand the complex hierarchy of the Order to which he had so recently attached himself.

The Draper

ONE of the first officers that the knight would deal with was the Draper who would collect his secular clothes upon joining the house. In return, the Draper would give the knight the garments he was to wear as a Templar: two shirts, two pairs of breeches, two pairs of hose and a small belt which was to be tied around his shirt.[1] Additionally, the knight was presented with a mattress, blanket and pillow for his bed. If the knight wanted to donate gold or silver, it was handed to the Draper who would keep ten bezants for the drapery and turn the rest to the house.

Although it might seem that the position of Draper was one of servitude, the office was actually an important one and entailed far more responsibility than merely distributing garments to new members. When robes were shipped from overseas or gifts were given to the brethren of the convent, it was the duty of the Draper to ensure that these were properly distributed. Additionally, he was to make sure that no brother had an excess of materials or was in possession of items that he was prohibited from having. Likewise, he was to ensure that the brethren were, at all times, properly dressed in accordance with the Rule of the Order. If they were not, he was to order the brethren to do so and they were to follow his orders to the letter. Next to the Master and Seneschal, the Draper was the highest-ranking member of the Order.[2]

Since the Draper was in a position of superiority over the knights, it was therefore necessary that he be chosen from among their ranks. As such he was awarded the benefits of his station, both within society and the Order itself. He was permitted to keep four horses, two squires and a man who was to care for the pack animals. These pack animals were used for transporting the tailoring equipment and tents used by the drapery.

Each of the lands of Tripoli and Antioch, and presumably the regions of the West, had their own Draper. The Draper stationed in the Kingdom of Jerusalem would appear to have been superior to the others for he was also permitted to have a pavilion similar to that of the Marshal of the Order.[3] The Rule mentions the office of Under-Draper. As no concrete details are provided as to his duties and powers, it is possible that, like the office of Under-Marshal, he may have been drawn from the ranks of the sergeants.[4]

Commanders

EQUIPPED with the garments given to him by the Draper, the knight would have been taken under the wing of a Commander of Knights or a Commander of Houses. The two positions, although carrying similar titles of office, seem to be based upon military and administrative roles respectively.[5] The Commander of a House was in charge of the conventual life of the knights under their charge and was to grant the new knight sleeping quarters and space to keep his horses. In the absence of a superior officer, he was to lead the chapter meeting and his orders were to be followed by the knights under his command as if the Master himself had given them.[6] To guard against any potential abuse of power, the Commander was not permitted to punish a brother for any harsh words that may have been exchanged between them without bringing it to the chapter – in such cases, the brother's words were to be as believed as those of the Commander.[7] However, the Commander was permitted to punish a knight who had disobeyed his orders without resorting to the usual disciplinary procedures. He could punish the knight by taking from him anything he pleased except his habit.

With the added responsibility of overseeing the knights in their charge, Commanders were granted a few privileges not afforded to his fellow knights. They were permitted to keep a locked bag and have two squires and one horse more than their brother knights to a maximum of four horses.[8] Additionally, he had some control over the possessions of the house. He was also permitted to distribute small sums of money to various officers as well as being granted the authority to contribute some of the house's food supplies to sister houses.[9]

The Rule makes provision for the knights to elect a commander from amongst their ranks, showing once again the democratic side of the Order:

> 'And if they have neither a commander of knights nor any other knight bailli brother, the brothers themselves by agreement may make one of the brothers in their number a commander of knights, he who seems to them most reasonable, and from whom henceforth they should obtain permission.' [10]

This same article makes provision for a group of sergeants to elect from amongst their number a brother sergeant to act as commander of the house. This provision was only acceptable in houses where there were no knights. In these houses, no member could be admitted to the Order unless a knight came from another house to conduct the ceremony of reception. Of course, his lofty position as a leader of sergeants did not allow much in the way of privileges but was allowed to have a horse like his fellow sergeants as well as a sergeant for a squire.[11] The casalier brothers, who were in charge of the Order's farms and drawn from the pool of sergeants, were even allowed to have two horses.

The Commander of Knights seems to have been most active on the field of battle where his duties are more clearly defined. He was to carry the black and white banner of the Order furled around his lance and he formed one of ten knights who accompanied the Marshal. If he were present on the field of battle, the turcopolier and all of his men were to fall under his command. The military aspect of this office and how it interchanged with the role of Commander of the House is perhaps best illustrated by the following passage of the Rule:

> 'If a brother goes to the land of Tripoli or Antioch, and he finds himself in Tyre or Tripoli, the commander of the house will give the orders. But in battle or if the alarm is raised outside the town, and they go, the commander of the house will be under the command of the commander of knights who governs those brothers.' [12]

But the chain of command did not end with these two seemingly interchangeable officers and the new knight brother soon learned that there were other members of the Order with a little more pull. These officers also carried the title of commander.

Commanders of Lands

The house that the new knight had joined was but one in a network of houses that made up a jurisdiction or baillie. Although the individual houses were presided over by a Commander of the House, the network fell under the control of a Commander of Lands. In fact, the officer was responsible for the administration of all the houses, castles and casals[13] in his jurisdiction. In the East, there were three districts: Antioch, Tripoli and Jerusalem, each with its own commander. As Jerusalem fell under Muslim control in 1187, it is clear that the Hierarchal Statutes governing this office were written before 1187.[14] Historians generally date the writing of the Hierarchal Statutes to be around the year 1165.[15]

The Commander of Lands was permitted to preside over any chapter meeting in his district, so long as the Master of the Order was not present, and whether in times of peace or times of war, all people who lived in the houses in his jurisdiction fell under his control.[16] In times of peace, the role was largely an administrative one and the Commander was to provide the castles in his jurisdiction with leather, wheat, wine, iron and steel. Additionally, it was his responsibility to ensure that sergeants were provided to guard the castle gates. Everything else that a castle might require was the providence of the castellan, the castle's equivalent to the Commander of Houses.[17] Although they were permitted to look into the treasury of any of the castles or houses in their domain, they were not allowed to take goods, etc, without the permission of the Commander of the House.[18] However, it was acceptable to take men from one house and send them to another so long as they stayed within their jurisdiction.[19] In fact, the Commander of Lands could appoint or remove a Marshal within his jurisdiction if it met with the approval of the chapter of the land and was given the same authority with respect to the region's Draper and castellans.

Like most senior officers within the Order, he was allotted a fairly large entourage. He was allowed to have four horses plus a mule or palfrey[21] as well as a sergeant with two horses and a deacon, turcopole[21] and Saracen scribe, each with their own horse. Although the Rule does not specifically mention it, it is likely he was permitted to have two squires. Additionally he was allotted one foot-soldier and a knight brother who served as a companion. The position, despite being one of power and authority, was not without a certain degree of humility. For each day that the Commander of Lands stayed in any given house, he was to feed three paupers for 'the love of God'.

The Commander of the Land of Jerusalem was senior to the Commanders of Antioch and Tripoli. As we have seen previously, until the loss of Jerusalem after the Battle of Hattin in 1187, the Holy City had served as the administrative headquarters of the Order in the Levant. As such, the Commander of the Land of Jerusalem, because of his placement in the city of Jerusalem, was an important figure for the Order's administrative tasks. His position afforded him a slightly larger entourage than his co-commanders: two foot-soldiers and a Draper were to travel with him as a companion. The Commander of the Land of Jerusalem was the Treasurer of the Convent and all belongings of the Order, whether brought from overseas or procured in the Levant, were to be brought to the treasury at Jerusalem. Here, the materials were to remain until such time as the Master had seen and counted them, after which the Treasurer would record the items in the Order's ledger books. This set of books could be viewed by any 'party of worthy men of the house'.[22]

As the port of Acre was within the Kingdom of Jerusalem, it also fell under the control of the Commander of the Land of Jerusalem, although the shipyard had its own commander who was drawn from the rank of sergeants.[23] However, the Rule makes no mention of how many ships the Order had stationed at Acre during this time.

Commander of the City of Jerusalem

Within the Land of Jerusalem was the Holy City of Jerusalem, which had its own commander. Of all the officers of the Templar hierarchy, this officer was perhaps the most interesting. For it is through him that we see that, despite many claims to the contrary, the Templars did not lose site of their original purpose and mission as they rose to wealth and power:

> 'The Commander of the City of Jerusalem should have ten knight brothers under his command to lead and guard pilgrims who come to the river Jordan; and he should carry a round tent and the piebald banner or flag, for as long as his authority lasts.'[24]

However, the Commander of the City of Jerusalem and his entourage had more to guard than pilgrims. This elite band of knights were charged with transporting and protecting the True Cross itself, arguably Christendom's most sacred holy relic which had been taken from the Orthodox Christians who held it soon after the crusaders had captured Jerusalem in 1099. When the relic was being transported, the knights were to camp as near to it as possible. At night, while ten knights were sleeping, two would keep watch in order to guard it.

What is puzzling about modern claims that the Templars found the Ark of the Covenant or mummified body parts of Jesus Christ is that one would have thought that they would be put on prominent display to further promote the Order. Being in charge of protecting the True Cross itself did the Order no harm, and the position of Commander of the City of Jerusalem was created, in part, to serve the task. The

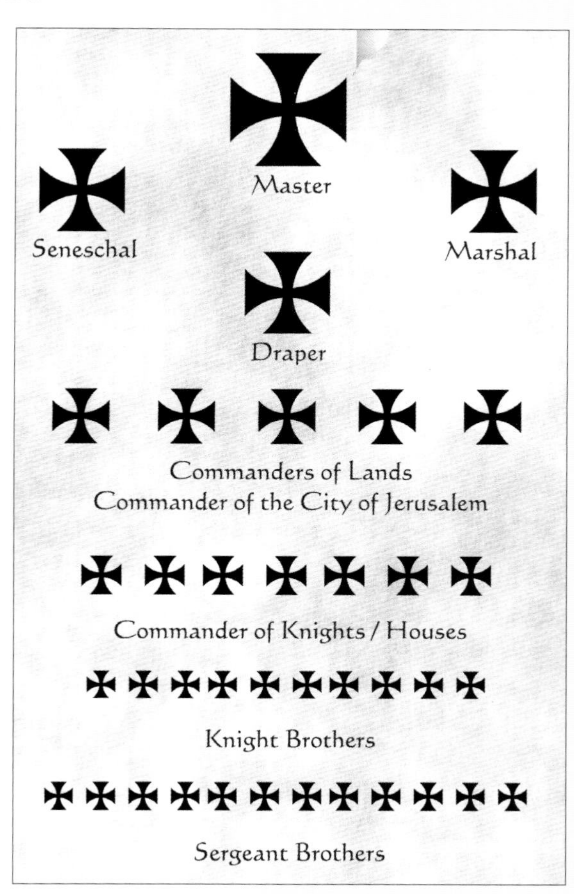

Diagram showing the approximate hierarchy of the Knights Templar. *Author*

special status of this commander is indicated by the fact that, like the commanders of much larger jurisdictions, he was granted a large entourage to accompany him and was allowed to keep half of the spoils of war taken beyond the river Jordan.[25] Additionally, he was in command of secular knights stationed at Jerusalem who had joined the order for set periods of time.

It is hard to imagine how other members of the Order viewed the commander and his elite band of knights. But given their sacred mission, the new knight must have looked up to them in awe, perhaps hoping one day to be considered worthy enough to be admitted to their number. But there were other positions of importance within the Order to which the new knight could aspire. And like the protectors of the True Cross they, too, were stationed at Jerusalem.

The True Cross was discovered in Jerusalem by Emperor Constantine's mother Helena. After the Christians captured the city in 1099 they took possession of the relic after torturing the Byzantine Christians to disclose where they had hid it. The object was carried into battle until it was lost in 1187 after the Battle of Hattin. *ClipArt.com*

Marshal

THE first of these was the Marshal. Although each of the Lands could have its own Marshal, this officer was their superior and is referred to in the Hierarchal Statutes as the Marshal of the Convent of the Temple. Some authors have suggested that the Marshal was the second highest-ranking officer in the Templar hierarchy.[26] However, the Rule lists him third but latterly indicates that the Draper was only subservient to the Master and Seneschal, which adds to the confusion in trying to create an accurate pyramid of Templar authority. This seemingly contradictory state of affairs is probably due to the dual role of the Order – militant and administrative – and with respect to the militant side of the Order, the Marshal stationed at Jerusalem certainly would be second in command, for his position is related primarily to the art of war.

The Marshal of the convent had a fair degree of autonomy, for if he happened to be in the Lands of Tripoli or Antioch, the Commander could offer him the marshalcy of the land; however, whether or not he accepted the offer was entirely up to him.[27]

Like other officers, the Marshal was granted an entourage to accompany him, but it was less substantial than other senior officers in the Order, its simplicity reflecting his military role. He was allowed four horses plus a fine turcoman or riding horse. To care for the horses as well as his other needs, he was allowed to have two squires. A sergeant and turcopole, each with their own horse, were also part of his entourage. Although he was equipped as any other knight under his command, he was entitled to a pavilion for himself as well as a tent for his squires.[28]

Whereas the Commander of the Land of Jerusalem was the treasurer and held the purse strings of the Order, the Marshal held the lock and key to the armoury, at least figuratively. Whether the weapons in the Order's possession were bought, gifted or captured in war, they fell under his care and command.[29]

Seneschal

BY contrast, the powers of the Seneschal are clearer in the Templar hierarchy as he was subservient only to the Master of the Order.

The position of Seneschal was dropped at the end of the twelfth century and replaced by the office of Grand Commander, which encompassed some of the duties of the previous office.[30] To add to the confusion that is the Templar hierarchy, there was a position in place with the same name when the Hierarchal Statutes were written; however, this Grand Commander was in charge of the election of the Grand Master as we will see in due course.

For a man who was clearly second in command, the Rule does not say a great deal about the office of Seneschal. There is a good reason for this. As the Seneschal was the Master's right-hand man and took on his duties when the Master was not present, they are virtually the same. In fact, the Seneschal was required to carry the same seal or bolle as the Master in order to fulfil those responsibilities.[31] The seal was similar to those used by officials of other religious Orders in that it validated the authenticity of documents and directives of the Order. The great seal used by the Master and Seneschal was double-sided depicting the symbolic two knights on a single mount on the front and the dome of the Holy Sepulchre on the reverse.[32]

An impressive entourage accompanied the Seneschal that exceeded those of other officers apart from the Master of the Temple. In addition to four horses and a palfrey, the Seneschal had two squires and a sergeant with two horses. His companion was drawn from the rank of knight with four horses and two squires of his own. Additionally, the Seneschal travelled with a deacon scribe who would help him observe the religious offices he was required to attend each day. A Saracen scribe, turcopole and two foot soldiers also travelled as part of the entourage.

When the company travelled in lands where the Master was not present, the Seneschal was to survey the situation, taking from them what he needed and transferring assets and manpower from one house to another in order to assist in balancing the needs of the houses.[33]

Master

While the Seneschal may have been the administrative head of the Order and the Marshal of the Convent the military head of the same, the Master was the overall head of the Order. The Master oversaw the triune aspects of the Templars: militant, administrative and spiritual. Although commonly referred to as the Grand Master, the Rule simply refers to him as Master.

As one would expect from the top man in the Templar hierarchy, the Master travelled with the largest entourage. Like many officers beneath him, he was allotted four horses plus a turcoman, but it is here where the similarities end. He was to travel with a clerk who was allotted three horses, a sergeant with two horses as well as a Saracen scribe and turcopole, each with their own horse. Additionally, the Master had his own cook, farrier and a valet, the latter of which was to carry his shield and lance. The valet must have been considered an important position, for the Master was permitted to make him a knight after he had served him well for a period of time. In addition to being accompanied by two sergeants, the Master was to have two knights to act as companions, but these knights were to be of such character that they would be included in all council meetings.[34] If one of the companions died, the Master was permitted to take any item of equipment he desired, but the remainder was to be turned over to the Marshal of the Convent.

Like the Commanders of Lands, he was entitled to a lock box for his personal effects, but was barred from holding the key to the treasury.[35] However, this did not mean he did not have some control over the contents of that treasury. The Master was permitted to lend with permission up to 1000 bezants, and if he were going to Antioch or Tripoli, he could withdraw 3000 bezants or more if he needed it to help the houses there. When assets came in from overseas, they were to be placed in the treasury but could not be distributed in any fashion by the Treasurer until the Master had seen and counted them. The same situation applied with respect to horses under the care of the Marshal. In fact, the Master could take any horse from a brother as he pleased and give it to any other, including a secular man if he thought the gift would benefit the house.[36]

Although the Master was the most powerful man in the Order, he was not without limitations. He was not allowed to give or sell land, nor was he allowed to take castles in the border regions, or march lands as they are referred to in the Rule. The reason for this was quite practical because outlying regions were difficult to defend and subject to frequent attack, something the Order would have been painfully aware after the fall of Edessa in 1144. Preserving and defending the Order's land holdings was of great importance and the Master was not permitted to start a war or make a truce on any land or castle that fell under the Order's seigniory without first consulting with the convent.[37]

But just as the position was not without limitations, it was also not without a certain degree of humility. The Master's old clothing was regularly given to lepers, and on Maundy Thursday,[38] he was to wash the feet of thirteen paupers and give to them shoes, clothing, two loaves of bread and two deniers. This act of humility was to symbolise the humility of Jesus Christ who had humbled himself in a similar fashion before his disciples and must have made an impression upon the officers, knights and sergeants under his command.

But this humility was to be expected. The Master was unquestionably a frontline man, and when present, led his brethren in matters of prayer, discipline and battle.

This popular illustration of three Templars is intended to show the dual aspect of the Order as warriors and monks. The cross is a Maltese cross, which was not used by the Order. ***ClipArt.com***

Election of the Master

Unlike other officers in the Templar hierarchy, the Master was elected for life and the election began with the death or departure of the previous Master of the Order. Although several of the Masters who led the Order of the Temple throughout its two hundred years of existence died in battle, there were two who left the Order for other reasons. In 1152, Everard des Barres resigned from his post and joined the Cistercian Order, and in 1171, Philip de Milly resigned and returned to secular life.[39]

After the death of the Master, a funeral event was held that was impressive in scale and not affordable to any other member of the Order. Many candles were lit in the Master's memory and his body was buried with the greatest of honour. Over the week that followed his death, each brother was to say two hundred paternosters in addition to the vast number they were required to recite each day, and the Order was to feed one hundred paupers dinner and supper for the sake of their fallen Master's soul. Although his equipment was to be distributed in the same fashion as any other deceased brother, the Master's clothing was to be donated to lepers, as was the custom with his old garments when he was alive.[40]

If the Master died in the Land of Jerusalem and the Marshal of the Convent was present at the time, the Marshal immediately took over for the Master.[41] This seems to indicate that, although the Seneschal was the second in command – at least administratively – the main priority of the Order upon the Master's death was preserving the Order's militant aspect. As several Masters died in battle, the Marshal would be the logical man to take over on the Master's death.

The Marshal's first duty as temporary head of the Order was to summon all key officers from Outremer to attend chapter, where a Grand Commander would be elected to replace the Marshal as head of the Order. Once a Grand Commander had been elected by either common consent or majority vote, he would set a date with the Commanders of the Lands for the election of the new Master. However, until that time, the Grand Commander fulfilled the duties of Master and carried the seal of the Order.[42]

Once the designated day arrived, the electoral process began as soon as the brethren had attended Matins. The Grand Commander was to summon the majority of the worthy men of the house to a chapter meeting where two or three of the Order's most worthy members would be put forth as candidates for the position of Commander of the Election. These brethren, chosen for their merit and good reputation, would be sent from the chapter so that those who remained could vote on which brother was most worthy of the honour. Once the council had made their decision, the Commander of the Election was assigned another knight to serve as a companion.[43]

While the other brethren returned to their beds until prime, the two brethren appointed to head the election were to remain in the chapel to pray for guidance in the task that lay before them. They were not to speak to any brother, nor was any brother to speak to them. In fact, they could only speak to each other if it pertained to the decisions they were to make with respect to the election. The election would reconvene after sext with the two brethren being cautioned by the Grand Commander as to the importance of choosing wisely those who would assist them in the election. The formula for choosing the thirteen Templars who would be given power to elect a new Master is laid out in the Rule and once again shows an inherent democracy present in the management of the Order:

> 'And these two brothers should choose another two brothers so that they are four. And these four brothers should choose another two brothers so that they are six. And these six brothers should choose another two brothers so that they are eight. And these eight brothers should choose another two brothers so that they are ten. And these ten brothers should choose and other two brothers so that they are twelve, in honour of the twelve apostles and the twelve brothers should elect together a chaplain brother to take the place of Jesus Christ; he should endeavour to keep the brothers in peace and in harmony: and they will be thirteen brothers. And of these thirteen, eight should be knight brothers, four sergeant brothers and the chaplain brother. And these thirteen brother electors should be as given above for the Commander of the election, from divers nations and countries, in order to keep peace in the house.'[44]

When the thirteen electors had been chosen, they returned to the chapter as a group. Here they asked the brethren present to pray to God on their behalf, and in response, the brethren would throw themselves on to the ground in prayer. This deviation from the normal prayer routine of the Order shows the importance placed on electing a new Master, for the head of the Order was not merely their military commander, but also their spiritual leader, and as such must be clearly chosen by God. With the assurance that God would assist them in their decision, the electors assembled elsewhere to hold the election.

Although preference was given to those brethren in the East, it was possible to elect a Master from the West if the electors felt that he was the brother most suited for the post. Additionally, tenure in the Order did not seem to be of great importance in electing a new Master, for both Robert de Sablé and Philip de Milly were elected to the helm of the Order after a relatively short period of service. De Milly, who had joined the Order between 1164 and 1165, was elected Master in 1169 after having served the Order for only four years. However, as we have seen with Philip de Milly, his Mastership would be equally brief as he resigned from his post after just two years, returning to the secular life he once enjoyed. After naming and discussing candidates for the position of Master, the electors would take a vote. In the event that the electors were split into different camps of opinion, the Commander of the Election would return to the chapter to ask for further prayers from the brethren.

When the majority had decided on the next Master, the Commander of the Election would go before the chapter and inform them of the electors' decision, asking their assent in the decision. Once the chapter had responded, the chief elector would ask the brethren if they promised to obey the chosen Master for the rest of their lives. This was followed by the Grand Commander, who until this point had been the temporary head of the Order, swearing to adhere to the decisions made, effectively relinquishing his powers of office to the duly elected leader of the Order.

Once the new Master had been officially proclaimed, the election concluded with a ritualistic ceremony, which dedicated the new leader to God's service:

> 'And the brothers should immediately rise and take the Master with great devotion and great joy, and carry him in their arms to the chapel, and offer him to God before the altar, whom He has provided for the governance of the house; and he should be kneeling in front of the altar while prayers are said to God for him.'[45]

Having been duly elected and ceremonially dedicated to God, the new Master was now prepared to take on his lifelong role as the spiritual, administrative and military head of his Order. As the Master was always based in the East (at Jerusalem until 1187, at Acre from 1191 to 1291 and on the island of Cyprus thereafter), it would have been far too easy to be focused purely on the military needs of the order. If not already aware of the fact, he would soon learn that in order for his Order to thrive and grow, he must not neglect the non-military work of the Order. As important as the knights and sergeants were in waging war in the East, none of the Order's military victories would be possible without the backbreaking efforts of the many serving brethren who toiled away in the fields of the West. It was these unsung members of the Order who kept the war machine turning and to whom much of the credit for the Templars' rise to power is truly owed.

References for chapter 8

1 Upton-Ward, *The Rule of the Templars*. p. 53 § 138.

2 Ibid. p. 51 § 130.

3 Ibid. p. 52 § 131.

4 Bruno, Salvatore, *Templar Organization: The Management of Warrior Monasticism*. p. 110.

5 Ibid. p. 127.

6 Upton-Ward, op. cit. p. 104 § 382.

7 Ibid. p. 52 § 134.

8 Ibid. p. 52 § 132. The Rule allows for the Commander of Houses to have four horses if the brethren had three, however, if the brethren had two horses, he was permitted to have three.

9 Ibid. p. 52 § 132-133.

10 Ibid. p. 92 § 328. Additionally § 575 of the Rule makes further provision for knights to elect from amongst themselves a commander if they enter a house, which has none and seems in danger from the Saracens.

11 Ibid. p. 62 § 180.

12 Ibid. p. 162 § 633.

13 The *casal* was a village or farm owned by the Order, which was attached to and under the control of an individual house or castle.

14 This is not meant to imply that prior to Zengi's capture of Edessa in 1144 that the Templars had properties in the County of Edessa, rather that had the county not have been captured, it is probable that the Order would have established some base of operations there by the time of the writing of the Rule.

15 Upton-Ward, op. cit. p. 13.

16 Ibid. p. 50 § 125.

17 Ibid. p. 50 § 126.

18 Ibid. p. 51 § 129.

19 Ibid. p. 49 § 119.

20 The palfrey is a type of horse rather than a specific breed. The palfrey was a light horse used for riding as opposed to a destrier, which was a heavy war horse used in a cavalry charge.

21 Turcopoles were mercenary cavalrymen recruited in the east on a required basis. They rode light horses and fought in the Eastern style.

22 Upton-Ward, op. cit. p. 47 § 111.

23 Ibid p. 49 § 119.

24 Ibid p. 49 § 121.

25 Ibid p. 50 § 123. The rest was to be turned over to the Commander of the Land of Jerusalem. The Jordan River had long been a place of Christian pilgrimage and it was while travelling to this sacred destination that 700 pilgrims were accosted at Easter, 1119. 300 were murdered and another 60 were carried off as slaves.

26 Bruno, op. cit. p. 101.

27 Ibid. p. 45 § 104.

28 Ibid p. 44 § 101.

29 Ibid p. 45 § 102. The exceptions to this rule were crossbows, which were to be given to the Commander of Lands, and Turkish arms, which were to be given to the brother craftsmen sergeants.

30 Nicholson, Helen, *The Knights Templar: A New History*. p. 117.

31 Upton-Ward, op. cit. p. 44 § 99.

32 Nicholson op. cit. p. 114.

33 Upton-Ward, op. cit. p. 44 § 100.

34 Ibid. p. 39 § 77-79.

35 Ibid. p. 40 § 81.

36 Ibid. p. 40 § 84.

37 Ibid. p. 40 § 85.

38 Maundy Thursday is also referred to as Holy Thursday in the Christian Calendar and as Great Thursday in the Eastern and Orthodox Churches. It is the Thursday before Easter and one of several feast days observed by the Templar Rule. It is said to derive from the first word in the Latin version of John 13:34, 'Mandatum novum do vobis ut diligatis invicem sicut dilexi vos' – 'A new commandment I give unto you, that you love one another as I have loved you.'

39 Nicholson, op. cit. p. 114 – Barber, Malcolm, *The New Knighthood*. p. 186. Barber lists Philip of Nablus, while Nicholson refers to the Master as Philip des Milly. They were the same Master. Philip des Milly was the Lord of Nablus.

40 Upton-Ward, op. cit. p. 67 § 199.

41 Ibid. p. 67 § 198.

42 Ibid. p. 68 § 203.

43 Ibid. p. 68 § 206-207.

44 Ibid. p. 69-70 § 211.

45 Ibid. p. 71 § 211.

Fields and Fortunes

'Every best gift and every perfect gift is from above, coming down from the Father of lights, with whom there is no change nor shadow of alteration.'

James 1:17 – Opening lines of the bull *Omne datum optimum*

Temple Bruer in Lincolnshire from a nineteenth-century engraving.
Author's collection

As the Templars gathered in the chapel on 24 May 1136, they did so with heavy hearts for Hugues de Payens, the first Master of the Order, had died in Jerusalem at the age of 66. For sixteen years, de Payens had faithfully served his Order as the spiritual, administrative and military leader, and during that time, had seen his beloved Templars evolve from an idea to reality. Under his leadership, the Templar organisation began to spread outwards from the Temple Mount as commoner and king alike gave grants of land and gifts of all kinds to the Order. While there can be no argument that Hugues had laid a firm foundation for the Order, it would be his successor, Robert de Craon, who would secure additional privileges for the Templars that Hugues could have only dreamed of.

The Second Master

Robert de Craon was the third son of Renaud de Craon and Ennoguen de Vitre and, as such, was born into the noble family of the Lords of Craon in Anjou. Like many early members of the Order, little is known of his life and what is known seems open to dispute among historians. Some claim that Robert was married and had, like his predecessor, joined the Order after the death of his wife, while others suggest that he did so after breaking his engagement with the daughter of Jourdain de Chabanais.[1] Regardless of de Craon's marital status before becoming a Templar, it is known that he entered the Order sometime during the 1120s; however, precisely when is a matter of conflicting accounts. Some historians are of the opinion that de Craon may have been one of the founding members while others place his joining closer to the Council of Troyes. Chief among those who hold to the latter theory is Malcolm Barber who cites a charter from Fulk of Anjou dated 22 September 1127. In this charter de Craon is listed as a witness, albeit under the name Robertus Burgundio, a name he was certainly known by. What is most interesting about the charter is that de Craon is referred to as 'miles Sancti Stephani Jerusalem', which would connect him with St Stephen's Church located near the Damascus Gate just outside the city of Jerusalem.[2] If de Craon was not a Templar in 1127 as the charter would seem to suggest, he certainly was by 1130, for by this time he had become Seneschal, placing him as the number two man within the Order – at least administratively.[3]

While de Craon's early involvement with the Templars may be open to question, his affiliation with Fulk of Anjou seems somewhat clearer, for as early as 1113, de Craon is seen acting on Fulk's behalf and the charter of 1127 is but one example of this.[4] As we looked at in an earlier chapter, the Templars had many friends in high places and Fulk of Anjou was certainly one of them. He had joined the Order as an associate member in 1120 while on pilgrimage to the East and paid the Order an annual allowance after his return to the West. Fulk continued to support the Order when he took up permanent residency in the East following his marriage to Baldwin II's daughter, Melisende.

As King of Jerusalem from 1131, Fulk was in a position to exert his influence on matters pertaining to his kingdom and often filled important positions with men he could trust.[5] Given his connections to de Craon and the Temple, it is not inconceivable to suggest that Fulk may have had a hand in a fellow Angevin being elected to the post of Master of the Temple. But even if de Craon's election was due, in some small part, to the political influence of King Fulk, the new Master was certainly not without merit. De Craon is remembered by history as an effective administrator, a skill he would have honed during his six years as the Order's Seneschal. Even William of Tyre, who was often critical of the Templars, spoke highly of de Craon, referring to him as a pious man, an excellent knight and a man who was noble in both the flesh and his personal conduct.[6]

Among de Craon's early administrative accomplishments was having the Rule translated from Latin to French, so as to make it more serviceable to the Order's use. It is believed that de Craon authorised this translation in 1139[7] and some historians are of the belief that the hierarchal statutes of the Order were also added around that time.[8] During de Craon's administration, the Templars seemed to have widened their recruiting nets: lowering membership standards by removing the probationary period for new members and by seeking out excommunicated knights as potential recruits.[9] However, these alterations to the Rule may have simply been a matter of necessity. The need for fighting men in the East continued, and as the Order continued to receive grants of land in the West, it became increasingly important to have the manpower to manage them.

While de Craon's modifications to the original Latin Rule may have played an important role in the Order's internal organisational structure, another document penned in 1139 would prove to be of incredible importance with respect to how the Order dealt with the outside world. This document, a bull issued by Pope Innocent II, was entitled 'Omne datum optimum' (every best gift) and gave the Templars powers and privileges that would secure the Order's autonomy. However, before examining this document, it is important to understand more on the man who wrote it and the chain of events that led to its creation.

Pope and Anti-Pope

Pope Innocent II was born Gregorio Papareschi, a member of the nobly born Guidoni clan. He was made a cardinal during the pontificate of Paschal II and went into exile with Paschal's successor Gelasius II, when the emperor installed his own anti-pope in Gelasius's place. It would not be the only period of exile Papareschi would experience during his lifetime. When Honorius II died on 14 February 1130, a number of cardinals arranged for a secret funeral and elected Papareschi as his successor the next morning. This seemingly underhanded move did not meet with the approval of the other cardinals and they moved to elect Papareschi's rival, Pietro Pierleone, as pope. Two weeks later, the two popes were consecrated on the same day: Papareschi, who took the name Innocent II at Santa Maria Nuova, and Pierleone, who took the name Anacletus II at St Peter's.[10]

Like Pope Urban II who had launched the First Crusade in 1095, Innocent II would soon find himself looking at Rome from the outside. The powerful Frangipani family who had lent support to Urban during his exile, sided with Anacletus and that was sufficient to ensure that Innocent would have to fight for his papal position. With the anti-pope Anacletus installed in Rome, Innocent removed himself from the city travelling to Pisa, then to Genoa and ultimately on to France. While in France, Innocent found many supporters, among them Louis VI, Abbot Sugar and Bernard of Clairvaux. In fact, through their united support, France swore its allegiance to Innocent II at Clermont, 35 years to the month after Pope Urban II had given his crusade speech at the conclusion of the Council held there. But France was not the only country to back the exiled pope. In the spring of the following year, King Lothair III arranged for a synod at Würzburg at which the German bishops swore their allegiance to Innocent.

This loyalty was repaid in part when Innocent crowned Lothair and his queen at Easter in 1131.[11] When King Louis's eldest son Philip died, Innocent went to Rheims to anoint Louis's younger son as heir to the throne, a position he would take after the death of King Louis VI in 1137. However, these papal honours were granted by a pope who was in exile. Although Innocent was able to return to Rome in 1133 in order to perform the imperial coronation on King Lothair, his stay in the city would not be long. When the emperor and his troops returned to Germany the following year, it became necessary for Innocent to retire, since he no longer had the military protection necessary to remain safely in Rome. For the next several years, he begged Lothair to liberate Rome so that he may take his rightful place, and in 1137, the emperor finally took action securing part of the city. However, Anacletus was not prepared to vacate the throne of St Peter and maintained enough control to prevent Innocent from achieving his goal.

Even when Anacletus died on 25 January 1138, his supporters moved quickly to elect a replacement, just as the cardinal-bishops had done when they elected Innocent eight years earlier. Their choice was Gregory Cardinal Conti who took the name Victor IV. But where Lothair had failed in removing an anti-pope by military force, another important member of Western Christendom was able to achieve the purpose by pure persuasion. Less than two weeks after he had been elected pope, Bernard of Clairvaux had exerted enough influence on Victor to convince him to abdicate in favour of Innocent II.[12]

Throughout the eight-year schism, Innocent had enjoyed the strong support of Bernard and the French clergy and it is doubtful that he ever forgot the loyalty shown to him during his struggles. The Templars, because of their association with Bernard, were doubtlessly considered a part of this loyalty. Innocent began to bestow his favour upon the Order as early as 1135 when, at the Council of Pisa, he granted the Order an annual allowance of an ounce of gold – an act of charity that was followed in lesser degree by his chancellor, the archbishops, bishops and the abbots who were loyal to him.[13] Of course, being exiled from Rome, the offering of monetary support to the Templars was the best the pope could do at the time. Innocent quickly made up for it, upon gaining control of Rome, by penning *Omne datum optimum*.

Every Best Gift

What is interesting about *Omne datum Optimum* – which some historians have referred to as the Magna Carta of the Knights Templar[14] – is that it was dated 29 March 1139, almost a full week before Innocent II convened the Second Lateran Council to sort out the problems caused by the schism. While this in no way proves that *Omne Datum Optimum* was repayment to Bernard and the Templars for earlier considerations, it does show that granting the Templars papal support was important enough not to be brushed of by other pressing Church matters. Indeed, as the prelude to the bull shows, Innocent II considered the Order to be of great importance to Christendom and the bull echoes the flowery language of Bernard's earlier letter praising the new knighthood:

> 'For by nature you were children of wrath, given up to the pleasure of the world, but now through the inspiration of grace you have become receptive to the message of the gospel and, having left behind worldly pomps and your own possessions and also the broad way that leadeth to death, you have humbly chosen the hard road that leadeth to life; and to prove it you have most contentiously sworn on your breasts the sign of the living cross, because you are especially reckoned to be members of the knighthood of God. In addition to this, like true Israelites and warriors most versed in holy battle, on fire with the flame of true charity, you carry out in deeds the word of the gospel in which it is said: Greater love than this no man hath, that a man may lay down his life for his friends. And, following the command of the chief shepherd, you are not at all afraid to lay down your lives for your brothers and to defend them from the pagans's invasions and, as you are known by name to be Knights of the Temple, you have been established by the Lord as defenders of the Church and assailants of the enemies of Christ.'[15]

Pope Innocent II was the author of *Omne datum optimum*, which granted the Templars special privileges.

As described in an earlier chapter, de Payens's Templars met with harsh opposition from some members of the clergy who could not understand the concept of an Order of religious men who took up arms against the infidels. This opposition was obviously strong enough to warrant a letter from Hugh the Sinner, written to bolster the Order's declining morale. However, *Omne datum optimum* effectively removed any doubts about the dual nature of the Order that might remain in the eyes of Christendom. For now the Templars had officially been taken under the wing of the very Church and faith they had vowed to defend. As such, they were an army of God under the direct authority of His earthly spokesman, the pope. Of course, an Order of such religious importance within the Church should be entitled to favours from the same and that is precisely what *Omne datum optimum* authorised.

Henceforth the Templars were answerable only to the Master of the Order and he was answerable only to the Pope. The Order was permitted to elect its Master from among the members without any influence from outside forces, and only the Master and the chapter were permitted to alter the customs and observances of the Order in any way. The brethren were to give no oath of loyalty to anyone outside the Temple and were required to remain members of the Order until their deaths. They were forbidden to join another Order or to return to secular life.[16] This did not apply to Templars who were expelled from the Order who were required to

The wheat barn at Temple Cressing in Essex is one of two surviving barns originally constructed by the Templars. This barn was constructed in the mid-thirteen century.
Mira Vogel

join stricter Orders. Certainly there were exceptions such as that of Philip de Milly who rejoined secular life after abdicating as Master of the Temple in 1171. Of course, these aspects of the bull were not much different than what had already been required of the Templars by their Rule, but Innocent's bull legitimised the practices by giving them the papal seal of approval.

One important area where the bull expands the Templars' privileges is with respect to the admission of priests into the Order. *Omne datum optimum* allowed the Order, for the first time, to have its own chaplains provided they obtained permission from the priests' bishops. However, this permission seems to have been nothing more than a courtesy gesture to the bishops, for if they refused the bull stated that the pope would overrule them. Once the priest had served the Order for a period of one year, he could be made a member of the Order by taking the vows of the Order and swearing loyalty to the Master.[17] In addition to making allowances for the Templars to have their own clergy, *Omne datum optimum* also granted the Order the right to construct their own oratories or private chapels where they could conduct their religious services unhindered by those outside the Order. On the grounds of these chapels, the Order was also permitted to bury its dead.

But the greatest gift of *Omne datum optimum* was the provision that excluded the Order from having to pay tithes to the Church – previously, the Order had been obligated to give the Church one tenth of all produce harvested from its lands. While the exclusion of paying tithes would prove to be of great economic benefit to the Order, it was but one half of the benefit, for the Order was now permitted to collect tithes from the laity or the clergy providing the bishops of the area approved.[18]

Give Me Land, Lots of Land

With the new privileges bestowed upon the Order by Innocent's bull, the Templars became a part of the feudal society that they had sought to leave. Instead of occupying land by tenure, as many of them had done before joining the Order, they now occupied their lands by possession, with the added benefit of a tax-free status. Sergeants, who in their secular lives may have broken their backs for their landlords with little or no personal benefit, now broke their backs for the common good of the brotherhood. In many cases, a sergeant could find himself in charge of a Templar property, the serving brethren and craftsman brethren who worked the lands it contained.

Important local lords and prelates, many who had a sincere interest in the Order's crusading efforts, often donated these lands that fell under Templar control. In some cases, these patrons joined the Order in the East as associate members and would be entitled to burial in a Templar cemetery.[19] But even those patrons who remained in the West were entitled to privileges from their donations to the Order. In exchange for the granting of land, the benefactor would be ensured that the Order would pray for them while they were living or dead. While this would hardly be an inducement to give land in modern times, it was highly regarded during medieval times and the Templars kept obituary rolls of those to whom prayers should be given.[20]

Once the Templars had accepted a piece of land, they would work the land as quickly as possible so as to maximise its economic benefit. Of course, the land grants were scattered throughout the territories, but the Order tried to build a network that linked the properties together where possible. Often smaller Templar holdings would be grouped around the largest preceptory in the area. For example, Richerenches was a preceptory located in south-east France in the Vaucluse region, which had eight smaller houses dependant on it. The main preceptory had between ten and twenty Templars in residence, while the smaller houses had two or three brethren, most likely sergeants, stationed at each. Similarly Mas-Deu in Roussillon had seven dependent houses under its control.[21] The arrangement was an effective one whereby the larger house could provide communal support to the smaller houses and the Order's resources such as men, horses and supplies could be shared between the houses in the network.

In areas where the Order had a number of houses, it was more efficient to cultivate the land themselves; however, in areas where they had small or few holdings, it made practical sense to let the land

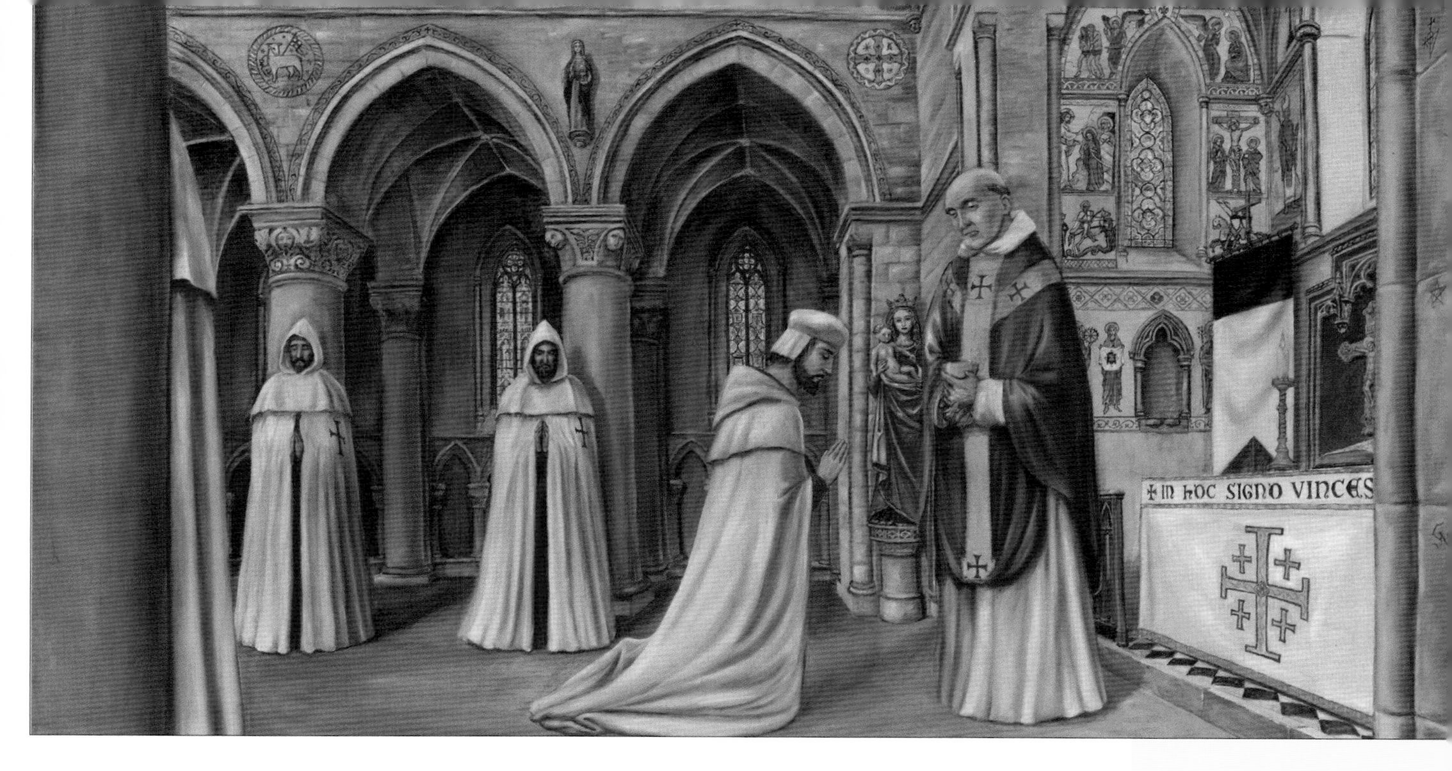

A Templar kneels before a priest in this modern interpretation of the Templars' religious observances.
Gordon Napier

and take a cut of the crop from their tenant. This arrangement was not only beneficial to the tenant but of great advantage to the Order who were able to amass large amounts of grain from the cumulative tithes of their outlying lands. However, even in areas where the Order had large quantities of land, small plots were often rented to tenants.

Temple Cressing in Essex, which had 85 tenants working small plots of land by 1185,[22] provides us with the finest surviving example of the shear magnitude of Templar farming. Eustace III, the count of Bolougne, who participated in the First Crusade alongside his relatives Godfrey de Bouillon and Baldwin of Bolougne, was the original owner of the manor of Cressing. Although Eustace decided to return to the West following the victory at Jerusalem, he was offered the Kingdom of Jerusalem upon the death of Baldwin I in 1118. However, by the time Eustace arrived in Apulia, he had received word that the throne had been occupied by his cousin Baldwin of Le Bourg, who was crowned King Baldwin II.

Upon Eustace's death, Cressing fell into the hands of his only daughter Matilda who was married to King Stephen of England.[23] King Stephen was the son of Stephen, Count of Blois, who had fled the city of Antioch just before the crusaders captured it in 1098. Matilda donated the manor to the Knights Templar in 1137 for the benefit of her father's soul [24] and the donation of Cressing is the first recorded Templar property outside of London,[25] the first being the Order's original headquarters at Holden. This grant was expanded a decade later when King Stephen added the neighbouring town of Witham making the donation one of the largest in England, measuring approximately 566 hectares (1,400 acres).[26]

Cressing is home to two surviving grain barns believed to have been built by the Order around 1206 and 1256 respectively.[27] The barley barn, which was constructed first, measures 36 metres in length and almost 14 metres in width, scaling to a height of just over 11 metres. Built fifty years later, the wheat barn measures 40 metres in length, 12 metres in width and rises to 11 metres. Records dating back to the Templars' suppression show the scale to which the property was being farmed. In addition to a substantial livestock population consisting of more than 700 animals, the property was reported to consist of 601 arable acres of which 121 were for growing beans, peas and drage (a course type of barley). A further 73 acres were sown with oats and 252 for growing wheat.[28]

As was explained earlier, a good deal of the farmland at Cressing was let out to tenants who rendered unto the Order set fees and services for the privilege of working the land. We are fortunate to have one extant example of the tenant arrangement from Cressing to provide an idea of how the Templars dealt with tenants:

> 'The heir of Walter Gardiner holds half a virgate of land in Cressing and will give two wardpennies at Hockday and will be quit of one work. At the feast of St Michael [29 September] he will give 2d., and two and a half pence of landgavel [land rent], and at Christmas he will give a halfpenny and at

Above left: **Despite popular opinion, not all Templar churches were round nor were all round churches Templar. The Church of the Holy Sepulchre at Cambridge is a perfect example of a round church that did not belong to the Templars. It was built by the confraternity of the Holy Sepulchre between 1114 and 1130.** *istockPhoto.com*

Above right: **The Templar Church in London, shown in this photo taken before the Second World War when the church was heavily damaged by German bombs, is an example of a round church built by the Order. The twelfth century pepperpot roof was not replaced in the post war resoration.** *ClipArt.com*

Easter a quarter ad savonem and on the Eve of the Lord's Ascension he will give one round measure of oats, which is called a mina, and two hens; and he will plough three acres of the winter crop and three acres of the summer sowing and for ploughing those acres he will have two loaves and four salt herrings or other food, and in exchange for the said ploughing he will be quit of six works at ploughing time and he will do ten works each month, whenever the commander wishes ... He ought to perform these customs from the feast of St Michael until the feast of St. Peter in chains [1 August] and from the feast of St Peter to the feast of St Michael, seven works each fortnight.'[29]

Wherever the Order was involved with grain crops, it required mills to process the harvest and Cressing was no exception – an inventory from 1308 shows that the Order had a windmill and watermill on the estate.[30] Although it is not known when the Cressing mills were constructed, by the time the Order was increasing its landholdings in the twelfth century, mills were few in number. Mills were difficult to maintain and few had the financial resources to construct them whereas the Templars and Hospitallers had the means to do so. The ancillary benefit of operating mills was that the military Orders could derive additional revenues by processing crops harvested by their tenants and other farmers in the area.

Occasionally, the Templars and Hospitallers operated mills near to one another, which could lead to conflict between the Orders. One such dispute took place at Acre in 1235 where the Templars and Hospitallers both operated mills on the River Belus. The Hospitallers mill was upstream from the Templars' and whenever the Templars would back the water to power their mill, it would flood the Hospitallers' fields. This caused the Hospitallers to hold back the flow of water altogether, which left little more than a trickle downstream that rendered the Templars' mill useless.[31] The dispute went on for some time to be settled in the papal court where the Master of the Temple and the Hospital reached an agreement.

The Templars were not always donated land that was suitable to grow crops. It was often the case that land, which was too difficult for the owner to cultivate, was handed over to the Order who had the means and men to work the land. An increasing number of properties donated to the Order required tremendous amounts of manpower to make them ready for farming and Temple Garway in Herefordshire on the Welsh border is one such example. This property, donated to the Order by Henry II, saw the Templars clearing more than 800 hectares of royal forest – a practice that would usually carry heavy fines. However, in the case of Garway, Henry pardoned the Templars with a charter granting them additional assart privileges in Shropshire, Oxfordshire, Northamptonshire, Bedfordshire and Huntingdonshire, totalling an additional 66 hectares of forest.[32]

Like the Cistercians, the Templars became adept at cultivating marginal land, and even where the land was not particularly suitable for crops, they would make the best use of it. One such property was Temple Bruer in Lincolnshire, which was given to the Order in the mid-twelfth century by William of

Ashby.[33] Located on a barren heath, the property was best suited for grazing and by the mid-thirteenth century, the Order had a flock of approximately 400 sheep.[34] Although the Templars were not as active in sheep raising as their Cistercian cousins, the Order did maintain substantial flocks in the Iberian Peninsula and in Yorkshire, England. In England, the Order established two water-powered fulling mills: one in the northeast at Newsham in Yorkshire and a second in the southwest at Barton on Windrush in Gloucestershire.[35] Fulling mills, which were used for manufacturing cloth, were among the first processes to be mechanised and, like the grain mills operated by the Order near their agricultural operations, were certainly used to full revenue earning potential.

As it expanded, the Order became particularly adept at involving themselves in every aspect of the process from field to fair. They grew the crops on their land, processed the crops at their mills and transported the grain with their own wagons or those of their tenants to the trade fairs and markets where they could be converted to cash. No matter what piece of land that they were given, the Templars would ensure that they extracted every ounce of revenue that they could from it. As the Order expanded throughout the twelfth century, the Templars engaged it a wide variety of economic activities including mining, smelting, glass manufacturing and salt production.[36]

Bisham Abbey in Buckinghamshire, despite its name was not an Abbey. Rather it was a manor house, which was part of a Templar preceptory. The land was donated to the Templars around the time of Cressing in Essex. *ClipArt.com*

As studied in an earlier chapter, many authors have put forth the idea that the Templars wealth and power came from a discovery made during their early years. If the Templars were in possession of any such discovery, it was the formula for creating a well-disciplined organisation capable of managing its many branches and business interests in the East and West. In this sense, the Templars were in many ways the medieval equivalent to a modern international corporation.

And like any modern corporation, they learned that when one acquires money and political power, the road to even greater wealth is smoothly paved.

References for chapter 9

1 Addison, Charles, *Knights Templar* p. 183. Addison suggests that de Craon was the son-in-law of Anselm, Archbishop of Canterbury and took Templar vows after the death of his wife. Napier, Gordon, *The Rise and Fall of the Knights Templar* p. 37-38. Napier agrees with Addison, but suggests that de Craon was the nephew of Anselm. This point of view is contradicted by Dr. Christian Tourenne who suggests that de Craon was engaged to the daughter of Jourdain de Chabanais; a marriage which would have made him the Lord of Chabanais and also Lord of Confolens. Tourenne suggests that the seizure of the two Lordships in 1121 prompted de Craon to rethink the value of his proposed marriage and he broke the engagement leaving soon after for the Holy Land.

2 Barber, Malcolm, *The New Knighthood*. p. 8.

3 Tourenne, Christian – Robert de Craon, *Templar History Magazine V. 3 N. 3* Issue 11 p. 19 2005.

4 Barber op. cit. p. 36.

5 Ibid p. 36.

6 Ibid p. 36.

7 Upton-Ward, *The Templar Rule*. p. 12. Ward basis this idea on the fact that several aspects of the translation include elements that were made possible by the papal bull *Omne datum optimum*, which was written in 1139.

8 Burman, Edward, *The Templars: Knights of God*. p. 39.

9 The translation of the Rule from Latin to French saw the removal of the probationary period for new recruits as well as a directive in the French version to seek excommunicated knights as opposed to the direct opposite injunction in the original Latin version, which stated specifically non-excommunicated knights. Ward suggests that the former may have been a clerical omission, but that the latter was clearly done with intent.

10 Coulombe, Charles, *A History of the Popes*. p. 236.

11 Ibid. p. 236

12 Coulombe op. cit. p. 236.

13 Barber, op. cit. p. 56.

14 Burman op. cit p. 41.

15 Ibid. p. 40.

16 Nicholson, Helen, *The Knights Templar: A New History*. p. 154

17 Ibid. p. 154.

18 Ibid. p. 154.

19 Barber op. cit. p. 257.

20 Ibid. p. 257. Barber references an obituary roll from the Templar Preceptory at Rheims, which ran to 42 pages of parchment.

21 Ibid. p. 254

22 Lord, Evelyn, *The Knights Templar in Britain*. p. 62. These tenants paid the Templars between 10 and 15s per virgate, which was approximately 12 hectares of land. Additionally the tenant would render other services to the Templars when required, such as ploughing, mowing and harvesting.

23 Cressing Temple – The documented History of Cressing Temple. www.cressingtemple.org.uk/History/CThist.htm accessed 16 February 2007.

24 Lord op. cit. p. 62.

25 Brighton, Simon, *In Search of the Knights Templar*. p. 86

26 Lord op. cit. p. 62.

27 Cressing Temple op. cit.

28 Lord, op. cit. p. 65-66.

29 The Military Orders and Economic Growth, Cardiff University: School of History and Archaeology www.cf.ac.uk/hisar/people/hn/MilitaryOrders/MILORDOCS9.htm#_ftnref31 Translated by Helen Nicholson.

30 Lord op. cit. p. 65.

31 Nicholson op. cit. p. 182-183.

32 Ibid. p. 171-172.

33 Lord op. cit. p. 94.

34 Ibid. p. 96.

35 Nicholson op. cit. p. 187.

36 Ibid. p. 187 At Castle Pilgrim on the Mediterranean coast, the Order operated a salting where they would distil seawater in order to manufacture salt.

The Engliſh Vſurer.

Caluin Epiſt. de Vſura.

In repub. benè conſtitutâ nemo fœnerator tolerabilis eſt, ſed omninò debet è conſortio hominum reiici : An Vſurer is not tolerable in a well eſtabliſhed Common-weale, but vtterly to be reiected out of the company of men.

This illustration from the seventeenth century, entitled The English Usurer, depicts the contempt with which money lenders were held by society.
ClipArt.com

The Borrowers and the Bankers

'But love ye your enemies, and do good, and lend, hoping for nothing again; and your reward shall be great, and ye shall be the children of the Highest: for he is kind unto the unthankful and to the evil.'

Luke 6:35

LIKE the notion that the Templars' wealth and power came from the discovery of buried treasure or a great secret that the Church wished to suppress, the idea that the Order invented the modern banking system as we know it was also built upon a faulty foundation. Although the Order engaged in a wide variety of financial activities, many of which have parallels in the contemporary banking world, the Templars did not operate as a bank in the modern sense of the word.

While it is certainly true that the Templars accepted deposits from their clientele, the Order did not pool monies and then lend them to other clients as banks do today.[1] As we will see in due course, the Templars had an absolute hands-off policy with respect to money given to their trust. In this sense, Templar banking, if it can be called that, was largely limited to the offering of safety deposit boxes – at least with their customer's money. This was certainly nothing new as other monastic Orders had long acted as depositories for documents and other valuable items.[2]

However, the Order did not lock their own strong boxes as tightly as they did those of their clientele and, as the Order's assets grew, they began to lend their money to others at interest. A common misconception about the Templars' involvement in interest loans is that they were the first moneylenders in Europe. Although this claim has been repeated in many modern books on the Templars, the truth is that the Jews of Europe had been engaged in money lending for many years before the Order became involved in the practice.

The First Money Lenders

THE social and economic status of the Jews in Europe changed for the worse towards the end of the eleventh century. In the largely agrarian society that existed prior to the First Crusade, the Jews had prospered as bankers, merchants and even landlords.[3] However, by the time of the First Crusade, Christianity had become more militant and Christian piety a popular pastime. With these changes in European society, anti-Semitism began to grow and the Jews found that their status as respected international merchants was on the wane. By the middle of the twelfth century, anti-Semitism had increased to the point where the Jews were being accused of engaging in the ritualistic murder of Christian children as the pagans had been before them.[4]

Concurrent with the growth of anti-Semitism was the growth of the merchant class in Europe, which, in keeping with the popularity of Judeophobia, began to shut the Jews out of enterprises in which they had previously thrived.[5] Christian merchants now travelled the trade routes once covered by Jewish merchants and the growing trade guilds began to bar Jewish craftsmen from membership.[6] Although some Jews continued to work as artisans or in the minor trades, many found themselves with financial assets, but no way to earn a living with it outside of lending it at interest.

Jewish money lenders were known to charge as much as fifty per cent interest; however the seemingly exorbitant rates were not so much a matter of greed but one of necessity. As the European economy became more mercantile, new businesses required new capital and, like many fledgling business enterprises, often folded as quickly as they began. Like financial institutions of today, the Jewish moneylenders levied interest according to the level of risk involved. There was a high likelihood that the loans would not be recovered when businesses went bust and it was not simply a matter of a Jewish lender taking the debtor to the small claims court. The Christians had a status in the courts that the Jews did not enjoy and the full recovery of a bad debt was nearly impossible.[7] However, the borrowers seldom understood the necessity of being charged high rates of interest and the Jews were further maligned in the eyes of Christendom as filthy usurers.

The modern definition of usury is a loan charged at a high rate of interest, but in medieval times, the term meant something else entirely. Usury was not defined by how much interest a loan carried, but rather if the loan carried any interest at all. Any amount charged above the principal was considered to be usury in the eyes of the Roman Church and the practice was forbidden between Christians. What is interesting is that in the East, no such prohibitions existed. The Byzantine Church not only allowed money lending, but the government set the rates of interest that could be charged.[8]

Although the Bible has several passages which would appear to forbid lending money at interest, the Roman Church's injunction against usury was taken largely from Luke 6:35: 'But love ye your enemies, and do good, and lend, hoping for nothing again; and your reward shall be great, and ye shall be the children of the Highest: for he is kind unto the unthankful and to the evil.' The key words in the passage are 'lend, hoping for nothing again' or in Latin as 'mutuum date nihil inde sperantes'. While the interpretation of the passage is open to question and may simply mean 'lend, without giving up hope that your loan will be returned', the Roman Church interpreted it as a hard and fast rule against Christians profiting by lending money to fellow Christians.

This understanding of the concept did not extend to non-Christians and allowed the Jews a loophole through which to earn a living at a time when most occupations were closed to them. In fact, until the Fourth Lateran Council in 1215, the Church had little to say about Jewish moneylenders – at least officially.[9] Of course, the Church's prohibitions against Christians engaging in the practice of usury did not stop Christians from lending each other money and charging for the service. Perhaps one of the most vocal opponents of usury within Christendom was Bernard of Clairvaux who once wrote that Christians who lent money were worse than Jews. Indeed, it was Bernard's belief that Christian usurers could scarcely be called Christians, but were more deserving of the label of 'baptised Jews' – a clear indication of the anti-Semitism prevalent in the Church at the time.[10]

Given the depth of the Templars' involvement in money lending, it is perhaps ironic that Bernard would be so vocal in his opposition. For around the time the Cistercian abbot was praising the Order in his *De Laude Novae Militiae*, the Templars were already making loans. Of course, Bernard could hardly have been critical of the Templars' involvement in money lending, for the Order did not charge their clients a penny of interest – at least not technically.

Templar Money Lenders

While the Templars have often been credited with great ingenuity with respect to international finance, an objective view of history shows that they were not so much innovators as they were opportunists. Quite simply, they were in the right place at the right time. After the victory of the First Crusade, the establishment of the Latin States and the evolution of the Military Orders, pilgrimage to the Holy Land multiplied. And along with the increase in the number of travelling pilgrims came the increase in opportunity to make a profit from them.

One of the earliest documented loans made by the Templars took place during the early years of the Order when Hugues de Payens was Master of the Temple. In 1135, a man named Petre Desde – wishing to make a pilgrimage from his home in Zaragoza (Saragoza), Spain to Jerusalem, to see the Holy Sepulchre – obtained a sum of 50 morabitins from the Templars to finance his journey. According to the document drafted for the sum, Desde was not being given a loan; rather the money was being provided to him by the Templars 'out of charity'.[11] In exchange for this act of Templar kindness, Desde agreed, upon his death, to give the Order his home, lands and vineyards in Zaragoza. While the Order could hardly be accused of taking interest on their loan of 50 morabitins, the post mortem pecuniary benefit of their charitable considerations far outweighed any interest they might have charged Desde while he was alive.

However, this clever ploy was not the only way that the Order skirted the Church's prohibition on usury and the Templars devised several ways of making money without claiming interest. One method they used was to take their fees up front. If a client wished to borrow 100 florins, 90 would be issued although the document would record the full 100 florins. When the loan was repaid, the Order would see a profit of ten florins on a 90 florin loan. This approach benefited both parties: the Templars made a profit and the borrower avoided a high rate of interest that Jewish moneylenders would have charged for a similar loan. Not all methods of lending money involved the need for the Templars to fudge their books. The loan department would often carry a clause where if the money depreciated between the time it was borrowed and repaid, the Order was to be compensated for the loss of assets. One example of this clause illustrates how the Templars could profit from a loan without breaking the rules on usury. In 1170, Raimon of Cornus and his nephew Ricart, pledged a farm to Elias, Master of the Temple of St Eulalia, in exchange for a loan of 200 sous Melgueil: 100 being given to each man. If the money depreciated before it was repaid, the men were to pay the Templars a silver mark for every 48 sous 'in love' until the loan was settled.[12] In addition, the document stated that although the Templars held the farm as security on the loan, its produce was to be secured by the Order and did not count towards the repayment of the loan.

Although the Templars did not limit themselves to lending money to pilgrims and farmers, their involvement in money lending was largely an ancillary activity to their original mandate of assisting pilgrims, as the 50 morabitins given to Petre Desde would seem to indicate. Within a decade of Desde's loan, the Order was now financing the crowned heads of Europe and their journeys to the Holy Land. However, they were not so much financing a pilgrimage to the Holy Land but that of a Holy War.

In 1147, during the Second Crusade, King Louis VII left France for the Holy Land accompanied by an army and 130 Templar knights, including Everard des Barres, the Master of the Order in France. By the time Louis and his army arrived in Antioch in the spring of 1148, the king had exhausted his financial resources set aside for the expedition and he needed to borrow money. Although the Templars and Hospitallers had lent the king money,[13] the Templars' contributions to the campaign nearly bankrupted the Order.[14] The massive debt was incurred on 10 May when Everard des Barres, who by this time had become a close confidant of the king, travelled from Antioch to Acre in order to procure the necessary funds from his brethren to allow Louis's crusade to continue.

King John of England (1199–1219) used the Templars and their financial services.
ClipArt.com

Later that year, the king wrote to his regents in France instructing them to find the money to repay the Order. As he told Abbot Sugar in his letter, had it not been for the financial support of the Templars he would not have been able to continue his campaign. Abbot Sugar was instructed to provide 2000 marks of silver, while Raoul of Vermandois was to find 30,000 livres parisis to repay the king's debt to the Order. This was not pocket money – 30,000 livres equalled around half the annual revenue of the French kingdom at the time.[15] When the regents had raised the necessary capital to repay the loan, it was the Templars who transported the money from France to the Holy Land where it was greatly needed to refill the Order's depleted coffers.

Templar Traveller's Cheques

The ability to move men, money and materials between locations had been well established by the time of the Second Crusade, due to the Templars' vast network of properties in the East and West. With the exception of the Cistercians, who had a large network of houses in the West, nothing like the Templar network existed in all of Christendom. The Franks were regionalised, fractionalised and still largely agrarian, while the Templars had evolved into a truly international organisation with landholdings in many territories and irons in many fires. What started as an internal system for keeping the Templar machine operating at peak efficiency was soon utilised by the Order to generate additional revenue. Because the Templars had such an extensive network, a pilgrim could deposit his valuables in a Templar preceptory in France or England and withdraw the funds in the appropriate currency when he reached his destination. If there was one area of financial activity in which

Right: **The Round Church of the London Temple as it appears today. In 1185 the London Temple became home to the royal treasure and in 1204, King John placed the crown jewels in the Templars' care for safekeeping.** *Author*

Below: **The Paris Temple, destroyed by Napoleon Bonaparte after the French Revolution, was used by the French monarchy from the late twelfth to early fourteenth centuries to store the nation's treasury.** *ClipArt.com*

the Templars were pioneers, it is in providing the 'lettre de change'.

While there is no question that the Templars performed such services, there is a great deal of misconception about just how the process worked. It has often been stated that the traveller was given an encoded document that could only be translated by another Templar. However, like so many aspects of the Templars' story, there is little evidence to support the claim – the theory being quoted from author to author until it became entrenched in the Templar legend. Surviving examples of these documents belie the notion, for they are not written in code, but in Latin. As the majority of people were illiterate or only able to read and write in their native tongue, it is understandable how a Latin document might be perceived as being composed of cipher code, unintelligible to the person holding it. As odd as it may seem, perhaps this is how the lettre de change was considered to be a coded document.

One example of this type of document was reprinted in 1884 in the book *Documents inédits sur le Commerce de Marseille au Moyen Age* by Louis Blancard. The lettre de change, dated 9 August 1229 indicated that Etienne de Manduel, who had travelled from the port of Marseille to Acre aboard a Templar vessel, had deposited a sum of 30 pounds of royal crowns (equal to 90 Saracen bezants) with a Templar named Bertrand de Cavaillon. The document indicated that de Manduel was to be paid the sum upon his arrival in the Holy Land.[16] The lettres de change would be stamped with the seal of the Order and the sealed lettre de change would then be carried on the person until it was redeemed at his destination. The Templars' profit in handling the transaction would have been in the form of a service charge or in the rate of exchange between currencies. What is interesting is that the devaluation of currency clause that the Templars wrote into their loan agreements does not seem to have been offered in their lettres de change.

Templar Safety Deposits

Not all money deposited with the Templars was to be collected by their owner on foreign shores. The Templars also safeguarded valuables such as coins, jewels or important documents while the owner was away. The owner's valuables would either be retrieved when he returned from his journey or to be collected from time to time. As we looked at earlier, the Order had a strict rule that money deposited with the Templars belonged to the depositor and could not be touched or used except by its rightful owner. To do so would constitute theft and the Templars' Rule of Order dealt with thieves in its ranks by expulsion. No member of the Order was to have money on his person that he was not entitled to carry[17] and should any be found amongst his belongings upon his death, he was to be denied a Christian burial.[18] In fact, if he had already been buried, the body was to be exhumed. It is doubtless that the Templars' strict adherence to their Rule of Order strengthened their reputation as men who could be trusted with money.

Their reputation for trustworthiness put them in the position to act as middlemen for parties who did not trust each other. One such situation occurred in 1214. King John of England, wishing to gain the support of some French barons offered to pay them a pension. However, the barons had little trust in the king so John placed the money in the Templar preceptory at La Rochelle with the directive to pay the pensions out to the barons as required.[19]

However, these regal deposits were not limited to pension funds. It was not long before larger centres of Templar activity such as London and Paris became home to the financial assets of entire kingdoms.

As early as 1185, the London Temple became home to the royal treasure, and in 1204, King John of England deposited the crown jewels there for safekeeping.[20] In France, kings Philip II (1180-1223) and Philip IV (1285-1314) used the Paris Temple to storehouse their treasures. Even when Philip IV created his own treasury at the Louvre in 1295, he still made use of the services of the Paris Temple.[21] In fact, just less than a decade before Philip IV organised his own treasury, the Templars were providing the king with a package of financial services that were chronicled in a massive document that ran to two hundred and ninety articles.[22]

An organisation that could be trusted with safeguarding and accounting the wealth of nations could certainly be relied upon to protect the valuables of citizens, merchant, farmer and peasant. However, these valuables could often take some unusual forms. The Templar preceptory of Gardeney in Aragon had a house of deposits, which was used by clients to hold agricultural produce, mules, horses and even Moorish slaves on occasion.[23]

Whatever was deposited with the Order, the client had the assurance of the Templars that it would be kept safe and secure until it was to be returned to its owner. Of course, like with so many aspects of the Templar Rule, there were occasions where the rules were bent and broken.

King Louis IX was captured during the Battle of Mansurah in February 1250.
ClipArt.com

A King's Ransom in Gold

In February of 1250, during the Seventh Crusade, the Templars were severely defeated at the Battle of Mansurah.[24] During the battle, one of the few survivors, King Louis IX, was captured. Negotiations moved back and forth, but it was decided that the French king would be traded for Damietta, which had been captured by the Christians the previous year. The survivors of Louis's army who had surrendered were to be traded for the sum of 400,000 livres.[25] While the negotiations were being arranged, Turanshah, the last Ayyubid Sultan of Egypt, was murdered by his Mamluk general. The new leader, Aybeg, not only inherited Egyptian power; he inherited a royal prisoner.

Upholding the previously negotiated treaty, Aybeg released the king from captivity once Damietta had been handed over to him. However, he would not permit Louis to leave Egypt until 200,000 livres of the requested ransom had been paid. Louis's men began to collect the money necessary to free their king but were short of 30,000 livres. It was suggested by Jean de Joinville, a nobly born Frank from the Champagne region who had travelled on a crusade with the French king, that the shortfall be borrowed from the Templars. Louis agreed.

However, when de Joinville met with the Commander and the Marshal of the Order, he found that his loan request was denied. Stephen de Otricourt, the Templar Commander told de Joinville, 'Sir de Joinville, this advice of yours is neither good nor reasonable; for you know that we receive our trusts in such a way, that we cannot by our oaths resign them to anyone except to those from whom we have received them.'[26] Instead of being impressed by the Templars' dedication to safeguarding their client's money, de Joinville was outraged and argued with de Otricourt. The Marshal of the Order, Reginald de Vichiers, gently suggested that what de Otricourt had said was true: the Templars were under oath to protect their client's belongings. But if de Joinville were to take the money by force, the Templars could not be held accountable for breaking their rules or violating their client's trust.

De Joinville was taken on a Templar vessel to the Order's chief galley where the treasury was kept. When de Joinville suggested that de Otricourt come

Nineteenth-century illustration showing the release of King Louis IX from captivity. The Templars provided 30,000 livres towards his release. *ClipArt.com*

down into the hold as a witness, the Commander replied that he would have no part of it. However, de Vichiers agreed to go in his stead to act as witness. In the hold, the men found that the Order's Treasurer was as dedicated to maintaining the rules as de Otricourt had been. When the Treasurer refused to hand over the keys, de Joinville flew into a rage, grabbed a hatchet and told him that the weapon would serve as the king's key.[27] When it seemed likely that de Joinville was going to smash open the strongboxes and take the money by force, de Vichiers took hold of his wrist and ordered the treasurer to surrender the keys.[28] The treasurer conceded and de Joinville obtained his 30,000 livres, which he later learned belonged to Nicholas of Choisy, one of the king's sergeants.[29] King Louis's freedom had been secured and de Vichiers was elected the Master of the Temple for raising the ransom money and bending the rules.

The dispute over the ransom money was not the only time that de Joinville would have trouble extracting money held in Templar coffers. However, the second time, he was trying to withdraw his own funds. In the summer of 1250, de Joinville deposited 360 livres in the Templar treasury while the army was stationed at Acre.[30] He had recently received a payment of 400 livres and decided that 40 were sufficient for his needs. Some time later, when de Joinville sent Father John Caym of St. Menehould to obtain another 40 livres, the priest returned empty-handed.[31] The Commander replied that not only did the Temple not have any of de Joinville's money, he also had never heard of him. Given the events of a few month's prior, it is hard to believe that the Commander would be ignorant of who de Joinville was.

While de Joinville may have not lost any sleep over depriving the Templars of money to ransom the king of France, he certainly did when the Order deprived him of his own money. Unable to get satisfaction in the matter, de Joinville approached Reginald de Vichiers who was Master of the Temple, largely due to the influence and gratitude of King Louis IX. Not only did De Vichiers not take de Joinville's dilemma seriously, he was incensed that he would dare to accuse the Order of being thieves. 'Sir de Joinville,' de Vichiers said. 'I love you well; but rest assured, that if you will not forego this claim of yours, I shall cease to be your friend; for you want to make people believe, that our brethren are thieves!'[32] Despite the Master's threat, de Joinville pressed the matter.

After four days of great anxiety where de Joinville said he felt like 'a man who has not a penny left to spend',[33] he was relieved to be told by de Vichiers

that his money had reappeared and the Templar commander had disappeared, having been transferred to the hamlet of Saffran.[34] It remains unclear as to exactly why de Joinville was denied his money. Perhaps the Templar Commander was ignorant of who he was. Perhaps it was in spite for de Joinville having taken money that was not rightfully his. Or perhaps it was one of the few instances where a Templar had violated the oaths of the Order by coveting a client's money for himself. Whatever the reason, the troubles de Joinville had in recovering his deposit, while certainly rare, were not without precedent. In 1198, the recently appointed Bishop of Tiberius had to bring a lawsuit against the Order to recoup 1300 bezants and other important items, which had been deposited with the Templars by his immediate predecessor.[35]

Taxes and Tithes

While there were times when people had difficulties in extracting money from the Templars, the Order had no difficulty in extracting money from the people. As such, the Order often acted on behalf of secular rulers and even merchants as collectors of taxes, tithes and debts. William Marshal, the earl of Pembroke, used a Templar as his almoner as did King Henry II. These almoners did not just dispense regal charity to the poor. During the time of King John of England, his almoner, Roger the Templar, was in charge of collecting freight duties from the king's shipping interests.[36] When crusader taxes were introduced in England in 1166 and again in 1188, both the Templars and the Hospitallers were utilised to collect the taxes. The best known of these taxes, the Saladin Tithe, was levied to help finance the Third Crusade, which was launched in 1188 as a response to the fall of Jerusalem the previous year. The taxation required that every person was to give one tenth of his rents and movable goods for the purpose of retaking Jerusalem; however, knights and members of the clergy who had taken the cross were exempted from the taxation as they were already supporting the cause.[37]

Article two of the taxation document shows the role that the Military Orders played in the process as well as the level of trust the Templars and Hospitallers were given in the final years of the twelfth century:

> 'Let the money be collected in every parish in the presence of the parish priest and of the rural dean, and of one Templar and one Hospitaller, and of a servant of the Lord King and a clerk of the King, and of a servant of a baron and his clerk, and the clerk of the bishop; and let the archbishops, bishops, and deans in every parish excommunicate every one who does not pay the lawful tithe, in the presence of, and to the certain knowledge of, those who, as has been said above, ought to be present. And if any one according to the knowledge of those men give less than he should, let there be elected from the parish four or six lawful men, who shall say on oath what is the quantity that he ought to have declared; then it shall be reasonable to add to his payment what he failed to give.'[38]

Although the Templars played a role in collecting English revenue during the Third Crusade, they did not become involved in the day-to-day financial administration of the English monarchies as they did with the crowned heads of France.[39] Still, there was money to be made, even in the collecting of taxes – whether it was on behalf of a king or a merchant, the Templars would have certainly charged a fee for providing the service. Under Pope Innocent III, the Templars derived an additional benefit from collected taxes. In 1202, he ordered that two per cent of the revenues from certain abbeys and religious orders should be sent to the Paris Temple for use in the Holy Land. Six years later he decreed that the alms of the Cistercians, plus two and a half per cent of the revenues

Of the nine effigies found in the London Round Church, the most famous is that of William Marshal, the Earl of Pembroke, who was made a Templar just before his death in 1219. It was common for the Order to receive men on their death bed for the love of God. These men often had been patrons of the Order and as such had financially assisted the Templars during their lives. *Author*

deposited by the Bishop of Paris, should be applied to the purpose and be used by the Patriarch of Jerusalem and the Masters of both the Temple and the Hospital.

As we have seen, the Templars' wealth and power did not come from some Holy relic or great dark secret discovered in the East, but from the fruits of their own labour. They had developed a well-organised, highly disciplined Order that spanned nations and owed allegiance to no earthly power save that of the Holy See. Papal favour and recognition had brought the Order donations of land and as such allowed the Order to generate revenue from produce or rent, often both. As the Order acquired financial resources, they were able to parlay their money into even more money by cleverly lending it out at interest and providing other financial services greatly needed in an emerging mercantile economy.

As their economic activities increased, bringing them great wealth, trust and power, accusations of greed were launched against the Order. An English satirist writing in the middle of the thirteenth century, while acknowledging the Templars for their resolute courage, nonetheless charged the Order with being too fond of pennies and looking after their own self-serving interests.[40] But the satirist's scathing remarks about the Order were not the only charges of greed, nor were they the earliest of the accusations levied against the Templars. Almost a century earlier, the Templars became involved in a scandal that had King Almaric of Jerusalem contemplating asking the pope to have the Order dissolved. In 1173,[41] Rashid ed-Din became governor of the Nosairi region, controlled by the Assassins (Hashshasin), a sect of Ismaili Muslims who specialised in terror and assassination. Rashid is better known by the name the Old Man of the Mountain and legends about him are almost equal to those of the Templars themselves.

The Templars and the Assassins had a common enemy in Nur al-Din who was growing in power and becoming an ever-increasing threat to Christian and Muslim alike. Rashid sent his negotiator Abdullah to King Almaric suggesting an alliance between the two groups against their common enemy and even went so far as to suggest that he and his followers were contemplating converting to the Christian faith.[42] There were other conditions of the alliance. At the time, the Templars stationed at Tortosa had been collecting an annual tribute of 2000 bezants from the neighbouring Muslim villages as a taxation to assure their protection. This tribute was in many ways similar to the jizyah,[43] which the Muslims had often charged non-Muslims living in their communities. However, Rashid did not see the similarities of purpose and wanted the Templars' taxation stopped. King Almaric, whether he believed Rashid's offer of conversion or not, was certainly glad for the assistance against Nur al-Din and sent Abdullah back to his leader with word that a Frankish contingent would follow soon after them.

By the time Abdullah had got north of Tripoli, he was ambushed by a group of Templars and killed. Runciman believed that a one-eyed knight named Walter of Mesnil had killed Abdullah and was acting on behalf of the Master of the Temple.[44] Outraged that his authority had been compromised, Almaric sent word to Master Odo de St Amand that he wanted those guilty of the murder handed over. De St Amand took full privilege of the autonomy granted to his Order by the pope and declined the king's request. Almaric decided this was not acceptable and moved north with some troops where he had Walter imprisoned at Tyre.[45]

While the murder of the Abdullah may have been a simple matter of seizing an opportunity to kill a few of Christ's enemies, others did not see it as such. William of Tyre, who was certainly no lover of the Templars, made the claim that the murder of the Assassin envoy was motivated by the Templars' pure lust for money. While it is true that the Templars seemed – and probably were – obsessed with making money, the popular opinion that the Order was amassing a fortune for their own greed was largely without foundation, at least in the years when Christendom was struggling to maintain a grip on the Holy Land. The need for the Templars to raise revenue in the West was directly proportional to their need to raise arms in the East. As the people knew all too well, whenever news arrived from the East, it was often about wars in which the Templars always seemed to be involved.

References for chapter 11

1 Nicholson, Helen, *The Knights Templar: A New History*. p. 162.

2 Barber, Malcolm, *The New Knighthood*. p. 266.

3 Cantor, *Norman Medieval History*. p. 431. In the early eleventh century the Jews occupied extensive estates in the south or France.

4 Potok, *Chaim Wanderings: Chaim Potok's History of the Jews*. p. 413. The blood libel was the myth that the Jews drank the blood of Christians and obtained the blood through ritualistic murder. Potok records the first instance of the accusation as having occurred in England in 1144. These accusations were commonly used by Christians to demonise non-Christians of all sorts.

5 Cantor op. cit. p. 432.

6 Potok op. cit. p. 414.

7 Cantor op. cit. p. 432.

8 Potok op. cit. p. 414.

9 Twelfth Ecumenical Council: Lateran IV 1215, Medieval Sourcebook. www.fordham.edu/halsall/basis/lateran4.html Canon 67 of the Fourth Lateran Council forbade the Jews from charging excessive rates of interest.

10 Burman, Edward, *The Templars Knights of God*. p. 83.

11 Ibid. p. 78-79.

12 The Military Orders and economic growth, Cardiff University, School of History and Archaeology. www.cf.ac.uk/hisar/people/hn/MilitaryOrders/MILORDOCS9.htm. Translated by Helen Nicholson. The phrase 'in love' seems to have been placed to point out that the silver mark was being paid to cover the Templars' losses and not as a financial gain on the loan.

13 Nicholson op. cit. p. 163.

14 Barber, Malcolm, *The New Knighthood*. p. 67.

15 Ibid. p. 68.

16 Blancard, Louis, *Documents Inedits sur le Commerce de Marseille au Moyen-Age*. Translation from the Latin by Dr. Christian Tourenne.

17 Upton-Ward, *The Templar Rule*. p. 92 § 329.

18 Ibid p. 147 § 566.

19 Burman op. cit. p. 82.

20 Ibid. p. 81.

21 Nicholson op. cit. p. 164.

22 Burman op. cit. pp. 88-89.

23 Ibid. p. 80.

24 The Crusade of 1248-1250 has sometimes been referred to as the Sixth Crusades by authors who do not consider the crusade of the Holy Roman Emperor Frederic II in 1229 to be an actual crusade.

25 Barber op. cit. p. 152. The ransom had originally been set at 500,000 livres, but was later reduced to 400,000 livres.

26 Wedgwood, Ethel, *The Memoirs of the Lord of Joinville: A New English Version*. pp. 191-192. http://etext.lib.virginia.edu/etcbin/toccer-new2?id=WedLord.sgm&images=images/modeng&data=/texts/english/modeng/parsed&tag=public&part=16&division=div2.

27 Ibid. p. 193.

28 Barber op. cit. p. 152. Nicholson op. cit. p. 163. Nicholson's account of the story is similar to Barber's; however, she does not indicate that de Vichiers made the suggestion of pretending to take the money by force. Barber draws his information from de Joinville's own account of the events, which makes the account certainly plausible if not probable.

29 Wedgwood op. cit. p. 193.

30 Ibid. p. 269. From 1187 when Jerusalem was captured by Saladin until 1291 when Acre fell to the Mamluks, the port city of Acre served as the Templars's headquarters in the east.

31 Wedgwood op. cit. p. 212.

32 Ibid. p. 212.

33 Ibid. p. 212.

34 Ibid. p. 212.

35 Burman ibid. p. 80.

36 Nicholson op. cit. p. 161.

37 Stubbs, William, ed. *Select Chartres of English Constitutional History*. p. 189. www.fordham.edu/halsall/source/1188Saldtith.html

38 Ibid. p. 189.

39 Nicholson op. cit. p. 164.

40 Ibid. p. 181. Nicholson quotes from a mid-thirteenth century work entitled *Sur les états du monde (On the classes of society.)* The work criticises the different aspects of medieval society from the clergy to the Military Orders.

41 Barber op. cit. p. 101 Runciman, Sir Stephen, *A History of the Crusades Vol. II*. p. 397. Sir Stephen gives the date of the event as 1163, which would be during the Mastership of Philip de Milly. However, Barber mentions Odo de St Amand's involvement, which puts Runciman's date in question as de Milly resigned from office in 1171.

42 Runciman op. cit. p. 397.

43 Armstrong, Karen, *Islam: A Short History*. p. 205. The jizyah was a poll tax levied by Muslims on non-Muslims to pay for military protection.

44 Runciman op. cit. p. 397.

45 Barber op. cit. p. 101.

A Knight Templar in travelling dress as depicted in this woodcut by the 16th-century German engraver Jost Amman (1539-1591).
Author's collection

Warriors and Monks

'I do not know if it would be more appropriate to refer to them as monks or as soldiers, unless perhaps it would be better to recognise them as being both.'[1]

Bernard of Clairvaux

The nobly-born Templar knight *(far left)* was dressed and armed differently than his ignobly born counterpart the sergeant. Because they were infantrymen, sergeants *(near left)*, did not receive full mail armour like their mounted counterparts. *Gordon Napier*

Bernard of Clairvaux, who supported the Templar ideal from its inception until his death in 1153, was the first to articulate the dichotomy that existed within the new knighthood. For in a single sentence in his *De Laude Novae Militiae*, quoted above, Bernard succinctly explained what was viewed in Christendom as an oxymoron; the idea that there could exist a group of men who lived as pious monks, yet fought as warriors for Christ.

In less than a century, the concept was not only accepted within Christendom, but had evolved into a standard to be emulated. Jacques de Vitry, the cardinal bishop of Acre, writing in the thirteenth century praised the Templars for the courage in a way that was certainly intended to inspire his readers:

> 'Thus they became so terrible to the enemies of Christ's faith that one of them sued to chase a thousand, and two of them ten thousand; when they were called to arms, they did not ask how many of the enemy there were, but where they were.'[2]

But in the nine centuries that have passed since Bernard's description of the Templars was penned, the concept of the nobly born, white-mantled soldier of God has evolved its own legend and elevated the Templars to warriors of superhuman status.

Much of what we have come to believe about the militant side of the Order is little more than a collection of romantic notions. Authors such as Chrétien de Troyes and Wolfram Von Eschenbach fashioned their grail knights after the Templars, and Freemasons like Andrew Michael Ramsay and Karl Gotthelf von Hund saw the Order as an opportunity to create a pedigree for their peculiar Masonic rites and observances.

As we will see over the next few chapters, our modern impression of the selfless Templar knight who would gladly give his life for the cause of Christendom is often based upon the ideal and not the reality of how they operated in the East. When the Templars are examined through the historical accounts of the many battles in which they were involved, we see an Order who lost more battles than they won. It was an Order that would often act in its own interests over those they were willing to protect and whose leaders were as impetuous as their secular counterparts. But most importantly, it was an Order that was every part as human as those who surrounded them on both sides of the field of battle – a fact that makes their story all the more interesting.

But before we examine the reality of life in the field and how the battles were conducted, it is important to have an understanding of how the militant side of the Order was intended to operate. No document provides us with a better illustration of that ideal than the Templars' own Rule of Order, which spends considerable time explaining what each member's duty was in the field.

Clothes and Armour Make the Man

As we looked at in an earlier chapter, there was a great distinction between the nobly born Templar knight and his sergeant brethren. The positions were

Above:
Contemporary depictions of the Order often show the Templars wearing a variety of crosses on their mantles.
Author

Above right:
Cross Pattée of the type believed to be used by the Templars found on the Uncastillo Church in Saragoza, Spain.
iStockPhoto.com Rafael Laguillo

distinguished by the roles they played in the convent to what they ate in the refectory and wore on their backs. The knights were issued with a white surcoat and mantle, while sergeants wore a black surcoat with a black or brown mantle.[3] What was common to both classes was the addition of a red cross on both the surcoat and mantle.

While the Templars were granted permission to adopt the white mantles for their knights at the Council of Troyes in 1129, the addition of the cross was a privilege believed by historians to have been granted two decades later at the time of the Second Crusade. According to William of Tyre, it was Pope Eugenius III who granted the Templars their red cross: an emblem that was symbolic of their willingness to suffer martyrdom in the defence of the Holy Land.[4] However, *The Chronicle of Ernoul and Bernard the Treasurer* states that even after the Templars left their association with the Church of the Holy Sepulchre, 'still they carry a part of the badge of the Sepulchre. The sign of the Sepulchre is a cross with two scarlet arms – such as the Hospital carries. And those of the Temple carry a cross which is completely scarlet.'[5] Although the Rule is specific as to when the cross could and could not be worn on the habit, it provides no detail as to what form the cross took, regardless of when the Templars first began to wear it. Unfortunately, contemporary and later depictions of the Templars are of little help in resolving the matter and illustrations of Templar knights have been produced over the centuries depicting various forms of the cross from the Greek or St George's Cross to the Maltese cross worn by the rival Hospitaller Order. However, it is generally agreed that the Order adopted the cross pattée which can take a variety of forms.

As well as the colour of their garments, the distinction in class was apparent in the different equipment each was to have. The knights wore a coat of mail, which included a coif to cover the head, iron hose and mail shoes, a helmet or chapeau de fer, a surcoat and arming jacket. The knight's weapons included a lance, sword, shield, Turkish mace and dagger.[6] By contrast, the sergeants were armed with swords, daggers, axes, Turkish maces and crossbows and were a little less protected than their white-mantled brethren; their mail shirts were sleeveless, their hose did not have mail shoes and they wore a chapeau de fer (steel kettle hat) instead of a helmet.[7] However, the differences in arms and protective covering, while favouring the highly prized knight, were not so much a class distinction as a case of having the right equipment for the job. The sergeants, who generally outnumbered the knights by a ratio of ten to one, were the foot soldiers while the knight's chief duty was the heavy cavalry charge, which required less mobility and greater protection.

Regardless of what equipment the Templar was issued, it was to be kept in a state of readiness at all times and its possession was not to be taken lightly. The Rule provides a couple of examples of just how

The Templars were one of several military orders who fought for Christendom during the Crusades. The Knights Hospitaller *(left)* began in the years prior to the First Crusade as an Order dedicated to caring for the sick, however eventually took on a militant role as well. The Teutonic Knights *(right)* began in the late twelfth century at Acre. The Hospitallers wore a black mantle with white a Maltese cross, which made them appear similar to Templar sergeants, while the Teutonic Knights wore a white mantle with a black cross, similar to that of the Templar knights. *Author*

valuable arms and armour were to the Order. A Templar brother stationed at Montpelier in Southern France had been practising with his sword when the blade snapped. When he came across the sea to answer the charges, he pleaded for mercy in chapter for having broken the sword.[8] The second example occurred when some Templars were out walking near Casal Brahim. One of the brethren threw his mace at a bird on the shoreline, but it missed its intended target and was lost in the water. The brother pleaded for mercy from the chapter for having lost his weapon.[9] Both instances were serious offences and punishable by a loss of habit, but both Templars were allowed to keep their habits 'for love of God' which was a lesser penance. But there was a practical reason to deal harshly with those who abused their equipment; it cost a great deal of money to equip an army and the brethren in the West worked hard to ensure that sufficient funds were raised to support the war efforts in the East. Although the Templars used weapons captured from their enemies and those gathered from their fallen comrades, the majority of their equipment was not readily available in the East and had to be imported from overseas.[10] As such, there could be no guarantee that a mace or sword lost today would be replaced by tomorrow.

But maces, swords and shields were not the only weapons in the Templars' arsenal for they had God Himself on their side and were, according to Bernard of Clairvaux, 'the picked troops of God, whom he has recruited from the ends of the earth.' [11]

In the Field

The chapel was central to the Templar way of life and this was no different in the field. When the Order made camp, the chapel tent would be the first to rise. The Brethren were to pitch their tents around it; however none were to do so until the command had been given and the Marshal, who was the chief officer in the field, had chosen his place.[12] Once the Templars had struck camp none were to leave the area without

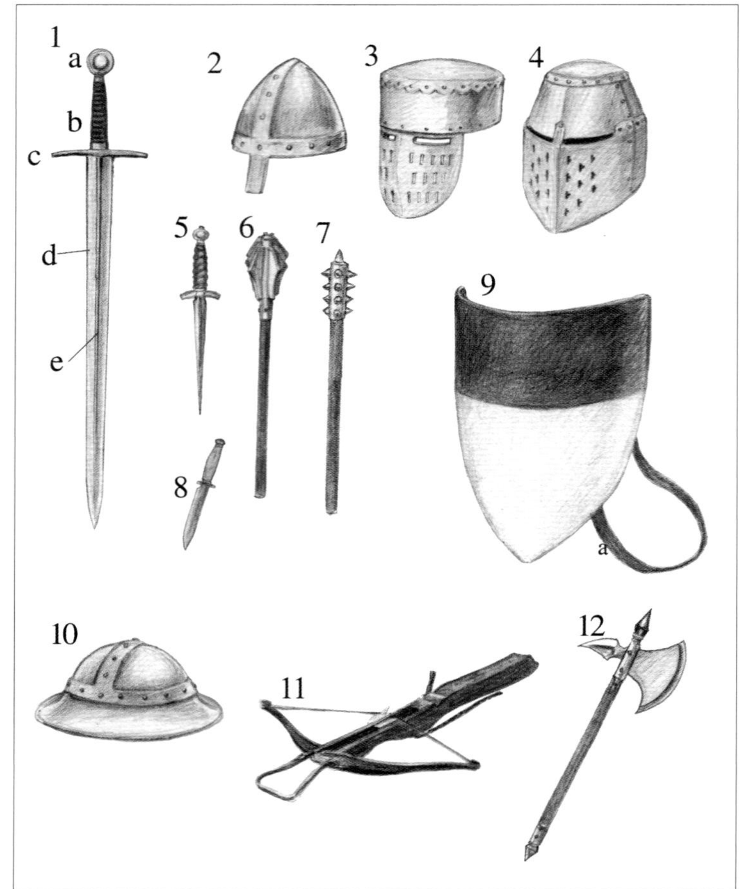

Illustration showing the various weapons used by the Templars as described in the Templar Rule of Order.
1: Sword: (a) pommel, (b) grip, (c) cross guard, (d) blade, (e) fuller (groove).
2: Helmet, early 12th century, riveted iron plates with nose guard.
3: Helmet, late 12th century with face guard.
4: Great helm, mid-late 13th century, fully enclosed.
5: Knight's dagger, with slender blade for stabbing through gaps in armour, e.g. eye slits in helmets.
6 & 7: Maces.
8: General purpose knife.
9: Shield of reinforced wood, with leather strap or 'guige' (a) and cover painted black and white.
10: 'Kettle hat' or 'chapel de fer' helmet of riveted iron plates.
11: Crossbow.
12: War axe.
Gordon Napier

permission, whether for pleasure or to gather wood, unless they stayed close enough to hear the alarm.[13] On sounding the alarm, those who were close by were to grab their shields and weapons and rush forwards to repel the threat; however, those who were not in close proximity were to assemble at the chapel and await the Marshall's commands. If the alarm was called outside the camp, no Templar was to raise arms without the permission to do so, regardless of its cause.[14]

When time had come for the Templars to break camp, the regimented discipline continued. No brother was to load his baggage or saddle his horse until the Marshal had given the command to do so; however, he could keep himself busy by picking up tent pegs, empty flasks and other small items like fishing nets.[15] When the Marshal gave the order to form the line of march, the Templars scoured the camp to make sure that nothing was left behind. When all was clear, the Templar knight loaded his baggage, saddled his mount and moved towards the line, his squire walking behind.[16] Once the line of march had been formed, the squire marched ahead of the knight carrying his lance. No brother was to leave the line for any reason without permission, not even to water his horse; however, if the Standard Bearer stopped to water his horse, the others were allowed to so. Should the alarm be called when in line, the knights were permitted to mount their horses and arm themselves with shield and lance but were to take no further action without being instructed to do so.[17] When the Templars formed into squadrons, they were not to move from one to another. When the squadron moved forwards, the squires who carried their knight's lances were in front, while those looking after the horses followed behind.[18] As the warhorse was the most important piece of equipment in the Templars' arsenal, they were to be kept fresh for battle – the knights travelled to their engagements on a mule or palfrey.[19] Although the Templars were not permitted to leave the squadron without permission, there were exceptions. If he wanted to try out his horse or to adjust the saddle, he could go a short distance; however, if he wished to take his shield and lance, he would need authorisation.[20] The second example illustrates how the Templars saw themselves as superior in skill and discipline over their secular counterparts:

> 'And if it happens by chance that any Christian acts foolishly, and any Turk attacks him in order to kill him, and he is in peril of death, and anyone who is in that area wishes to leave his squadron to help him, and his conscience tells him that he can assist him, he may do so without permission, and then return to his squadron quietly and in silence.'[21]

Whether in the line of march or aligned in their squadrons, discipline was essential, especially when the Order was preparing to make a charge. When the time had come to prepare for battle, the Marshal would take up the Order's banner and gather as many as ten knights around him to help guard it.[22] Among their number was the Commander of Knights who had a second banner furled around his lance in case the Marshal's banner should fall or become damaged.[23]

The Beauséant

LIKE the cross pattée, the Templars' banner has been a source of confusion and speculation, especially with respect to its etymology. Among today's many neo-Templar Orders, the banner is most commonly referred to as the Beauséant, which has led some modern authors to offer a variety of fanciful speculations as to what the word may have meant.[24] However, the Templar Rule refers to the standard as a piebald banner or 'confanon baucon', which not only provides the most logical explanation for Beauséant, but also describes what the banner actually looked like. The standard was divided into two halves: one part white, the other black, but different depictions of the banner place the colours in opposite sections. In the work of Matthew Paris, the chronicler of St Albans Abbey in Hertfordshire, the banner was portrayed as being black over white, while templar frescoes, such as that of the church of San Bevignate in central Italy, depict the banner as white over black, with the addition of the cross pattée in the midst of the white field.[25]

Whatever its true orientation, what is most important is that the banner was the central rallying point for the Templars after the charge was made. Throughout their existence, the Templars relied on the power of the heavy cavalry charge to destroy their enemies' lines, but knights would often find themselves scattered throughout the field in the mêlée that followed. While the knights selected to guard the banner were to stay as close to it as possible, the remainder were commanded by the Rule to attack the enemy in whatever direction they felt best in harassing their foe.[26] If a knight found himself in a position where he could not see the Order's banner, he was to protect the first Christian banner he saw in the field. If said banner happed to belong to the Hospitallers, he was to inform the squadron leader of his situation and fight by their side until he could rally around his own banner.[27]

Although the Standard Bearer was to look after the banner and keep it aloft, his principal job was to look after the squires, which were also arranged into squadrons. When the knights made their charge, the squires would follow in order to provide their lords with fresh horses should they be required.[28] With fresh horses at the ready, the knights could continue the battle and rally around the standard to regroup.

Even if it appeared as though the Christians had been defeated, as long as the piebald standard was held aloft, no Templar was to leave the field: to do otherwise was to suffer the penalty of expulsion from the Order.[29] It has often been stated that the Templars were to remain in the field of battle unless outnumbered three to one. The origin for this theory may have evolved from the praise heaped on the Order by chroniclers such as Jacques de Vitry who suggested that the Templars were not concerned with how many enemies remained, but where they were on the battlefield. There is no instruction in the Rule on the ratio of opposing forces required to retreat, rather the sole emphasis is on the presence of the banner. Not only could a brother be punished for fleeing the field while the banner was aloft, he could also face harsh discipline if he were to lower it:

> 'For if the banner is lowered, those who are far off do not know why it is lowered, for good or ill, for a Turk could more easily take or seize it when it is lowered than when it is aloft; and men who lose their banner are very afraid, and may suffer a very great defeat, and because of this fear it is forbidden so strictly.'[30]

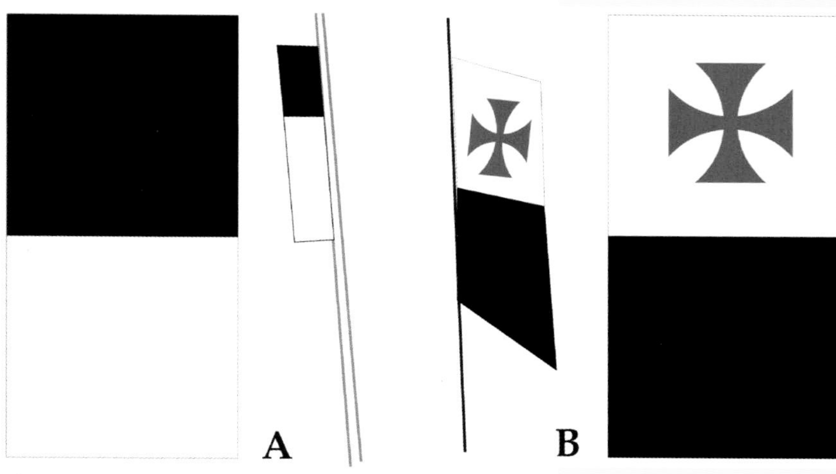

Two depictions of the Templars' banner taken from contemporary sources. The depiction on the left is from an illustration by Matthew Paris, while that on the right is patterned after one of the Templars' own frescoes in central Italy.

The Turcopoles

The Templars were aided in the field of battle by the Turcopoles: local fighting men who were employed as required and paid a mercenary's wage. These men – who were often recruited on a campaign-by-campaign basis – were under the command of the Turcopolier, who was also in charge of the Order's sergeants when they were in the field. Although not solely employed by the Templars, the Turcopoles formed a considerable part of the Order's military activities. They were, in the words of Runciman, 'raised locally and armed and trained after the model of the Byzantine light cavalry, whose name they took'.[31] As such, they would have played a vital role in the field, especially in early campaigns when the

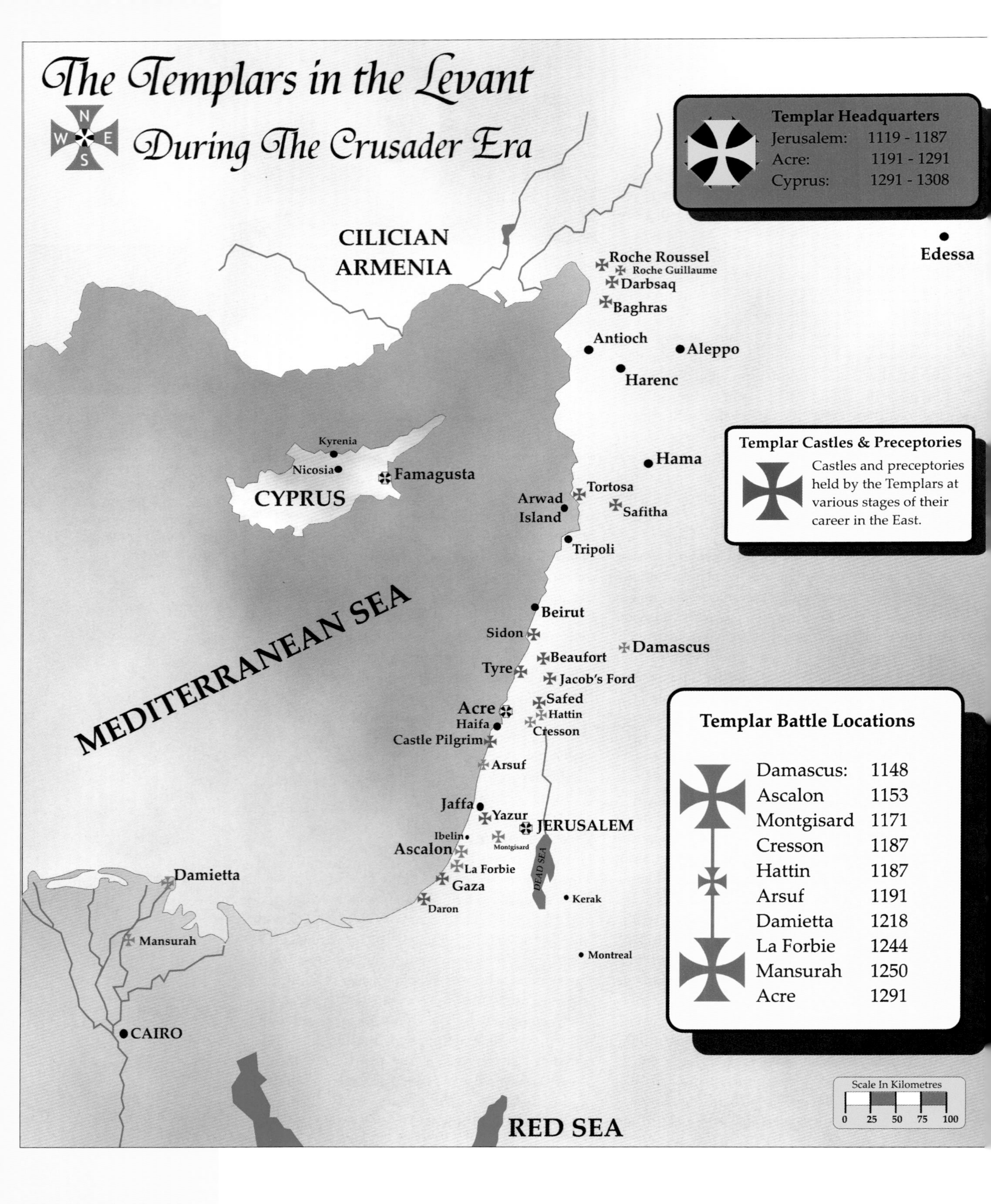
The Templars in the Levant
During The Crusader Era
N
W
E
S
Templar Headquarters
Jerusalem: 1119 - 1187
Acre: 1191 - 1291
Cyprus: 1291 - 1308
CILICIAN ARMENIA
Edessa
Roche Roussel
Roche Guillaume
Darbsaq
Baghras
Antioch
Aleppo
Harenc
Templar Castles & Preceptories
Castles and preceptories held by the Templars at various stages of their career in the East.
Kyrenia
Nicosia
Famagusta
CYPRUS
Hama
Tortosa
Arwad Island
Safitha
Tripoli
MEDITERRANEAN SEA
Beirut
Sidon
Damascus
Beaufort
Tyre
Jacob's Ford
Safed
Hattin
Acre
Haifa
Cresson
Castle Pilgrim
Arsuf
Templar Battle Locations
Damascus: 1148
Ascalon 1153
Montgisard 1171
Cresson 1187
Hattin 1187
Arsuf 1191
Damietta 1218
La Forbie 1244
Mansurah 1250
Acre 1291
Jaffa
Yazur
JERUSALEM
Ibelin
Montgisard
Ascalon
DEAD SEA
La Forbie
Gaza
Damietta
Daron
Kerak
Mansurah
Montreal
CAIRO
Scale In Kilometres
0 25 50 75 100
RED SEA

Far left: **This late nineteenth or early twentieth-century painting shows what appears to be the Templars' piebald standard flowing in the background.** *ClipArt.com*

Near left: **The Templars had to contend with the lighter and faster horses used by Muslim archers who could attack and retreat with far greater manoeuvrability than the heavy horses used by the Christian cavalry.** *Author*

Order was trying to adapt to how the Muslims waged war. The backbone of the Franks' military strategy was the heavy charge, but their opponents were often mounted on lighter and faster horses that could evade the Templars' assault if not executed with precision. Additionally, the Muslims relied on skilled archers who could harass the Templars while maintaining a safe distance: a tactic that would cause the Order to lose many men and horses. Therefore, the inclusion of the Turcopoles into the Templars' fighting force who could engage in the Eastern style of combat helped level the playing field, while maintaining the Order's advantage of the heavy charge.

The success of the Templars' military ideal relied on a well-trained and disciplined army, in which every man knew his position, duty and the fact that he was never to act in his own interest, but that of the Order and the cause of Christendom. At least this is how the standard was envisioned, but on the battlefield, events seldom went according to the rulebook.

References for chapter 11

1 Bernard of Clairvaux, De Laude Nova Militae translated by Conrad Greenia.

2 Burman, Edward, *The Templars: Knights of God*. p. 59.

3 Upton-Ward, Judith, *The Templar Rule*. p. 54 § 141.

4 Barber, Malcolm, *The New Knighthood*. p. 66. Barber suggests that the most likely date for this was during a Templar chapter meeting held in Paris on 27 April 1147, which was attended by King Louis VII and Pope Eugenius III.

5 Nicholson, Helen – Contemporary reactions to the foundation of the Templars – www.deremilitari.org/resources/sources/templars1.htm

6 Upton-Ward op. cit. p. 53 § 138.

7 Ibid. p. 54 § 141.

8 Upton-Ward op. cit. p. 156 § 607.

9 Ibid. p. 156 § 605.

10 Nicholson, Helen and David Nicolle, *God's Warriors: Templar Knights, Saracens and the Battle for Jerusalem*.

11 Bernard of Clairvaux op. cit.

12 Upton-Ward op. cit. p. 56 § 148.

13 Ibid. p. 56 § 149.

14 Ibid. p. 57 § 155.

15 Ibid. p. 58 § 156.

16 Ibid. p. 58 § 157.

17 Ibid. p. 58 § 159.

18 Ibid. p. 59 § 161.

19 Ibid. p. 63 § 179.

20 Ibid. p. 59 § 162.

21 Ibid. p. 59 § 163.

22 Ibid. p. 59 § 164.

23 Ibid. p. 60 § 165.

24 Robinson, John J., *Dungeon, Fire and Sword*. p. 45 Robinson suggested that Beauseant was not only the name of the banner, but also a rallying cry meaning 'be noble' or 'be glorious.'

25 Nicholson, Helen, *The Knights Templar: A New History*. p. 118. Dr Nicholson suggests that the banner depicted in the Templar fresco may be that of the Master of the Order, while the one depicted by Matthew Paris may have been the one used in the field.

26 Upton-Ward op. cit. p. 60 § 164.

27 Ibid. p. 60 § 167.

28 Ibid. p. 63 § 179.

29 Ibid. p. 60 § 168.

30 Ibid. p. 157 § 611.

31 Runciman, Steven, *A History of the Crusades Vol. II*. p. 293.

Self-Serving Soldiers

'Do not the heathen say: 'Where is their God?' Nor do I wonder, for the sons of the Church, those who bear the label, 'Christian' have been laid low in the desert and have either been slain by the sword or consumed by famine ...' [1]

Bernard of Clairvaux's apology to Pope Eugenius III for the Second Crusade

Gustave Doré's impression of the crusaders crossing Asia Minor during the First Crusade. Louis's army suffered similar difficulties at the commencement of the Second Crusade and survived due to the discipline of the 130 Templars who had accompanied the campaign.
ClipArt.com

On the morning of 19 March 1148, a number of Byzantine ships arrived on the shores of St Symeon in the principality of Antioch. Aboard were the remnants of an army that included the Master of France, Everard des Barres and one hundred and thirty of his Templar knights. More importantly, also present were King Louis VII of France and his queen, Eleanor of Aquitaine.

The Franks were met with the warm hand of friendship by Eleanor's uncle, Raymond of Antioch, who took the royal couple and their entourage back to the capital where they were shown several days of fine Eastern hospitality. As was so often the case in the East, Raymond's generosity and graciousness was not so much a matter of practising Christian charity as it was positioning for political favour, for as soon as it appeared that Louis had recovered from his journey, Raymond was bending his ear about a new campaign against his Muslim enemies.

It would be unfair to unduly criticise Raymond in attempting to garner the king's support. Louis and Eleanor had not travelled east on a holiday or for a family reunion and Raymond was well aware of that fact. The king had journeyed to Outremer for a crusade and the prince was eager to get on with it. Four years earlier, the Christians had lost the first of the so-called Crusader States when Zengi, the governor of Aleppo, captured Edessa. The loss of Edessa in 1144 had prompted Pope Eugenius III to call for the new crusade. Bernard of Clairvaux enthusiastically promoted the cause with a zeal equal to that of Urban II's preaching of the First Crusade half a century earlier. It was through Bernard's influence that King Louis decided to take up the cross himself.[2]

Raymond told the French king that in the four years that had passed, the Muslims had not been satisfied with capturing Edessa – in fact, things had got progressively worse. Zengi's second son and successor as governor of Aleppo, Nur ad-Dīn,[3] had established himself firmly along the Christian landscape from Edessa to Hama. And worse, during the previous Autumn, he had begun to seize Christian fortresses east of the Orontes River.[4] With Nur ad-Dīn coming ever closer to his territory, Raymond was painfully aware that the Principality of Antioch could easily be the Muslim leader's next target and the prince hoped to set things right by hitting him on his own turf at Aleppo.

While Raymond could hardly be faulted for seeking help in dealing with the dangers facing the Principality of Antioch, it might have been avoided had he done something to address the situation in 1144. At the time Zengi was planning to take Edessa, the political situation that existed in the Latin East certainly worked in Raymond's favour. King Fulk of Jerusalem had died the previous Autumn and his heir, Baldwin III, was still a child very much under the tutelage of his mother Melisende. Count Raymond of Tripoli was only slightly concerned with Edessa's troubles; the county was someway distant from his own. Closest to the troubled county, and most able to

Right: **Medieval manuscript depicting the marriage of King Louis VII of France to Eleanor of Aquitaine in 1137 and their embarkation for the Second Crusade a decade later.**
ClipArt.com

Above:
Pope Eugenius III (1145–1151) called the Second Crusade. He is believed to be the pope who granted the Templars the right to wear a red cross on their mantels.
ClipArt.com

offer assistance was Raymond of Antioch; however, there was a strong animosity between Count Joscelin of Edessa and himself, and as such, Raymond was not prepared to assist. In fact, Raymod actually took pleasure in Joscelin's plight. It was a course of action that he would ultimately regret, if he hadn't already. In his *History of Deeds Done Beyond the Sea*, William of Tyre laid the blame for Edessa's downfall firmly at Raymond's feet:

'Thus while the Prince of Antioch, overcome by foolish hatred, delayed rendering the help he owed to his brothers and while the count awaited help from abroad, the ancient city of Edessa, devoted to Christianity since the time of the Apostles and delivered from the superstitions of the infidels through the words and preaching of the Apostle Thaddeus, passed into an undeserved servitude.'[5]

However, Raymond of Antioch was not the only Latin prince looking for the support of the French king and his army. Raymond of Tripoli had hoped to recover Montferrand which had been lost to Zengi in 1137 during a battle where, amidst heavy Christian losses, only eighteen Templars survived.[6] Perhaps most eager for the king's assistance was Joscelin of Edessa who was living in Turbessel, in what was once the County of Edessa. The exiled count desperately wanted Louis to retake Edessa, for after all, it was the fall of Edessa that had brought the crusaders east in the first place. Despite being tugged in several directions at once, the king said he was not prepared to take any course of action until he had fulfilled his crusader vows by visiting Jerusalem and seeing the sites sacred to his faith.

In his history of the Crusades, Sir Stephen Runciman claimed that Louis's insistence on seeing the sacred sites was an excuse to cover his indecision.[7] However, if the king had any doubts about what course of action to take, they were not without good reason, for the journey thus far had not gone as smoothly as he'd hoped and his confidence must have been shaken. Louis arrived in the East virtually penniless having exhausted his resources getting there and had to borrow heavily from the Templars in order to continue. But the loan was not the only time the French king had been bailed out by the Templars during the journey east.

In January of 1148, the crusaders were making their way through the mountainous terrain that led to Attalia in Asia Minor. The journey would be difficult in the best of times, but given the storms common to the season, the journey was hard and treacherous. As the Franks made their way, they passed the corpses of

German soldiers who had perished there several months earlier. If the sight of rotting bodies was not enough to sink the Franks' morale, the poor state of their supplies surely was. Horses were becoming scarce and food supplies scarcer. However, unlike the undisciplined crusaders, most whom were unaccustomed to long journeys, the Templars with their institutionalised practice had rationed their supplies.[8] As the party made its way ever closer to Attalia, the Franks were attacked and harassed by Turks who saw an advantage over the weakened troops. Louis, seizing upon the one strength he had at his disposal, handed control of the army over to the Templars who organised the army into units of fifty men, each under the direct control of a Templar knight.[9]

This was perhaps the best decision Louis made during his time in the East, for it allowed what was left of his army to reach Attalia where the king procured the ships that brought him and his entourage to St Symeon in mid-March. The king would never forget the Templars' help and his gratitude and later support of the Order, particularly to Everard des Barres, was as much due to the Templars' discipline in the field of battle as it was to the money in their treasury.

Regardless of the real reasons for Louis's reluctance in choosing a plan of attack, his queen did not seem to share in his indecisiveness. She placed her full support behind Raymond and was becoming increasingly vocal about what her husband should be doing. However, there may have been more to her support than seeing the sense in her uncle's plan. As time passed, the queen – who had a reputation for being flirtatious – was spending more and more time with her uncle and rumours began to circulate that the prince's interest in his niece had turned carnal.[10] Whether the allegations of an incestuous affair were true or not, Louis left for Jerusalem as planned, forcefully dragging his queen along against her will.

King Louis VII kneels at the feet of the Cistercian abbot Bernard of Clairvaux, who preached the Second Crusade called by Pope Eugenius III. *ClipArt.com*

The Council of Princes

DESPITE his sudden departure for Jerusalem, Louis was one of the last westerners to arrive in the city. Conrad III of Germany had landed at Acre in mid-April and set out for the Holy City, where King Baldwin III and his mother, Queen Melisende, warmly welcomed him. Over Easter, the German King spent a few days with the Templars at their headquarters on the Temple Mount[11] where the Order no doubt advised him as to the coming campaign. Alfonso Jordan, the Count of Toulouse, had arrived in the East a few days after Conrad, where his arrival was also greatly celebrated, largely due to the fact that he was the son of the legendary Raymond of Toulouse, one of the leaders of the First Crusade. Alfonso set out for Jerusalem to join his fellow crusaders, but during a brief stop in Caesarea, he suddenly took ill and died in the land in which he had been born forty-five years earlier.[12] Although his untimely death may have been due to appendicitis, allegations soon began to circulate that Raymond of Tripoli or Melisende of Jerusalem had poisoned him.[13] Once Louis finally arrived at Jerusalem his crusader vows were fulfilled and the Westerners were invited to travel to Acre for a war council.

The assembly, held on 24 June 1148, was an impressive gathering. In attendance were King Baldwin III and Fulcher, the Patriarch of Jerusalem as well as the Archbishops of Caesarea and Nazareth. Conrad was accompanied by a number of his country's higher and lower nobility as was King Louis. Also in attendance were Robert de Craon, the Master of the Templars and Raymond du Puy, the Master of the Hospitallers. Conspicuous in their absence were the other leaders of the Latin East. Raymond was angry at Louis's sudden departure from Antioch and shunned any participation, while Joscelin of Edessa was in no position to travel anywhere for fear of losing further ground against his enemies. Raymond of Tripoli's absence was largely due to the death of Alfonso Jordan and the insistence of the deceased's bastard son, Bertrand, that Raymond was involved in

Louis VII of France, Baldwin III of Jerusalem and Conrad III of Germany are seen seated at the Council of Acre in the top panel of this medieval illustration. The lower panel depicts their disastrous campaign against Damascus. *ClipArt.com*

his father's death.[14] Once again the defence of Christendom would be undertaken with the majority of the Crusader States turning their backs and hoping for the best.

History does not record precisely what was said during the great council at Acre in the summer of 1148 or who was in favour of taking what course of action. The crusade had been called in response to the fall of Edessa, but Nur ad-Dīn had murdered its remaining Christian inhabitants and destroyed its fortification in 1146 when Joscelin had tried to retake the city. There was little to recover and the crusaders must surely have ruled it out as an option. Another potential target was Ascalon to the south on the Mediterranean coast. As the last port city in the region still under Muslim control, it would have been a welcome addition to the kingdom; however, there may have been some reluctance on the part of Baldwin III, who saw its capture as a possible future benefit to his younger brother Amalric.[15] This left two options: Aleppo to the north and Damascus to the northeast. Ultimately, to the disappointment of the northern princes, the crusaders opted to strike Damascus.

The city was of great religious importance to the Christians. It was on the road to Damascus that St Paul had converted to Christianity; it was in Damascus that the tomb of St John the Baptist resided and there were many other Holy Sites sacred to the Christian faith in the region. Damascus was also an important centre of trade and communication and its capture would be as great a benefit to the Christians as its loss would be a drawback to the Muslims. For an entire generation, the Kingdom of Jerusalem had coveted Damascus as a possession, repeatedly attempting to keep it under its thumb through conquest or treaty. However, the most recent treaty between the Kingdom of Jerusalem and Damascus had deteriorated and the Damascenes were growing a little too friendly with Nur ad-Dīn. Ultimately the Damascus campaign was to be a pre-emptive strike in order to gain control of the city before their adversary from Aleppo did. It would prove to be a humiliating disaster.

The Fiasco at Damascus

The Crusaders set out from Galilee in the middle of July with the largest army the Franks had ever put into the field. The Arab chronicler Ibn al-Qalãnsi put the number of Franks at fifty thousand between cavalry and infantrymen,[16] however, as we have seen, chroniclers on both sides often exaggerated the numbers of combatants. Whatever the real number, the army of Louis VII and the Templars made up the bulk of the troops. Because the locals were more familiar with the territory, it was decided that Baldwin and his men would lead the march, followed by King Louis and his men in the centre and Conrad and his army to guard the rear against attack.[17]

On 24 July 1148, the crusaders approached Damascus from the southwest, where they encountered the thick orchards that surrounded the city. The orchards were like a dense forest interlaced with mud walls which served to separate individual farmers' land as well as acting as a protective fortification for the city. The entire set-up created a labyrinth of narrow roads and pathways, which, while not a hindrance for the local farmers, proved to be difficult terrain for the crusaders to pass through. The decision to take this route was in order to fulfil the dual purpose of securing the fortified part of the city first and to provide the crusaders with a supply of food and water during their siege of the city.

However, there was more than lush fruit awaiting the crusaders amidst the trees. The Damascenes had hidden themselves there and began harassing King Baldwin and his troops as they made their way through the narrow paths. As the army slowly marched on, the Muslims shot arrows down on the crusaders and stabbed at them with lances through slits in the mud walls.[18] Although many men fell to the ambush, the crusaders persevered and slew or captured as many of the enemy as they could.

As the army pressed towards a nearby stream they were met by cavalrymen on the other side who began launching arrows to prevent the crusaders from reaching the stream. Parched from the journey and the battle, the army moved on towards the river, where they were met by an even larger force, which caused the line to halt. Unable to see the cause of the blockage, Conrad demanded to know what the hold up was. When he heard that the enemy was blockading the river, he charged through the line with his lieutenants, dismounted and began to engage the enemy in hand-to-hand combat. In his account of the battle, William of Tyre told of the German king's courage at arms:

> 'In this combat the Lord Emperor is said to have performed a feat which will be remembered through the ages. It is related that one of the enemy was resisting manfully and vigorously and that the Emperor with one blow cut off this enemy soldier's head and neck with the left shoulder and arm attached, together with part of his side – despite the fact that the foe was wearing a cuirass. At this deed the citizens, both those who witnessed it and those who learned of it from others, were thrown into such a fright that they despaired of resisting and even of life itself.'[19]

With the river secured in front of them and the orchards cleared behind them the crusaders set up camp. Both the Franks and Damascenes began erecting barricades for the battle ahead. The siege continued for several days after which the crusaders' efforts took a turn for the worse.

While the reasons differ greatly between accounts, it is universally agreed that the crusaders left their supply of food and water on 27 July, for the other side of the city; a position which afforded them far less advantage than their previous base of operations. Runciman claims that the crusaders were driven from their position by the arrival of fresh reinforcements who had come to assist the city. However, the early chroniclers were less generous. William of Tyre claimed that the Damascenes bribed some of the crusaders to lift the siege, while the Arab chronicler Ibn al-Athīr made the claim that the Emir of Damascus Mu'in ad-Dīn appealed to the Eastern Franks questioning their loyalty to the Western Franks. According to the Emir, if the Western Christians captured Damascus they would keep it for themselves and the Eastern Christians' possessions on the coast would also soon fall to the greedy Westerners. In addition, according to this account, the Emir said that if it looked like he was going to lose Damascus, he would simply hand it over to the more powerful of his fellow Muslim neighbours, and then the entire region would be in danger.[20]

The Crusaders are seen battling their way towards Damascus in this modern interpretation of the campaign. *ClipArt.com*

Regardless of their motivations for moving their position, the crusaders quickly went from the offensive to the defensive and despite, having not yet captured the city, began quarrelling amongst themselves as to what would be done once the city was seized. Jerusalem expected the city to be incorporated into its territory, while Thierry, Count of Flanders, who had travelled East with Louis wanted to hold it for himself. Baldwin, Louis and Conrad were in agreement, which raised the ire of the Eastern barons and lowered their willingness to continue the fight.[21] As rumours of bribery and treachery began to pass between the troops, the crusaders learned that Nur ad-Dīn and his men were on their way. The local barons began to persuade their Western brothers that the time to retreat was now. Louis and Conrad, though puzzled by the blatant disloyalty among their fellow Crusaders, ordered the retreat.

The eastern gate of the old city of Damascus as it appeared in the 1800s. The crusaders abandoned their position on the west side of the city and relocated near to this area, which ultimately led to their defeat. *ClipArt.com*

As the crusaders made their way back to Jerusalem, the Muslims harassed them with a greater zeal than they had during their approach to Damascus. In his account of the battle, Ibn al-Qalānsi told of the further devastation of the Frankish army:

'They showered them with arrows and killed many of their rearguard in this way, and horses and pack animals as well. Innumerable corpses of men and their splendid mounts were found in their bivouacs and along the route of their flight, the bodies stinking so powerfully that the birds almost fell out of the sky.'[22]

Aftermath and Accusations

The failure to capture Damascus effectively brought the Second Crusade to a disastrous and unproductive end. The alliance between the Western kings was over; Conrad returned at once to his homeland by way of Constantinople, and although Louis would spend another year in the East, he made no attempts to engage in further military activities. From Attalia to Damascus, the East lay littered with the bloated and rotting corpses of dead crusaders, left to bake under the Levantine sun. The decision to attack Damascus instead of Aleppo, as Raymond of Antioch had desired, ultimately allowed Nur ad-Dīn's base of power to grow and strengthened his alliance with Damascus. In 1149, the united efforts of Aleppo and Damascus led to Raymond's death at the Battle of Inab[23] and in 1150 Nur ad-Dīn captured and imprisoned Joscelin of Edessa, where he spent the last decade of his life.

The inability of the barons of the East to set aside personal differences and work towards a common goal and against a common enemy was beginning to push the Eastern Franks closer and closer towards the Mediterranean Sea. It would only be a matter of time before they would be forced to cross it. As with all military disasters, there needed to be someone to blame for the failures and William of Tyre had no problem laying that blame at the feet of his own people:

'Thus a company of kings and princes such as we have not read of through all the ages had gathered and, for our sins, had been forced to return, covered with shame and disgrace, with their mission unfulfilled. They returned to the kingdom by the same route over which they had come. Henceforth, so long as they remained in the East, they regarded the ways of our princes with suspicion. With good reason they turned down all their wicked plans and henceforth the leaders of the Crusade were lukewarm in the service of the Kingdom. Even after they had returned to their own lands they constantly remembered the injuries they had suffered and detested our princes as wicked men. Nor were they alone affected. For they also caused others who had not been there to neglect the care of the kingdom, so that henceforth those who undertook the pilgrimages were fewer and less fervent. Even today [1170s] those who come are careful lest they fall into a trap and they strive to return home as soon as possible.'[24]

Some claimed that the failure to take Damascus was due to the Templars' desire for money, pride and even their jealousy of the Western crusaders. Among those who took this point of view was Ralph of Coggeshall, an English Cistercian chronicler who wrote that the Templars had urged the crusaders to retreat after being offered a bribe from Nur al-Dīn himself. Another contemporary chronicler, Gervase of Canterbury held to the same belief, and added that when the Templars received their bribe, they found jars full of copper rather than the valuable coin they had expected. This was, according to Gervase, a miracle from God rather than treachery from the Muslims.[25]

What is interesting about the accusations is that as early as the Second Crusade, the Templars were being used as a scapegoat in the West to explain the failures of the East. We may never truly know if the Templars forfeited the Siege of Damascus in favour of financial gain, but just five years later, the Order would engage in another campaign where they would be again accused of acting in their own interests. However, this time, the accusations were not entirely without foundation.

The Templars at Gaza

Two years after the fiasco at Damascus, Baldwin III made the decision to refortify the city of Gaza, the ruins of which lay to the south of Ascalon. He gave the location to the Templars so that they could use it as a base of operations to guard the South and to eventually pave the way for an attack on the port city of Ascalon. Although Egypt attempted to seize Gaza in the spring of 1150, they were successfully repelled and from that point forward their activities in the region were greatly reduced. No longer did they fuel Ascalon with supplies by land; instead materials were brought around the back by sea.[26]

However, the Templars, in their newly acquired base did no such thing and regularly made raids on Ascalon's territory, just as Ascalon had done so often

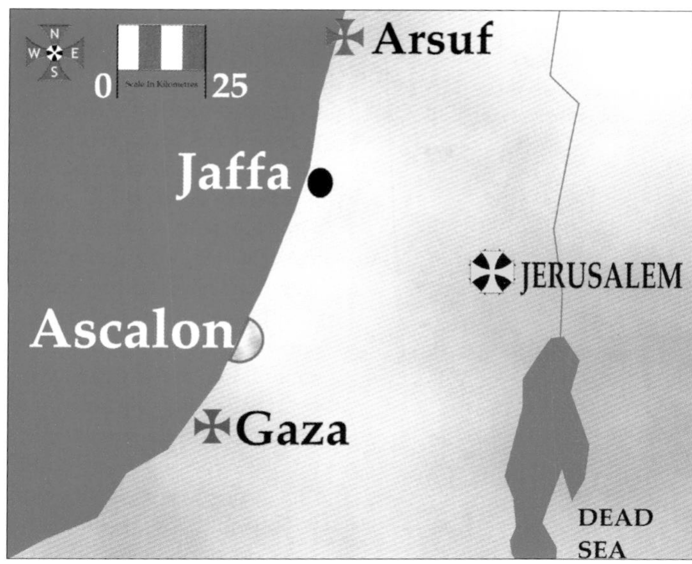

During the Siege of Ascalon in 1153, Bernard de Tremeley and a number of Templars lost their lives. The city eventually fell into King Baldwin's hands who gave it to his younger brother Amalric. ***Author***

before on Christian held land. William of Tyre, who we have seen was not one of the Order's biggest fans, spoke highly of the Templars at Gaza when he said, 'Again and again they [the Templars] have vigorously assaulted Ascalon, sometimes openly and again by attacks from Ambush.'[27] What is particularly interesting about William's praise of the Order is the fact that he mentions that the Templars engaged in an ambush against the Ascalon garrison. This shows that by this stage of the Order's military evolution that they had become quite comfortable with utilizing the Eastern methods of warfare, which had often been used against them.

Although Baldwin had been of great help to the Order by giving them their first major castle within the Kingdom of Jerusalem,[28] his own position within the realm was being put to the test. When King Fulk died in 1144, his wife Melisende gained control of the Kingdom of Jerusalem on behalf of her son. Even when Baldwin had reached the age of maturity, Melisende held onto the reins and her reluctance to give up control to her son brought the kingdom to the brink of civil war. When Baldwin was 22 years of age he demanded that the kingdom be divided.[29] While Melisende did grant her son a sizeable slice, her share included Jerusalem. Baldwin felt that holding Jerusalem was essential if he were to successfully protect the kingdom from Nur ad-Dīn's ever increasing power. Melisende did not see things that way and fortified the walls of the city to keep her son out.[30] However, the citizens of Jerusalem were against her and she soon turned the city over to her son.

It was precisely this type of power struggle and infighting among the Muslims that had allowed the Christians to gain so much ground during the First Crusade. But Christian disunity began to change things in the years before and after the Second Crusade, which allowed the Muslims, who were drawing closer together, to begin to make major advances in Outremer. However, with a potential civil war quelled, the Kingdom of Jerusalem was able to secure one final victory, before things began to spiral downward.

The Siege of Ascalon

On 25 January 1153 the Commander of the City of Jerusalem, along with the ten knights under his command, was guarding the True Cross as an army of Templars, Hospitallers, seculars and ecclesiastics made the march toward Ascalon. The massive army arrived at the walls of the port city with as many siege towers as King Baldwin could gather for the war that lay ahead.[31]

Ascalon was situated on the Mediterranean coast and its fortifications were like a half circle; the radius on the shoreline and the semicircle on the landside facing eastward. William of Tyre described the city as being like a basin, that sloped seaward, girded round with artificial mounds, on which were built walls, studded with towers. The stone work, according to William's account was held together with cement, which made them very strong. There were also four gates in the circuit of the city's walls and one wall was flanked by two high towers.[32]

The Franks besieged the city for months, their number added to at Easter with the arrival of pilgrims, including many knights and sergeants.[33] The Fatimid garrison at Ascalon was aided in June by the arrival of troops from Egypt who had come by ship to bring fresh supplies. With fresh forces on both sides of the battle the siege continued on through the summer.

The largest of the Franks' siege towers was so big that it rose a good distance above the city walls and allowed the Christians to rain volleys of missile fire down on the city with greater precision and accuracy.[34] On the evening of 15 August, some members of the garrison snuck outside and set the massive tower ablaze.[35] However, they did not allow for the direction of the wind and soon the flames were

Eleanor of Aquitaine as depicted in a Victorian illustration. Upon her return to France, Eleanor had her marriage to Louis annulled and soon after married Henry II of England. Richard I of England, who was a major participant of the Third Crusade, was a child of her union with the English monarch. *ClipArt.com*

not only destroying the tower, but weakening the city's walls.

The next morning the walls had become so weakened from the heat and several months of Christian battering that they collapsed, creating a breach that gave the Franks their first opportunity in nearly seven months to capture the city. When the dust began to clear the Christians were greatly excited that a victory was at hand and immediately picked up their arms to enter the breach.

However, Bernard de Tremeley, who had succeeded Everard des Barres as Master of the Temple when the later resigned his post in 1152, arrived at the wall first along with a number of his Templars. In his account of the siege, William of Tyre said that de Tremeley would not let anyone into the breach except his own men so that they could have first pick in obtaining the spoils of war.

Although William was in France during the actual siege of Ascalon and writing as much as a quarter century after the actual event, the custom at the time was still the same as it had been when Ascalon was besieged. Whenever a city was captured by force, whatever a man seized belonged to him and his heirs in perpetuity. So there was certainly precedent for the practice among secular knights and although the Templars were vastly different to secular knights in many ways, it is reasonable to assume that de Tremeley would have wanted to obtain as much reward for his Order's efforts as possible. In fact the papal bull *Omne datum optimum* had among its many privileges expressly given the Templars the right to keep booty captured from the Muslims and it is certain the Templars would have taken full advantage of this privilege.

De Tremeley entered the breach with about forty of his Order, and it was said that those who remained outside the breach did so to keep others from getting in until the Templars got their share of the booty. Unfortunately for de Tremeley and his men, forty Templars, no matter how well trained, were no match for the awaiting garrison who slew the invaders to a man as soon as they realised that the odds were in their favour.

Realising that no further Christians were following, they moved quickly to secure the breach by piling beams and other pieces of good sized timber across the hole. As the fire of the previous night had now died out, they once again resumed their positions in the towers and renewed their defence immediately. Soon the Muslims were not the only ones looking down on the Christians from above – the slain Templars were tied to ropes and hung over the city's walls to taunt the Christians.[36]

As was often the case in medieval warfare, a truce was called so that each side could bury its dead. Although the battle later resumed, the Muslims had soon had enough and terms of surrender were sought. The Christians accepted the proposals and gave the citizens of Ascalon three days to vacate the city. They were gone within two and the captured city was given to Baldwin's younger brother Amalric.

Although it would be easy to accept William of Tyre's assertion that Master Bernard de Tremeley and his Templars acted in their own interests at Ascalon, his is the only account of the battle to make such a claim. Given that William was not an eyewitness to the events and did not always see eye to eye with the Templars, it is possible that his account, derived from second hand sources, was manipulated to deliver his own message. What is known is that the Templars lost a number of men during the siege, including their Master Bernard de Tremeley.

Once again, as they had several times previously, the Order assembled thirteen of their number to elect a new Master and this time chose the Order's Seneschal, Andrew de Montbard, perhaps the last of the Order's founding members, to be the Templars's fifth Master.

Although de Tremeley was dead, accusations that the Order was acting in its own interests in the field of battle were certainly not.

Gold from Cairo

IN THE same year that the Franks were attempting to capture Ascalon, Egypt was experiencing its own internal power struggle at Cairo. The conflict ended with the murder of the reigning caliph by his vizier Abbās, who wished to install his son, Nāsir al-Dīn, in the murdered caliph's stead. However, the vizier's plan did not go as he had hoped; revolt broke out and soon the father and son were fleeing Egypt with as much gold as they could carry.[37]

As the fugitives made their way towards Damascus in June of 1154, they were ambushed by a Christian army; Abbās was killed in the conflict, but Nāsir al-Dīn was captured. Once again, because the Templars had more knights in the field, the lion's share of the spoils went to them. Among the booty captured was Nāsir al-Dīn. After holding him captive for a short period of time he was sold back to the Egyptians, who desperately wanted his head, for a sum of 60,000 bezants. The ransom was a death sentence, for as soon as he returned to Egypt, Nāsir was torn to pieces by an angry mob.

The Templars' return of their hostage to the enraged Egyptians was not without criticism. According to William of Tyre, prior to his release Nāsir had expressed a desire to become a Christian and had begun the process of conversion. Once again William saw a willingness on the part of the Templars to act in their own interests, especially where money was concerned, but the reality of the matter is that, even if the Templars believed his wish to become a Christian, the Order probably felt that gold won for the defence of the Kingdom of Jerusalem was of far greater value than one soul won for the Kingdom of God.

Gaza continued to be as important to the Templars as Ascalon would be for the young Amalric. When he came to the throne after Baldwin's death in 1162, Ascalon became an important base of operations for the new king's invasion of Egypt – a series of campaigns in which the Templars showed little interest. But just as Baldwin's failure to capture Damascus in 1148 allowed Nur ad-Dīn to expand his base of power, Amalric's failure to make inroads into Egypt allowed another Muslim leader's power base to build. However, if the Christians had thought Nur ad-Dīn to be a formidable enemy, they had not yet met Saladin and soon they would wish they hadn't.

References for chapter 12

1 *St. Bernard: Apologia for the Second Crusade*, Medieval Sourcebook translated by Prof. James Brundage www.fordham.edu/halsall/source/bernard-apol.html.

2 Payne, Robert *The Crusades* p. 156. Bernard wrote a number of scathing letters to the French king criticising the way he was living and suggesting that if he continued on his present path, his soul would spend an eternity in hell. The correct path, Bernard told Louis, involved penance and that penance could surely be won if the king would only go on crusade. Other accounts suggest that Louis and Eleanor took up the cross after hearing one of Bernard's sermons on the new crusade.

3 When Zengi was assassinated in 1146, his kingdom was divided between Nur ad-Dīn, who took control of Aleppo and his older brother, Saif ad-Dīn, who took control of Mosul.

4 Runciman, Sir Stephen, *A History of the Crusades: Volume II*. p. 278.

5 William of Tyre, *Historia rerum in partibus transmarinis gestarum* [History of Deeds Done Beyond the Sea], XIV, 4-5, *Patrologia Latina* 201, 642-45, Translated by James Brundage, *The Crusades: A Documentary History*, (Milwaukee, WI: Marquette University Press, 1962), 79-82 www.fordham.edu/halsall/source/tyre-edessa.html.

6 Barber, Malcolm, *The New Knighthood*. p. 35

7 Runciman op. cit. p. 279.

8 Barber op. cit. p. 67

9 Ibid. p. 67. The individual groups were in turn under the command of a Templar commander named Gilbert.

10 Runciman op. cit. p. 279. Tyerman, Christopher, *God's War*. p. 331. Tyerman acknowledges the claim that Eleanor may have been having an affair with her uncle, but suggests that the matter is coloured by the fact that the couple divorced in 1152.

11 Barber op. cit. p. 68 Otto of Freising, *The Deeds of Frederick Barbarossa*. p. 102.

12 Runciman op. cit. p. 280. Alfonso Jordan was born in 1103 at Mount Pilgrim while his father was laying siege to Tripoli.

13 Ibid. p. 280. The allegations that Raymond murdered Alfonso Jordan was due to the fact that Raymond of Tripoli was an illegitimate son and may have been afraid that the Count of Toulouse might put in a claim for Tripoli, which would have been hard to refuse on feudal grounds. Queen Melisende's involvement was rumoured to have been at the request of Raymond's wife Hodierna.

14 Ibid. p. 280 Tyerman, Christopher, *God's War*. p. 331.

15 Tyerman op. cit. p. 332.

16 Gabrieli, Francesco, *Arab Historians of the Crusades*. p. 57

17 *Tyre, William of The Fiasco at Damascus 1148*, Medieval Sourcebook Translated by Prof. Brundage. www.fordham.edu/halsall/source/tyre-damascus.html.

18 Ibid.

19 Ibid.

20 Gabrieli op. cit. p. 61.

21 Runciman p. 283.

22 Gabrieli op. cit. p. 59.

23 Tyerman op. cit. p. 189.

24 Tyre op. cit.

25 Nicholson, Helen, *The Knights Templar: A New History*. p. 73.

26 Barber op. cit. p. 73.

27 Burman, Edward, *The Templars: Knights of God*. p. 67.

28 Barber, op. cit. p. 73.

29 Billings, Malcolm, *The Cross and the Crescent*. p. 94.

30 Runciman op. cit. p. 334.

31 Ibid. p. 338.

32 William of Tyre, Historia rerum in partibus transmarinis gestarum, XVII, 22-25, 27-30, Patrologia Latina 201, 696-708, translated by James Brundage, The Crusades: A Documentary History, http://www.fordham.edu/halsall/source/tyre-cde.html#ascalon

33 Ibid.

34 Runciman op. cit. p. 339.

35 Barber op. cit. p. 74.

36 Tyre op. cit.

37 Barber op. cit. p. 75.

A contemporary depiction of Saladin from the 12th century.
Author

A Formidable Foe

'Almighty God has said, "And those who fight for Our cause, We shall guide them in Our path, and God is with those who act with nobility," and the sacred works are full of passages referring to the Holy War. Saladin was more assiduous and zealous in this than in anything else.' [1]

Bahā' Ad-Dīn

On 15 May 1174, Nur ad-Dīn's right hand, which had held so much power during his 28 year reign, suddenly clutched his throat as he fell to the ground. It was here at Damascus, where his father had been murdered nearly three decades earlier, that the 60-year-old Nur ad-Dīn would also meet his end his life, felled not by the dagger of his enemies, but complications arising from tonsillitis.[2]

Before his untimely death, he had been planning to invade Egypt in order to take it away from an old associate of his named Saladin, whom Nur ad-Dīn, despite his previous esteem for the man, now viewed as a coward.[3] Nur ad-Dīn himself had sent Saladin to Egypt to work on his behalf, but lately had formed the opinion that Saladin had made not made enough progress against his Christian enemies to the north. Nur ad-Dīn saw this as Saladin attempting to maintain a buffer between himself and his master.[4] True or not, Saladin was certainly no coward.

The Rise of Saladin

Salah al-Din, or Saladin as he is known in the west, was born Yusuf ibn Ayyub, the third son of Najm ad-Dīn Ayyub, a Kurd who had served Nur ad-Dīn's father Zengi. When Zengi captured Baalbek from Damascus, it was Ayyub who held the keys to the city for his master. However when Zengi was murdered by a slave's dagger in 1146, Ayyub quickly seized the opportunity to ally himself with Damascus by giving Baalbek back to them. Nur ad-Dīn was not amused by what he must have seen as disloyalty, but his displeasure was not sufficient to break his ties with Ayyub's brother, Shirkuh, who continued to serve the Turkish leader.[5] In fact it was Shirkuh who killed Raymond of Antioch at the Battle of Inab in 1149.[6]

Five years later, Shirkuh arrived at Damascus as Nur ad-Dīn's ambassador, but the governor of the city would neither let him in nor go outside the city to meet with him. Nur ad-Dīn, insulted at the treatment of his ambassador, descended on the city with a sizeable army, which was inside the city gates within a week, having been granted entry by the citizens of Damascus themselves.[7] He instructed his men not to pillage the city, but instead filled the markets with much-needed produce and returned to Aleppo, leaving Ayyub in charge as the conquered city's new governor. With the capture of Damascus, Nur ad-Dīn had succeeded in achieving with ease what the crusaders had failed utterly to do less than a decade earlier.

It was in Damascus that the young Saladin received his early education. Once he reached the age of 14 he entered military service at Aleppo under the tutelage of his uncle Shirkuh, returning to Damascus four years later in an administrative capacity. Saladin continued to serve Nur ad-Dīn as part of his personal entourage and ultimately replaced Shirkuh as vizier of Egypt, upon his uncle's death in March of 1169.[8]

In November of 1170, Saladin, who had been at war with the Christians sent to invade Egypt, decided to strike back at them on their own turf and marched on the Templar fortress at Daron. The Templars received

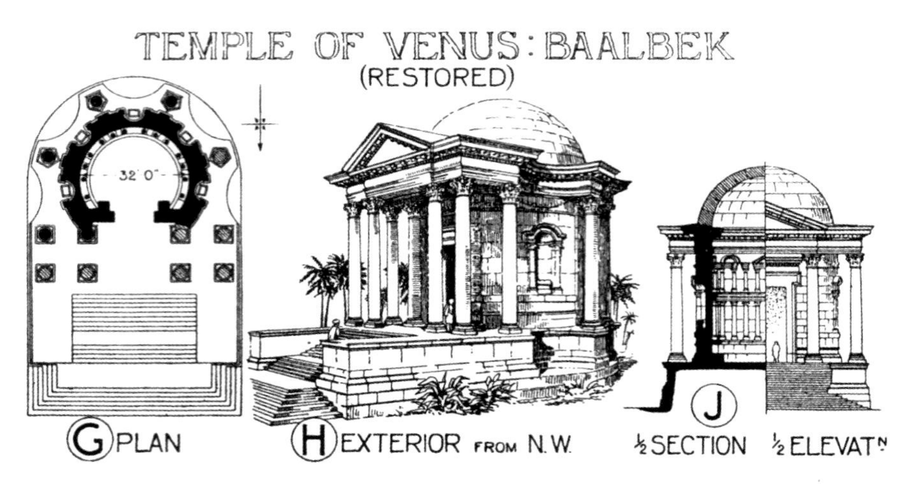

Diagram of the Temple of Venus at Baalbek. The city was ancient even in Zengi's time.
ClipArt.com

assistance from King Amalric and a group of their brethren from the garrison at Gaza. Although the Templar army was able to lift his siege of Daron, Saladin immediately marched on Gaza, where he massacred the citizens of the lower town but made no efforts to attempt to take citadel.[9] Soon after, Saladin returned to Egypt where he would continue to strengthen his position, while trying to minimise that of Damascus.

By August of 1171, Nur ad-Dīn had sent word to Saladin that he wanted the country's Fatimid government and caliph gone and that if his representative in Egypt was not prepared to handle the job, he would have no problem making the journey in person.[10] Despite Saladin's reluctance to comply with Nur ad-Dīn's orders, just a month later, two hundred years of Shia Fatimid rule came to an end when the caliph, al-Adid, died. Within a week Saladin had what was left of the Fatimid royal family rounded up and imprisoned and set out on a campaign to attack the crusader castle at Montreal.

Saladin's siege of Montreal began well. Amalric received poor advice on the situation and left Jerusalem too late to be any help. As a result, the garrison at Montreal was all but ready to surrender when word arrived that Nur ad-Dīn was nearby at Kerak.[11] Saladin immediately lifted the siege with the excuse that word had just arrived of problems in Upper Egypt which required the army's immediate attention.[12] The reality of the situation was that a confrontation with Nur ad-Dīn could have consequences for Saladin's position within Egypt; a position, which he had worked hard to obtain and was unwilling to compromise.

For the next three years, Saladin followed his father's advice to lie low and sent frequent tributes to Aleppo to smooth things over with Nur ad-Dīn. But the treasure and riches sent from Cairo were not enough to appease Nur ad-Dīn and in 1173 he ordered Saladin to besiege the Christian fortress of Kerak. Once again, as he had at Montreal, Saladin lifted the siege the moment he heard Nur ad-Dīn was on his way to assist. However, this time he had a more legitimate reason for returning quickly to Egypt. His aging father Ayyub had been thrown from his horse and was seriously wounded. The old man died before Saladin reached Cairo.[13]

While Nur ad-Dīn was saddened by the death of his long-time servant Ayyub, he was nonetheless angered by Saladin's disloyalty and vowed to move on Egypt the following spring.[14] But as the seasons of 1174 passed, so too did Muslim power in Syria. By spring, Saladin's rival Nur ad-Dīn lay dead at Damascus; by summer word of his death had arrived in Cairo and

Kerak of Moab in present day Jordan was an important crusader castle and one often confused with Krak des Chevaliers, which is located much further north. Saladin was ordered to besiege the castle in 1173, but eventually captured it in 1189 after the Battle of Hattin and Fall of Jerusalem.
iStockPhoto.com Paul Cowan

Saladin was now sultan. By the autumn the new sultan of Egypt was on the march to Damascus, where he was received with open arms as regent for Nur ad-Dīn's heir, As-Salih.

By 1175 Saladin succeeded in adding Homs, Hama and Baalbek to his conquests and during 1176 further added to his territory by taking Manbij and Azaz. Aleppo, however, would remain beyond his grasp, despite his efforts to take the city. Upon his return to Damascus that year, he further taunted Nur ad-Dīn from this side of the grave by marrying one of his widows, Asimat ad-Dīn.[15] By fall he was back in Cairo – not only with the title Sultan of Egypt, but also King of Syria.

The Citadel of Aleppo was first constructed in the tenth century AD and was greatly expanded during the thirteenth.
istockPhoto.com Simon Gurney

Confusion in Christendom

It was not only the Muslim world that was experiencing a shift in power. Concurrent with Saladin's victories in the North, Christendom was experiencing difficulties of its own in the South.

On 11 July 1174 King Amalric of Jerusalem, who had spent much of his rein trying to make inroads into Egypt, died of dysentery.[16] This left his 13-year-old son, Baldwin, as heir to the throne. As if his age was not problematic enough, the future king was also a leper.[17] Despite his obvious shortcomings, four days after his father's death, he was crowned Baldwin IV in the Church of the Holy Sepulchre. It was clear, however, that the Kingdom of Jerusalem would need a regent.

That role, in all but name, was initially performed by Miles de Plancy, who was the deceased king's closest friend and Seneschal. However, de Plancy was not well liked and his unpopularity with the local barons paved the way for Raymond, Count of Tripoli, who was the king's closest male relative, to take over as regent.[18] Three weeks later Miles de Plancy was assassinated at Acre. Raymond was a suspect. Raymond may have been more popular with the local barons but he, like de Plancy, was not without his opponents. In fact his regency divided the kingdom into two factions. Raymond's party consisted of the local barons such as the Ibelins and the Hospitallers, who sought ways to work cooperatively with their Muslim neighbours, while the other camp was composed of Westerners and the Templars, who sought a more militant approach to dealing with the same problems.[19]

Among those to side with the Templar's was a man named Reynald de Châtillon, who was released from prison in Aleppo in 1176 with a rabid hatred for Islam. Reynald's position was as much personal as ideological. A few months after his release from prison, Reynald married de Plancy's widow, Stephanie, and through the marriage became Lord of Oultrejordain. Since de Plancy's widow was convinced that Count Raymond had played a hand in her husband's murder, it was clear which faction they had aligned themselves with.

Likewise the Templars's problems with Count Raymond were, at least in part, personal. In 1173, a Flemish knight named Gerard de Ridefort came to Tripoli and entered into Raymond's employ. In exchange, Raymond had promised de Ridefort the hand in marriage of his first eligible heiress. However, when that opportunity arose a few months later, Raymond seemingly forgot his promise. Instead of marrying her off to de Ridefort, Raymond gave her hand in marriage to a rich Pisan who literally offered the Count the princess's weight in gold.[20] Soon after Gerard de Ridefort joined the Templars, but he would never forget Raymond's slight.

The rift between the factions spread almost as rapidly as Baldwin's leprosy and with equal damage. It was well-known that Baldwin would not have a long life and it was therefore necessary to secure the future of the Kingdom of Jerusalem quickly. Baldwin had two step-sisters Isabella and Sibylla, neither of whom had husbands. Sibylla, the eldest, was the first to marry, uniting with William de Montferrat in October of 1176. However, just three months after the marriage, William died of malaria, leaving Sibylla pregnant with his child.[21] Although the powers that be tried to find a husband for Sibylla in the person of Philip of Flanders, the Count was more interested in

Construction of Saladin's Citadel in Cairo began in 1176, soon after he became Sultan of Egypt. Shown here is one of the citadel's towers.
istockPhoto.com Ranjan Chari

Hama, shown in this illustration, was one of several Muslim cities captured by Saladin in 1174-1175. *Clipart.com*

marrying off his two cousins than entering a marriage himself.[22] It would be a few years before Sibylla would ultimately choose her own husband and in so doing seal the fate of the Kingdom of Jerusalem.

The Battle of Montgisard

WHEN King Baldwin reached the age of 16 in 1177, Raymond's regency of the Kingdom of Jerusalem came to an end. Now in power, the leper king immediately became involved in military campaigns, despite his growing illness. When Philip of Flanders decided to go north to help Raymond of Tripoli in a campaign against the Muslims, Baldwin sent one thousand knights and two thousand foot soldiers to assist, as well as a number of Templars.[23] This left the kingdom with far fewer men than they had sent[24] and Saladin quickly learned of the kingdom's weakened condition.

On November 18 1177, Saladin crossed into Christian territory with a massive army said to have been composed of twenty-six thousand light cavalry, eight thousand men on camels and an additional one thousand men who formed Saladin's bodyguard.[25] Knowing that his army greatly outnumbered the Christians, Saladin confidently began his northward march up the Palestinian coast. However, the kingdom was not without its own intelligence and as soon as word arrived that the sultan was on the move, Odo de St Amand, who was then Master of the Templars, ordered every knight he could gather to move south to Gaza to fend off the Muslims.

Saladin, perhaps realising that the Templars would respond in such a manner, sailed on past Gaza and set out to besiege Ascalon, which had been captured two decades earlier. Baldwin, who had been able to gather about five hundred knights, headed straight for the port city, arriving a few hours before Saladin and his army[26] But Saladin once again changed his plans. Since the Templars were guarding Gaza and the king and his men were guarding Ascalon, the sultan realised that the road between him and Jerusalem lay empty of his Christian enemies. Leaving a small contingent to keep Baldwin occupied, Saladin moved north towards Jerusalem, his mouth surely salivating at the prospect of capturing the Holy City. But overconfidence caused Saladin to let his guard down. The normally tight rein he kept on his men was loosened and they were allowed to wander and pillage the countryside.

Baldwin somehow managed to get word to the Templar garrison at Gaza as to what was happening. His messenger told the Templars there to abandon Gaza and head north to Ascalon to help their king.

When the Templars arrived at Ascalon, Baldwin along with Reynald de Châtillon and the army flew out of the city and the united Christian forces moved north to Ibelin, where they swung inland towards Jerusalem.[27]

Exactly one week after he had crossed over from Egypt, Saladin and his army were crossing a ravine near Montgisard, southeast of Jerusalem, when the Christians came crashing down on them from the north. Saladin had no idea what was coming his way.

With the element of surprise on their side, the Christians, despite being incredibly outnumbered, were able to send Saladin's army from the field of battle. The victory was owed to the Templars and their heavy charge, led by Odo de St Amand and eighty of his brethren. Ralph of Diss in chronicling an eyewitness account of the Battle of Montgisard wrote of the devastating effect of the Templars' charge:

> 'Spurring all together, as one man, they [the Templars] made a charge, turning neither to the left nor to the right. Recognising the battalion in which Saladin commanded many knights, they manfully approached it, immediately penetrated it, incessantly knocked down, scattered, struck and crushed. Saladin was smitten with admiration, seeing his men dispersed everywhere, everywhere turned in flight, everywhere given to the mouth of the sword.'[28]

Many of Saladin's men left the field before the first wave of the Templars' charge hit; those who had the courage to hold their positions were all but destroyed by the Christians. Soon the Egyptian army was in flight, abandoning not only the booty they had captured as the pillaged their way towards Jerusalem, but also many of their own weapons.[29] If the humiliation in the field was not enough, the journey home only added to it. As the army crossed the Sinai Desert, they were regularly harassed by Bedouins, while others who stopped in villages to beg for food and water were slain or handed over to the Christians as captives.[30]

As for Saladin, ever concerned that his position of power might be upset, he sent messengers ahead to Egypt, mounted on speeding camels, to let everyone

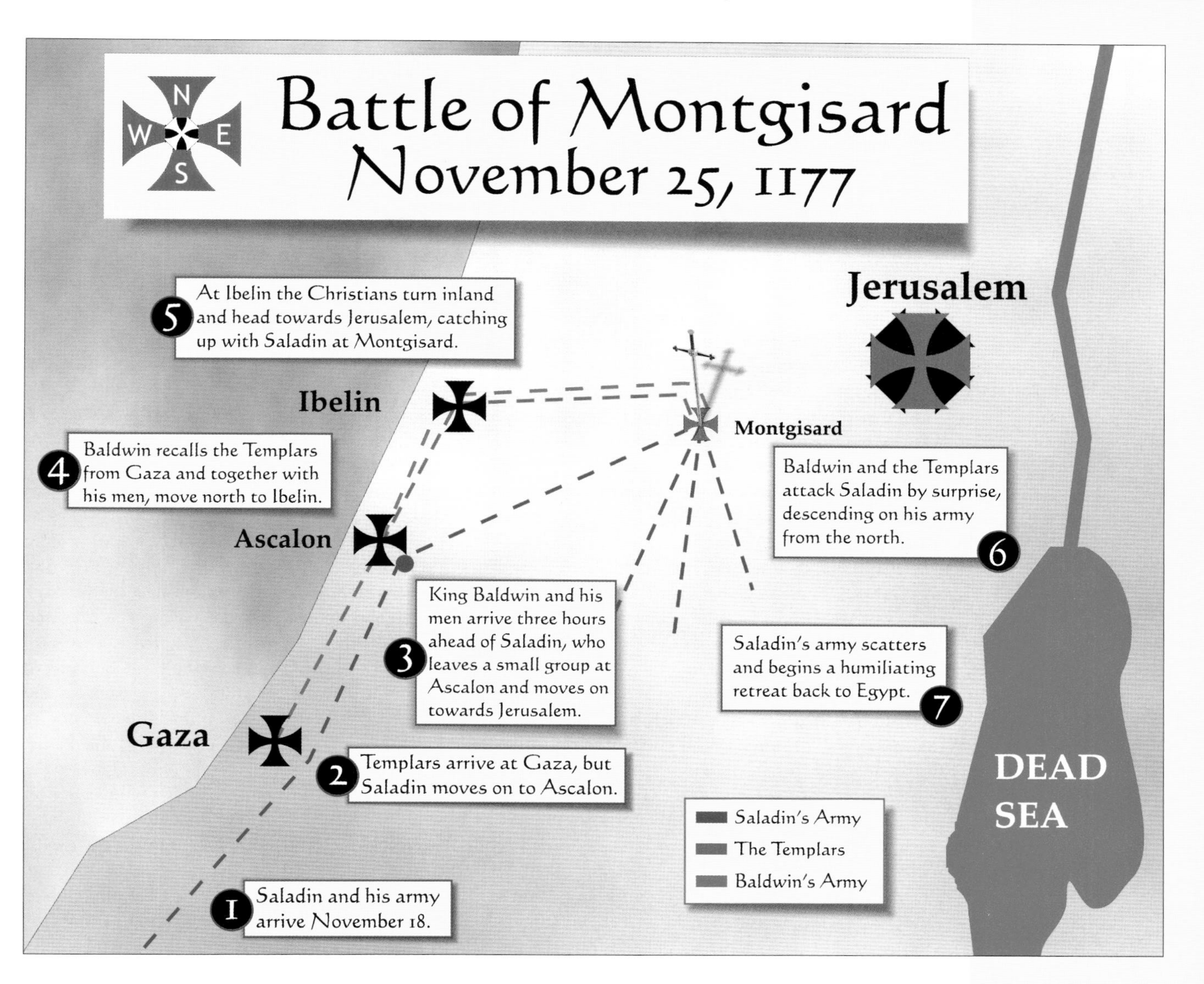

know that he was very much still among the living. Upon his return carrier pigeons were sent throughout the land to let the Egyptians know that their sultan had returned.

In the end, Saladin failed to capture Jerusalem as he had hoped, largely due to the courage of Jerusalem's leper king and the skill and discipline of the Templars under Odo de St Armand. However, whatever humiliation Saladin had faced at Montgisard in the autumn of 1177, it would be long forgotten a decade later when the Holy City would finally be his.

The Seeds of Destruction

Saladin did not sit idle during the decade between his great defeat at Montgisard and what would be his greatest victory at Jerusalem. In 1179 the sultan succeeded in capturing the Templar Master, Odo de St Amand, as well as Baldwin d'Ibelin, who had also fought at Montgisard. Baldwin's ransom was set at 150,000 dinars plus the return of one thousand Muslim prisoners being held by the Christians. The Templar Master was to be exchanged for but one Muslim prisoner, albeit one whom the sultan considered to be of great importance.[31] Unwilling to admit that any man was his equal, de St Amand remained in prison at Damascus, until his death a year later. De St Amand was succeeded by Arnold de Torroja, who had served as Master of the Order in Spain. As such, de Torroja was unfamiliar with the politics of the East and spent a considerable amount of time trying to mediate between the various factions.[32] He died in 1184, during a trip to the West to drum up support for what was left of the Crusader States. De Torroja was in turn succeeded in 1185 by Gerard de Ridefort, the man who had joined the

Templars after being denied the hand of the princess of Botron. Although it would be de Ridefort, who would carry much of the blame for the loss of Jerusalem, the seeds of destruction were actually planted several years earlier.

Intrigue in the Kingdom

KING Baldwin was dying and his sister Sibylla had still not found a husband. Although she had fallen in love with Baldwin d'Ibelin and planned to marry him, he had been captured by Saladin along with Odo de St Amand at the Battle of Marj Ayun. When Baldwin was released from prison, Sibylla informed him that she could not possibly marry him when he was in debt. However, by the time Baldwin had secured the money to pay his ransom debt, Sibylla had found another man, a knight from Poitou named Guy of Lusignan. The couple were married at Easter 1180 and Guy was given Ascalon and Jaffa as his fief.[33]

A month later the king entered into a two year truce with Saladin, which allowed both sides to pass freely through each other's lands. Not everyone in the kingdom was prepared to honour the truce, however. Reynald de Châtillon saw the rich Muslim caravans that passed by his home as too great an opportunity for booty and began raiding them. Saladin was outraged and took the matter to King Baldwin, who although agreeing that Reynald was violating the truce, was nonetheless unable to force the Lord of Oultrejordain to make amends.[34] Saladin obtained a further bargaining chip a few months later when a group of pilgrims, forced to make port at Damietta in bad weather, were captured. Saladin offered the fifteen hundred pilgrims in exchange for the caravan booty Reynald had taken, but de Châtillon was still unwilling to make amends. In fact Reynald had become so bold that he actually planned to launch a squadron to Mecca by way of the Red Sea. It was his intent to attack Islam's holiest city, bring the Kaaba to the ground and rob the tomb of the Prophet Muhammed in Medina. Although he did not make it as far as he'd hoped, his incursion was sufficient to seal his fate as far as Saladin was concerned.[35]

De Ridefort's Revenge

DE RIDEFORT'S administration began as the political instability that had plagued King Baldwin's reign was coming to a close. The leper king finally succumbed to his illness in March 1185, and was replaced by his nephew, Baldwin V, who died a little more than a year later at the age of eight.[36] Prior to his death, Baldwin IV had written in his will that should his nephew die before he reached the age of ten, Raymond was to resume his position as regent; however, there were those within the Kingdom of Jerusalem who did not wish to see the will fulfilled. With the assistance of de Ridefort and the Templars, Sibylla and Guy staged a coup in September of 1186 that ensured that they, and not Raymond of Tripoli, would rule the kingdom.

There were three keys to the box, which held the crown jewels. The Patriarch and de Ridefort, both of whom supported Sibylla, each held one, while the third was held by the Master of the Hospitallers Roger des Moulins. Des Moulins refused to turn over the key, but ultimately threw it from his window in a fit of utter disgust over the matter.[37] De Ridefort eagerly snatched the key from the dirt, seeing it not so much as the key to unlocking the crown jewels as the key to unlocking his revenge on Raymond of Tripoli. As the Templars guarded the city gates to keep Raymond out, Sibylla was crowned queen of Jerusalem by the city's Patriarch and immediately the new queen crowned Guy as her king. According to some accounts, as de Ridefort left the Church of the Holy Sepulchre, he cried out that the crowning was payback for the marriage of the princess of Botron.[38] It would not be de Ridefort's only move against Raymond of Tripoli.

Throughout the winter of 1186, de Ridefort tried to persuade King Guy to march on Raymond and take Tiberius in order to bring him back into the fold. In a countermeasure, Raymond entered into a truce with Saladin to protect Tripoli and Galilee.[39] King Guy, who tended to take whatever council was offered him at any given moment, may have made the move had he not been persuaded by Balian d'Ibelin to take wiser council. Instead of marching on Tiberius with arms, it was decided to march with diplomats and on 29 April 1187 the archbishop of Tyre together with the Master of the Temple and the Master of the Hospitallers set out for Tiberius. The plan was to pick up Balian at his castle at Nablus, but the younger Ibelin brother was tied up and sent the party north, promising to meet up with them at the Templars' castle at La Féve.[40]

Concurrent with the embassy's move northward, Saladin's son al-Afdel had requested that Raymond allow a scouting party from his army to move south. The request was little more than a polite formality as the truce Raymond had entered with Saladin could permit him but one answer. However, it did not prohibit the count from sending word to the embassy to let them know what to expect. What should have been a friendly warning would soon turn to unnecessary bloodshed. Upon receiving word that Muslims were afoot, de Ridefort moved immediately into action by summoning as many of his Templars as he could quickly gather.

The Springs of Cresson

On 1 May, the army made up of ninety Templars, another fifty knights including the Master of the Hospitallers, Roger des Moulins and three hundred foot soldiers arrived at the Springs of Cresson, a little north of Nazareth. Below them was an army of Muslims said to be seven thousand strong, but which in reality probably numbered no more than seven hundred.[41] If the numbers are to be believed, for every Christian on the hill, there were fifty Muslims waiting below. Even if there were only seven hundred, the Christsians were outnumbered five to one.

Des Moulins and the Templar Marshal James de Mailly, seeing the unfavourable odds, urged de Ridefort to retreat, but he would have none of it. Instead of taking his Marshal's council, he taunted him, telling him that he was too fond of his own blonde head to risk losing it. The Marshal responded that he would die in battle a brave man, while his Master would flee the field of battle like a traitor.[42] It was a prophecy that would come true sooner than de Mailly could have known. Gerard, insulted by his Marshal's insubordination, spurred his horse at once and led the charge down into the valley where the Muslims were waiting.

When the battle was over, both the Marshal of the Templars and the Master of the Hospitallers, who had urged de Ridefort to retreat, lay dead in the field. Alongside their corpses lay the bodies of the one hundred and forty knights and three hundred sergeants.[43] Of those who had entered the field only three men survived, one of whom was de Ridefort.

The massacre at Cresson was without a doubt a disaster brought on by de Ridefort's impetuous nature and, although the Templar Master was solely responsible for sending ninety of his men to their deaths, an unexpected benefit of their martyrdom was the unification of the two political factions. After all it had been Raymond who had allowed the Muslims to cross his land in the first place and, as such, part of the blame lay at his doorstep. Shortly after the massacre at Cresson, Raymond and King Guy patched things up, the truce with Saladin was ended and the Muslim garrison stationed at Tiberius was expelled.[44] For the first time in many years, it seemed like Christendom was once again prepared to turn their attentions towards a common enemy and Guy was able to assemble an army from Tripoli, Antioch and his own Kingdom of Jerusalem the likes of which had never been seen.

Unfortunately, it would prove to be too little too late.

A romantic depiction of de Ridefort's impetuous charge against the Muslims at the Springs of Cresson on 1 May 1187.
Author's collection

References for chapter 13

1 Gabrieli, Franscesco, *Arab Historians of the Crusades* p. 99. This is a quote from Bahā' Ad-Din on Saladin's zeal in waging holy War.

2 Runciman, Steven, *A History of the Crusades Vol. II*. p. 398. Gabrieli, Francesco, *Arab Historians of the Crusades*. p. 69-70. The account of Ibn al-Athīr gives the cause of death as a heart attack.

3 Ibid. p. 69.

4 Ibid. p. 69.

5 Hindley, Geoffrey, *Saladin* p. 47.

6 Ibid. p. 48.

7 Runciman, Steven, *A History of the Crusades Vol. II*. p. 341.

8 Hindley op. cit. p. 61.

9 Runciman op. cit. p. 390.

10 Hindley, op. cit. p. 65.

11 Runciman op. cit. p. 394.

12 Hindley, op. cit. p. 66.

13 Ibid. p. 67.

14 Runciman op. cit. p. 396.

15 Hindley op. cit. pp. 79-86.

16 Runciman op. cit. p. 374.

17 It was William of Tyre who had discovered Baldwin's leprosy when he was the boy's teacher. The young heir to the throne had been playing a game of endurance with his friends where they would dig their nails into each other's arms to see who would be the first to yield to pain. The young Baldwin won, the contest not for his courage, but because he could not feel anything.

18 Runciman op. cit. p. 404.

19 Ibid. p. 405.

20 Ibid. p. 406. Payne, Robert, *The Crusades*. pp. 183-184. Barber, Malcolm, *The New Knighthood* pp. 109-110. Barber gives a later date of 1180, suggesting that de Ridefort had served as Marshal of Jerusalem in 1179 and joined the Templar Order in 1180.

21 Payne op. cit. pp. 184-185.

22 Runciman op. cit. p. 415.

23 Nicholson, Helen, *The Knights Templar: A New History*. p. 66.

24 Payne op. cit. p. 188.

25 Ibid. p. 187.

26 Runciman op. cit. p. 416.

27 Ibid. p. 417.

28 Nicholson op. cit. p. 66.

29 Runciman op. cit. p. 417.

30 Payne op. cit. p. 187.

31 Runciman, op. cit. p. 420.

32 Barber, Malcolm, *The New Knighthood*. p. 109.

33 Runciman op. cit. p. 424.

34 Ibid. p. 431.

35 Ibid. p. 437.

36 Barber op. cit. p. 110.

37 Runciman op. cit. p. 448.

38 Ibid. p. 448.

39 Barber, op. cit. p. 111.

40 Ibid. p. 111.

41 Ibid. p. 111. Nicholson, Helen David Nicolle, *God's Warriors: Knights Templar, Saracens and the Battle for Jerusalem*. p. 66. Barber gives the number as 7000 as does Nicholson and Nicolle; however, the latter indicate that the larger number is an exaggeration – 700 being more realistic.

42 Runciman op. cit. p. 453 Barber op. cit. pp. 111-112.

43 Tyerman, Christopher, *God's War: A New History of the Crusades*. p. 367.

44 Ibid. p. 367.

A nineteenth-century depiction of the final battle at Hattin.
Author's collection

The Fall of Jerusalem

'The number of dead and captured was so large that those who saw the slain could not believe that anyone could have been taken alive and those who saw the prisoners could not believe that any had been killed.'[1]

Ibn al-Athir on the Battle of Hattin

Right: **The murder of Thomas Becket on 29 December 1170 led to Henry II sending money to the Templars to be held in trust to help finance a crusade.** *ClipArt.com*

On 29 December 1170, four knights entered England's Canterbury Cathedral where they assassinated the Archbishop, Thomas Becket. In cold blood and with cold steel, the knights had answered a simple question asked by their king: 'Who will rid me of this meddlesome priest?'

While it is unlikely that King Henry II of England, the grandson of King Fulk of Jerusalem, had intended for his words to be taken literally, he was nonetheless forced to atone for the priest's murder. Part of that atonement was to send a large sum of money to Outremer, where it was to be banked by the Templars against a crusade that the king had sworn to undertake.

In June of 1187, Henry's coffers in the Templar treasury at Jerusalem were opened by Gerard de Ridefort; not to aid the king's planned and long delayed crusade, but to hire mercenary troops. As always there was a reason for breaking the Order's policy on protecting a client's money and in this case de Ridefort felt the move necessary to avenge the shame the Muslims had brought on Christendom in general and himself in particular the month previous at Cresson.[2]

Indeed the Kingdom of Jerusalem was on the brink of facing even greater shame, for Saladin was bringing in troops from Aleppo, Mosul and Mardin[3] and when combined the Muslims had amassed fifty thousand men.[4] On 26 June Saladin reviewed his troops at Ashtera and arranged them in marching formation, Taki-ed-Din, Saladin's nephew, taking the right wing, Kukburi, the Emir of Harran, the left wing and Saladin himself the centre column. The army marched north from Ashtera to Khisfin and then southward around the southern tip of the Sea of Galilee, where they stayed for five days while gathering intelligence on the Christians.[5] Saladin crossed the River Jordan on July 1 and sent half of his troops north to lay siege to Tiberias while the other half moved west to Cafarsset where they set up camp.

Concurrent with Saladin crossing the Jordan, King Guy held a council meeting at the port city of Acre to lay plans for the Christian's plan of attack. Raymond

Henry II of England was the son of Geoffrey, Count of Anjou and Matilda. As such he was the grandson of Fulk of Anjou who became King of Jerusalem after the death of Baldwin II.
ClipArt.com

of Tripoli knew that the summer heat would be a problem for both sides in the coming conflict, but realised that the army who attacked would be at an immediate disadvantage. As such, it was his suggestion that the Christian army, which numbered some thirty-eight thousand men[6] including the mercenary troops hired with King Henry's money, should take a defensive stand. Saladin could not, Raymond told the council, press the fight for long in the parched region and would be forced to retreat.[7] Reynald and de Ridefort accused Raymond of cowardice and suggested a more militant approach. As was so often the case, Guy was blown by the wind hitting his ears and gave the Order to march towards Tiberias.

The Christian army arrived at Sephorie, northeast of Nazareth, on 2 July and set up camp. Like the orchards outside of Damascus the spot was an excellent place to make camp. There was plenty of water, pastures for the horses and the location would give them the advantage in the coming battle. But like the fiasco of Damascus, the king would soon be persuaded to change locations.

That evening a messenger arrived informing the Christians that Saladin had besieged Tiberias. Raymond again recommended the same defensive strategy he had offered earlier. Even though Tiberias belonged to him and his wife was in the city's citadel, he was willing to let it fall for the greater good of saving the kingdom. This time King Guy took Raymond's advice and spread the word that the camp would hold their position. However, later that night, Gerard de Ridefort returned to Guy's tent intent on bending his ear and making him abandon his plan. The Templar Master asked the king if he were prepared to trust a traitor; in de Ridefort's eyes, that is what his old adversary, Raymond of Tripoli, was. It was a disgrace to sit idle while a Christian city so close by fell to the infidels. De Ridefort even threatened the king that should he remain inactive, the Templars would be forced to hang up their habits; the deaths of the brethren at Cresson must be avenged.[8] Again the malleable Guy was persuaded by the last voice to reach his ears and gave the order that the camp would march at dawn. Of course there was little he could say in opposition to Gerard's requests. Had it not been for the Master of the Temple and his brethren, it would be Raymond of Tripoli and not he making the decisions.

When the sun rose the next morning, the Christians broke camp and left their favourable position at Sephorie for Tiberias, moving northeast towards Tourran. As the army was travelling through Raymond's fief, he, according to feudal custom, took the vanguard position. King Guy and his men made up the centre column, while Balian d'Ibelin, Reynald de Châtillon and the Templars formed the rearguard. The divisions were made up of cavalry and each unit would have been protected on all sides by the foot soldiers who accompanied the army. In the centre of the line of march was the sacred relic, the True Cross.

Saladin, having received word of the Christians' movement, broke camp at Cafarsset and, along with his army, began to move in the same direction. Although detachments were sent to harass the line of march, Saladin's army did not have any major contact with the Christian army until they had arrived at Tourran around mid-morning.

As the Christians continued towards Tiberias, Muslim light cavalry began to skirmish the army, picking off horses and men one by one. As if the harassment was not enough to sap their morale, they were now suffering from the heat, unable to quench the thirst that had been building since they had left Sephorie that morning. By noon, the army had all but come to a full stop.[9]

It was at this point that Raymond suggested to King Guy that the army change course and move towards the village of Hattin, six kilometres away, where the army could take water at the springs, make camp and set out for Tiberias the following morning. Guy agreed and the army moved off in that direction. However, as the Christians were travelling downgrade towards the two hills known as the Horns of Hattin, Saladin had the advantage of being able to see what they were doing and ordered Taki-ed-Din to move in to block their approach to Hattin.

With the vanguard halted, Saladin had his other wing harass the Christian rearguard, which caused Raymond to order a second halt of the army. The Templars charged their Muslim tormentors in

ClipArt.com

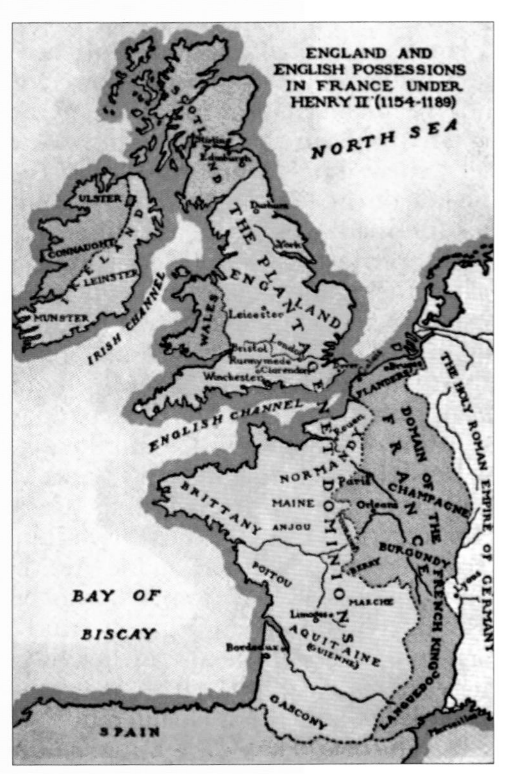

The Horns of Hattin viewed from the north-east towards the ridge and the southern Horn. It was here that Saladin crushed the Christian forces on 4 July 1187. *iStockPhoto.com Linda Winkler*

the hopes of driving them away, but the charge failed to deliver the desired result and the army, now exhausted from the abundance of heat and lack of water, decided to make camp where they were. It was at this point, according to a contemporary account of the battle that Raymond cried out, 'Alas, Lord God, the battle is over! We have been betrayed unto death. The Kingdom is finished!' [10] The account continues by describing the hardships the Christian army faced throughout the night:

> 'And so, in sorrow and anguish, they camped on a dry site where, during the night, there flowed more blood than water. The sons of Esau [Saladin's army] surrounded the people of God [The Christians] and set fire to the desert [brush] round about them. Throughout the night the hungry and thirsty men were harassed further by arrows and by the fire's heat and flame.' [11]

When the soldiers, who were able to sleep amid the evening's torment, awoke they were even dryer than the night before and the first thing on their minds must have been to find water. Saladin's men, on the other hand had water to spare as the army had employed a caravan of camels to transport water from the lake to their encampment.[12]

The Battle of Hattin

Fighting broke out almost as soon as the army began to move forward, with Saladin sending his men in to attack the parched Christians. This was met with a counter-charge from the Templars. Although the charge was effective, the Templars lost a number of horses. As the fighting continued, the infantrymen who were to protect the knights lost morale and broke off from the main army in ever increasing numbers heading towards the body of water glistening to their right, despite it being further away than it must have appeared. It was water they would never drink as many of the infantry were slaughtered, the rest captured to later be sold as slaves.

With their protection destroyed there was little the remaining knights could do. Not even the better disciplined Military Orders could gain much ground without the assistance of the infantry. The anonymous writer of *De Expugatione Terrae Sanctae per Saladinum* tells of the chaos and carnage that followed:

> 'The Templars, Hospitallers, and Turcopoles, meanwhile, were engaged in a fierce rear guard action. They could not win, however, because enemies sprang up on every side, shooting arrows and wounding Christians. When they had gone on for a little bit, they shouted to the King, asking for some help. The King and the others saw that the infantry were not going to return and that they themselves could not hold out against the Turkish arrows without the sergeants. Accordingly, by the grace of the Lord's cross, they ordered the tents to be put up, in order to block the Saracen charges and so that they could hold out more easily. The battle formations were, therefore, broken up. The units gathered around the Holy Cross, where they were confused and intermixed here and there. The men who were with the Count of Tripoli in the first group saw that the King, the Hospitallers, the Templars, and everyone else were jumbled together and mingled with the Turks. They also saw that there was a multitude of the barbarians between themselves and the King, so that they could not get through to return to the Lord's cross. They cried out: "Those who can get through may go, since the battle is not going in our favour. We have now lost even the chance to flee." Meanwhile, thousands and thousands of Syrians were charging at the Christians, shooting arrows and killing them.' [13]

Many knights now fought on foot; the weight of their chain mail hauberks and leggings putting them at a huge disadvantage, their only additional protection being the corpses of their fallen mounts and slain comrades. Raymond of Tripoli had fled the battle, as did Balian d'Ibelin and Reynald of Sidon. However, there was little the count could do. When he led his

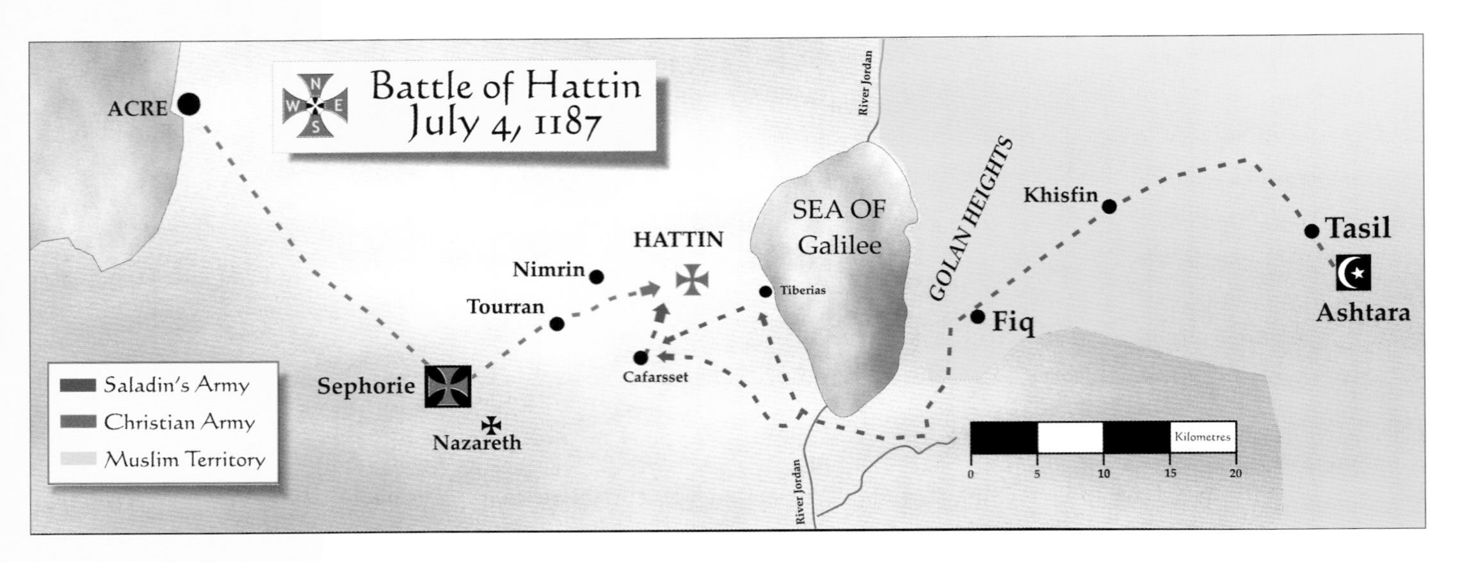

Map showing the direction of the opposing forces.
Author

men in a charge against the Muslims, Taki-ed-Din opened his ranks, allowing the charge to pass through and then closed his formation just as suddenly. Raymond saw that charging uphill again would be as impossible as it would be futile and set off for Tyre.

King Guy was also seeing that things were quickly going downhill and moved what was left of his troops uphill to the southern horn, where he set up the royal tent, perhaps hoping that its bright red colour would serve as a rallying point for the troops.

Watching the last moments of the Christians' fight from a distance was Saladin and his son al-Afdel. The Arab chronicler Ibn al-Athir told the story of the Franks' fall from al-Afdel's perspective:

> 'I was at my father Saladin's side during that battle, the first that I saw with my own eyes. The Frankish king had retreated to the hill with his band, and from there he led a furious charge against the Muslims facing him, forcing them back upon my father. I saw that he was alarmed and distraught, and he tugged at his beard as he went forward crying: "Away with the Devil's lie!" The Muslims turned to counter-attack and drove the Franks back up the hill. When I saw the Franks retreating before the Muslim onslaught I cried out for joy: "We have conquered them!" But they returned to the charge with undiminished ardour and drove our army back toward my father. His response was the same as before, and the Muslims counter-attacked and drove the Franks back up the hill. Again I cried: "We have beaten them!" but my father turned to me and said: "Be quiet, we shall not have beaten them until that tent falls!" As he spoke the tent fell, and the Sultan dismounted and prostrated himself in thanks to God, weeping for joy.' [14]

The loss of the king's tent must have been as great a source of misery to the Christians as it was a source of joy to the Muslims. However, it was not the only symbol of Christian authority to fall that day. Soon after Guy's tent was pulled to the ground, the True Cross was wrestled from Christian hands. Imad ad-Din, another of the Arab chroniclers who told the story of the Battle of Hattin wrote of the loss of the most sacred of Christian relics:

> 'Its capture was for them more important than the loss of the King and was the gravest blow that they sustained in that battle. The cross was a prize without equal, for it was the supreme object of their faith. To venerate it was their duty, for it was their God, before whom they would bow their foreheads to the ground, and to which their mouths sang hymns.' [15]

The earthly remnants of Christ's suffering and sacrifice were not all the Muslims had succeeded in capturing from the Christians. King Guy, Reynald de Châtillon, Gerard de Ridefort and William Borrell, the Master of the Hospitallers, as well as many other nobly born Franks were now Saladin's captives. Given the sheer magnitude of the slaughter, it is hard to imagine if they considered themselves lucky for having survived, or if they longed for the death their soldiers had met. As Imad ad-Din described the carnage:

> 'The dead were scattered over the mountains and valleys, lying immobile on their sides. Hattin shrugged off their carcasses, and the perfume of victory was thick with the stench of them. I passed by them and saw the limbs of the fallen cast naked on the field of battle, scattered in pieces over the site of the encounter, lacerated and disjointed, with heads cracked open, throats slit, spines broken, necks shattered, feet in pieces, noses mutilated …' [16]

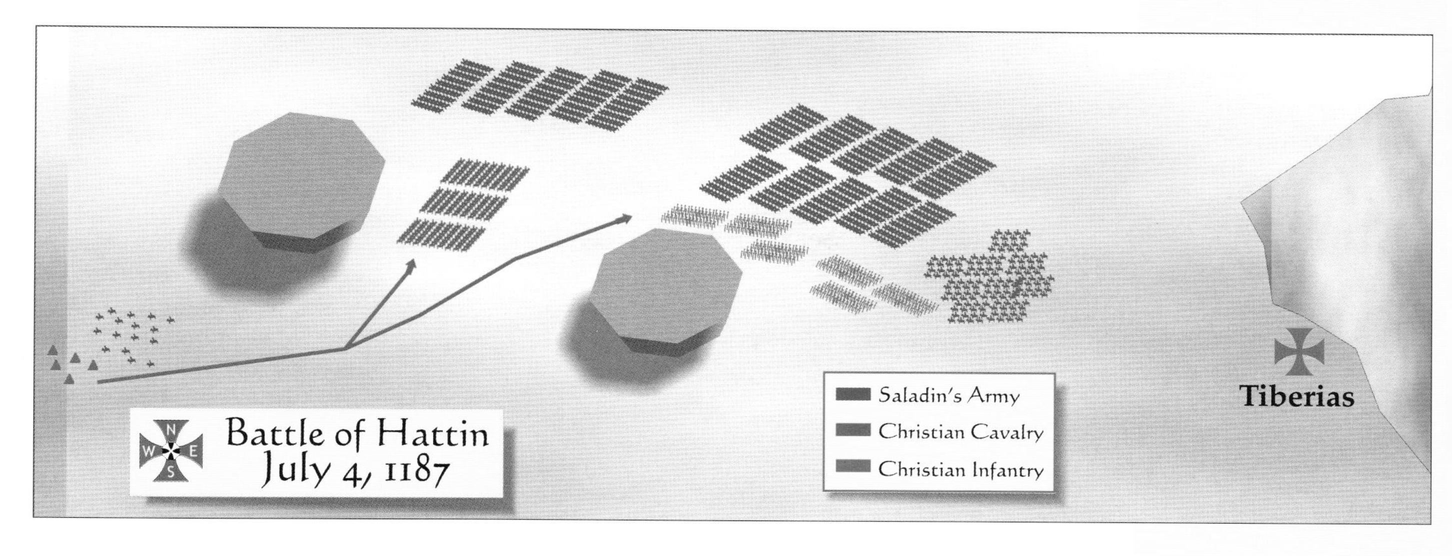

Saladin's Revenge

When the Franks had been brought to Saladin's tent, the Sultan offered King Guy a glass of cool water, the first he had tasted since he had left Sephorie two days earlier. After Guy had his fill, he passed the cup to Reynald de Châtillon; however, the offering was not as welcomed by the Sultan as it was by Reynald. 'This godless man did not have my permission to drink and will not save his life this way,'[17] Saladin said. Muslim custom dictated that if a man were offered food or drink, his protection was assured. This was a privilege which Reynald was not entitled to, especially since Saladin had vowed to kill him for his continued attacks on Muslim caravans and his plan to invade Islam's Holiest cities. After being reminded of his many transgressions against the Muslims, Reynald was beheaded and Saladin dipped his fingers into the slain Frank's blood smearing it on his own forehead.[18] In some accounts Saladin himself beheaded Reynald while others indicate he ordered the job to be done, but regardless of who actually beheaded the Lord of Oultrejordain, Saladin had taken his revenge on his enemy at long last.

Seeing his friend beheaded before his eyes did little to quell King Guy's fear and he began to tremble anticipating a similar fate. Saladin reassured him that his life would not be taken. Instead he was thrown in prison along with Ridefort, the Templars' Master.

Those Templars who had survived the ordeal did not share their Master's fate. The men who survived Hattin had been rounded up like any other captured booty and treated as a marketable commodity. The Turcopoles would have been of little value to the Muslims and most likely met with instant death for having betrayed their faith.[19] The Templars and Hospitallers, however, would have been highly prized by their captors, who anticipated a great ransom. Saladin was well aware of this and offered fifty Egyptian dinars for each Templar or Hospitaller who had been captured. The sum was sufficient to ensure that two hundred of Christendom's best fighting men were brought before him. Quite simply, Saladin was not interested in seeing the Templars as slaves; he wanted them gone, although each was given the choice of conversion or death.[20] As Ibn al-Athir explained the matter, 'He [Saladin] had these particular men killed because they were the fiercest of all the Frankish warriors, and in this way he rid the Muslim people of them.'[21]

The Kingdom Falls

As the remaining months of 1187 passed from one to another, so too did the various cities, towns and castles of the Levant pass from Christian to Muslim hands. Saladin's strategy was wise in that he struck at the Christian's coastal holdings first, effectively depriving any future Christian army arriving from the West of access by sea. Within a week of the Muslim victory at Hattin, the port city of Acre had surrendered to Saladin's army and within a month Toron, Sidon, Gibelet and Beirut had also caved. Writing sometime between the surrender of Acre on 10 July and the surrender of Beirut on 6 August, the Templar Grand Commander Terricus told Pope Urban III and all who would read his letter of the grave situation facing the Latin East:

> 'For at the present moment they [the Muslims] are besieging Tyre with all their might, and cease not to assault it either night or day, while so vast are their numbers, that they have covered the whole face of the land from Tyre, as far as Jerusalem and Gaza, just like swarms of ants.

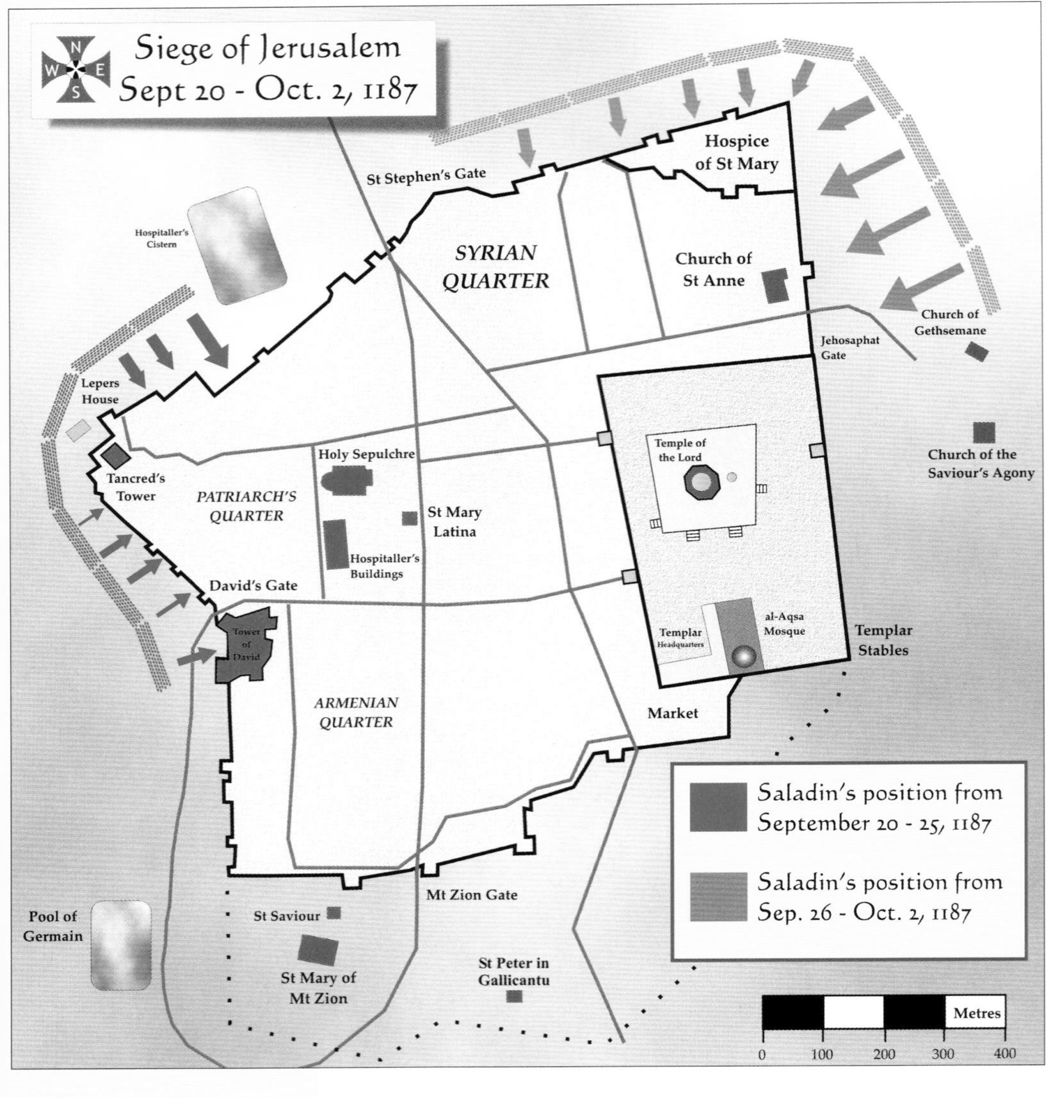

> Deign, therefore, with all possible speed, to bring succour to ourselves and to Christianity, all but ruined in the East, that so through the aid of God and the exalted merits of your brotherhood, supported by your assistance, we may be enabled to save the remainder of those cities.'[22]

The Templar Grand Commander's letter would not be his only missive to the West; his second letter, written in January of 1188, would tell of even greater losses to Christendom than his first.

Ascalon, which had taken the Crusaders several months to capture in 1153, had surrendered to Saladin on 5 September 1187 after being besieged for less than two weeks. However, in the case of Ascalon, Saladin had some Christian help. The sultan brought King Guy and Gerard de Ridefort along to convince their co-religionists to surrender.[23] Guy did as he was told, aided by the Templar Master, but their pleas were not well received by those behind the city walls who hurled insults at the men while Saladin's mangonels hurled projectiles at the walls.

Although de Ridefort's plea may have fallen upon deaf ears at Ascalon, his Templars stationed at Gaza did not take the same attitude a year later when their Master informed them to vacate the fortress. They were, by their very Rule of Order, obligated to obey his commands and it was the surrender of Gaza that bought Gerard his freedom.[24]

Nothing remained of the kingdom's coastal holdings except Tyre, where many who had fled Saladin's onslaught were now huddled. Saladin could now turn his full attention on Jerusalem.

Prior to the siege, Balian d'Ibelin who was at Tyre sent a request to the Sultan asking to be given safe passage to retrieve his family from Jerusalem. Saladin agreed on the condition that Balian would stay in the city for no longer than one day, collect his family and leave again. However, when he arrived at Jerusalem, he found a city incapable of manning a defence against the coming siege and was persuaded to take the leadership role in the battle that lay ahead.[25] He had given his word to Saladin, but now his duty to his people put him in the unfortunate position of having to betray his word. He wrote to the sultan explaining his position and Saladin not only accepted his apology but even sent his own men to escort Balian's family back to Tyre.[26]

The situation in the Holy City, which had been headquarters to the Templars since their inception nearly seven decades earlier, was grim. The knights who once filled the al-Aqsa were now vastly outnumbered by the ghosts of the brethren who had fallen at the Battle of Hattin two months earlier. In fact, in all of Jerusalem there were but two secular knights and men were in short supply.[27] Balian knighted every nobly born male over the age of sixteen and even knighted men of lower station.[28] Those who were able to bear arms were given them.

On 20 September, Saladin's army arrived at Jerusalem and began its attack on the western side of the city the following day. For five days Saladin's mangonels hurled boulders and Greek fire at the walls, but the walls failed to give. On 26 September he withdrew to the northern side of the city, which gave the inhabitants of Jerusalem hope that Saladin had lifted the siege. However, their hope, like the city's walls were soon reduced to rubble, as the sultan's mangonels resumed their volleys.

As Jerusalem received its punishment, Saladin's miners worked on the walls, finally opening a breach on 29 September. The Patriarch and other nobles offered five thousand bezants to any man who would move to guard the breach, but there were no takers.[29] It was realised that a continued fight would only cost more lives in defence of a city that could no longer hold off Saladin's army.

On 30 September, Balian left what little safety the crumbling walls of Jerusalem afforded him and sought an audience with Saladin in order to negotiate the terms of surrender. Saladin informed Balian that the city was already lost and the only option was unconditional surrender; however, Balian told the sultan that unless the Christians were assured of favourable terms they would destroy what was left of the city before his army could take it. The Dome of the Rock and al-Aqsa Mosque would be razed to the ground and the Muslims inside the city would be slaughtered just as they had been when the city was captured nearly a century earlier.

With the prospect of entering a city in ruin, Saladin set the terms of surrender at ten dinars for every man, five for every woman and one for every child.[30] However, within the city were many of Christendom's poor who could not afford the ransom. Balian bought the freedom of seven thousand for the sum of thirty thousand dinars, taken from not only the city's own treasury, but also those of the Templars and Hospitallers. The Military Orders were not pleased with the decision to use their money to free the poor.[31]

On 2 October, after besieging the city for less than two weeks, Saladin entered Jerusalem bringing to an end the Christians' eighty-eight year hold on the Holy City. However, unlike the Christian capture of Jerusalem in 1099, Saladin and his army entered the city with their swords sheathed. As the Muslims entered the gates, the Christians left in the opposite direction. Some had bought their freedom, others had their liberty bought for them and still others faced the prospect of a life of slavery. But even in this the Saladin showed compassion by granting many of them freedom without ransom,[32] although many spent their lives as Muslim slaves.

A decade had passed since the sultan had first marched on Jerusalem, only to be thwarted by the heavy charge of the Templars at Montgisard, but now the Templars had been removed from the Holy City and Saladin moved quickly to erase any memory of the Christian's presence on the Temple Mount. The great golden cross that once rose above the Dome of the Rock was torn down, the Holy sites were cleansed with rose water to remove the pollution caused by the Christians, and the al-Aqsa, which had been granted to the Order by Baldwin II in 1120, was restored to its pre-Templar purpose.[33]

Jerusalem was once again in Muslim hands and once again news from Outremer arrived in the West within a fortnight. Two weeks after the Christians conquered the city in 1099, Pope Urban II lay dead, having never learned of the good news. Two weeks after the Christians lost the city in 1187, Pope Urban III also lay dead, having died soon after hearing the bad news.

References for chapter 14

1 Gabrieli, Francesco, *Arab Historians of the Crusades*. p. 123 Translation of Ibn al-Athir's account of the Battle of Hattin.

2 Barber, Malcolm, *The New Knighthood*. p. 112.

3 Runciman, Steven, *A History of the Crusades Vol. II*. p. 454.

4 Dickie, Iain, *Hattin 1187 Battles of the Medieval World*. p. 40.

5 Runciman op. cit. p. 455.

6 Dickie op. cit. p. 40.

7 Runciman op. cit. p. 455.

8 Barber op. cit. pp. 112-113. This is the version of the story according to the account of Bernard the Treasurer.

9 Nicholson, Helen & David Nicolle, *God's Warriors: Knights Templar, Saracens and the Battle for Jerusalem*. p. 62.

10 *De Expugatione Terrae Sanctae per Saladinum* Medieval Sourcebook translated by Professor James Brundage. www.fordham.edu/halsall/source/1187hattin.html.

11 Ibid.

12 Nicholson op. cit. p. 64.

13 Brundage Ibid.

14 Gabrieli op. cit. pp. 122-123. Translation of Ibn al-Athir's account of the Battle of Hattin.

15 Ibid. p. 132.

16 Ibid. p. 135.

17 Ibid. p. 124-125. Taken from the account of Ibn al-Athir.

18 Nicholson op. cit. p. 72.

19 Ibid. p. 72.

20 Ibid. p. 72.

21 Gabrieli op. cit. pp. 124-125.

22 The Letter of Terricius, Master of the, Temple, on the Capture of the Land of Jerusalem, Roger of Hoveden: *The Fall of Jerusalem*, 1187, Medieval Sourcebook www.fordham.edu/halsall/source/hoveden1187.html.

23 Runciman op. cit. p. 462.

24 Ibid. p. 462.

25 Ibid. p. 463.

26 Ibid. p. 463.

27 Ibid. p. 463.

28 Ibid. p. 464.

29 Nicholson op. cit. p. 79 The authors add that some citizens proposed a suicide mission preferring to die in battle than in the city; however, they were dissuaded from the idea by the Patriarch who felt their deaths would leave the women and children victim to the Muslims.

30 Runciman op. cit. p. 465.

31 Nicholson op. cit. p. 79.

32 Runciman op. cit. p. 466.

33 Gabrieli op. cit. p. 144.

Acre: The Final Century

'It occupied a large site on the sea, like a castle. It had at its entry a tall, strong tower and the wall was thick, twenty-eight feet wide.'[1]

The Templar of Tyre's description of the Templar Fortress at Acre

Left: **Richard and Philip ride through the streets of Acre after it is captured on 12 July 1191.** *ClipArt.com*

Right: **Frederick I, Barbarossa, is shown mounted on his horse in this heroic statue. Frederick had come east during the Second Crusade with his uncle Conrad III.** *ClipArt.com*

IN June of 1190 a grieving son arrived at the walls of Antioch carrying the remains of his dead father preserved in vinegar.[2] The dead man was the Holy Roman Emperor Frederick I Hohenstaufen, better known as Barbarossa or red beard. Barbarossa had participated in the disastrous Second Crusade when he was then Duke of Swabia. Upon hearing of the fall of Jerusalem in 1187, he had sent an envoy to Saladin demanding the return of the Holy City but the best the sultan was prepared to offer was the release of his Christian prisoners and the release of the Christian abbeys to the monks who had once occupied them.[3] The offer was not good enough. In May of 1189, the emperor assembled a massive German army and began the long march to the Holy Land.

Frederick's army was met with the same difficulties as those who had taken the land route in previous crusades – conflicts in Byzantine territory, hunger and thirst, inclement weather conditions and the ever present assault of Turkish arrows. Despite numerous casualties, the emperor and his army succeeded in defeating the sultan's son who had been sent to halt their progress and pressed their way to the river Calycadnus. As the emperor rode ahead of his bodyguard and began to cross the river, he lost his life. Whether he had paused to cool himself in the river or had been thrown from his horse at the crossing and suffered a heart attack from the shock of the water, the end result was that the emperor drowned, having been weighted down by his armour.

The loss of the Holy Roman Emperor was devastating, and although his son Frederick, the Duke of Swabia, took control of the army, he did not have the commanding presence of his father and soon the army fell apart.

Those who managed to continue the crusade arrived in the Levant to find the political climate had changed. King Guy, who had been held responsible for the massacre at Hattin and subsequent loss of Jerusalem, had been ousted by Conrad of Montferrat, one of Barbarossa's kin, who had been able to keep Tyre in Christian hands during Saladin's conquest of the coast. When Guy was released from prison in 1188 he had arrived at Tyre intent on being received as king, but instead found the city's gates closed in his face. A second attempt to secure his throne in April of

Barbarossa drowned while crossing the river Calycadnus on his way to the Holy Land. His body was carried to Antioch by his son Frederick, who had assumed command of the German Army. *ClipArt.com*

1189 was met with a similar response and after camping in front of the city for four months, Guy finally broke camp and marched on Acre with the intent of laying siege to the city.

The deposed king arrived at Acre on 28 August 1189 and set up camp two kilometres east of the city near the river Belus, so that his men would have an ample supply of water. If Hattin had taught him anything, it was the importance of water. But Saladin soon moved in to oppose him. On 4 October, Saladin's nephew Taki-ed-Din, who had fought the Templars at Hattin, once again tried to lure them into battle, but the manoeuvre took Saladin by surprise and he weakened his centre column by rushing to rescue his nephew. The Franks charged on Saladin's right and centre lines and put them to flight; however, the left flank was not occupied and charged on Guy's scattered troops, while a sortie from the Acre garrison also joined the battle. Although many were able to return to safety behind the Christian lines, the Germans and Templars suffered heavy losses. During the battle, Gerard de Ridefort, the Master of the Temple, was captured for a second time. This time it cost him his life.[4] It would be almost two years before the Templars would find a replacement.

The Lionheart

When Richard I of England arrived at Acre in the spring of 1191, he found a city that had been under siege for nearly two years. He also found that his late father's enemy, Philip Augustus, the King of France had preceded his arrival by seven weeks. Both Philip and Richard had left the West around the same time and met up with each other in Italy, but the passage between there and Acre had been decidedly different for the two nobly born Franks. Richard's fleet had encountered bad weather and was forced to make stops at Crete and Rhodes. Two of the ships had been wrecked on the coast of Cyprus, while another carrying the king's sister Joanna and his fiancé was forced to land at Limassol, a port on the island's southern coast. The island's self-appointed ruler, Isaac Ducas Comnenus, who was an ally of Saladin, had the shipwrecked passengers imprisoned. However, Joanna refused to leave the ship. When Richard arrived on 8 May, he was not in a good mood from the journey, and the treatment his people had received did little to improve it. Although Isaac had initially agreed to return what he had taken from Richard's fleet, he later retracted his offer, thinking that the English king was weaker than he had first thought. It would prove to be a big mistake, for Richard had sent one ship to Acre to announce his arrival. Three days later another returned with Guy, his brother Geoffrey and a number of Templars. Despite the death of de Ridefort two years earlier, the Order still remained loyal to the deposed king. When the remainder of the English fleet arrived the following day Richard began a conquest of the island, which was aided by the fact that Isaac was not popular with his subjects.

Isaac Ducas Comnenus, the self-appointed ruler of Cyprus, surrenders to Richard in this interpretation of the event. *ClipArt.com*

The Capture of Acre

On 5 June 1191, the English fleet set sail from Famagusta on the eastern coast of Cyprus and landed the next day at Tyre, where they were refused entry to the city by orders of Conrad of Montferrat and Philip

Augustus. The dispute over the Kingdom of Jerusalem was still going on; Richard was a supporter of Guy's cause, while Philip had sided with his cousin Conrad.[5] On 8 June, Richard's twenty-five galleys arrived at Acre. Although Philip had arrived almost two months earlier, he had made little progress in gaining ground on the city that had already been long under siege when he arrived. Despite a fondness for his siege engines, which had been battering at the city's walls since his arrival, Philip lacked the qualities needed to finally conquer the city. However, the arrival of the King of England brought both a fresh outlook and fresh troops to the battle.

Richard Coeur de Lion having the Saracens beheaded – a nineteenth-century illustration by Alphonse de Neuville. *ClipArt.com*

It would be another month before the city was to be captured as sickness in the camp, infighting between the rival factions and repeated attempts of Saladin's men to break the siege would all play a role in thwarting the Frankish efforts. On 3 July, the catapults finally managed to create a substantial breach in the wall, but all attempts to enter through it were repelled, as was a second attempt launched eight days later. However, by this time the garrison had already been prepared to offer their surrender as reinforcements promised by Saladin had yet to arrive. The terms of the surrender were set: 200,000 bezants were to be paid to the crusaders for the lives of the city's Muslim inhabitants, fifteen hundred Christians held captive by Saladin were to be returned along with the True Cross, which had been captured at the Battle of Hattin, four years earlier.[6] On 12 July 1191, the Muslim inhabitants of Acre moved out of the city bound in shackles as the Christians moved in bound with joy.

As was the case in previous conquests, the nobly born Franks tripped over one another to lay their claims. Richard claimed the royal palace on the north side of the city, while Philip occupied the Templars' former holdings on the tip of the city's peninsula. After Barbarossa's son had been killed during the siege, Leopold, the Duke of Austria, took control of the German army. As such it was his belief that he should be entitled to a claim equal to that of the other monarchs. However, when he hoisted his banner near to Richard's the English snatched it up and flung it into the sea below. It was an insult that would not soon be forgotten and three days later, Leopold set sail for home.

With the city in Christian hands the nobles met to resolve the dispute over the Kingdom of Jerusalem. It was decided that Guy would retain the crown until his death and thereafter it would pass to Conrad of Montferrat and his wife Isabella, the daughter of King Almaric of Jerusalem. Soon after Philip returned to France complaining of illness, though his departure was viewed as cowardice by the English.

But there were other matters to deal with as Saladin had still not paid the ransom on the Muslim captives. On 2 August, an embassy was sent to Saladin's camp to suggest that the payment of the ransom and the return of the Christian captives should be made in three monthly instalments. Two weeks later the first batch of money and captives was sent to Richard's camp. Although the money was the specified sum, the captives were not; the sultan had failed to return the prisoners of rank that had been requested. As a result Richard refused to complete his end of the deal. This led to a standoff over the terms of the original agreement and as neither Richard nor Saladin trusted each other, neither man was prepared to budge. After declaring that Saladin had broken the agreement, and wanting to leave Acre to march on Jerusalem, Richard decided to deal with the prisoners in his own way. On 20 August, the two thousand seven hundred Muslim captives held in Acre were marched outside the city

A thirteenth-century depiction of Richard the Lionheart and Saladin in battle. *ClipArt.com*

walls and massacred. Bahā ad Din, a contemporary Arab chronicler who entered Saladin's service after the fall of Jerusalem wrote of the massacre:

> 'Then they [the Franks] brought up the Muslim prisoners whose martyrdom God had ordained, more than three thousand men in chains. They fell on them as one man and slaughtered them in cold blood, with sword and lance.'[7]

The Battle of Arsuf

Two days after the massacre, Richard set off with his army for Jaffa. His goal was Jerusalem, but it would first be necessary to capture the port city as a base of operations. As the army marched down the coast they stayed close to the shoreline to benefit from the cool breeze and the support of the ships that followed the march down the coastline. The army was divided into three columns. The first column was comprised of knights, and kept to the shore, while the remaining two columns, made up of infantrymen, took the land-side position. In the vanguard were the Templars, whom Richard relied on throughout his crusade. In fact it had been through his influence that Robert de Sablé, an Angevin who had travelled east with the king, had been elected to succeed de Ridefort as Master of the Order, despite the fact that he was not a Templar when he left England.[8]

As the crusader army marched down the coast their movement was shadowed by Saladin's light mounted archers who launched a series of attacks on the Christians, riding in close enough to shoot and then retreating again as quickly as they had come. Despite the torments of Saladin's arrows, the army managed to maintain their discipline and the crusader infantry, armed with crossbows took out a number of the Muslim archers.

Although the knights and their heavy charge often receive the bulk of attention in discussions of medieval conflicts, the discipline of the infantry is every bit as worthy of mention. For while the knights were cooled by the sea breeze and protected by two lines of human targets, the infantrymen in those lines sacrificed their lives to protect their nobly born counterparts and their horses. The medieval war horse was the tank of its day and the loss of even one horse was a great cost to an army. It is for this reason that the Templar Rule went to such lengths to ensure that no harm would come to them.

After two weeks of marching, Richard's army had covered less than half the distance to Jaffa and on 6 September they passed through a wooded area about 16 kilometres north of Arsuf. Although they had been tormented throughout the march, the Muslims had inflicted little real damage. That would all change the next morning.

On 7 September, as the crusaders began their march towards Arsuf, Saladin began his march towards victory. Throughout the morning the Muslims assaulted the Christians using the tactics they had employed throughout the march. However, just before noon they began a fully fledged assault. The crusaders continued to resist their attacks, once again thanks to the discipline of the common foot soldiers. Between the Muslims and the knights were two rows of infantrymen. The front line knelt with spear and shield, while the crossbowmen returned the attack. When the crossbowmen rearmed, the spearman stood with their shields to provide them with cover.[9]

Meanwhile the knights were aligned in battle formation behind the front line. The Templars were at the southern end of the line forming the right flank along with the Bretons, Angevins and King Guy and his party. King Richard and his English and Normans troops made up the centre assisted by Flemish and French troops. In the rearguard were the Hospitallers.[10] In total the crusader army was made up of approximately twelve hundred knights and ten thousand infantrymen, while the Muslims numbered twenty thousand men equally split between cavalry and infantry.[11]

As the day progressed it became increasingly difficult for the infantrymen to maintain a line. The Muslim attacks came closer and closer, ultimately close enough to replace their bows and arrows with lances and swords. Soon the Christian infantry were falling in increasing numbers.

Hoping to draw the crusaders into an early charge, Saladin's troops focused their attacks on the Hospitallers division. The attacks began to take their toll on the Hospitallers and on several occasions Garnier of Nablus, the Master of the Order, approached Richard begging him to give the signal to charge, but Richard continued to urge patience. Finally the Muslim assaults proved too much and the Marshal of the

Order and one of his knights broke rank and began the charge. Although the signal had not been given, all the Hospitallers assumed it had and charged after their comrades. Within seconds horses were spurred down the Christian line as knight after knight joined the charge.

Richard, seeing that there was no choice but to join the battle lest those who were already in it be slaughtered, ordered the Templars and the Bretons and Angevins in their line to attack Saladin's left flank.[12] Finally the Templars were able to release the frustration that the Hospitallers had been unable to contain and their charge drove the Saracens from the field, stunned by the Hospitallers impetuousness and mopped up by the Templars's discipline. Although the losses had been relatively light on both sides of the field of battle, the Muslims had been repelled and following so close on the capture of Acre, the battle must have been a morale-boosting victory for the Christians in general and the Templars in particular. It had been the first open battle since Hattin four years earlier and the Templars would not have forgotten the role their Order played there.

A statue of Richard I, which stands outside the Palace of Westminster (Houses of Parliament) in England. *iStockPhoto.com Paul Cowan*

In October of 1191, Richard wrote to the abbot of Clairvaux informing him of the success of his crusade:

> 'With God's guidance we reached Jaffa on 29 September 1191 and fortified the city with ditches and a wall with the intention of protecting the interests of Christianity to the best of our ability. After his defeat [at Arsuf] Saladin has not dared to face the Christians, but like a lion in his den has been secretly lying in hiding and plotting to kill the friends of the Cross like sheep for slaughter.
>
> 'So when he heard that we were swiftly heading for Ascalon, he overthrew it and levelled it to the ground. Likewise he had laid waste and trampled on the land of Syria.'[13]

The Saladin Truce

Soon after writing to the abbot, Richard entered into negotiations with both the Templars and Saladin; with the former it was over the purchase of Cyprus, while with the latter it was over the surrender of Jerusalem. However, he soon found his allies to be more agreeable to his terms than his enemies. Saladin had sent his brother al-Adil to handle the negotiations and returned to the sultan with Richard's first offer, which was really a demand. The king wanted Jerusalem, all of its land west of the Jordan and the return of the True Cross. The offer was refused.[14] Richard's second offer must have seemed as incredulous. Al Adil should receive all of Palestine currently controlled by Saladin, while Richard's sister, Joanna, should receive all the area captured by the king thus far. Al Adil and Joanna should get married and live in Jerusalem and access to the Holy City should be open to Muslims and Christians alike. Additionally, the True Cross was to be returned to Christendom and the Templars and Hospitallers were to be restored with all of their properties captured after Hattin.[15] Saladin was not the only one who thought Richard's proposals were a joke; Joanna had no intentions of marrying a Muslim and while Saladin was amused, Joanna was outraged.

Shortly after Christmas 1191 Richard's army was within 19 kilometres of Jerusalem and although those who had come on crusade wanted to lay siege to the Holy City, the Masters of the two Orders urged caution. The consensus was that even if they succeeded in taking the city by force, it would be virtually impossible to hold once the crusaders returned west. Richard took the council, perhaps hoping that a peaceful solution was still possible, and spent the next four months at Ascalon rebuilding the city Saladin had razed to the ground following his defeat at Arsuf.

From March until August Richard and Saladin alternated between fighting and negotiating with each other. The common stumbling block in the negotiations was Ascalon, which Saladin wanted destroyed once and for all. While Saladin and Richard were trying to come to terms over Jerusalem, the Franks were trying to come to terms over who should wear the crown that bore its name. Although the matter had been decided some time previously, it had not been widely accepted and to this end Richard called a council of the barons to decide the matter. When presented with the choice between Conrad and Guy, the council unanimously chose the former, which shocked the latter. Three days after receiving the favourable news, Conrad was murdered in the streets of Tyre by two Assassins. The marquis's murder, however, did not mean that Guy regained his crown. Although Conrad was dead, his widow Isabella was the rightful heir to the throne and soon after she chose Henry, Count of Champagne as her new husband. Although Guy had lost one kingdom he would soon gain another; for the following month, Richard sold Cyprus, which the Templars had been unable to control, to the deposed king.[16]

On 28 August 1192, three years to the day that Guy had begun his siege of Acre, al Adil's courier delivered Saladin's final offer to Richard. The terms were to last five years and their contents were more favourable than earlier efforts. The Christians were to keep the coastal cities as far south as Jaffa, Jerusalem as well as other sites sacred to the faith would once again be open to the Christians, and both sides were free to travel through each other's lands. However, there was one caveat: Ascalon was to be destroyed. Richard, although agreeable to the terms, was not prepared to swear an oath; he was after all a king. However, on 2 September Hugh of Champagne, Balian d'Ibelin and both the Master of the Temple and the Hospital, taking Richard's hand, swore on his behalf adding their names to the document. The next day the Third Crusade came to a close when Saladin added his own signature completing the truce.

For the first time in nearly five years Jerusalem was once again open to Christians and many of the crusaders who had come east to rescue the city took advantage of visiting the Holy City. Richard was not among them.[17] On 9 October, the King of England, set sail for home, having never seen the city he had come to rescue.

The journey west would prove to be every bit as eventful as the journey east had been. Shipwrecked near Aquileia, the King of England soon found himself in the hands of the Duke of Austria – the very man whose banner he had thrown into the sea. Richard would spend more than a year in prison, having initially been accused of Conrad's murder by the duke. Five years later, on 6 April 1199 Richard's life would come to a close. After surviving a volley of arrows aimed directly at his body while in the Holy Land, the King of England would fall to but a single stray arrow shot from the ramparts of a rebel castle in his own land.

The Templars and the Crusades

Richard's life had ended, but the city he had helped to capture during the Third Crusade remained very much alive. The Templars, who had used the Temple Mount as a base of operations for 67 years, now occupied the peninsula of the port city of Acre as their main headquarters in the East. From this base of operations, the Order would be led by eleven Masters, starting with Robert de Sablé who, like others before him and after him, obtained his post due as much to a monarch's will as that of the brethren charged to elect him. Just as kings had long supported the Templars, so too would the Order continue to support the monarchs and the crusades they came east to fight.

Although these crusades would draw the Templars into a number of military conflicts over the next century, the most significant battles were fought in Damietta in 1218 and 1249, La Forbie in 1244 and Mansurah in 1250.

Of the four campaigns, two were victories, while the other two were crushing defeats. The campaign in Damietta in 1218 saw the Templars lose their Master, William of Chartres, not in battle, but through illness. However, the death did not prevent the Templars from playing a vital role in capturing the city. At the Battle of La Forbie in 1244 the Templars also lost their Master, Armand de Périgord, although it remains uncertain if he was killed in battle or captured alive. What remains certain, however, is that the Order lost between two hundred and sixty and three hundred men during the campaign.[18] Although the Siege of Damietta in 1249 was initially a victory for the crusaders, the city would be lost a year later after the crusaders were defeated at the Battle of Mansurah.

In that campaign the Templars lost two hundred and eighty men, including the Master of the Order, William de Sonnac.[19]

In the disastrous Battle of La Forbie the Templars were defeated by a young Mamluk emir named Baibars. Within a decade of the Battle of Mansurah, Baibars had secured, by conquest, the position of sultan of the Mamluk Empire. In 1263, when Thomas Bérard was Master of Order, the sultan agreed to a truce with the Christians on the condition that a number of Muslims held in captivity be released; however the Templars and Hospitallers, who were using the prisoners as skilled craftsmen, refused to release them.[20] This brought the negations to an abrupt close and the sultan marched into Frankish territory where he sacked Nazareth, destroyed the Church of the Virgin and launched an attack on Acre. Although the sultan managed to sack the suburbs, he never actually laid siege to the city itself. However, three decades later the Mamluks would succeed in taking the city from the Christians forever.

Political Interlude

William de Beaujeu, who succeeded Bérard as Master in 1273, joined the Templars within a few years of the Battle of Mansurah. He was distantly related to the French monarchy through the marriage of his paternal great grandmother's sister, Isabel of Hainault, who was the first wife of Philip Augustus. However, de Beaujeu had closer and less complicated connections with the French crown, for it is probable that he had come east with Philip's grandson, Louis IX, when he went on crusade in 1248.[21] Louis's brother, Charles of Anjou, who was also the King of Sicily from 1262 to 1282, often referred to de Beaujeu as *consanguineous* or 'of the same blood' and this, combined with the fact that de Beaujeu had been Preceptor of southern Italy and Sicily prior to his election, makes it all the more probable that Charles had a hand in de Beaujeu's appointment as Master.[22] It is also this familial connection – as distant as it may have been – that prompted de Beaujeu and the Templars to continue their support of Angevin interests in the East.

Above: **Charles of Anjou (1227–1285) was the brother of Louis IX and king of Sicily from 1262 to 1282.** *ClipArt.com*

Although elected in 1273, William did not arrive in Acre until 1275 – the year after the Council of Lyon, where he had sat next to the pope to discuss the prospects of a new crusade.[23] Upon his return he led the Templars in supporting Charles of Anjou who had sent his representative to Acre in 1277 with a letter from the pope stating that Charles was now the King of Jerusalem. This policy, which the Templars endorsed, put the Order in conflict with Hugh III of Cyprus, who had previously held the claim. When Hugh tried to gain control of Acre in 1279, the Templars stepped in to stop him and, in retaliation, he destroyed a number of Templar properties on Cyprus.[24] It is doubtful, however, that the Templars realised that within another generation, they would be forced to operate from the very island whose ruler they now opposed. Beore that happened, however, de Beaujeu would be dead and his Templars evicted from the city his distant relatives had helped to capture a generation earlier.

The Fall of Acre

In January of 1289 Badr al-Din, a Mamluk informant working for the Templars, approached William de Beaujeu with the news that the Mamluk sultan Qalawun was preparing to attack Tripoli.[25] De Beaujeu wasted no time and immediately informed Tripoli of the dangers that awaited them. However, de Beaujeu's warning was not believed. The city fell to the Mamluks three months later on 26 April. Two years later, Qalawun's son al Ashraf Khalil attacked Acre.

Khalil arrived at Acre on 5 April 1291 and began his siege of the city the following morning. For the first week the battle largely consisted of skirmishes outside

Upper left: **Eighteenth-century engraving of the Siege of Damietta in 1249.**

Lower left: **Sixteenth-century impression of crusaders under Louis IX disembarking prior to the siege.** *ClipArt.com*

Right: **The port city of Acre as it appeared in 1291 when it was captured by the Mamluks: A) the Accursed Tower. B) Hospitallers' compound; C) Teutonic Knights' compound; D) Templars' headquarters.** *Author*

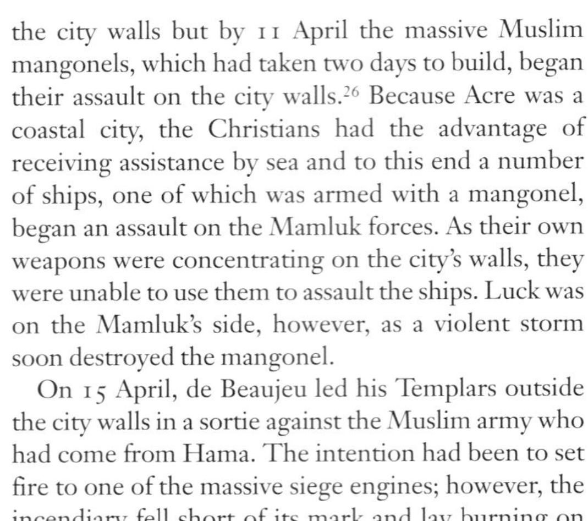

the city walls but by 11 April the massive Muslim mangonels, which had taken two days to build, began their assault on the city walls.[26] Because Acre was a coastal city, the Christians had the advantage of receiving assistance by sea and to this end a number of ships, one of which was armed with a mangonel, began an assault on the Mamluk forces. As their own weapons were concentrating on the city's walls, they were unable to use them to assault the ships. Luck was on the Mamluk's side, however, as a violent storm soon destroyed the mangonel.

On 15 April, de Beaujeu led his Templars outside the city walls in a sortie against the Muslim army who had come from Hama. The intention had been to set fire to one of the massive siege engines; however, the incendiary fell short of its mark and lay burning on the ground. In the process many Templars were either killed or captured. Three days later, a second sortie was launched, led by the Hospitallers backed by a few Templars, but this attempt was also thwarted by the Muslims and once again Christian lives were lost in the skirmish. This brought the sorties to an end due to the number of lives already lost.[27]

The siege continued for another two weeks at which point the citizens of Acre began to lose hope. However, the arrival of Henry II of Cyprus on 4 May with a fleet of forty ships containing one hundred knights and two thousand foot soldiers, soon restored their faith that the city could be saved.[28] Henry, however, despite bringing a sizeable contingent of combatants, soon felt that the best solution was a peaceful one.

To this end, a cease fire was called and two Templars, William de Cafron and William de Villiers, were sent to meet with the sultan to propose a truce. When the Templars arrived at the sultan's tent the first words out of his mouth were to ask if the Templars had brought him the keys to the city. Khalil went on to tell the Templars that it was the city and not the citizens he was interested in and that if the city would surrender, the citizens would be spared. No sooner had he spoken than a crusader mangonel from inside

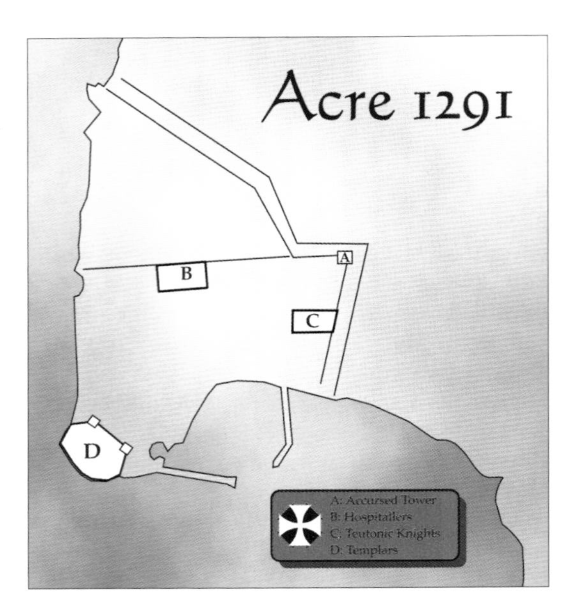

the city flung a rock, landing close by the tent. Khalil was outraged and threatened to kill the Templars, but was stopped by one of his men. The Templars returned to the city and Khalil returned to his siege. Soon after, three thousand of Acre's nobility fled the city to take refuge on Cyprus.[29]

Over the next few weeks the sultan's miners continued to work on the city's towers. By 15 May the defenders were preparing to defend the city from inside its inner walls, while the sultan's men were building a rampart to be able to scale the rubble of the city's outer walls, which had finally collapsed. Three days later the battle was brought to the streets of Acre.

On 18 May the Mamluks focused their assault on the Accursed Tower, which was being defended by Henry's troops from Acre and Cyprus. They were assisted by the Templars and the Hospitallers. Despite their efforts, the tower soon fell to the Mamluks, who pressed their way further into Acre. It was during the battle that ensued that de Beaujeu lost his life. According to the account of the Templar of Tyre, de Beaujeu was fighting without a shield and as he raised his arm he was struck by a javelin, which lodged itself a hand's width under his armpit.[30] The Master, now mortally wounded, was carried by his bodyguards throughout the city seeking refuge, ultimately arriving at the Templar castle on the peninsula. It was here in the Templars's courtyard that the last Master to rule the Order from Acre died in the arms of a Hospitaller named Matthew de Claremont, who had been left to care for the fallen Templar.

Those who remained in the city received no more mercy from the Muslims than the Muslims had

Below: **Gustave Doré's impression of the Siege of Acre in 1291.** *ClipArt.com*

received 192 years earlier when the crusaders stormed Jerusalem at the end of the First Crusade. Those who managed to escape the slaughter gathered at the Templars' headquarters and it was here that the era of the Crusader States would come to a close.

On 20 May the Hospitallers and Teutonic Orders both surrendered their fortified towers. Soon after a Mamluk negotiator was sent to the Templars' fortress to ensure that they followed suit. The Templars accepted the terms and let the Mamluks into the compound. However, once they entered things did not go according to the agreement and the Muslims began to harass the inhabitants. Both Christian and Arab sources confirm the event. The Mamluk chronicler Abu Al-Mahasin, who wrote one of the most detailed and interesting of the Muslim accounts of the Siege of Acre,[31] provides us of the details of what happened after the Templars surrendered their fortress:

> 'He [the sultan] sent them a standard, which they accepted and raised over the tower.
> The door was opened and a horde of regulars and others swarmed in. When they came face to face with the defenders some of the soldiers began to pillage and to lay hands on the women and children who were with them, whereupon the Franks shut the door and attacked them, killing a number of Muslims. They hauled down the standard and stiffened their resistance.
> The siege continued.'[32]

At some point over the next week, as the Templars continued to defend their compound, The Marshal Peter de Sevrey sent some civilians and the Order's treasury to Cyprus, where a large number of refugees had already gathered. On 28 May the sultan once again offered terms of surrender; however, when the Marshal and some of his brethren emerged to discuss the matter, they were executed for having killed the Muslim prisoners.[33] No sooner had the Marshal's body hit the ground than it was followed by those of five Muslim prisoners thrown from the Templars' tower in retaliation for their Master's execution. It was not long after that the sultan's miners succeeded in bringing the fortress's walls crashing to the ground and with them, the Christians' hold on the city.

The old walls of Acre as they appear today.
istockPhoto.com Dorit Jordan Dotan

Ancient Crusader fortress in old Acre (Akko).
istockPhoto.com Michal Anna Safker

References for chapter 15

1 Nicolle, David, *Acre 1291: Bloody Sunset of the Crusader States*. p. 82.

2 Runciman, Steven, *A History of the Crusades Vol. III*. p. 16.

3 Read, Piers Paul, *The Templars*. p. 167.

4 Runciman op. cit. p. 26.

5 Ibid p. 49.

6 Ibid p. 50, Read op. cit. p. 171.

7 Gabrieli, Francesco, *Arab Historians of the Crusades*. p. 224.

8 Barber op. cit. pp. 119, 123. Barber indicates that de Sablé was a layman when he travelled east with Richard I.

9 Dougherty, Martin, *Battles of the Medieval World: 1000-1500*. p. 56.

10 Runciman op. Cit. p. 55.

11 Dougherty op. cit. p. 52.

12 Ibid p. 59.

13 Hallam, Elizabeth, *Chronicles of the Crusades*. p. 191.

14 Runciman op. cit. p. 59.

15 Ibid p. 59.

16 Barber op. cit. p. 120. While it is known that Guy purchased Cyprus, various historians seem in disagreement as to whether he bought the island from the Templars or from Richard. The Order had paid 40,000 bezants of its 100,000 bezant purchase price, but never paid the balance. Some believe that Guy bought the island for the balance still owed by the Templars.

17 Runciman op. cit. p. 74.

18 Barber op. cit. p. 147.

19 Ibid pp. 149, 151.

20 Runciman, op. cit. p. 317.

21 Barber op. cit. p. 169.

22 Ibid p. 169.

23 Ibid pp. 170-171.

24 Ibid p. 173.

25 Nicolle op. cit. p. 45.

26 Ibid p. 57.

27 Runciman op. cit. p. 416.

28 Nicolle op. cit. p. 68.

29 Ibid pp. 68-69.

30 Ibid p. 77.

31 Gabrieli op. cit. p. xxxvi

32 Ibid p. 348.

33 Nicolle op. cit. p. 84.

Jacques de Molay, the last Master of the Knights Templar, was born in AD 1244 and joined the Order in France in 1265. He was elected to his post in 1293.
Author's collection

The End of an Era

'A bitter thing, a lamentable thing, a thing, which is horrible to contemplate, terrible to hear of, a detestable crime, an execrable evil, an abominable work, a detestable disgrace, a thing almost inhuman, indeed set apart from all humanity …'[1]

– Opening of Philip IV's order to arrest the Templars

TODAY, much of what remains of the Templars's headquarters at Acre has been flooded by a rise in sea level, but in the days that followed its capture in 1291, it was Mamluks and not water that flooded the streets; the end result of the rising tide of Islam that the crusaders had come eastward two centuries earlier to fight. Unlike the men who had swarmed the Mediterranean coast in 1099, many who had fled the city of Acre in 1291 were not invaders, but rather people who had been born in the very city they were now forced to flee. To them the loss of Acre was not so much a political or religious defeat as it was a personal one. They had lost their homes, their possessions, and most tragic of all, their loved ones. The Templars had also experienced great loss at Acre; for not only had they lost their Master and many of their companions, they had also lost their headquarters, which they had occupied for the last century.

Those Templars who had left before the city fell moved 100 kilometres north to Sidon where the Order still had a fortress. It was here that Theobald Gaudin was elected to replace William de Beaujeu as Master. Soon after the election, he removed to Cyprus to recruit help; however, the reinforcements never came and on 14 July 1291, the Templars abandoned the fortress at Sidon and joined their brethren on the island.[2]

Almost as soon as word of the fall of Acre arrived in the West, Pope Nicholas IV began to make arrangements to take back the Holy Land. In August of 1291 he called for a number of provincial councils to be held in February of the following year, where the clergy would gather to discuss the challenges of undertaking a new crusade, including the possibility of uniting the Military Orders. The concept was certainly nothing new. The notion had been tossed around at the Council of Lyons in 1274, but was rejected largely because the Spanish kings were concerned that a united Order would be too powerful.[3] However, Nicholas died in March of 1292, before he had an opportunity to hear the council's report. A month later, the Templars mourned the passing of another spiritual leader when Theobald Gaudin, who had served as Master of the Order for less than a year, died.[4] His successor, Jacques de Molay, would be the last Templar who would hold the office.

The Last Grand Master

DE MOLAY was a Burgundian by birth having been born in the village of Molay in the Haute-Saône department of what is today eastern France. Although the exact date of his birth is unknown, it is generally believed to be sometime between 1244 and 1245. When de Molay was questioned after the arrests of 1307, he indicated that he had been received into the order forty-two years previously.[5] This would mean that he had joined in 1265, during the administration of Thomas Bérard. Given that many Templars joined the Order as knights and knights were generally dubbed at the age of 21, we arrive at a possible date of birth of 1244. If this is the case, de Molay would have been 47 when he was elected as Master of the Order.

The twin chapels of the Templars and Hospitallers are located in northern Famagusta. Although there is some disagreement as to which was owned by which order, the general consensus seems to be that the chapel on the left was built by the Templars. Both eventually became the property of the Knights Hospitaller and today serve as an art gallery and theatre.
Simon Brighton

Alain Demurger, in his book *The Last Templar*, suggested that de Molay probably went east somewhere between 1273 and 1282, during William de Beaujeu's reign as Master of the Order. In fact, it is possible that de Molay came east with de Beaujeu when he returned from the West in 1275.[6] What is certain is that the new Templar Master was in the East during the fall of Acre and had lived to tell the tale, although there is no evidence to indicate that he was an active participant in the battle.

De Molay left Cyprus in the spring of 1293, shortly after his election, and for the next three years travelled throughout England, France, Aragon and Italy drumming up support for his plan to recapture the Holy Land and to reform the Order so that it would be better prepared to lead the charge.[7] It has been a long-held belief that the fall of Acre in 1291 brought the Templars's *raison d'être* to a sharp, crisp end; however, de Molay's presence in Europe five years after the capture of Acre shows that such was not the case and that the Order was still dedicated to its cause. The same was true of the Hospitallers who remained on Cyprus along with the Templars until they succeeded in capturing Rhodes in 1309.[8]

However, de Molay's presence in the West was not for the purpose of recruiting crusaders, but merely support to aide his cause – arms, horses and other supplies to replace those lost in recent years. As the secular rulers liked to charge a duty on anything entering or exiting their ports, de Molay had also hoped to establish some trade leniencies in that regard.[9] To this end Pope Boniface VIII, whose coronation de Molay had attended in 1295, granted the Templars the privileges they sought via a series of bulls written in 1297.

The additional favours bestowed upon the Order by the pope disprove the notion that the Order was falling out of favour with the Church in the days that followed the loss of Acre. There were certainly those among the populace who had a hatred for the Templars, but this was nothing new. As early as 1160 Pope Alexander III had issued a bull which prohibited people from pulling Templars off their horses and mistreating the Order in other ways.

While it is certainly true that the Military Orders took a portion of the blame for the tragic events of 1291, they were not alone in receiving criticism; then as now a scapegoat must be offered up whenever there is a military defeat. To many Europeans, the failure of the pope in providing assistance was to blame. So, too, was the ineffectual leadership of Henry II, the King of Cyprus. Even the citizens of Acre were blamed for the destruction of Christendom's last Eastern city, some seeing it as a direct result of the sins of its populace.[10]

The Templars on Cyprus

Little is known of de Molay's activities between his return to Cyprus in 1296 and his visits to Armenia in 1299 and subsequent coastal raids launched at the turn of the century, which resulted in the Templars being driven from the island of Ruad in 1302. However, it is possible that a good deal of his time was spent trying to deal with the King of Cyprus. As we saw in the previous chapter, in the years prior to 1291, the relationship between the Templars and the Kingdom of Cyprus became strained due to the Templars support of Charles of Anjou over Hugh III of Cyprus in their rivalry for the Kingdom of Jerusalem.[11] Henry II was the younger son of Hugh III and came to power upon his brother John I's death in 1285. Soon after the Templars and Hospitallers had evacuated to the island of Cyprus, Henry began to interfere with their privileges there. Both Orders were prohibited from acquiring any new property on the island, regardless of whether it was purchased or donated and a tax was levied, which further reduced their revenues.[12]

It was a situation, which de Molay inherited from his predecessor Tibauld Gaudin and matters had certainly not improved in the interim. In fact the friction between the Templars and the King of Cyprus became so extensive that Boniface VIII was forced to attempt to mediate between the parties, reminding the king that the Templars were an important part of his island's defence and reminding the Templars that the king had taken them in after the fall of Acre.[13]

Matters came to a head in 1306 when Henry's brother Amaury assisted by a number of the Cypriot nobility deposed the king. According to one account de Molay and the Bishop of Limassol had drawn up the papers, while another indicates that the Templars had lent Amaury 50,000 bezants, implying that the Templars financed the coup.[14] Although de Molay did not orchestrate the move against Henry, he and the Templars were nonetheless involved, and their involvement would have consequences. Amaury was assassinated in 1310 and when Henry regained the throne, he had the Templars's central convent on the island destroyed in retaliation for the support they had given his brother.[15] However, by this time the Templars had far bigger problems to deal with.

The Pontiff and the King

Many popular works on the Knights Templar tell a well-known, now almost mythical account of the demise of the Order. Suddenly one fall morning, after de Molay had been summoned to France, the Templars were rounded up by order of the king and imprisoned. Helping him in his nefarious plan was a subservient pope who ruled not from Rome, as popes ought to do, but from France, where he could be controlled by the king. While there is some truth in this account, there are other aspects which are misleading. To understand what happened to the Templars after de Molay was summoned to France, we must first understand a bit about the personalities involved and why he was summoned in the first place.

Philip IV of France, known as le Bel.

The King

Philip IV came to the throne of France in 1285; the eleventh in a continuous line of male heirs, which traced its lineage back to AD 987, when Hugh Capet, the founder of the Capetian Dynasty took the throne. Perhaps more than any of his ancestors, Philip regarded his throne as having been given to him in trust by God and, as such, felt it his duty to govern by the strictest of Christian principles.[16] Of course it didn't hurt that his grandfather was proclaimed a saint during his reign. Philip's grandfather was King Louis IX, whom the Templars had ransomed after he was captured in 1250 during the Battle of Mansurah. In fact, despite being captured in his first outing, Louis went on crusade again in 1270 and it was there that the crusading king took ill and died. In 1297, the twelfth year of Philip's reign, Pope Boniface VIII proclaimed Louis to be a saint.

Throughout his reign, Philip was known as *le Bel* or the fair, due not to his accommodating personality, but due to his handsome countenance. In fact a summary of his various actions as king indicate that he was often anything but fair. In a quest for money, to support the growing costs of military operations and to relieve the massive debts accumulated by his father's war with Aragon, Philip fiddled with the currency, persecuted the Jews and Lombards and even levied a tax on the clergy in his lands. This last action prompted Boniface VIII to issue the bull *Clericis laicos* in 1296, which prohibited secular rulers from taxing the Church without the pope's approval. Philip's response was to forbid the clergy on his lands from sending any money to Rome. Boniface was not amused and began the process of excommunicating the French king in 1303. However, William de Nogaret, one of Philip's ministers, and Sciarra Colonna, one of the pope's Italian enemies, descended on the pontiff and had him arrested. Although he was freed from prison, he died soon after the humiliating ordeal. Philip had turned on the very man who had made his crusading grandfather a saint. As such, it should come as no surprise that he would turn on the men who had helped free his grandfather when he was in an Egyptian prison.

Pope Clement V became Pope in 1305 and ruled from France, finally settling in Avignon in 1309.
ClipArt.com

The Pope

BERTRAND de Got, who would take the papal name Clement V, was born in 1264 at Villandraut in Gascony and prior to his coronation served as Bishop of Bordeaux, which made him a subject of the King of England rather than the King of France.[17] Although Bertrand and Philip had been childhood friends,[18] Bertrand remained a strong supporter of Philip's enemy Boniface VIII. On the death of Boniface's successor Benedict XI, who had reigned for eight months, Bertrand was elected by the College of Cardinals with a two thirds majority vote. His election was a long drawn out affair, which took eleven months to resolve due to politics and controversies that still hung over from Boniface's reign. But Bertrand was not related to the Colonna or Orsini families who had caused Boniface problems, his status as Bishop of Bordeaux made him acceptable to the anti-French factions and the fact that he was a Frenchman by made him acceptable to the King of France.[19]

Upon his election, Bertrand was invited to Rome for his coronation, but ordered that the ceremony be held in Lyons instead. In fact Clement would serve his entire reign in France, ultimately choosing Avignon as his base of operation in 1309; a base that would be used by his successors until 1378. While this resistance to reigning in Rome has been used as evidence of Clement's subservience to the King of France, the fact remains that like Pope Urban II, who launched the First Crusade, the political situation in Rome was such that the new pope did not feel safe in Italy.

The United Military Orders

JACQUES de Molay left Cyprus for France in the fall of 1306, the year after Clement became pope, and never returned to the island again. He, along with the Master of the Hospital, Fulk de Villaret, had been summoned to France by Clement in order to offer the pontiff their views on the prospects of a new crusade and the unification of the two Orders. Many popular works on the Templars have claimed that de Molay was summoned by the pope to lead him into Philip's trap. However, the presence of the Hospitaller Master and the evidence of de Molay's report to the pontiff show that this was not the case.

As we have seen earlier, the idea of uniting the Military Orders had been presented at the Council of Lyons in 1274, and was also suggested by several other Westerners, such as Ramon Lull, who wrote several treatises on recapturing the Holy Land. In 1292 Lull suggested that the Orders should be united under a *Bellator Rex* or War King, who would serve as the leader of the united organisation. Thirteen years later, Philip expressed a desire to renounce his own kingdom in exchange for being given the leadership role in a new Order to be called the Order of the Knighthood of Jerusalem. Successive leaders of this Order would be the sons of kings or royal appointees, should the king die without a male heir.[20] However, these plans by men who had never tasted the Levantine sun on their backs must have seemed impractical if not outright foolish to de Molay.

De Molay's report to the pope in May of 1307, although presenting the pros and cons of the concept, was largely opposed to the idea. The two Orders had existed separately for many years and men who joined them chose to join one or the other. Additionally, there had been a long rivalry between the two Orders, which had been beneficial since one Order tried to out due the other in its defence of Christendom. Perhaps most importantly, the unification of the Hospitallers and the Templars would see the creation of a new Rule for the new organisation. The Templars Rule was stricter than that of the Hospital and de Molay did not want to see his Order softened by the introduction of Hospitaller ideas. By contrast, Villaret offered no ideas on the unification of the two Orders, largely due to the fact that his Order was just beginning its conquest of Rhodes. As such, he hoped that with the pope's assistance he could resist the French king's rising ambitions.

Rumours of Heresy

THE talk of a united Order was not the only rumour about the Templars being circulated. While the Master was discussing his ideas with the pope, rumours were running through the streets that this great Order of Christian knighthood was a little less Christian than they'd like their co-religionists to believe. The rumours were circulated by a man who had been a member of the Order, a renegade Templar named Esquin de Floryan. De Floryan had, according to some accounts, been a prisoner and spread the rumours to his fellow inmates.[21] His accusations against the Order, which he eventually brought to Philip's attention in the hope of lessening his sentence, consisted of four allegations. Esquin told the French king that when the Templars were received, they were instructed to deny Christ and spit on His Holy Cross. During their reception they were made to kiss the receptor on the buttocks, navel and mouth and because the Templar Rule prohibited them from having sex with women, the new brethren were told that it was permissible to engage in sexual activity with each other. But perhaps most horrifying of all, the Templars did not worship God, but rather an idol.[22] It was not Esquin's first attempt to bring the Order into disrepute, for he had previously made such suggestions to James II, King of Aragon,[23] but the monarch did not believe the accusations. Whether he believed the accusations or not, Philip would prove to be a different sort of monarch.

After hearing the renegade Templar's account, Philip informed the pope of what he had learnt and turned the matter over to his right hand man, William de Nogaret, who began an investigation into the Templars, interviewing a number of brethren who had been expelled from the Order. Additionally, a survey was conducted to ascertain just what properties the Templars owned. To avoid their suspicions, the assessment was broadened to include all religious Orders who held land in the kingdom.

On 24 August 1307, Clement wrote to Philip informing him that he was planning to launch an investigation into the recent accusations levelled against the Templars, but that the investigation would not begin until October.[24] However, Philip had no intention of waiting that long; his mind was already made up on the matter and there was a possibility that de Molay could set sail for Cyprus at any time. On 14 September the king issued a letter to his bailiffs throughout the kingdom outlining the Templars' crimes and ordering their arrest at a later date, which was to be kept secret until the time had arrived.

The Arrest of the Templars

In the early morning hours of Friday 13 October 1307 Philip's men acted upon the orders they had received a month earlier. In a series of simultaneous raids on Templar properties throughout France, virtually every Templar in the country was taken into custody. The king's men would certainly have been well acquainted with such a practice – they had previously acted upon similar orders when Philip had the Jews and Lombards rounded up.[25] Although the dawn raids were a huge success in capturing the Templars, there were those who managed to escape. The official sources record twelve Templars evading the bailiff's irons, although there may have been as many as four dozen. Among those who fled was Gérard de Villiers, the former Master of France, who along with a number of brethren and Imbert Blanke, the Master of Auvergne crossed over into England.[26] There were other brethren of lower rank who managed to escape, but ultimately most found themselves imprisoned one way or another; even Blanke was later captured and went on to play a role in defending the English Templars.

It has long been theorised by modern authors that the Templars learnt early on of Philip's arrest orders and as such escaped in large numbers to re-establish the Order elsewhere. Many scholars such as Barber, Nicholson and Demurger are of the belief that the Order had little to no advance notice of the planned arrests, although Demurger provides evidence that de Molay was aware of the allegations and rumours circulating about the Order.[27]

A question that is often asked regarding the arrests is why didn't the Templars fight back. The most logical answer, apart from the fact that many of the houses were populated with serving brethren, is that the Templars were convinced of their innocence and as such felt that their incarceration would be short

A modern interpretation of the arrest of the Templars on 13 October 1307 by American graphic artist Stephen McKim.
Stephen McKim

Domme in France was one of the locations in which the French Templars were imprisoned.
iStockPhoto.com Rafael Laguillo

lived. In short, the Templars had been under the Church's sanction since the Council of Troyes in 1129 and had every confidence that nothing had changed since that time. This is reaffirmed in a letter dated November 1307 from a Templar in the pope's curia, which was sent to the Templar Commander at Ascò:

> 'Holy Father, we are not afraid, because you will defend us and preserve justice, and because all we brothers of the Temple are good Christians, Catholics and strong in the faith. And the brothers of the Templar have always died and fallen prisoner to the Saracens for the Catholic faith, and still do so today.'[28]

But the Templars were not in the pope's hands; they were in the hands of the King of France. Three days after imprisoning the Templars, Philip wrote to the other Western rulers explaining the actions he had taken against the Order and the reasons why. Although he urged them to take similar actions upon the Templars in their lands, they refused to do so. While Philip was undoubtedly surprised by their reaction, Clement was appalled, not by their failure to comply but rather by Philip's failure to seek his permission before arresting the Templars. Yet there was little the pontiff could do, the Templars were already being interrogated and Philip was not about to let them loose.

The Templars who were imprisoned at Domme left behind a number of geometrical carvings, which have led to speculations of un-Christian practices within the Order. However, the vast majority of carvings are of a clearly Christian nature, as shown in this illustration.
Author's collection

The Interrogation of the Templars

Within a week of their arrests, Philip put the Templars through a series of interrogations, the purpose of which was to extract confessions that confirmed the accusations levelled against the Order. On 19 October, the one hundred and thirty-eight Templars arrested in Paris began to issue testimony. The process of interrogation was politically brilliant. While the depositions were to be sent to the king in sealed enclosures, he also wanted the details circulated to the populace in order to swing public opinion on the Order. To ensure that only the right information was received in the Templars's depositions, the jailers were instructed to keep the brethren in isolation, to inform them that both the king and pope were aware of the scandalous nature of their reception and that they would be pardoned if they confessed to the accusations against them, while refusal to do so would result in death. To help persuade the Templars to comply, the jailers were instructed to use threats and torture before the brethren were sent to meet with the inquisitors. The tactic worked and the king got the confessions he desired.

One must wonder how a group of knights, who were trained to withstand the rigours of battle and who would rather suffer death than abandon their faith, could cave to such tactics. However, it is important to remember that the vast majority of the Templars who made up the Western houses were not battle hardened knights; rather they were simple serving brethren who were charged with the task of working to support the knights who were still fighting the enemies of Christ in the East. Of the one hundred and thirty-eight extant depositions from the Paris inquisitions of October and November 1307, only four Templars were able to resist the tortures inflicted upon them.[29] Even Jacques de Molay, the Master of the Order, confessed on the fear of the tortures that awaited him if he refused.

A contemporary, but anonymous writer, who believed the Templars to be innocent, wrote a letter to the doctors and scholars of the University of Paris in 1308, explaining how the Templars's confessions had been extracted through torture:

> 'But when the brothers refuse to produce these lies, although they know absolutely nothing about them, the torments of the attendants who press them daily force them to speak the lies, saying that they must recite them before the Jacobins and assert that they are true if they wish to preserve their lives and obtain the king's plentiful grace.'[30]

The letter goes on to indicate that 36 Templars in Paris had died as a result of the tortures inflicted upon them.[31]

The Charges against the Order

Esquin de Floryan had muttered but four accusations against his former brethren to the King of Aragon and France. By August of 1308, when the charges against the Order had been formally drawn up they had been greatly embellished and expanded. What is interesting about the articles of accusation is that they were a clever blending of standard charges of heresy similar to those issued against the Cathars and Waldensians of France as well as some misinterpretations about actual Templar practices.

There was the standard fare offered by de Floryan that the Templars denied Christ and defiled His Holy Cross, that they engaged in sodomy, kissed their receptor on the buttocks and worshipped idols. Added to the list were other charges: that they did not believe in the Mass and other holy sacraments of the Church, that they believed the Master and other high-ranking officers could absolve them of their sins and that they were even permitted to confess their sins to a brother of the Order.[32]

The idol that de Floryan claimed the Templars worshipped evolved into the claim that the Order venerated a bearded head, which they touched with cords that they wore around their waists. The reality of the matter is that the bearded head simply didn't exist. However, this did not mean that the Templars did not own a head or two. Among the many holy relics acquired by the Order was a head believed to have belonged to one of St Ursula's eleven thousand virgins as well as the head of St Euphemia. The former was kept in Paris, while the latter was housed in the East.[33] However, these relics, neither of which would have had beards in life or in death, were well-known as were all the relics owned by the Order. The Templars did indeed wear a cord around their waists as a symbol of chastity and the cincture or girdle, as it is called, is still a part of liturgical attire to this day. It would not have been uncommon for the Templars to touch their relics with the cord and, as strange as the idea may seem today, there was nothing unusual about it at the time. Religious Orders didn't keep holy relics because they believed them to be powerless. As we have seen in previous chapters, the relic of the True Cross and the Holy Lance were both used in battle because they were believed to contain divine powers.

But the Templars did confess to these and other charges that were levelled against them and on 27 November 1307 Pope Clement issued the bull *Pastoralis praeminentiae*, which ordered the arrest of the Templars throughout Christendom. However, compliance with the pope's directive had different results in different places.

In England the Templars were reluctantly rounded up, but they did not receive the same treatment as in France; even after Clement ordered that they be tortured, none were willing to comply.[34] On Cyprus, King Amaury was reluctant to arrest the Templars because they had supported him in his coup against his brother, and even when he did, the Templars were confined to their own estates. In Venice the investigations into the Order were conducted by the state, while the Templars remained free. In Naples, torture was used; notably, Charles II was a relative of Philip IV. In Germany the Templars arrived at the council in Mainz armed and accompanied by the local barons who swore to their innocence, and as a result they were set free. In Aragon the Templars proclaimed their innocence while entrenched in their castles and although James II besieged the castles and arrested the Order, they were freed in 1312 and granted pensions. But in France they did not receive any fairness from Philip the Fair.

Finally Clement demanded that the matter in France be turned over to the Church's authority and in February of 1308, he suspended the trial. Philip continued to garner public support against the Order and lobbied the pope to resume the trials. Clement finally capitulated in July, but insisted that the trials continue under the direction of the clergy. In August of 1308, Clement issued the bull *Regnans in coelis*, which called for a general council to be held on 1 October 1310 at Vienne in order to deal with the matter of the Templars and to that end the Order was instructed to send suitable *defensores* to the council. The second series of investigations began in 1309, but the Templars were unwilling to defend themselves, largely out of fear of further torture. Although de Molay initially volunteered to defend the Templars

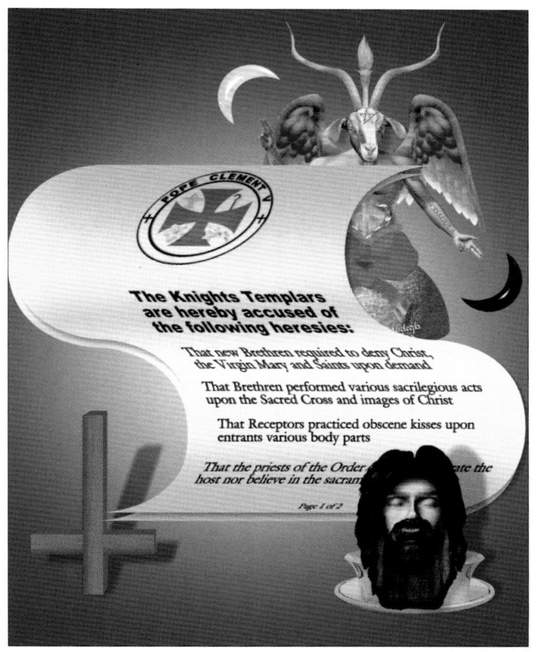

The Articles of Accusation of August 1308 greatly expanded on the original charges levied against the Order. In this modern interpretation by Stephen McKim we see an inverted cross, symbolising the unorthodox Christian practices the Order was accused of, the bearded head the Order was accused of worshipping and a modern interpretation of the Baphomet; a name used to describe the alleged idol in but two of the depositions.
Stephen McKim

Among the two heads known to be in the Templars' possession was that of St Euphemia of Chalcedon, an early Christian martyr.
ClipArt.com

providing he had legal assistance, he later withdrew the offer stating that he would only give his deposition directly to the pope.

The interrogations of Philip's inquisitors had been conducted with the clear intention of getting the Templars to tell them what they wanted to hear; however, the papal commission seems to have been sincerely interested in getting to the truth. A call was sent out requesting that those who wished to testify and defend the Order should assemble at Paris and although the movement was slow to build steam, by February of 1310 some six hundred Templars had expressed a desire to comply.[35]

However, in so doing they created a bigger problem for themselves since the majority of them had previously confessed during the initial inquiry. Philip's camp came to the forefront arguing that the Templars had confessed at one trial, yet contradicted themselves at the other. By withdrawing their confessions, Philip argued, the Templars had become lapsed heretics and the punishment was death. On 12 May, fifty-four of their number were handed over to Philip's men and burnt at the stake in Paris. Similar executions took place elsewhere in France until finally those who remained alive also remained silent.

The Council of Vienne

The general council, which had been called for the autumn of 1310, was postponed another year, finally opening on 16 October 1311. The reason for the delay was not papal procrastination, but rather the fact that the papal commissioners working in Paris were having a hard time getting confessions that matched. One witness would contradict another witness and sometimes even managed to contradict themselves. In the end the Papal commission determined that the Templars were orthodox. Those who had acknowledged the unworthy aspects of the reception ritual were absolved of their sins and restored their privileges in the Church.[36] However, it would be necessary to ensure that the Order was reformed and its Rule brought in line with orthodoxy. The commission believed that the Rule, which they had copies of, was fine, but that unwritten and unorthodox practices had been attached to it. It was these observations that were to form the basis of the Council of Vienne.

The Church fathers who had gathered at the council to deal with the matter of the Templars were for the most part doubtful of the Order's guilt and seemed genuinely interested in hearing what its members had to say. However, Philip had no intention of allowing this to occur and continued to apply pressure on the pope. On March 20, matters were brought to an abrupt end when the king, along with a sizeable army, assembled at Vienne. Two days later Clement held a meeting with a number of cardinals and his special commissioners, who voted by a four fifths majority to dissolve the Order. The result of the meeting was the bull *Vox in excelso*, which was read publicly on 3 April. It was clear that Clement knew that the bull would be met with resistance and that those present would want to debate the matter; however, with Philip's army nearby and Philip sitting beside him in the council, Clement was not prepared to take any chances. Before he delivered his bull, a clerk rose in council and stated that anyone who spoke without permission would be excommunicated.

In the end it was the Templars's defamed reputation and not their alleged guilt that dissolved the Order. After fighting for Christendom for nearly two centuries the Templars were destroyed, not by their enemy's sword, but by their benefactor's quill:

> 'Therefore, with a sad heart, not by definitive sentence, but by apostolic provision or ordinance, we suppress, with the approval of the sacred council, the order of Templars, and its rule, habit and name, by an inviolable and perpetual decree, and we entirely forbid that anyone from now on enter the order, or receive or wear its habit, or presume to behave as a Templar.'[37]

In the end Philip had succeeded in destroying the Templars, but he had failed to acquire any of its properties, which seems his likely motive given that he had conducted a survey of their holdings in France in the autumn of 1307. On 2 May 1312, Clement issued a second bull, *Ad providam*, which turned the Templars' property over to the rival Order of the Hospitallers:

> 'In order that we may grant them [The Hospitallers] increased support, we bestow on them, with the approval of the sacred council, the house itself of the Knights Templar and the other houses, churches, chapels, oratories, cities, castles, towns, lands, granges, places, possessions, jurisdictions, revenues, rights, all the other property, whether immovable, movable or self-moving, and all the members together with their rights and belongings, both beyond and on this side of the sea, in each and every part of the world, at the time when the master himself and some brothers of the order were arrested as a body in the kingdom of France, namely in October 1307.'

Properties outside of France in the Kingdoms of Castile, Aragon, Portugal and Majorca were exempted from the bull's decision.[38]

But what of the Templars themselves? Their Order was now dissolved, their possessions and properties had been turned over to the Hospitallers and they were not getting any younger. At the time the Order was arrested in France, the average age of the members captured was 42 years old,[39] but by 1312, the average age was nearly 50. Is it likely that these men, mostly in their middle years and pacific in their station within the Order fled to some foreign land to start anew as many modern accounts suggest?

In the bull *Considerantes dudum*, issued on 6 May 1312 Clement made special provisions for those members of the Order who had been found innocent or had confessed and been reconciled with the Church. They were still regarded as being tied to their monastic vows and were not permitted to return to secular life; however, they were permitted to live in the Order's former properties, now in possession of the Hospitallers and were to receive a pension derived from the assets transferred to the Hospitallers.[40] This was certainly known to have occurred in France, England and Aragon. In some cases the Templars of Aragon joined the Order of Montesa, as they did in Portugal with the Order of Christ; two Orders that were granted former Templar lands. These new Orders, although sanctioned by the Church, were under the control of secular rulers.

However, the Templars on Cyprus were not as lucky. In 1311, Henry II, who had resumed his throne the previous year, learnt of a plot to once again take control of the Kingdom. Amaury's oldest son was to take the crown while Ayme d'Oselier, the Templar Marshal, was to be given control of the government. When the plot was revealed, Ayme was drowned and many Templars were imprisoned, where they would spend the final years of their lives.[41]

But the Templars on Cyprus were not the only living members of the Order who were condemned to die in prison. Clement's bull of 6 May 1312 had reserved for himself the fate of the leaders of the Order, namely The Master Jacques de Molay, the Visitor of France Hugh Pairaud, the Commander of Normandy Geoffrey de Charney and the Commander of Aquitaine and Poitou Geoffrey de Gonneville.[42] However, it would be another two years before their fate would be pronounced and when it was the Templar myth would begin.

The rotunda chapel of the Convento de Cristo in Tomar, Portugal, was constructed in the mid-twelfth century and passed to the Order of Christ, which was formed after the Templars were dissolved in 1312.
istockphoto.com Mel Bedggood

References for chapter 16

1 Barber, Malcolm, *The Trial of the Templars*. p. 45.

2 Nicholson, Helen, *The Knights Templar: A New History*. p. 198.

3 Barber, Malcolm, *The New Knighthood*. p. 283.

4 It has long been believed that Gaudin died in April of 1293, but Demurger believed that the date must be 1292 and sites a letter of that year published by A. Forey in 1973 to support the claim.

5 Demurger, Alain, *The Last Templar*. p. 2.

6 Ibid p. 28, Barber, *The New Knighthood*. p. 171. Barber records de Beaujeu returning to Acre in 1274.

7 Demurger op. cit. pp. 78-82.

8 The Teutonic Order, which had held a presence in the Levant since its formation nearly a century earlier, left the region entirely, going first to Venice and latterly to Marienburg in Prussia. It nonetheless continued a successful career as a Christian Military Order.

9 Ibid p. 86.

10 Nicholson op. cit. p. 205.

11 Demurger op. cit. p. 117.

12 Ibid p. 112.

13 Barber, *The New Knighthood*. p. 289.

14 Ibid pp. 289-290.

15 Nicholson op. cit. p. 237.

16 Barber, *The Trial of the Templars*. p. 27.

17 Coulombe, Charles A., *A History of the Popes*. p. 287.

18 Ibid p. 287.

19 Nicholson op. cit. p. 201.

20 Barber, *The New Knighthood*. p. 285.

21 Ibid p. 157.

22 Nicholson op. cit. p. 215.

23 Barber, *The Trial of the Templars*. op. cit. p. 51.

24 Demurger op. cit. p. 173

25 Barber, *The Trial of the Templars*. p. 46

26 Ibid p. 46 Demurger op. cit. p. 175. Barber references an additional twelve above the twelve mentioned in the official sources, while Demurger indicates that 40 Templars accompanied Gérard de Villiers, the former Master of France.

27 Demurger op. cit. pp. 155-156

28 Ibid p. 187

29 Barber, *The Trial of the Templars*. pp. 54-55.

30 Anonymous, Lament for the Templars, The ORB On-Line Reference Book for Medieval Studies, translated by Helen Nicholson www.the-orb.net/encyclop/religion/monastic/anonlamt.html

31 Ibid.

32 Barber, *The Trial of the Templars*. pp. 248-252 Barber provides a translation of the full Articles of Accusation against the Templars.

33 Nicholson op. cit. p. 213.

34 Ibid p. 226.

35 Demurger op. cit. p. 177.

36 Ibid p. 178.

37 Vox in excelso, A History and Mythos of the Knights Templar www.templarhistory. com/exelso.html.

38 Ad providam, A History and Mythos of the Knights Templar, www.templarhistory.com/providem.html

39 Barber, *The Trial of the Templars*. p. 54

40 Considerantes dudum, A History and Mythos of the Knights Templar www.templarhistory.com/consider.html.

41 Nicholson, op. cit. p. 230.

42 Considerantes dudum op. cit.

The Templar Legend

'The whole history of civilization is strewn with creeds and institutions which were invaluable at first, and deadly afterwards.'

Walter Bagehot

Left:
Church at Temple, Midlothian. Until the sixteenth century, the area was known as Balantrodoch. Although many believe that the Templars built the church in the twelfth century, it is possible that it was not constructed until the land passed into the hands of the Hospitallers after 1312.
Gordon Napier

Right:
The front of Notre Dame Cathedral in Paris. It was in front of these steps that Jacques de Molay and the other Templar leaders heard their sentence.
iStockPhoto.com David Lentz

The story of the final hours of Jacques de Molay's life, like so many aspects of the Templars' story, has been greatly embellished over the years; however, contemporary chroniclers did not give it a great deal of attention at the time. Writers such as Jean de St-Victor, and Bernard Gui, who was the inquisitor in the Toulousain during the Templar trials[1] and who would go on to write a guide for other inquisitors in the 1320s, mentioned de Molay's execution only in passing, providing us with few details to draw upon. The most reliable of the contemporary accounts is that of the anonymous monk who continued the chronicle of Guillaume de Nangis.[2]

From his account we learn that on the feast of St Gregory, 18 March 1314, de Molay and the other leaders were brought to the front of Notre Dame Cathedral in Paris to hear the decision of the three cardinals who had been assigned to determine their fate. As the four men and those who had gathered to witness the event listened intently, the cardinals read their sentence. The former Templars were to spend the rest of their lives in prison. Hugh Pairaud and Geoffrey de Gonneville received their sentence in silence; however, Jacques de Molay and Geoffrey de Charney stood and interrupted one of the cardinals. Both de Molay and de Charney stubbornly defended themselves and denied the confessions they had previously made. Upon retracting their confessions, they were handed over to the provost of Paris, a royal agent, who took the men into custody until the cardinals could deliberate further on the matter the following day. However, when Philip learnt of their recanted confessions he moved into action without consulting the clergy. That evening de Molay and de Charney were taken to a little isle on the Seine between the royal garden and the Augustinian's house and burnt at the stake. According to the continuator of Guillaume de Nangis's chronicle, de Molay and de Charney endured the flames with a dignity befitting their rank:

> 'They were seen to be so prepared to sustain the fire with easy mind and will that they brought from all those who saw them much admiration

and surprise for the constancy of their death and final denial ...'[3]

These words, of a man who may have been an eyewitness to the actual events, should have been sufficient bring the tragic story of the Knights Templar to a close. However, the story of de Molay's heroism and valour soon gave rise to more colourful retellings, which have endured to the present day. Among them were conflicting accounts of what happened to the templar leader's burnt remains. In one account the remains of de Molay and de Charney were snatched up as holy relics almost as soon as the fire's embers had begun to die out, while in another the remains were consumed by the flames until they were reduced to ashes.[4] Geoffrey de Paris, one of the king's clerks and an eyewitness to the immolation of the Templar leaders was perhaps the first to introduce de Molay's dying words. In his account, written in verse, Geoffrey suggests that de Molay requested that his hands remain free so that he could join them in prayer. The poem goes on to suggest that the last Master said that God would avenge the Templars's deaths, for he knew who was truly in the wrong.[5]

Above: **Nineteenth-century illustration depicting the immolation of de Molay and de Charney.** *ClipArt.com*

Right: **A depiction of the execution of de Molay and de Charney. It was alleged that while the last Master of the Order was consumed by flames, he uttered a curse that would end the life of Philip IV and Clement V.**

But the most perennial of the embellishments relates to another version of the speech made by the last Master as the pyre was lit beneath him. As the flames licked his garments, de Molay was alleged to have said that before the year was over both Philip and Clement would be summoned by God to answer for their crimes. It is certainly true that both men did die within the prophesied time; Clement on 20 April as a result of his long illness and Philip on 29 November after being thrown from a horse while hunting. However, it was not the curse, which was responsible for the timing of their deaths, rather it was the timing of their deaths that was responsible for stories of the curse.

Amongst those sources written closest to the actual events, there is simply no mention of de Molay's curse outside of Geoffrey de Paris's indication that de Molay believed that God would enforce the laws of righteousness. In fact the earliest version of the curse story was written in 1330 by an Italian chronicler named Feretto de Ferretis.[6] However, in de Ferretis's rendition it was not de Molay, but an anonymous Templar who uttered the curse. Although others repeated de Ferretis's account, it would not be until the sixteenth century that the words of the

The point of L'Ile de la Cité where de Molay was executed. *iStockPhoto.com*

anonymous Templar would be uttered from de Molay's mouth, in a book published in 1548 by Paul Émile entitled the *De rebus gestis francorum*.[7] But Émile's book was not a work of fiction or a poetic chronicle, rather it was a book of history and as such his account was picked up either directly or indirectly by subsequent historical writers, such as the English historian James Anthony Froude who wrote in 1886:

> 'There was thenceforward a universal conviction that the Templars had been unjustly dealt with. The popular feeling shaped itself into a tradition (possibly it was a real fact) that as the flames were choking him, the last Grand Master summoned the pope and the king to meet him before the tribunal of God. Clement died in agony a few weeks later. A little later Philip the Beautiful was flung by a vicious horse, and he too went to his account.'[8]

To his credit, Froude presents the de Molay curse story as a tradition rather than an historical fact, although he remains open to the possibility that it may have actually happened. However, other authors were not as discerning as Froude in their recitation of the famous curse. Charles Addison, in his 1842 book on the Templars renders a full dialogue of the event along with some theatrical embellishments of his own:

> 'A pile was erected on the island in the Seine where the statue now stands – or lately stood – of Henri Quatre [Henry IV], and here on the same evening they were led forth to execution before a crowd greatly outnumbering that of earlier assemblages, and the Grand Master addressed the citizens thus: "France remembers our last moments. We die innocent. The decree which condemns us is an unjust decree, but in heaven there is an august tribunal to which the weak never appeal in vain. To that tribunal within forty days I summon the Roman Pontiff." A violent shudder ran through the crowd, but the Grand Master continued: "Oh, Philip, my master, my King! I pardon thee in vain, for thy life is condemned. At the tribunal of God within a year, I await thee."'[9]

Seventy-seven years later, de Molay's martyrdom would serve as the inspiration for a new organisation created by a member of the Masonic fraternity. In 1919 a mason named Frank S. Land, concerned about the number of boys left fatherless after World War I, decided to create a new organisation to fill the void. According to the organisation's official web site, 'The group needed its own identity and its own name. After Dad Land related the story of Jacques DeMolay, [sic] the group decided to name itself for this historical figure connected with Masonry.'[10] Two years later, when the organisation became official, H. L. Haywood, one of the best-known and respected of Masonic scholars of his day, was commissioned to write a book entitled, *A Story of the Life and Times of Jacques de Molay*. The book was written to introduce the young members of this new fraternity to their namesake and the Order to which he belonged. Although Haywood was clear to point out that the de Molay curse story was a

An engraving from the 1815 edition of Les Templies by the French poet and playwright François Juste Marie Raynouard shows de Molay's hands freed from their ropes.

tradition, he did introduce the young men to other erroneous information about the Templars's last Master. In recounting de Molay's trip to Armenia in 1299, the author offers the following account of de Molay's military exploits:

> 'After that, and working in conjunction with a Tartar [Mongol] general, de Molay had the good fortune to retake a few of the cities that had been lost to the Saracens, Jerusalem among them, where the Templars celebrated Easter.'[11]

This erroneous piece of information was not the only Masonic publication to repeat the claim. In 1944, William Moseley Brown wrote a book for the Grand Encampment of Knights Templar in the United States entitled, *Highlights of Templar History* in which the claim was again given widespread coverage:

> 'When Acre fell, the Templars retired to Cyprus, which they had purchased from Richard the Lionheart. They had one more day of glory when, in 1299, they again entered the Holy City and worshipped at the Holy Sepulchre.'[12]

Although Haywood and Brown's accounts of the story no doubt stuck in the memories of many Freemasons and young men who later went on to become Freemasons, their intentions were not malicious. The fact is that the story, popular in the West at one time, related to a Mongol general by the name of Mûlay and not the last Master of the Templars, de Molay.[13]

Sadly the same cannot be said of other Freemasons, who were largely responsible directly or indirectly for much of the Templar legend as it exists today.[14] As early as the 1730s, little more than a decade after Freemasonry took its organised form in 1717, Andrew Michael Ramsey, a Scottish Jacobite living in exile in France put forth the notion that the first Freemasons had been operative stone masons working in the Holy Land at the time of the crusades. These stone masons, according to Ramsey, 'agreed upon several ancient signs and symbolic words drawn from the well of religion in order to recognise themselves amongst the heathen and Saracens.'

Although Ramsey did not tie a Masonic apron around the Templars' waist, he did connect the Freemasons with the Order of the Hospitallers, and it was for this reason, Ramsey claimed, that Masonic lodges were dedicated to St John. It would be the German Freemasons, who would add the Templar angle via the Rite of Strict Observance, which started in the late 1740s and was strengthened by the efforts of Karl Gotthelf, Baron Von Hund. The German Masons made the claim that when the Templars had occupied the Temple of Solomon, they acquired magical powers and secret wisdom, which de Molay passed on to his successor prior to his execution.[15]

Just who the alleged successor of de Molay was, depends upon the division of Templar Masonry one wishes to subscribe to. The French claim was that upon his death de Molay passed the reins to John Mark Larmenius, who continued on in secret.[16] There was also the claim that the Templar torch was passed to Pierre d'Aumont, who had fled to Scotland, where the exiled Templars established Freemasonry. From Scotland it returned to France and thence on to Germany. In Scandinavian countries, the Masons drew their lineage through the Order of Christ in Portugal, which was a real Order; however, added to the lineage was the claim that de Molay's nephew had carried his ashes to Stockholm, buried them there, and latterly established the Swedish Templar Order. There was also the claim that the Templars had assisted Robert the Bruce in the Battle of Bannockburn, who later established the Order of Heredom on their behalf as a repayment.[17]

None of the accounts have so much as a kernel of truth in them, but as the Masonic author Burton E. Bennett wrote in 1926:

> 'These fabrications were made for the purpose of establishing an Order not only that nobles of all countries could join, but that all who joined would believe they became ennobled. Designing men took advantage of it to obtain both money and power through "lost secrets", occultism and magic. It was an age that believed not only with personal contact with God, but also with the devil; and the supposed secrets of the Ancient Masons furnished the seed for all this tremendous growth.'[18]

Sir Knight Abelard Reynolds was the prelate of Monroe Commandery No. 17 in Monroe New York. This cabinet photo taken in the late 1800s shows the regalia worn by American Templars after the American Civil War. It is a uniform, which has seen little change since that time. *Author*

In the United States and Canada, Masonic Templarism consists of three Orders: the Illustrious Order of the Red Cross; the Order of Malta (Hospitallers); and the Order of the Temple. Despite the popularity of the theory among Masons, the Masonic organisation makes no claim of direct descent from the original Templars. *Author*

The Port of La Rochelle in France, where many authors claim the Templars sailed off into the sunset aboard eighteen Templar galleys; effectively escaping Philip's persecutions in 1307. *iStockPhoto.com Jacques Croizer*

But Bennett was not the first to condemn the work of his earlier Brethren. Albert Mackey in his *History of Freemasonry* wrote disparagingly of the theory adopted by von Hund's Strict Observance:

> 'Of this rubbish is the legend of Peter d'Aumont and his resuscitation of the Order of Knights Templar in Scotland. Without a particle of historical evidence for its support, it has nevertheless exerted a powerful influence on the Masonic organisation of even the present day. We find its effects looming out in the most important rites and giving a Templar form to many of the high degrees. And it cannot be doubted that the incorporation of Templarism into the modern Masonic system is mainly to be attributed to ideas suggested by this d'Aumont Legend.'[19]

But these theories about Scotland, eventually took root there and in 1837 the Chevalier James Burns wrote a book entitled *The Knights Templars of Scotland*, which created a direct lineal descent between the Templars and the Freemasons that has been accepted by many people, among whom are to be found a number of Freemasons themselves. In his book *The Rosslyn Hoax*, Robert Cooper explained that Burns invented the myth 'for his fellow Freemasons who were interested in creating a Masonic Order which mirrored their own attitudes and their own 19th century chivalric ideals.'[20] Burns, in crafting his history of the Templars in Scotland, made use of the d'Aumont connection stating that he along with other refugee Templars 'continued to carry on the mysteries of the Order.'[21]

More than a century after Burns wrote these words, legends of post-dissolution Templar survival continue through a variety of equally fictional accounts, written by mason and non-mason alike, but presented as historical fact. Starting with a common theme that large numbers of Templars had escaped the arrests of 1307, these authors have put forth a variety of final destinations for the Order ranging from America on one side of the Atlantic to Scotland on the other. In almost all theories the Templars managed to escape by sea on eighteen galleys that were waiting for them in the harbour of La Rochelle.

The source of this theory lies in the testimony of a serving brother named Jean de Châlons, who testified in 1308 that Gérard de Villiers had managed to receive advance warning of the arrests and escaped with fifty horses. De Châlons went on to state that he had heard that de Villiers had set sail with eighteen galleys.[22] De Châlons's testimony regarding the Templar galleys was not based on first hand knowledge, rather it was a recitation of a rumour and, given that the rest of his testimony was damning of the Order, it is doubtful that there was any truth to his claims. In fact after the dissolution of the Templars in 1312, the Hospitallers became more involved in naval warfare; however, at that time they are recorded as having only four galleys.[23] It therefore becomes less likely that these galleys existed among the Templars in the numbers suggested by either de Châlons or the modern authors who have used his testimony as the basis for entire books.

Of course, on board the galleys was the Templars' treasure, which the fleeing brethren had managed to get out of the Paris Temple without anyone noticing. The most common destination for the galleys and the treasure that was alleged to be in their holds was Scotland, home to the earlier Masonic Templar fantasies of the eighteenth and nineteenth century. For here after landing on the Isle of Mull off Scotland's western coast, the modern authors contend that the Templars went on to do great things.

The argument that is most often presented is that the Templars chose Scotland because Robert the Bruce was excommunicated at the time and therefore would have harboured them from the pope. But as we

Rosslyn Chapel began construction 134 years after the Templars were suppressed. This fact has not stopped the legend that the Templars assisted in its construction. *Linda Berthelsen*

have seen in a previous chapter, although Clement V was aware of Philip's allegations against the Order, he did not intend to begin an investigation until October.

Additionally, he would not have been angered by Philip's pre-emptive strike had he known that he was going to arrest them. Therefore, if the Templars had advance warning, it was the king and not the pope they were fleeing from and Robert's status with the Church would not have benefited them one way or the other. Not only did the Templars flee to Scotland where they could fall under Robert the Bruce's protection, but some would have us believe they also assisted him at the Battle of Bannockburn, despite there being no mention of it in the many contemporary accounts of the battle and historical resources derived from them.[24]

However, the most perennial of the claims related to the Templars in Scotland is that the Order built the enigmatic Rosslyn Chapel, 139 years after they escaped Philip's clutches. It was here that the Templars, who by this time were now Freemasons, carved their secret knowledge into the chapel's walls and pillars. Although Rosslyn Chapel was first mentioned in a Masonic context in 1738 with the publication of Anderson's revised constitutions,[25] it would be another two and a half centuries before it would come to be associated with the Knights Templar. In their 1982 book *The Holy Blood and the Holy Grail*, authors Michael Baigent, Richard Leigh and Henry Lincoln mentioned Rosslyn in passing, connecting it directly to Freemasonry and the Rose-Croix, but indirectly by mentioning that it was geographically close to the Templars headquarters in Scotland, Temple Balantrodoch.[26] Of course, the Templar connection was further implied by repeating the previous information in their brief biography of Marie de St Clair, one of the alleged Grand Masters of the mysterious Prieuré de Sion, and an ancestor of the man who built Rosslyn Chapel.[27]

This Prieuré de Sion, which has long since been proven to be a work of fiction created by a Frenchman named Pierre Plantard, was the main thrust of Baigent, Leigh and Lincoln's bestselling book. This fictitious organisation was, of course, connected to the Templars. According to the authors the Prieuré de Sion and Templars shared a common leader until 1188 when they went their separate ways and chose

Nineteenth-century illustration of the interior of Rosslyn Chapel. *ClipArt.com*

their own leader. The reason offered for the split between the two groups had to do with a dispute over an elm tree near Gisors in France. Cutting their way through the 'garbled accounts' relating to the event the authors tell us that Henry II of England and Philip II of France had met in a 'sacred field' where the elm tree stood, but for unknown reasons the tree became the object of a 'bloody contention.' Without citation, the authors reference a medieval chronicle, which indicated that the French, who outnumbered the English, began to attack. When the English sought refuge in Gisors, the French cut down the tree and Philip stormed back to Paris claiming that he didn't come to Gisors to be a woodcutter.[28]

Of course the reality of the matter is that the accounts were not garbled at all. There really was a meeting between Henry and Philip at Gisors in January of 1188. The two had been at war with each other for two years and the purpose of the meeting was to call a truce. Jerusalem had been captured by Saladin the year previously, and the time had come to turn towards a common enemy. While the kings were discussing the matter they were met by Josias, the Archbishop of Tyre, who had travelled to the West to gain support for the Third Crusade. Josias, through his eloquence, was able to persuade both kings to take up the cross and it was agreed that the two armies should march together.[29] Of course six months later war resumed between England and France, which delayed the proposed crusade even further. Although Henry died in 1189, his successor Richard I would eventually join Philip on crusade and it was largely to their credit that Acre was captured in 1191 as we saw in detail in a previous chapter.

But not only did *The Holy Blood and the Holy Grail* connect Rosslyn to the Templars and create a pedigree for the Order that tied it to the fictitious Prieuré de Sion, they were also responsible for accelerating the notion that the Templars were the secret guardians of the true grail, which was the bloodline created by Christ's marriage to Mary Magdalene. The idea was certainly no more controversial among the Christian faithful in 1982 than it was a generation later when Dan Brown picked up on the idea for *The Da Vinci Code*. In fact the latter's meteoric rise up the sales charts may have made it more controversial than the book that first popularised the myth. However, in writing his bestselling novel, Brown succeeded in engraving the fictionalised story of the Knights Templar on the minds of a new generation of readers, which has in turn opened the door for many other fictionalised accounts of the history of the Knights Templar.

Among the many intricate carvings in Rosslyn Chapel is one which many authors have used as proof of a Templar connection. Seeing what they wish to see, these authors have suggested that the carving is of two knights on a single horse. A close examination reveals that the second figure is standing behind the horse and what some claim is the second rider's leg, is actually the horse's tail.
Author

It is perhaps ironic that seven hundred years ago the Templars were destroyed by false information, yet today, it is largely false information rather than historical fact that has kept their memory alive. As Napoleon Bonaparte once said, 'What is history, but a fable agreed upon?' Actually he said, 'History is the version of past events that people have decided to agree upon', but as the former is so much more quotable, it is that which has become the accepted version, which only serves to prove his point.

References for chapter 17

1 Barber, Malcolm, *The Trial of the Templars*. p. 21.

2 Demurger, Alain, *The Last Templar* p. 196. De Nangis died in 1300 and his history was continued by an anonymous writer.

3 Barber, op. cit. p. 241.

4 Demurger op. cit. p. 199 .

5 Ibid pp. 197-198.

6 Ibid p. 202 Barber, op. cit. p. 315.

7 Demurger op. cit. p. 202.

8 Froude, James Anthony, *The Knights Templars*. p. 52.

9 Addison, Charles G., *Knights Templars*. p. 418.

10 Frank S. Land: The Founder of DeMolay, DeMolay International http://www.demolay.org/history/people/land/index.shtml.

11 Haywood, H. L., *The Story of the Life and Times of Jacques De Molay*. p. 27.

12 Brown, William, *Highlights of Templar History*. p. 27.

13 Demurger op. cit. p. 204.

14 Barber op. cit. p. 317, Nicholson, *The Knights Templar: A New History*. p. 240, Read, Piers Paul, *The Templars* p. 303.

15 Barber, Malcolm, *The New Knighthood*. p. 318.

16 This claim would also be used by Bernard Raymond Fabre-Palaprat when he launched his neo-Templar Order in 1804.

17 Bennett, Burton E., *The Rite of Strict Observance*, The Builder, October 1926.

18 Ibid.

19 Mackey, Albert G., *The History of Freemasonry*. p. 262.

20 Cooper, Robert L. D., *The Rosslyn Hoax*. pp. 245.

21 Ibid p. 300.

22 Barber, Malcolm, *The Trial of the Templars*. p. 101 Burman, Edward, supremely Abominable Crimes p. 225.

23 Nicholson op. cit. p. 192.

24 Cooper op. cit. pp. 217-218. Cooper provides a page and a half of contemporary or near contemporary sources related to the Battle of Bannockburn – 23/24 June 1314.

25 Cooper, op. cit. p. 123.

26 Baigent, Michael, *The Holy Blood and the Holy Grail*. p. 152.

27 Ibid p. 373.

28 Ibid p. 90.

29 Runciman, Steven, *The Crusades Vol. III*. pp. 5-6.

Bibliography

Abbott, Lyman. *The Recovery of Jerusalem*. Harper's New Monthly Magazine Volume XLIII June – November 1871: 195-206.

Addison, Charles G. *Knights Templars*. New York: Masonic Company, 1874.

Armstrong, Karen. *Islam: A Short History*. New York: The Modern Library, 2000.

Baigent, Michael, Richard Leigh and Henry Lincoln. *The Holy Blood and the Holy Grail*. London: Jonathan Cape, 1982.

Barber, Malcolm. *The New Knighthood*. New York: Cambridge UP, 1996.

Barber, Malcolm. *The Trial of the Templars*. New York: Cambridge UP, 1978.

Billings, Malcolm. *The Cross and the Crescent: A History of the Crusades*. New York: Sterling Co., 1990.

Boyle O'Reilly, Elizabeth. *How France Built Her Cathedrals*. New York: Harper & Brothers, 1921.

Bredero, Adriaan H. *Bernard of Clairvaux: Between Cult and History*. Grand Rapids: William B. Eerdmans Company, 1996.

Bright, John. *A History of Israel*. Philadelphia: Westminster P, 1960.

Brighton, Simon. *In Search of the Knights Templar*. London: Weidenfeld & Nicolson, 2006.

Brown, William M. *Highlights of Templar History*. Greenfield: Wm. Mitchell Printing Co., 1944.

Bruno, Salvatore T. *Templar Incorporated*. New York: BookSurge, 2006.

Bruno, Salvatore T. *Templar Organization: The Management of Warrior Monasticism*. New York: 1st Books, 2000.

Burman, Edward. *Supremely Abominable Crimes*. Chatham: Alison & Busby, 1994.

Burman, Edward. *The Templars: Knights of God*. Rochester: Destiny Books, 1986.

Cantor, Norman F. *Medieval History: The Life and Death of a Civilization*. New York: Macmillan, 1963.

Catherwood, Christopher. *A Brief History of the Middle East*. New York: Carrol & Graf, 2006.

Comay, Joan. *The Temple of Jerusalem: With the History of the Temple Mount*. London: Weidenfeld & Nicolson, 1975.

Cooper, Robert. *The Rosslyn Hoax*. London: Lewis Masonic, 2006.

Coulombe, Charles A. *A History of the Popes: Vicars of Christ*. New York: MJF Books, 2003.

David, Nicolle. *Acre 1291: Bloody Sunset of the Crusader States*. Oxford: Osprey, 2005.

Demurger, Alain. *The Last Templar: The Tragedy of Jacques De Molay Last Grand Master of the Temple*. London: Profile Books, 2004.

Dunan, Marcel, ed. *Larousse Encyclopedia of Ancient & Medieval History*. Middlesex: Hamlyn, 1972.

Dunlop, Ian. *Burgundy*. London: Hamish Hamilton, 1990.

Forey, Alan. *The Military Orders: From the Twelfth to the Early Fourteenth Centuries*. Toronto: University of Toronto P, 1992.

Fox-Davies, Arthur C. *Complete Guide to Heraldry*. London: Wordsworth, 1925.

Freising, Otto. *The Deeds of Frederick Barbarossa*. Trans. Charles C. Mierow. New York: W. W. Norton & Co., 1953.

Froude, James A. *Knights Templars*. New York: John B. Alden, 1886.

Gabrielli, Franscesco, trans. *Arab Historians of the Crusades*. 1993: Barnes & Noble.

Gies, Frances. *The Knight in History*. New York: Harper & Row, 1984.

Gui, Bernard. *The Inquisitor's Guide: A Medieval Manual on Heretics*. Trans. Janet Shirley. Welwyn Garden City: Ravenhall Books, 2006.

Hallam, Elizabeth, ed. *Chronicles of the Crusades*. New York: Weidenfeld & Nicolson, 1989.

Haywood, Harry L. *A Story of the Life and Times of Jacques De Molay*. St Louis: The Order of DeMolay, 1925.

Hindley, Geoffrey. *Saladin: A Biography*. London: Constable, 1976.

Howarth, Stephen. *The Knights Templar*. New York: Barnes & Noble, 1982.

Karageorghis, Jacqueline. *Cyprus: There is an Island*. Nicosia: C. J. Philippides & Son, 1987.

Keen, Maurice. *Medieval Europe*. London: Penguin, 1969.

Keller, Werner. *The Bible as History*. New York: William Morrow & Company, 1956.

Knight, Christopher, and Robert Lomas.

Knight, Christopher, and Robert Lomas. The Second Messiah: Templars, the Turin Shroud and the Great Secret of Freemasonry. London: Century, 1997.

Laidler, Keith. *The Head of God: The Lost Treasure of the Templars*. London: Weidenfeld & Nicolson, 1998.

Lord, Evelyn. *The Knights Templar in Britain*. Edinburgh: Pearson, 2004.

Mackey, Albert. *The History of Freemasonry*. New York: Gramercy Books, 1996.

Maier, Paul L., trans. *Josephus: The Essential Writings*. Grand Rapids: Kregel, 1988.

Meadows, Denis. *A Saint and a Half: The Remarkable Lives of Abelard and St Bernard of Clairvaux*. New York: The Devin-Adair Company, 1963.

Napier, Gordon. *The Rise and Fall of the Knights Templar*. Staplehurst: Spellmount, 2003.

Nicholson, Helen, and David Nicolle. *God's Warriors: Knights Templar, Saracens and the Battle for Jerusalem*. Oxford: Osprey, 2005.

Nicholson, Helen. *The Knights Templar: A New History*. Pheonix Mill: Sutton, 2004.

Oldenbourg, Zoe. *The Crusades*. New York: Pantheon Books, 1966.

Paris, Matthew. *The Illustrated Chronicles of Matthew Paris*. Trans. Richard Vaughan. Phoenix Mill: Allan Sutton, 1993.

Payne, Robert. *The Crusades*. Kent: Wordsworth, 1984.

Potok, Chaim. *Wanderings: Chaim Potok's History of the Jews*. New York: Fawcett Crest, 1980.

Ralls, Karen. *The Templars and the Grail*. Wheaton: Quest Books, 2003.

Read, Piers Paul. *The Templars*. London: Phoenix P, 1999.

Robinson, John J. *Dungeon, Fire & Sword: The Knights Templar in the Crusades*. New York: Evans, 1991.

Runciman, Steven. *A History of the Crusades Volume 1: The First Crusade and the Foundation of the Kingdom of Jerusalem*. London: The Folio Society, 1994.

Runciman, Steven. *A History of the Crusades Volume II: The Kingdom of Jerusalem and the Frankish East 1100-1187*. New York: Cambridge UP, 1954.

Runciman, Steven. *A History of the Crusades Volume III: The Kingdom of Acre and the Later Crusades*. New York: Cambridge UP, 1954.

Savage, Anne, trans. *The Anglo-Saxon Chronicles*. Surrey: Coombe Books, 1995.

Seward, Desmond. *The Monks of War*. London: Penguin, 1972.

Southern, R. W. *The Making of the Middle Ages*. London: Arrow Books, 1953.

Spilling, Michael, ed. *Battles of the Medieval World: 1000-1500*. London: Amber Books, 2006.

Strayer, Joseph R., and Dana C. Munro. *The Middle Ages: 395-1500*. New York: Appleton-Century-Crofts, 1959.

Tobin, Stephen. *The Cistercians: Monks and Monasteries of Europe*. New York: Overlook P, 1995.

Tyerman, Christopher. *God's War: A New History of the Crusades*. London: Penguin, 2006.

Upton-Ward, Judith, trans. *The Rule of the Templars*. Woodbridge: The Boydell P, 1992.

Urban, William. *The Teutonic Knights: A Military History*. London: Greenhill Books, 2003.

Wise, Terrence. *Medieval Warfare*. London: Osprey, 1976.

Index

Pictorial references are in **bold**.

1177 Baldwin IV comes of legal age and assumes the throne.

On 25 November the Templars under Baldwin IV defeat Saladin at the Battle of Montgisard.

1779 Odo de St Amand, Master of the Order is captured by Saladin at the Battle of Marj Ayun. Upon his death in prison the following year he was succeeded by Arnold de Torroja.

1180 King Baldwin IV's sister Sibylla marries Guy of Lusignan at Easter and is given Ascalon and Jaffa as his fief.

1181 Baldwin signs a two-year truce with Saladin. Soon after Reynald de Châtillon begins violating it by raiding Muslim caravans near Kerak of Moab.

1184 Arnold de Torroja dies during a trip to the West to drum up support for the East.

1185 Gerard de Ridefort becomes Master of the Order.

Baldwin IV, the Leper King, dies and Raymond of Tripoli becomes regent of the Kingdom of Jerusalem for Baldwin V.

1186 On the death of King Baldwin V, Guy of Lusignan becomes King of Jerusalem after a political coup, which was assisted by de Ridefort and the Templars.

1187 Gerard de Ridefort uses King Henry's money to hire mercenary troops to help fight Saladin.

Templars defeated by Saladin's men at the Springs of Cresson. De Ridefort leads his men and the Master of the Hospitallers to their deaths.

Templars defeated at the Battle of Hattin on 4 July.

Jerusalem surrenders to Saladin on 2 October ending 88 years of Christian rule. Two weeks later Pope Urban III dies shortly after hearing of the city's fall.

1188 Saladin tithe introduced to finance a new crusade.

Gerard de Ridefort is freed by Saladin in exchange for the Templar fortress as Gaza.

1189 Guy of Lusignan begins siege of Acre on 28 August. Soon after Gerard de Ridefort was captured during a skirmish and died later.

1190 Frederick Barbarossa drowns crossing the river Calycadnus.

1191 Richard I captures Cyprus.

Robert de Sable, who accompanied King Richard on crusade, joins the Templars and is made Master of the Order soon after – with the king's assistance.

Acre is captured by Richard and Philip of France on 12 July. A short time later 2,700 Muslim prisoners are beheaded by Richard after negotiations for their surrender break down.

The Battle of Arsuf on 7 September is a victory for the crusaders.

1193 Death of Saladin.

1199 Death of Richard I.

1244 Probable date of Jacques de Molay's birth.

Templars defeated at La Forbie by Baibars.

1249 Damietta is captured by Louis VII. Templars participate in siege.

1250 Louis IX captured at Battle of Mansurah. Templars provide part of his ransom.

1265 Year de Molay joined the Templars according to his own testimony.

1270 King Louis IX takes ill and dies while on his second crusade.

1274 Council of Lyons meets to discuss possibility of uniting the Military Orders.

1285 Henry II becomes King of Cyprus.

Philip IV becomes King of France.

1291 Acre falls to Mamluks on 28 May. William de Beaujeu, the Master of the Order, is killed in the battle and is succeeded by Theobald Gaudin.

1293 De Molay elected Master of the Order – leaves for Europe in search of support for the Order.